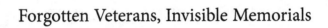

Forgotten Veterans, Invisible Memorials

WAR, MEMORY, AND CULTURE

Series Editor

STEVEN TROUT

Advisory Board

JOAN BEAUMONT

PHILIP D. BEIDLER

JOHN BODNAR

PATRICK HAGOPIAN

MARA KOZELSKY

EDWARD T. LINENTHAL

KENDALL R. PHILLIPS

KIRK SAVAGE

JAY WINTER

Series published in cooperation with

THE CENTER FOR THE STUDY OF
WAR & MEMORY
at the UNIVERSITY OF SOUTH ALABAMA

http://www.southalabama.edu/departments/research/warandmemory/
Susan McCready, Content Editor

Forgotten Veterans, Invisible Memorials

How American Women Commemorated the Great War, 1917–1945

Allison S. Finkelstein

The University of Alabama Press   Tuscaloosa

The University of Alabama Press
Tuscaloosa, Alabama 35487-0380
uapress.ua.edu

Typeface: Minion

Cover image: Detail of the poster "Five Thousand by June / Graduate Nurses Your
Country Needs You" designed by Carl Rakeman, New York: Rand McNally & Co.,
c. 1917; courtesy of the Library of Congress, Prints and Photographs Division
Cover design: David Nees

Cataloging-in-Publication data is available from the Library of Congress.
ISBN: 978-0-8173-2101-7
E-ISBN: 978-0-8173-9368-7

In memory of my beloved grandparents:
George Hoffman, US Army, World War II, ETO
Rose Edith Hoffman
Lewis Finkelstein, US Navy, World War II, ETO
Clara Finkelstein

Contents

Illustrations

Acknowledgments

In the nearly ten years that have elapsed since the origins of this book, I have relied on a network of scholars, colleagues, archivists, friends, and family who have supported me every step of the way. It is my pleasure to finally thank them for helping to make this book possible.

This book began during my time in graduate school at the University of Maryland, College Park. The Department of History there generously supported my academic studies and research through various teaching assistantships, grants, and fellowships. I benefited from the guidance and training of many professors and staff members in the department and elsewhere at the university, including Jodi Hall, Dr. Michael Ross, Dr. Richard Bell, Dr. Clare Lyons, Dr. Jon Sumida, Dr. Marsha Rozenblit, Dr. Daryle Williams, Dr. Julie Greene, Dr. Sonya Michel, and Dr. Marian Moser Jones (School of Public Health). Dr. Saverio Giovacchini, Dr. Robyn Muncy, and Dr. Donald Linebaugh (School of Architecture, Planning & Preservation) have remained steadfast supporters of my work even after graduation. I am grateful for their continued guidance, advice on this book, and friendship. As my former adviser, Dr. Giovacchini has believed in this project from the very beginning, and his unceasing support and belief in my potential has played a key role in my success as a historian. Every historian should be so lucky to have an adviser such as him. Thank you.

Outside the University of Maryland, many other scholars have supported this book over the years. Dr. Jennifer Wingate encouraged me to build on her own wonderful work in this field. I appreciate all the time she put into this project, especially her trip to College Park to serve on my dissertation committee. Likewise, Dr. Steven Trout has long championed this project, and it is due to his support that I got the opportunity to work with the University of Alabama Press. I appreciate his friendship and encouragement. Many other scholars have also supported this book in various ways, including Dr. Pearl James, Dr. Michael Neiberg, Dr. Christopher Capozzola, Dr. Mark Levitch,

Dr. Mitchell Yockelson, Dr. Michael Matheny, Dr. Barton C. Hacker, and the late Margaret Vining. At the College of William & Mary, Dr. James Whittenburg and the late Dr. Richard Palmer inspired me to become a historian and pushed me to fulfill my scholarly potential. I continue to benefit from Dr. Palmer's wisdom and I dearly miss him.

The publication of this book would not have been possible without the help of numerous archivists, public history professionals, and institutions who have guided my research and provided access to collections. I would especially like to thank Jonathan Casey, Stacie Peterson, and Lora Vogt at the National WWI Museum and Memorial; Britta Granrud and Marilla Cushman at the Women In Military Service For America Memorial Foundation, Inc.; Laura Cutter and Trenton Streck-Havill at the National Museum of Health and Medicine; Susan Watson, Whitney Hopkins, Jean Shulman, and Shane MacDonald at the American Red Cross Archives, National Headquarters, Washington, DC; Casey Castro-Bracho and the library staff at the Kentucky Historical Society; Marisa Bourgoin at the Archives of American Art; Tom McAnear and the staff at the National Archives, College Park; the staff at the National Archives Building, Washington, DC; Christian Belena at the Franklin D. Roosevelt Presidential Library; Lewis Wyman and the staff at the Library of Congress Manuscript Division; the staff of the Naval History and Heritage Command, Archives Branch; and Natalie Kelsey and Laurie Ellis at the Schlesinger Library.

The staff at the University of Alabama Press gave me the incredible opportunity to publish this book and I am thankful for all of their work to make it a reality. My editor, Dan Waterman, has been a font of wisdom, and I am grateful for his advice and leadership of this project. I also appreciate the contributions of Jon Berry, Blanche Sarratt, Clint Kimberling, and others at the press, as well as my copyeditor, Laurel Anderton. Thank you as well to the *Journal of the Vernacular Architecture Forum* for giving me the opportunity to publish my first scholarly article, which formed the basis of a chapter in this book.

Throughout the time I spent writing this book, I have been fortunate to work with colleagues at several jobs who have supported my goal of completing this project. My current colleagues at Arlington National Cemetery have cheered me on during the final stages of publication and given me opportunities to be part of commemoration on the ground. I would like to thank the entire Arlington National Cemetery team, particularly Dr. Stephen Carney, Tim Frank, Rod Gainer, Justin Buller, Robert Quackenbush, and contractors Kevin Hymel and Dr. Jenifer Van Vleck. Stephen Carney supported this project from its earliest iteration and I am grateful for his belief in my abilities and his advice about book writing. Jenifer Van Vleck also provided valuable wisdom about the book completion process and I appreciate all of her encouragement. At the US Citizenship and Immigration Services History Office and Library, Marian Smith, Zack Wilske, and Charlaine Cook constantly supported my effort to complete this manuscript. During my time on their team, they expanded my scholarly horizons, and I am thankful for their continued encouragement and friendship.

Past and present staff members at the American Battle Monuments Commission gave me the opportunity to learn about the ABMC from the inside and encouraged this project for years. Many of them provided access to records and expertise that aided my research. Thank you to the entire team, especially Senator Max Cleland, Michael Conley, Rob Dalessandro, Michael Knapp, Tim Nosal, John Marshall, Alan Amelinckx, Edwin Fountain, David and Bibiane Bedford, Jay and Amy Blount, Martha Sell, Craig and Lorna Rahanian, Angelo Munsel, Mike Coonce, Geoffrey Fournier, and Annelle Ferrand. Mike Shipman generously helped with archival photographs, and Alec Bennett served as a valuable sounding board for my ideas. Brigadier General John S. Brown (USA, Ret.) took me under his wing and became a trusted adviser and friend, along with his wife, Mary Beth—I am grateful to them both. I would also like to thank my colleagues from my time at the Department of Defense Vietnam War Commemoration Program who taught many important lessons about leading commemoration projects. Likewise, the staff and volunteers of the US World War I Centennial Commission and my fellow members of the Arlington County World War I Commemoration Task Force gave me once-in-a-lifetime opportunities to memorialize World War I and put the ideas of the women of this book into action. Thank you.

I am lucky to have many wonderful friends who have encouraged me through the long process of publishing this book—I thank them all. I especially want to thank those who have somehow helped me with the project, whether by providing a shoulder to lean on or historical advice to consider. They include Elizabeth Hyman, Lindsey Crane, Richard Hulver, Amy Meyers Eskay, Varnika Roy, Rohan Fernandes, Joshua Walker, Harrison Guthorn, Meghan Ryan Guthorn, Alda Benjamen, Sara Black, Laura Steadman, and Sara Steinberger. Peter Booth, Ian Kerr, Tom Shedden, and Simon Matthews are responsible for my interest in World War I commemoration and I am thankful for the incredible opportunities they gave me to explore British commemorative culture. Richard Azzaro and the late Neale Cosby taught me about the living memory of World War I and inspired me to stay the course on this project.

Most importantly, the love and support of my family enabled me to complete this book. I have dedicated it to the memory of my beloved grandparents, who always believed in me. My sister helped me with images and technological questions in addition to being my constant cheerleader and forever friend. There are not enough words to express my gratitude for all that my parents have done throughout this long process. My mother encouraged me with her patient phone calls, cheered me up with her good humor, and constantly reminded me of her confidence in my abilities. My father, a regular army officer and historian, inspired me to become a historian and provided years of advice that improved this project. I appreciate all of their love and support. My husband has lived with this project for several years and allowed it to take up much space in our lives. He has spent countless hours talking through my arguments with me and provided valuable insight that strengthened the manuscript. I am eternally grateful for his support, understanding, patience, wisdom, and love.

Finally, I must thank the pioneering women of World War I who form the central focus of this book. Reading their words and learning about their activism has inspired me and shaped my own views of commemoration. For too long, their contributions have been overlooked. It has been my honor to tell their stories in print. I hope this book stands as a living memorial to their service and reassures them that they have not been forgotten after all.

Abbreviations

ABMC	American Battle Monuments Commission
AEF	American Expeditionary Forces
ARC	American National Red Cross
AWM	American War Mothers
CFA	Commission of Fine Arts
IWM	Imperial War Museum
WAAC	Women's Army Auxiliary Corps
WAC	Women's Army Corps
WOSL	Women's Overseas Service League
WWRAA	World War Reconstruction Aides Association
YMCA	Young Men's Christian Association
YWCA	Young Women's Christian Association

Forgotten Veterans, Invisible Memorials

Introduction

For the whole earth is the sepulchre of famous men; not only are
they commemorated by columns and inscriptions in their country,
but in foreign lands there dwells also an unwritten memorial of
them, graven not on stone but in the hearts of men. Make them your
examples, and, esteeming courage to be freedom and freedom to be
happiness, do not weigh too nicely the perils of war.

 —Funeral oration of Pericles from *The Peloponnesian War* by
 Thucydides, translated by Benjamin Jowett

In 1924, in the French commune of Issy-les-Moulineaux, just outside Paris,
work began on a memorial to Katherine Baker, an American woman who volunteered as a nurse in Europe during World War One. Initially, Baker aided
wounded French soldiers. She later worked with the American Red Cross to
care for American troops, and she continued her nursing work even after she
became ill. She never recovered, and she died in 1919 upon her return to the
United States. Baker's death did not remain forgotten among the community
of American women who served in World War One. Ada Knowlton Chew,
who also served overseas during the war and after the war helped to found the
Women's Overseas Service League (WOSL), formed a committee of mostly
American women who joined forces with a French committee to memorialize Baker's life. Instead of erecting a stone statue or a formal monument, these
two committees decided to construct a living memorial building that housed
an orphanage for destitute French girls impacted by the war. They preferred
to build a memorial that could help the war's survivors, rather than construct
a traditional statuary monument.[1] This preference for service-based memorials instead of statues represented a method repeatedly pursued by the American women who served and sacrificed in the Great War.

As the story of Baker's memorial indicates, the commemoration of the

First World War deeply impacted American culture between 1917 and 1945 and incited a contentious debate about the best forms of military memorialization. As leaders in this debate, all kinds of American women participated in commemorative projects alongside men, the government, veterans, and the military.

In the postwar era, American women who participated in World War One formed new female organizations that defined community service and veterans' advocacy as forms of commemoration. They often pursued these alternative commemorative methods in addition to, or sometimes instead of, more permanent forms of commemoration. In keeping with women's contributions to the war effort and their Progressive era service and reform work, many American women chose to engage in service-based commemorative projects so they could serve the nation in ways normally prohibited to them because of gender-based restrictions on their citizenship.

This book investigates how the American women who served and sacrificed during the First World War commemorated this conflict during the interwar years and through the end of World War Two. It argues that during this period, these female activists considered community service and veterans' advocacy to be more effective and more meaningful forms of commemoration than traditional practices, such as statuary memorials. Specifically, they frequently preferred projects that helped a broadly defined group of male and female "veterans" as an alternative to physical monuments and memorials.

I created the term "veteranism" to describe the overarching philosophy of these women, whom I call "veteranists." Female veteranists believed that in the aftermath of war, supporting, aiding, and caring for veterans needed to be a priority of American citizens, civic groups, and the government. In keeping with the tenets of veteranist ideology, female veteranists often rejected traditional monuments and placed the plight of male and female veterans at the center of their memorialization efforts.

Veteranism did not address solely the veterans of official military service. Rather, these women broadened their definition of a veteran to encompass anyone who served or sacrificed during the war. Their classification of a veteran often included women who served overseas or on the home front but outside the official military apparatus, Gold Star family members who lost relatives in the conflict, and the families of present and former members of the military, among many others.

By uncovering the veteranist activities of the generation of American women connected to World War One, this book uses women's experiences to analyze the war's impact, instead of the male perspective often employed to examine matters of military memory. In doing so, it exposes a unique and somewhat avant-garde method of commemoration that will change the way scholars and practitioners understand American commemorative practices.

Female veteranists pioneered an alternative form of commemoration and tried to revolutionize American memorialization practices. Their actions forced Americans to rethink their standard commemorative rites and provided a different way to conceptualize the definition of a memorial. Through their outspoken support of veteranism, these female innovators promoted a type of commemoration that included intangible actions, human bodies, and ephemeral activities as crucial parts of the commemorative process. In doing so, female veteranists changed the course of American military commemoration, even though their memorialization methods did not gain the widespread acceptance they hoped for.

Defined broadly, the commemorative activities embraced by veteranism included any type of community service, philanthropy, relief, welfare, donation, charity, aid, or advocacy work done to honor or memorialize an individual man, woman, group, or event related to the war. These activities could be both intangible and tangible, permanent and impermanent. They also sometimes incorporated more traditional statuary memorials and ceremonies, or elements of them.

World War One created new communities of veterans, widows, surviving family members, and wounded warriors whom female veteranists sought to support through their work. Their projects involved activities as wide ranging as helping disabled veterans, advocating for veterans' rights, supporting the families of military casualties, enabling relatives to visit battlefield graves, pursuing peace efforts, and making monetary donations to a variety of charitable causes, including utilitarian memorials and living memorials.

Utilitarian memorials and living memorials formed a foundation from which the veteranist ideology initially emerged. Many of these projects began to develop around the turn of the nineteenth century and became even more popular during and after the First World War. A utilitarian memorial or living memorial refers to any memorial structure or activity that serves a useful purpose in a community at the same time that it operates as a monument. This purpose differentiates it from a statuary memorial, which usually has only an aesthetic, artistic, or commemorative purpose. After World War One, utilitarian and living memorials often took the form of structures such as stadiums, bandstands, auditoriums, theaters, gymnasiums, observation towers, bridges, hospitals, schools, museums, and churches. Living memorial buildings that commemorated World War One, sometimes also called "liberty buildings," became especially popular since they could both contribute to a community or a cause and be designed to include the decorative elements that made statuary monuments so popular.[2]

During the interwar period, some female veteranists supported the use of utilitarian and living memorials as a way to combine elements of statuary memorials with the community service values central to their veteranist ideology. They viewed living memorials as a middle ground where they could straddle the line between traditional memorial practices and the more unconventional elements of veteranism. Yet other female veteranists disagreed and rejected living memorials in favor of entirely service-based commemoration projects; this incited an ongoing debate among the female veteranist community.

The more purely service-based commemorative projects preferred by some female veteranists were often temporary and ephemeral; they lasted only as long as the women who led these efforts lived. Rooted in women's bodies, these commemorative projects remained distinctly corporeal. In contrast to inanimate statues, veteranist commemorations embodied the memory of the dead in the actions of the living. They remained at once connected to and the antithesis of the more traditional statues and funerary monuments that proliferated during the interwar period, since female veteranists sometimes participated in traditional commemorative rites. But because of the intangible nature of so many veteranist memorial projects, most left little permanent evidence on the landscape. This absence of physical evidence obscured the importance of women's interwar memorialization activities, their impact on the commemorative discourse, and the overall significance of the First World War in American culture.

Somewhat aware of the fleeting nature of their commemorative work as well as the nation's short memory regarding women's service in World War One, female veteranists fought to include the history of American women's contributions to the war in the historical and commemorative narrative. They wanted American women to be honored and memorialized for their wartime services and sacrifices alongside American men. In particular, the women who served in uniform wanted to be considered veterans, even if they did not officially serve in the military and did not meet the government's definition of a veteran. Women correctly feared that history might obscure the legacy of their wartime contributions, and they did their best to prevent such historical amnesia.

While the government and the military sometimes supported female veteranists' efforts to commemorate women's wartime roles, they allotted women only a temporary and partial place in the official military memory of the war. They also reduced women's postwar opportunities for military service. It was not until the Second World War, when the government needed women to support the armed forces again, that women's services to the military became more accepted. As an example, during World War Two, Representative Edith

Nourse Rogers (R-MA), a member of the Women's Overseas Service League who served overseas with the Young Men's Christian Association (YMCA) and the Red Cross during World War One, passed legislation in 1942 and 1943 to create the Women's Army Auxiliary Corps (WAAC) and its successor, the Women's Army Corps (WAC).[3] The WAC finally allowed women more opportunities to serve in the army and obtain many of the veterans' benefits previously denied to them. Yet even as Rogers and the women who served in World War One advocated on behalf of the women serving in World War Two, the younger generation of women started to overshadow the historical legacy of their predecessors.

Political advocacy formed an important way that women acted on their veteranist ideology. Veteranist women activists tried to influence military policy, national defense, and the evolving veterans' welfare state. They reminded the nation that women had fulfilled the duties of martial citizenship in wartime even before all women obtained the franchise. By continuing their wartime service after the Armistice, they demonstrated women's commitment to national service and their desire to gain the equal citizenship rights and opportunities for military service still denied to them. Although they hoped that the First World War had truly been "The War to End All Wars," they still wanted the next generation of American women to obtain more equal opportunities for military service.[4]

Female veteranists did not achieve a clear victory over traditional memorials, and their modes of commemoration did not become the dominant form of memorialization during the interwar era. Their more modernist veteranist memorialization ideas were often used in conjunction with or in addition to more conventional commemorative activities. Nor did female veteranists always completely reject traditional types of commemoration. They took steps forward and backward as they promoted and developed veteranism, and they frequently disagreed with each other about how to best pursue veteranist projects.

Although veteranist commemorations profoundly impacted American culture and society and continued to be used during the Second World War and beyond, this story has no clear-cut before and after. These women activists formed the avant-garde faction of the Americans involved in the interwar commemorative discourse. Even as they tried to disrupt traditional memorialization practices, they understood that their preferred methods of commemoration were often viewed as alternatives to the popular and more mainstream traditional statuary memorial projects that continued to flourish. Yet female veteranists still strongly believed in their veteranist ideology.

They also believed that the women who served and sacrificed during the war should be considered veterans, just like men who officially served in the armed forces. A key part of their veteranist ideology included advocating for women who contributed to the war effort but were not officially veterans. Veteranists created a broad and inclusive definition of women's wartime services and sacrifices. This definition incorporated all forms of women's contributions to the war effort. They expanded the meaning of military service to include diverse types of women's wartime activities, and they defined these as a category of martial citizenship equivalent to men's official military service. Of course, some American men also contributed to the war effort outside the military and lacked veteran status, such as men with the YMCA and other civilian groups.[5] However, these men chose to serve in this capacity and did not face government restrictions on their opportunities for military service based on their gender, thus differentiating their situation from that of women.

The service category included all of the women who officially or unofficially served overseas or on the home front in any way. This encompassed the women who served in the Army or Navy Nurse Corps, the navy Yeoman (F), the women marines, and any of the dozens of civilian welfare organizations such as the American Red Cross (ARC) and the YMCA. It encompassed the civilian women employed by the military in clerical work, communications, health-care work in physical or occupational therapy, and in other capacities and with different organizations. This definition also sometimes included all forms of women's unpaid volunteer work and paid labor on the home front, from knitting bandages to working in a factory or farming. Motherhood constituted a wartime service, since according to the ideals of republican motherhood, American women served the nation by raising strong, moral sons to join the military.[6] Widows, military wives, and families also fit into this definition of service. As long as a woman somehow contributed to the war effort, female veteranists believed that her service needed to be acknowledged.

Veteranists defined women's wartime sacrifices just as broadly and included women who made sacrifices of their own free will as well as women whose sacrifices were involuntary because of a wartime tragedy. Forms of sacrifice varied widely, from women who lost their lives or endured physical injuries, illnesses, or emotional distress because of their wartime service, to women who donated their time or money and put their country before their own needs. The sacrifices of Gold Star mothers or widows who lost a child or husband during the war received special attention. Veteranists believed that the losses of Gold Star women and their family members constituted a sacrifice made in service to the nation.

After World War One, many women formed organizations based on their wartime services and sacrifices, and they pursued veteranism through these groups. Such organizations included the Women's Overseas Service League (WOSL), the American War Mothers (AWM), the American Gold Star Mothers, Inc., the National Yeoman (F) (NYF), the World War Reconstruction Aides Association (WWRAA), and the National Organization of World War Nurses, among others. However, not all women who served in the war formed such organizations. For example, the telephone operators employed and paid by the US Army Signal Corps—known colloquially as the Hello Girls—did not form their own specific organization. Instead, many became active in the WOSL.[7]

Throughout the interwar period, female veteranists interacted and cooperated with a variety of groups and people. These included the American Legion; the Veterans of Foreign Wars (VFW) and their auxiliaries; other women's organizations unrelated to the war, such as the National Society of the Colonial Dames of America and the Daughters of the American Revolution; independent female and male supporters; and the government and military, among others. Organizations without direct ties to female veteranists also sometimes pursued aspects of veteranism.

Although both the American Legion and the VFW created women's auxiliaries that frequently engaged in veteranist activities, their membership criteria exclude them from the group of women investigated in this study. Members of these auxiliaries gained admittance based on the organizational membership and military service of a husband, father, brother, or son, not based on a woman's own services and sacrifices.[8] While these female auxiliaries emerged because many of their members supported the war effort and wanted to continue that service, and although their male counterparts valued their service, these organizations were still based on a man's membership in the main organization. At the 1925 American Legion national convention, the auxiliary's president, Mrs. Claire Oliphant, explained this difference. She declared that "we are unique among women's organizations because we are the only women's organization that takes its entire program of activity from a man's organization."[9] Likewise, membership in the Ladies Auxiliary to the Veterans of Foreign Wars was also based on a familial relationship to a male member.[10] This membership distinction differentiated these auxiliaries from the organizations that veteranist women established based on their own wartime actions, distinct from any connections to men. Nevertheless, these auxiliaries and their male counterpart organizations still conducted veteranist commemorations, sometimes in conjunction with organizations of female veteranist activists. The American Legion Auxiliary and the VFW Auxiliary, for example, provided support to their parent organizations' poppy sales, which supported disabled veterans.[11]

Some eligible women who officially served in the military did join the American Legion and the VFW, and they sometimes formed all-female posts.[12] In order to gain membership, these women had to be official veterans of the war according to the government's requirements. The limited groups of women who qualified included the Yeomen (F) and female marines—the first women to ever officially enlist in the US military—and the Army and Navy Nurse Corps. The former members of the Yeoman (F) even formed their own veterans' organization in the postwar years, the National Yeoman (F).[13] While the National Yeoman (F) and all-female units of the American Legion and VFW did often embrace veteranism and became a part of the greater veteranist community, they do not form a large part of the story told in this book. While important, their official military and veteran status distinguished them from the veteranist women who also had to fight for recognition of their wartime service.

These unrecognized female veterans form the main focus of this book because their lack of official status colored their distinct interpretation of veteranism and their dedication to this ideology. Because the government did not consider them to be military veterans, they felt even more compelled to continue their service after the war as a way to prove their dedication to the nation. They hoped their veteranist service activities would help justify their claims to veterans' benefits. They also felt an even greater sense of urgency to preserve the memory of their wartime experiences because their status outside the official military narrative put them at greater risk of being forgotten or overlooked.

Despite these differences between official and unofficial veterans, female veteranists' commemorative projects were all distinguished by their uniquely feminine attributes that developed from, and often continued, the work done by women before and during the war. Women's wartime work emerged from the sex-segregated wage labor performed by women in the early twentieth century such as nursing, clerical jobs, and telephone operation. These workers had important skills required by the military during the war.[14] Women also utilized expertise from their Progressive-era reform work that focused on aiding children, families, the needy, the infirm, immigrants, and the disabled.[15]

Women veteranists' focus on service activities, and their use of the word "service," held several layers of significance for turn-of-the-century America, not all of which they agreed with. Service could refer to military service like that of the men in the armed forces, as these women often professed was the case. It could also denote unpaid volunteer and community service similar to women's Progressive-era undertakings, which often dovetailed with their wartime work and postwar commemorative activities. But service also alluded to women's domestic work as servants, and women's unpaid labor at home serving and caring for their families. Female veteranists often disliked these last two connotations because they tried to define their wartime work as military service and assert their professionalism beyond the traditional feminine sphere.[16]

Likewise, the word "volunteer" had two meanings during this period. First, in the military context, it could refer to people who volunteered for paid military service as opposed to those drafted into service. Second, in the civilian context, it could refer to people, frequently women, who volunteered to do unpaid work, often referred to as "voluntarism."[17] During the Progressive era and throughout World War One and its aftermath, many women pushed to professionalize the unpaid activities they did in the spirit of voluntarism. In doing so, they often mixed paid professional employment with voluntary activities. Especially after the war, many women built paid careers from their unpaid volunteer work as they tried to professionalize their fields and assert the monetary worth of their skills.[18]

Before the war, many of the women who participated in the war effort and later championed veteranism had connections to the Progressive movement and the suffrage campaign.[19] Many were politically active, committed volunteers while others were paid, career-oriented professionals. Quite a few learned about memorialization from their mothers and grandmothers who had commemorated the Civil War.[20] For example, Lena Hitchcock, who served overseas with the army as an occupational therapist and became a national president of the WOSL and a dedicated member of the World War Reconstruction Aides Association, came from a prominent family in the elite society of Washington, DC. Prior to the war, she followed the lead of her mother, Virginia White Speel, an active Republican, volunteer, and daughter of a US officer in the Civil War. In 1916, Lena served as the chair of the third precinct of the Washington, DC, branch of the suffragist Congressional Union, the predecessor of the National Woman's Party.[21]

Like Lena Hitchcock, many, but by no means all, female veteranists came from the middle and upper classes. Women from the lower and middle classes joined forces with more elite women such as WOSL member First Lady Lou Henry Hoover, American Red Cross leader Mabel Boardman, Representative Edith Nourse Rogers, and Representative Helen Douglas Mankin (D-GA). From Toledo, Ohio, to Paris, France, women from all walks of life banded together to pursue veteranism. Although wartime stereotypes frequently presented the women who served as mostly wealthy members of the upper classes, the accuracy of this remains questionable. Many women who served overseas during the war came from lower-middle-class backgrounds, held paid jobs, and supported themselves financially.[22] One such woman was Merle Egan Anderson, an active member of the Seattle WOSL Unit. Before the war, she worked as a telephone operator in Montana. She volunteered to go to

France in 1918 as a telephone operator and joined the ranks of the women called Hello Girls. Anderson later served as the chief telephone operator for the Paris Peace Conference. In 1926 as she volunteered with the WOSL to help hospitalized veterans, she discovered that unlike the women who served in the Yeoman (F), telephone operators had an undefined wartime status that made them ineligible to receive the World War One Victory Medal and veterans' benefits. That year, she began to lead what became a long, but ultimately successful, fight to gain veteran status for the female telephone operators.[23]

Despite the participation of working-class women in many types of wartime service, overseas service in particular remained limited mostly to White, native-born women. Some Jewish women and an even smaller handful of African American women did serve overseas, as discussed below.[24] But on the home front, all types of women could support the war effort. Even with racial segregation and other restrictions, many minorities gained more opportunities to participate in the war effort at home; this enabled a limited number of them to become veteranists after the war, although their participation can sometimes be difficult to track because of the ad hoc, grassroots nature of some home front activities.

For African American women, however, segregation and discrimination greatly curtailed numerous opportunities for formal wartime service and thus reduced the number of Black women eligible to formally participate in veteranist organizations after the war. Although many African American women wanted to support their nation during the war, they faced exclusion from many of the organizations that utilized women's paid labor and volunteer services.[25] The military mostly prohibited African American women from officially serving in the armed forces, except for a small group of Black women who enlisted in the navy as Yeoman (F) and served in the muster-roll section; they became known as the "Golden Fourteen."[26] Both the federal government and the American Red Cross remained reluctant to utilize African American nurses during the war.[27] Despite the founding of the National Association of Colored Graduate Nurses in 1908, no African American nurses were allowed to serve in France; only after the onset of the influenza epidemic and the signing of the Armistice were eighteen African American Red Cross nurses accepted for service at military bases in the United States with the Army Nurse Corps.[28]

Very few African American women gained the opportunity to serve overseas; perhaps only three African American women went to Europe during the war and about another dozen arrived in April 1919.[29] Alice Dunbar-Nelson, a Black writer and activist who served as a field representative for the Women's Committee of the Council of National Defense and documented Black women's wartime work, reflected on this in 1919 when she wrote that "colored women since the inception of the war had felt keenly their exclusion from overseas service."[30]

Civil rights activists Addie Waites Hunton and Kathryn M. Johnson published a joint memoir in 1920 about their time serving with the YMCA in France during and after the war, where they supported African American troops at YMCA recreation huts.[31] Titled *Two Colored Women with the American Expeditionary Forces*, the book chronicled both their work in France and their observations of the experiences of African American members of the military, much of which exposed the racism encountered by these soldiers.[32] In the illustrated edition published around 1920, Hunton and Johnson dedicated the book to "the women of our race, who gave so trustingly and courageously the strongest of their young manhood to suffer and to die for the cause of freedom."[33] This dedication can be understood to demarcate this book as a veteranist memorial created by Hunton and Johnson to memorialize the African American women who sent their sons, husbands, and brothers to fight for a country that denied them equality. The foreword of the book indicates that they also intended it to function as a memorial to the African American men who served in the war. They explained that they wrote the book because they believed that "an effort to interpret with womanly comprehension the loyalty and bravery of their men seems not only a slight recompense for all they have given, but an imperative duty."[34] After the war, Hunton became a dedicated peace activist involved with the Women's International League for Peace and Freedom (WILPF), likely inspired by her wartime experiences.[35] This trajectory and support of the peace movement resembled that of other female veteranists, such as American War Mothers founder Alice French, and provides further indication that Hunton's postwar activism and work, such as the book, may have been a type of veteranism, albeit one conducted independently from the predominantly White female veteranist organizations.[36]

On the home front, African American women faced restrictions but also carved out their own opportunities for wartime service. Although many organizations excluded Black women from their ranks at home, the Young Women's Christian Association (YWCA) and the YMCA represented two exceptions. They included African American women in their wartime efforts, although in limited ways, such as the staffing of segregated hostess houses for African American men at stateside bases.[37] According to Alice Dunbar-Nelson, some Black women in northern cities worked with White women as a part of Red Cross activities, while in the South, Black women had to form separate Red Cross auxiliaries; overall, opportunities for Black women to work in the Red Cross remained limited across much of the country.[38] More commonly, though, African American women on the home front supported the war and African American service members through their own grassroots efforts in their communities, preexisting groups such as women's clubs, and the creation of new wartime organizations like the Circle for Negro War Relief, dedicated to "promoting the welfare of Negro soldiers and their dependent families."[39] They also participated in Liberty Bond drives, purchased War Savings Stamps, collected donations for the American Red Cross, worked in war industries, and took part in other activities, similar to White women.[40] Likewise, African American women became involved with national efforts such as the War Work Council, the Women's Division of the Council of National Defense, and in state and local projects, usually in separate "colored" divisions or committees.[41]

The racial restrictions that limited African American women's opportunities for wartime service thus led to their exclusion from many of the formal, organized activities of White female veteranists after the war, since most Black women could not meet the eligibility criteria to join veteranist organizations. Compounding this, even when eligible, White female veteranists often segregated their organizations and restricted Black women's participation. Like many women's organizations before the war, most female veteranist organizations segregated African American women into separate chapters, if they allowed them to be members at all.[42] The government also adhered to segregationist policies in its interactions with female veteranists, most notably when it segregated the Gold Star pilgrimages of widows and mothers to overseas cemeteries, a choice that angered and divided the African American community.[43]

While White female veteranists frequently argued about the best way to accommodate African American women, they rarely reached a consensus and often disagreed about racial policies. Some White members believed in segregation and did not want to incorporate African American women. Other White members took a more welcoming stance and pushed to include African American women alongside White women. Especially as the 1930s progressed, the efforts of African American women to be included in veteranist groups meant that White women could not ignore the question of race, even if they could not determine a solution. Meanwhile, Black female veteranists participated in veteranism as much as they could, especially with the American War Mothers and the Gold Star pilgrimages.

Of course, Black women also pursued the ideals of veteranism outside the predominantly White female veteranist organizations explored in this book. Mary Church Terrell, a prominent civil rights leader and women's suffrage activist who helped organize both the National Association of Colored Women and the National Association for the Advancement of Colored People

(NAACP), provides an important example.[44] During World War One, Terrell worked for the War Camp Community Service, a group that organized recreational programs for soldiers stationed at military camps, but she later quit because of the lack of resources provided for her work with African Americans.[45] After the war, she supported the campaign begun before the war to create the National Negro Memorial in Washington, DC, a living memorial building with museum exhibits and educational components intended to commemorate the military service of African Americans throughout US history, among other topics.[46] On February 1, 1928, she testified during a House of Representatives hearing about the memorial building. She explained that "a memorial building in which a record of the achievements of the colored American might be kept and exhibited would be the means of educating old and young alike concerning the important role this group has played in the history of the United States."[47] As a woman who supported the war effort, she aligned her thinking with the tenets of veteranism while she also promoted civil rights, for she wanted this memorial to serve as a teaching tool rather than just a static statuary monument.

Other African American female leaders also embraced the ideals of veteranism, usually from outside the predominantly White veteranist organizations. Like White women, Black women knew that much of the task of rehabilitating service members and recovering from the war fell to them. Alice Dunbar-Nelson highlighted this within *Scott's Official History of the American Negro in the World War*. After describing the work of various wartime relief organizations formed by Black women, she explained their situation after the Armistice. According to Dunbar-Nelson, these groups found themselves "facing a still larger field, the returning soldiers coming from scenes of horror and devastation with problems and needs. Like all of the war organizations of the women of the race, they found their work had only just begun."[48] Similarly, Ora Brown Stokes (later Perry), a prominent African American leader in Richmond, Virginia, continued her wartime work through postwar commemorative projects.[49] During the war, she chaired the Colored Women's Section of the Council of National Defense of Virginia, served as the secretary of the fifth liberty loan and the secretary of the food conservation field agent of Virginia, and supported the Committee on Training Camp Activities, among other endeavors.[50] After the war, she served as a field agent for the Virginia War History Commission, an official state project to collect and preserve the history of Virginia's participation in the war, including individual service records.[51] Stokes particularly tried to get recognition for Black Virginians who served in the war, efforts that placed her within the realm of veteranism as a woman who supported the war effort and tried to commemorate and help veterans afterward.[52] Other examples of Black female veteranists beyond the groups included here can likely be found but remain outside the scope of this book.

Although veteranism as described in this book maintained a uniquely American attitude, it did have some international reach. Since many female veteranists worked and interacted with women from the Allied countries during the war, they often maintained those friendships in the postwar era. They sometimes even collaborated with their overseas counterparts or supported their projects. The WOSL maintained ties with the Ligue des Femmes Alliées de la Grande Guerre—the League of Allied Women of the Great War. Formed in France and composed of international members, this organization aimed to "tighten the lines of sisterhood between the women that worked voluntarily in the hospitals, the canteens, or other works for the Allied cause in the war, without distinction of condition or religion" and encouraged them "to continue the fight for peace against those who seek to weaken the militaries of France and the Allies."[53] WOSL founder Mrs. Ada Knowlton Chew corresponded with this organization, attended its conventions, and even spoke alongside her husband at its June 1924 meeting. She shared some of the ideals of veteranism with the audience at that meeting. She told them, in French, that their organization now had "a beautiful chance to do something very important. They have the opportunity to work for their country as they did during the war."[54] With this speech, Mrs. Chew helped spread the ideology of veteranism among her fellow female veterans in Europe.

Likewise, some women from the Allied nations also tried to preserve the memory of women's wartime service through veteranist memorial projects, just like their counterparts in the US. Almost from its inception, Great Britain's Imperial War Museum (IWM) formed a women's subcommittee to include the story of British women in the museum's narrative.[55] The committee had two aims: first, to acquire artifacts to exhibit in the IWM, and second, to form a record of the war that showcased the "activities of women by means of a collection of photographs, pamphlets and manuscript reports from all women's organisations and outstanding private individuals."[56] The committee also created a record of all British women who died because of the war, whether during active service near the front, in munitions plants, or in other circumstances.[57] Extremely active and well organized from the outset, even before the IWM had a permanent building, the committee organized an exhibition of photographs that depicted women's war work, which were exhibited in October 1918 at the Whitechapel Art Gallery. This exhibit served as a memorial to the British women who died in service.[58] It represented a type of British veteranist memorial focused on telling the story of women's service and demonstrated the parallels between American women's veteranism and international iterations of this ideology. While more examples like this can certainly be found, an international examination of veteranism remains outside the purview of this book, which must by necessity be focused on the uniquely American version of veteranism that developed after the First World War.

This book stems from the rich field of scholarship on American historical memory and proposes that historians should expand the definition of commemoration to include community service and advocacy activities.[59] It especially follows the lead of other scholars who have investigated the cultural importance and contentious nature of American military memory and commemoration, as well as the broader field of memory studies. In doing so, this book builds on the small body of literature about the American memory of World War One and approaches it from the perspective of the women who served and sacrificed.[60] It also draws on the extensive scholarship regarding the memory of the First World War in Europe, Canada, and Australia, particularly the work of Jay Winter.[61] I agree with and expand Winter's argument that cultural commemorations of the Great War are more complicated than the "modernist" versus "traditional" explanations that are often used and actually represent an overlap of the two.[62] I continue to employ the terms "traditional" and "modernist" merely for the ease with which they describe and categorize statuary monuments and memorials. The American women I study simultaneously rejected and interacted with more traditional forms of memorialization. Their tendency to combine service-based memorial projects with statuary monuments, or to support some conventional memorial activities, demonstrates the interplay between the "modernist" and "traditional" memorial rituals that Winter discussed. Traditions and cultures do not change overnight, and during the interwar period, many female veteranists and their allies clung to older memorial forms even as they advocated for utilitarian memorials and promoted veteran-centered commemorations. These women did not achieve a decisive veteranist victory that purged the commemorative culture of statuary memorials. Female veteranists did not want to do so, even if they sometimes preferred veteranist commemorations. Rather, they wanted to complicate the commemorative discourse, challenge older forms of memorialization, and ask Americans to consider experimenting with veteranism in their commemorations.

Accordingly, instead of rejecting it, my work complements and expands the existing interpretation of memorials and monuments, since the women I study did not always completely discard these forms of commemoration. Rather, this book encourages scholars to include veteranist commemorations alongside other forms of memorialization and to think about different understandings of living memorials. It posits that living memorials had a bigger impact on interwar commemorative culture than previously granted.[63]

By revealing the veteranist traditions of creating intangible and ephemeral memorials based on acts of service that do not exist today, this book also argues that the memory of World War One in America exerted a greater impact than previously thought.

As a study of cultural memory and commemoration, my work does not examine the history of American women's participation in the First World War in detail. It is chiefly concerned with what these women did *after* the war.[64] It does, however, touch on the origins of female veteranism in the Progressive era and the way these women transferred their prewar experiences with reform work, politics, policy, and suffrage to their wartime service and postwar commemorative activities. For example, the suffragist and political activist Molly Dewson and her partner Polly Porter served with the Red Cross in France during the war, like many other women who translated their Progressive era experience into wartime service.[65]

Community service and voluntarism constituted an important part of Progressive women's activities, especially through women's organizations and settlement houses. Female veteranists drew on these experiences both during and after the war.[66] Some women veteranists, particularly those involved with the Gold Star pilgrimages and the American War Mothers, also took inspiration from long-standing American ideas about republican motherhood, maternalism, and the civic roles of mothers in the nation.[67]

Female veteranists' instinct to organize themselves into associations after the war frequently stemmed from their involvement in women's clubs, female organizations, and volunteer groups before the war. They used their experiences and skills with these groups during both their wartime service and their postwar memorialization work. Their participation in commemorative organizations and activities after the war was the natural extension of their earlier experiences.[68] Veteranist organizations such as theirs reveal another way that Americans fulfilled their citizenship obligations through extragovernmental groups.[69]

My investigation of how these female activists argued for their right to be recognized as veterans of war and pushed for veterans' benefits during the interwar period allows me to make a gendered intervention into the scholarship on veterans' politics.[70] Previously, much of this field has focused on male veterans and their struggles to procure government benefits. This book contends that women also participated in veterans' politics and shaped the debates about the privileges earned by American veterans as they sought to be recognized as veterans. Thus, this book includes women veterans in the overall trajectory of the history of veterans' politics in the US. More specifically, it investigates their role in the contentious struggle for veterans' benefits before, during, and immediately after the New Deal. With more women serving in the military today, such a historical investigation remains relevant to the US as the military seeks to integrate women more fully into the armed forces.

This book's theoretical perspective relies on Pierre Nora's idea of *lieux de mémoire* (sites of memory), Maurice Halbwachs's concept of collective memory, and Benedict Anderson's imagined communities.[71] Nora's *lieux de mémoire* frame the book's focus on sites of memory such as memorials, landscapes, cemeteries, and buildings as key ways to understand commemoration. Halbwachs's theory of collective memory supports the assertion that the memory of women's World War One service, and women's intensive commemoration of that conflict, survived through the community of female veteranists and often faded after their deaths.[72] Benedict Anderson's definition of the nation as an imagined political community and the importance of military memory to nationalism influenced the analysis of how women defined their nationalism in relation to each other.[73]

Of course, commemorative service was not new after World War One. It had been pursued in various iterations for decades, especially after the Civil War, and it accelerated in popularity during the World War One era. The Progressive era's focus on community development and improvement led to an increased desire for some Americans to serve society while memorializing a person or event. At the turn of the century, living memorial buildings dedicated for use by a particular community began to come more into vogue. For example, Brevet Major General George Washington Cullum left a bequest in his will to construct a hall at his alma mater, West Point, for the use of the officers and graduates of the United States Military Academy. Opened in 1900 and designed by Stanford White, it contained numerous commemorative plaques and memorialized Cullum while also serving the West Point community, as it continues to do today.[74] In 1917, the American Red Cross opened the Memorial to the Heroic Women of the Civil War in Washington, DC, a living memorial building constructed to house its headquarters. These buildings and others set a precedent for future living memorial buildings dedicated to ongoing service missions.

Veteran-centered commemorations began before the end of the war and before the US entrance into the conflict. After the widely publicized German execution of British nurse Edith Cavell on October 12, 1915, a group of Bostonians held a memorial service for her and decided to commemorate her life in a meaningful way. They raised money to send an "Edith Cavell Nurse from Massachusetts" to serve with the British in France in honor of Cavell's memory. They selected Alice L. F. Fitzgerald for the position. In 1916, Fitzgerald went to France wearing a specially created medal that identified her as the "Edith Cavell Memorial Nurse."[75] Excerpts from her letters were published in the US to raise funds to support her overseas work. Through Fitzgerald's service as a nurse, she and this committee exemplified the ideals of veteranism even before the war's conclusion.

Another American woman, artist Anna Coleman Ladd, also executed a veteranist commemoration project that aided disabled soldiers in France during the war. A professional sculptor, Ladd established the American Red Cross Studio for Portrait-Masks in Paris in 1917 to create copper masks for wounded soldiers with facial disfigurations (figs. I.1 and I.2). Awarded the French Legion of Honor for her work, Ladd embraced veteranism early on. With the team in her Paris studio, she used her talents as a sculptor to help wounded soldiers, rather than pursue only purely artistic projects that did not help those affected by the war.[76] She transferred her skills as a maker of memorials and sculptures to the mission of healing and re-creating human bodies mutilated by combat. She explained that her mission in her mask work "was not simply to provide a man a mask to hide his awful mutilation, but to put in that mask part of the man himself—that is, the man he had been before tragedy intervened."[77] During the war, the human body became Ladd's medium. Her masks served as corporeal memorials to the men she aided, making them into living memorials to their own wartime services and sacrifices, perhaps in the purest sense of the concept.

After the war, Ladd returned to her work as an artist and designed several memorials to the First World War, which, given her intimate experiences with the conflict's destruction of the human body, graphically depicted the war's horrors.[78] Ladd's prewar sculptural work had already portrayed war in a negative light. Her overseas experiences further inspired her to represent the ugly realities of war and pacifist sentiments in her war memorials.[79] As a member of the Boston WOSL Unit, Ladd continued to support veteranism at the same time that she created traditional statuary memorials. She even designed a medallion for the WOSL that the organization presented to Marshal Foch.[80] Although some of Ladd's sculptural memorials survive today, her intangible work as a veteranist, and the living memorials embodied in the reconfigured faces of the soldiers she helped, survived only as long as the men who wore them.

The chapters that follow are organized thematically. They demonstrate the myriad ways that female activists influenced the interwar discourse and debate on the legacy of the First World War and the American women who participated in it. Chapter 1 focuses on the Women's Overseas Service League (WOSL), an organization composed of women who served overseas during the war in a variety of capacities and who considered themselves veterans. It argues that because of their unique wartime experiences, these women pre-

Figure I.1. Before and after images of a wounded soldier wearing one of Anna Coleman Ladd's masks. American Red Cross photographer. Anna Coleman Ladd Papers, Archives of American Art, Smithsonian Institution.

Figure I.2. Some of Anna Coleman Ladd's masks for disfigured soldiers displayed in her Paris studio. Note how they resembled sculptural memorials. Circa 1918, American Red Cross photographer. Anna Coleman Ladd Papers, Archives of American Art, Smithsonian Institution.

ferred commemorations based on veteranism rather than traditional statuary memorials, which they often rejected.

Chapter 2 analyzes the Memorial Building to the Women of the World War, a living memorial building constructed by the American Red Cross (ARC) to honor women's services and sacrifices in World War One. Intended to house ARC service activities while it commemorated women, this building represented an attempted compromise between traditional statuary commemoration and veteranism that some women viewed as a failure. Chapter 3 recounts the history of the World War Reconstruction Aides Association (WWRAA), an organization composed of women who served as physical and occupational therapists during the war. Devoted to veteranism and keenly aware of their status as pioneers in their fields, they spent decades fighting to gain veterans' benefits and proper recognition of their wartime service and legacy.

Chapter 4 investigates the American War Mothers (AWM), an organization of mothers of World War One service members. These women believed their role as war mothers constituted national service, and they pursued veteranist commemorations to continue their national duties. Chapter 5 turns to the Gold Star mothers and widows pilgrimages of 1930 to 1933, a government-sponsored program that sent the mothers and widows of deceased service members to visit their loved ones' overseas graves. This chapter reframes the pilgrimages as a form of commemorative veteranism performed by the government for the Gold Star women at their own behest. These women believed that such a trip was the most appropriate way to honor their sacrifices and their deceased relatives.

By drawing on eclectic examples of women's interwar veteranist commemorations, I demonstrate these women's far-reaching impact on American culture and society. Irrevocably changed by their wartime experiences, female veteranists actively sought to promote a form of memorialization that honored their wartime service and helped to heal the wounds of war. They had little patience for commemorative practices that seemed to only pay lip service to the personal destruction caused by the war. Although women veteranists often left little permanent physical evidence of their work, their importance cannot be underestimated, and their lasting legacy must be understood. They reconceptualized American commemorative practices and challenged the definition of military service and veterans in ways that remain relevant to the nation over one hundred years after the end of the Great War.

1

Carry On

*The Women's Overseas Service League
and Veteranist Commemorations*

Re-Dedication:

As only those
Who dared War's horrors:
Who felt War's pain;
Who shared War's terrors;
Who saw War's slain:
Who bear War's scars
Of flesh and brain,
Can know War's awful Truth
And wholly realize
The noble sacrifice
Of those who gave their lives to Glory,—

Who with them, hour by hour,
Guarded the Faith which gave them power
Gladly to die,
Can surely see and humbly feel
The sacred trust their deaths reveal.

Then,
While today
We celebrate
The victory to them denied,

Let us, our lives, re-dedicate
To keep alive the Faith which led
Those glorious Legions of the Dead.[1]

—M' Edna Corbet, ARC searcher, Meuse-Argonne Offensive, Kansas
City Unit, Women's Overseas Service League (WOSL), *Carry On*,
November 1926

IN HER POEM "Re-Dedication," published on the front cover of the November 1926 issue of *Carry On*, the national magazine of the Women's Overseas Service League (WOSL), M' Edna Corbet explained the postwar commemorative mission of this organization of American women who served overseas during the First World War.[2] When these women returned to the US, they realized that their wartime experiences had changed their ideas about military commemoration and who could be considered a veteran. As the title of Corbet's poem indicates, rather than just build war memorials, they rededicated their lives to service projects in memory of the war dead, while they simultaneously argued that as those "who dared War's horrors," they too should be considered veterans.

The members of the WOSL strongly embraced and promoted veteranism and often acted as leaders in the movement. They believed they could best memorialize the First World War through service to the living, especially male and female veterans, including themselves. By defining community service as an alternative form of commemoration, they chose to honor the past by positively influencing the present and the future, rather than glorifying war by only constructing monuments. Their veteranist commemorative agenda focused on support for male veterans, serving and advocating on behalf of former overseas women whom they considered veterans, and spearheading a campaign to include women in the national historical narrative of the war. The WOSL's support for female veterans became especially important since many were ineligible for government benefits. This inspired the WOSL to create its own forms of social welfare to aid them.

By continuing their national service, WOSL members reminded the nation that they too had served in the war and gone above and beyond the accepted duties of women's citizenship, even before many could vote. The group staked a claim for women in the interwar commemorative culture and tried to include the memory of women's overseas service in the war's history. After all women gained the franchise in 1920, the organization created space for women to support the armed forces, despite restrictions on their military participation. In the process, the WOSL helped redefine commemoration to include service, advocacy, and social welfare. It demonstrated that memorials could be formed from human actions just as they could be carved from stone. Through this work, it also argued for a new definition of "veteran" that included the women who provided critical wartime support to the military from outside its official ranks.

A BRIEF HISTORY OF THE WOMEN'S OVERSEAS SERVICE LEAGUE

The WOSL became one of the most important women's organizations related to the First World War in the United States. It continued the bonds of sisterhood among overseas women and provided them with a way to serve the nation through community service, commemoration, advocacy, and patriotic work.[3] The WOSL evolved from local groups of former overseas women that formed upon their return to the US. Mrs. Ada Knowlton Chew, who drove an ambulance in the French hospital service from 1916 to 1919, decided to unite these groups into a national organization.[4] She helped plan the first national convention in Philadelphia in May 1921 to officially organize the national WOSL.[5] According to its 1925 Articles of Incorporation, membership was open to any American woman who served overseas, or any foreign woman who lived in America and served "for the success of the Allied Cause during any part of the World War between August the first, nineteen hundred and fourteen, and January the first, nineteen hundred and twenty."[6] To organize a national league, the WOSL arranged its self-governing local units into nine Corps Areas that corresponded to the War Department's Army Corps Areas.[7] A national board of officers and committees planned the annual national conventions, published a magazine titled *Carry On*, and coordinated other matters.

The WOSL intended to become more than just a friendly social association of former overseas women: it focused on serving others. The Articles of Incorporation stated that "the object of this association is to keep alive and develop the spirit that prompted overseas service, to maintain the ties of comradeship born of that service and to assist and further any patriotic work; to inculcate a sense of individual obligation to the community, state and nation; to work for the welfare of the Army and Navy; to assist, in any way in their power, the men and women who served or were wounded or incapacitated in the World War; to foster friendship and understanding between Americans and Allies in the World War."[8] The WOSL thus united its members to serve their local communities, states, and the nation according to these principles. Although the members appreciated the work done by women on the home front, they excluded them from membership because they felt that by going overseas they experienced unique hardships that created what Mrs. Chew described as a "feeling of sistership among those who went over there."[9] They used this sisterhood and the unique legacy of their wartime experiences to continue their service in the postwar era. As much as it could, the WOSL tried to be apolitical and concentrate on service. In 1923, national president Louise Wells explained how she hoped that "men may say of us, not, 'They support this or that'; not 'They oppose this or that'; not 'They want this or that'; but 'They serve.'"[10]

The WOSL saw itself as a sister organization to the American Legion, with which it often cooperated. In 1923, the American Legion's national commander, Alvin Owsley, even described the WOSL as the American Legion's "comrades in service."[11] Although the few women who officially served in the military could join the American Legion or Veterans of Foreign Wars, many women served overseas with civilian organizations or in other capacities and remained ineligible for membership because they did not officially serve in the military. The creation of the WOSL allowed these women to join a similar veterans' organization. Mrs. Chew even admitted that they intended to create an organization based on the same principles as the American Legion, and the legion endorsed the WOSL's bill that sought a national charter, although this failed.[12]

As highly trained and experienced women, WOSL members wanted to continue using their skills to support the nation after the war. Mrs. Chew envisioned the league as serving the US government "in case of future wars, catastrophes, or need of any kind, to have a body of women trained in the Great War, in service of every kind; organized and ready for action so that they can be called upon at a moment's notice . . . in other words, it is a reserve army for the United States government."[13] Members did not want to fully retreat back to the traditional female domestic sphere; they wanted to use their skills in the public sphere. As Louise Wells explained in 1922 while serving as the national service chair, when the overseas women came home, "something said to us—I suppose it is the maternal instinct in every good woman which said that the women had served well over there, and that we had no families, no children, and we wanted to continue to serve. We came back wanting to work, wanting to carry on."[14] By grounding their need to continue their service in the traditionally feminine term "maternal instinct," Wells relied on accepted notions of femininity to expand women's opportunities in civic society. WOSL members frequently embraced the often feminine nature of their work, but, newly armed with the vote and fresh from their wartime experiences, they also yearned for new ways to continue their national service beyond traditional female roles. Through the league, they created space for women to engage in national defense and expanded women's opportunities for civic leadership. Their advocacy for women's opportunities, especially with the military, occupied a transitional moment teetering between traditional and more modern roles for women.

Advocating for and serving male and female veterans became the WOSL's most important mission and soon partially overtook its initial intention to also serve as a reserve army. Mrs. Chew described WOSL women as wanting "to go on with the service that we have started. These women, who gave their services willingly during the World War, now wish to continue their services to humanity and their country." She explained that WOSL members wished "to help and are already helping the soldier and sailor injured during the World War and those of their own ranks who are suffering or in need."[15]

The WOSL embodied its focus on service in the title of its organizational magazine: *Carry On*, a phrase that became an unofficial WOSL motto and was often repeated within the larger network of female veteranists. An advertisement for the American Red Cross (ARC) featured on the back cover of the August 1925 edition of *Carry On* epitomized this maxim. Titled "The Greatest Mother Still 'Carries On,'" it includes a photograph of two female nurses assisting two severely disabled veterans, one in a wheelchair and the other a double amputee who rests on a wheeled board (fig. 1.1). The image is captioned "In the Homes, in the Government Hospitals, and the Veterans Bureau Offices it is Serving Those Who Served." This image and its caption played on both the Red Cross's wartime nickname of the "World's Greatest Mother," a phrase commonly featured in wartime propaganda posters, and the WOSL magazine's title, *Carry On*. The caption demonstrates the overlapping missions of the ARC and the WOSL, which included former and present ARC members, and shows how both organizations acted as leaders in veterans' care.

WOSL members placed special importance on serving and commemorating women like themselves whom they believed to be veterans.[16] They advocated for overseas women to receive government benefits that many were denied because they lacked official veteran status. They consistently memorialized the women who died overseas and commemorated women's wartime service alongside men's. In doing so, they tried to prevent their contributions from being forgotten and argued for their inclusion as official veterans. Louise Wells described how the WOSL women "took overseas with us a torch we lighted in our own hearts, and it was our purpose to keep that burning, which we did, and when we came back we wanted to preserve that spirit."[17] The idea of a torch of service appeared in the league's emblem, which featured a lit torch spreading its light, an apt symbol for how the WOSL spread the light of its service through its postwar activities (fig. 1.2). Wells worried that "if that spirit . . . is to be allowed to die out without some permanent form

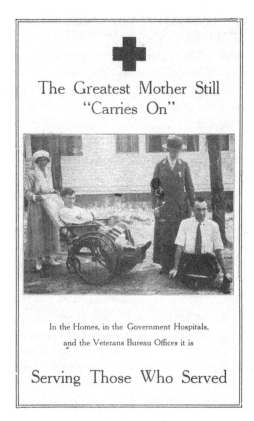

The Greatest Mother Still
"Carries On"

In the Homes, in the Government Hospitals,
and the Veterans Bureau Offices it is

Serving Those Who Served

Figure 1.1. Back cover of *Carry On*, vol. 4, no. 3 (August 1925). *Carry On* Periodical Collection, Gift of Carolyn Habgood, Military Women's Memorial Collection.

of record, without something which can be handed down to our successors, I think that the country will have lost a very precious thing."[18] She believed that the history of American women's overseas service needed to be preserved in the historical record so future generations could learn how women served their country even before they could all vote, officially enter every branch of the military, or receive veteran status. Recording this history might help future generations of women gain more opportunities to serve in the military and receive veteran status.

Over sixteen thousand American women are estimated to have served overseas during World War One.[19] This provided a large population of women from which the WOSL recruited members. Members represented over one hundred different organizations with which women served overseas. The annual rosters published as supplements to *Carry On* usually contained an entire page listing these organizations.[20] These rosters even included some foreign organizations such as Great Britain's Queen Alexandra's Military Nursing Service and the French Red Cross. American women who served abroad with

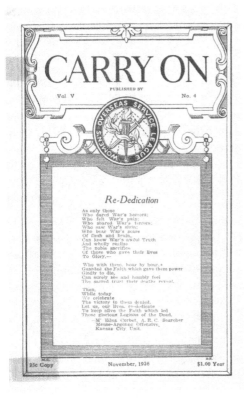

Figure 1.2. Women's Overseas Service League (WOSL) emblem from the cover of *Carry On. Carry On* Periodical Collection, Gift of Carolyn Habgood, Military Women's Memorial Collection.

foreign groups, often before the US entered the war, and European women who moved to the US after the war, could all become WOSL members.[21]

The league's broad membership captured the diverse ways that American women served overseas, and WOSL members took pride in uniting women across regional, economic, social, and religious differences.[22] By 1925, 2,086 women had joined the WOSL, and they constantly worked to increase their membership.[23] Members recognized and appreciated the league's attempted inclusivity. Miss Blanton, a member from Richmond, Virginia, explained how during the war, "those of us who were born and bred in a brier patch have been broadened by having contact with other parts of the world and with women from the West and from the North."[24] She praised how the WOSL brought these women together after the war. For southern women like Blanton, raised in the shadow of the Civil War, the WOSL aided the ongoing process of national reconciliation.

The league tried to keep dues affordable so that women of all social and economic classes could join.[25] In contrast to the popular image of the women who served overseas as coming mostly from wealthy, upper-class backgrounds, many women actually came from lower-middle-class backgrounds and worked as wage earners before and after the war; the WOSL wanted to remain accessible to them.[26] Nonetheless, numerous members did come from White, Christian, middle- and upper-class backgrounds. Their privileged upbringings may have enabled them to more easily devote time to the WOSL after the war, while working women often had to return to jobs, leaving less time to be involved.

Despite its intention to be an inclusive organization, the WOSL racially segregated its membership. The Articles of Incorporation specifically stated that "colored women in each state shall form their own separate units."[27] In reality, the WOSL probably did not need such a statement given how few African American women actually served overseas; most were prohibited from overseas service. Historian Susan Zeiger estimated that three African American women served in France as YMCA secretaries during the war; several dozen others joined them after April 1919.[28] No African American nurses were permitted to serve overseas.[29] Even though only a handful of African American women served overseas, the WOSL still felt compelled to include this segregation policy and prevent even the few eligible African American women from joining together equally alongside their White colleagues.[30] With so few Black women eligible for membership, forming their own separate state chapters likely would have been almost impossible. In keeping with the customs of Jim Crow, the WOSL, like the military, did not believe that the services and sacrifices of African Americans necessitated their equal treatment as citizens in the postwar social order or their participation in an organization focused on service and philanthropy. The WOSL's policies abandoned the small number of African American women eligible for membership and prevented them from benefiting from the league's advocacy or taking part in its veteranist work.

Many WOSL members volunteered for wartime service because of their Progressive era involvement in voluntarism and reform work.[31] During the Progressive era, women expanded their traditional roles by becoming leaders and active participants in social work, settlement houses, and volunteer organizations. At the same time, they pushed for the professionalization of their fields and pursued careers as paid employees. When World War One began, many of these women transferred their leadership experience and skills to organizations that supported the war effort overseas. Afterward, many joined the WOSL and connected their Progressive era service work to their postwar commemorative activities and careers. Two such women were Rose Glass and Lena Hitchcock.

Rose Glass organized the Seattle WOSL Unit and served as its charter

Figure 1.3. WOSL Seattle Unit members, November 11, 1968. From left to right: Mrs. Edna Lord (ARC), Mrs. I. M. (Anna) Palmaw (Army Nurse Corps), Miss Rose Glass (YMCA), and Miss Blanche Wenner (YMCA). Women's Overseas Service League Collection, National WWI Museum and Memorial Archives, Kansas City, Missouri, USA.

president. Highly educated, she graduated from the University of Washington in 1904 and attended graduate school at Columbia University. She then worked in a New York City settlement house before she volunteered with the YMCA as the entertainment director for the American Expeditionary Forces (AEF) in France. After the war, Glass settled in Seattle, where she worked as a teacher for forty years. She never married and received support in her old age from a trust fund established for her by a relative, evidence of her privileged background.[32] Influenced by Progressivism, Glass took her leadership roles seriously and devoted her life to being an educator and supporting the Seattle WOSL Unit (fig. 1.3).

Lena Hitchcock served as the WOSL national president from 1927 to 1929 and similarly devoted her life to her career and the advancement of women's service and leadership.[33] Hitchcock came from a privileged family involved with Republican politics, and she spent her youth as a volunteer and suffrage activist in Washington, DC. During the war, she served in France with one of the first groups of occupational therapist Reconstruction Aides attached to the Army Medical Corps.[34] As a pioneer in this field, she worked as a private occupational therapist in Washington, DC, after she returned home. She later supported the establishment of the occupational therapy department at the city's Children's Hospital, where she served as chair from 1935 to 1952. Hitchcock then helped lead the occupational therapy program at the Society for Crippled Children until 1967, all while remaining an active leader with the WOSL and the World War Reconstruction Aides Association (WWRAA).[35] Hitchcock made helping others the focus of her career. She explained in a 1982 oral history that volunteering remained important to her throughout her life.[36] Women like Lena Hitchcock and Rose Glass, who came of age during the Progressive era, drew from their early experiences and transformed their volunteer service into professional careers. They understood veteranism as complementary to their commitment to aiding others, acting as community leaders, and establishing careers.

SERVICE AS COMMEMORATION

The WOSL's veteranist commemoration activities encompassed a variety of service projects and advocacy. Service projects included any form of community service, volunteer work, fundraising, or philanthropy. Advocacy work encompassed lobbying and advocating on behalf of male and female veterans, especially former overseas women who tried to gain government benefits.

As Americans built hundreds of World War One monuments in the US and Europe, the WOSL chose another course of action with its preference for veteranist commemorations.[37] According to the WOSL's organizational historian Helene M. Sillia, the WOSL felt that "any memorial to our women war-dead should be in this country rather than overseas and that it should take the form of living service to our own."[38] The WOSL repeated this mantra throughout the interwar period to justify its abstention from traditional memorial projects. For example, on the front cover of the May 1923 edition of *Carry On*, it printed Edgar Guest's poem "Memorial Day," which asserted that the living must "Pledge ourselves as warriors true / Unto the work they died to do." Guest wrote:

> The finest tribute we can pay
> Unto our hero dead to-day
> Is not of speech or roses red,
> But living, throbbing hearts instead,
> That shall renew the pledge they sealed
> With death upon the battlefield.[39]

In a less abstract way, during its 1937 annual national radio broadcast, service chair Mrs. J. Nathaniel Steed, known by her nickname "Mother Steed," reminded the WOSL of its motto, rooted in veteranism: "The greatest memorial to the dead is service to the living."[40]

The WOSL remained committed to veteranism even during the Great Depression. In the August 1933 issue of *Carry On*, national president Faustine Dennis reminded the WOSL of the increased importance of its service work during these trying times. She told WOSL members that they must "carry on our Service—this word that is to us the very breath of our League Life!"[41] Referring to the recent action taken at the convention to establish an emergency fund to help WOSL members in need of temporary aid because of the Great Depression, she explained: "I cannot adequately express my happiness that through convention action another service to our women is at last made possible—financial assistance to those who, although not physically disabled, are no less in need of a helping hand over an economic crisis."[42] The WOSL stepped in when the government did not and provided support to its members, no matter the cause. In doing so, it commemorated these women for their wartime service.

The WOSL would last as an organization only as long as its members lived; eventually, the women who served in World War One would die and the league would not be able to pursue its missions.[43] The life of the organization was extended only when the US entered World War Two and the WOSL opened membership to the next generation of women who served overseas. Nevertheless, by commemorating World War One through acts of service, WOSL members physically embodied the concept of a living memorial that existed only while they could carry on their service work. In fact, some WOSL units became memorials themselves when they chose unit names that honored a local woman who died in wartime service or a recently deceased member of their unit.[44]

Despite its preference for veteranist commemorations, the WOSL did not prohibit or discourage traditional statuary memorials, but it prioritized them below service. While it pushed for a more modernist approach to commemoration, it occupied a more transitional stance and still incorporated a variety of traditional commemorations and social events into its activities, many of which were fairly standard for veterans' organizations of the time.[45] Local WOSL units participated in parades, memorial services, funerals, and social activities in addition to their service work. For example, on Memorial Day in 1925, members of the Toledo, Ohio, WOSL Unit marched in the local parade; some members even wore their old uniforms. Later that day, they attended services at a Presbyterian church.[46] The WOSL also had its own "Order of Service," a document that outlined a memorial service held at each annual national convention to honor women who died overseas during the war as well as recently deceased WOSL members.[47]

In its early years, the WOSL even considered supporting some memorial projects that combined aspects of statuary memorials with service, such as the George Washington Victory Memorial Building and the American Red Cross Memorial Building to the Women of the World War. Begun in 1898 to memorialize George Washington in the nation's capital, the George Washington Memorial Building faced a series of problems that prevented its completion.[48] In an attempt to revive the project, commemoration of the victory in the World War was added to its mission and the project was renamed and reconceived as a living memorial with themed memorial rooms. The WOSL received an offer to purchase one of these rooms as its national headquarters and a memorial to the women who died during their overseas service.[49]

The WOSL briefly considered participating in this project but learned it had been a source of nationwide controversy and condemned by the American Legion. The legion explained to Irene M. Givenwilson, chair of the WOSL Memorial Committee and an American Red Cross leader, that it opposed the erection of any public building commemorating the war until "proper and adequate legislation has been enacted for the relief of the disabled, first; the unemployed, second; and adjusted compensation."[50] The American Legion agreed with the WOSL's prioritization of service projects before the construction of monuments and encouraged it to reject the offer, which it did, a wise choice since the building was never completed.[51]

The decision not to participate in the George Washington Victory Memorial Building reflected the WOSL's intensifying preference for commemorations rooted in veteranism during the 1920s. In her 1923 report about this decision, Givenwilson concluded that the Memorial Committee believed it to be "far more important at the present time to increase our membership than to decide upon a permanent memorial, since we have enrolled to date only about 10% of the women who actually served overseas."[52] Increasing the WOSL membership took precedence over building memorials because the more women who became members, the more veterans they could assist. The WOSL continued to reject offers to participate in physical memorials, such as in 1924 when it declined an invitation from a potential war mothers' memorial with the explanation that its "particular care at present" focused on "disabled women."[53]

The WOSL's focus on service captured attention even in France. During the WOSL's 1930 national convention in Paris, the president of France, Gaston Doumergue, addressed WOSL national president Mrs. Taubles and several other national officers at the Élysée Palace and praised the league for its service work. As published in *Carry On*, President Doumergue noted how the "women of your organization have done your share of service in time of war, but now, when womanhood has come into her own, there is still as great a service to render to the cause of peace, a constant service, that of bringing gradually continued peace on earth."[54] Doumergue understood that by pursuing veteranism, the WOSL aimed to make the world a better, more peaceful place.

To conduct its agenda of veteranist commemorations, the WOSL instituted service programs at the national and local unit levels. Service at the national level took place through two national standing committees: the Service Committee and the Fund for Disabled Overseas Women Committee. The Service Committee worked on the issues of "Rehabilitation; Hostess Service of the United States Army; Government and Soldiers' Homes; Loans and Grants from the Fund for Disabled Overseas Women; and other service incidental to purposes of the League." The Fund for Disabled Overseas Women Committee specifically focused on running the national fund that aided overseas women and became one of the WOSL's most important ongoing projects.[55]

Local units devoted most of their time and resources to service activities. They often focused their service work on the main projects outlined by the national committees, such as raising money for the Fund for Disabled Overseas Women, doing army hostess work, volunteering at veterans' hospitals, and aiding other overseas women. No standard protocol existed for local units to follow; they could choose the causes they wanted to support, and their service activities varied.

At all levels of the organization, the WOSL focused on the three main categories of service that originated in its mission: service to former overseas women and other female veterans, service to male veterans, and advocacy that aided former overseas women and aimed to include them in the war's historical narrative. With the onset of the Great Depression, the growing political power of veterans, and the aging of veterans, these categories of service became even more vital.

HELPING THEIR OWN: SERVICE PROJECTS IN SUPPORT OF OFFICIAL AND UNRECOGNIZED FEMALE VETERANS

The men who served in the American armed forces successfully gained some government veterans' benefits such as the Bonus, vocational rehabilitation training, and hospitalization benefits for those with service-related disabilities, while the majority of former overseas women remained ineligible for veteran status and government aid.[56] The WOSL did not leave these women to fend for themselves. It helped its members and other White former overseas women, especially since these women often had no other means of assistance. By aiding former overseas women, the WOSL commemorated their service, showed its appreciation for their sacrifices, and defined them as veterans, even when the government did not.

Because so many overseas women served in voluntary organizations and not in "official" government service since those opportunities often prohibited women, many women received no government benefits. An undated document about the league's history explained that although the women who served overseas outside the official government apparatus "had shared the hardships of the armed forces and many came home with impaired health, only the Army and Navy nurses were entitled to government compensation. None of the welfare organizations made any provision for their disabled workers after the war. Even the Red Cross nurses who served in Army hospitals were not eligible for aid from any source."[57] These women had supported the American armed forces but because they did not officially serve in the military, they could not obtain government veterans' benefits. This became an extremely contentious policy that the WOSL worked to overturn. At the same time, it spearheaded several initiatives to provide its own social welfare to women and asserted that they should be given veteran status.

The WOSL established the Fund for Disabled Overseas Women to provide loans and financial aid to any disabled, ill, or economically unstable former overseas woman. This fund became especially important during the Great Depression. It was created through a resolution passed at the 1923 national convention that asked each member to contribute one dollar to the fund every year. The fund was intended to "serve as an emergency fund for any unit which may be unable to care for some case arising in its territory and also to serve as a fund for worthy cases of disabled ex-service women who may need help and who are too distant from any unit to make it practical for that unit to help."[58] Grants could also be issued to women who could not repay a loan; in fact, the term "loan" was used even when repayment seemed unlikely in order to provide encouragement to the recipient, or to persuade women to accept money they might have refused if they thought it was charity.[59]

The WOSL established a national committee to operate the fund. During the national convention in San Francisco in July 1924, the committee's chair, Mrs. Eugene K. Sturgis, outlined the three resolutions from the 1923 convention that guided the league's policies on disabled ex-servicewomen.[60] First, the WOSL resolved to undertake "a definite and comprehensive program" to alleviate "the suffering now existing among disabled ex-service women and that this program be continued for as long a period as there shall be any disabled ex-service women who are in need of help." Second, it would take on the care of all "disabled ex-service women, who, for some technical reason, are debarred from receiving aid from the US Government or from a welfare organization, and also of those women whose disability may not be directly traceable to their service overseas." Third, they pledged to try to secure under the new Veterans Bureau "a national home and hospital for disabled and sick ex-service women, which shall be open to ex-service women exclusively, upon the same terms that such national homes maintained by the US Government are open to men." Sturgis highlighted her committee's success with a few of these goals and felt "tempered by enthusiasm and a fine recognition of the joy which comes in serving one's own disabled comrades." But even as she lauded these accomplishments, she emphasized that many women needed assistance in proving their claims to the Veterans Bureau.[61] In order to assist them, around 1924 the WOSL sent out twelve thousand questionnaires to its members and other former overseas women asking about disabled women's needs. It hoped to identify struggling disabled women and learn what assistance they required.[62] These questionnaires helped the WOSL better assist disabled women and enabled it to recruit new members who could benefit from its support.

Local WOSL units constantly worked to raise money to support the fund. The May 1927 edition of *Carry On* contained a short article from the national service chair about local units' contributions. It was titled "Does This Look as Though the W.O.S.L. Had Forgotten?" and listed the contributions of twelve different units, with donations ranging from $10 from Mississippi to $100 from San Francisco.[63] Some units raised money for the fund in very creative ways, such as a unit in New York that raised $2,000 through a benefit performance of a play written by member Mrs. August Belmont.[64]

WOSL members and local units used *Carry On* to promote campaigns for the fund that members could participate in nationwide. The Omaha Unit sponsored a trip to Paris, France, to benefit the fund and advertised it on the back cover of the February 1928 edition of *Carry On*.[65] In another example of imaginative fundraising, in 1931, the WOSL national leadership urged members to participate in "The Christmas Card Club." In lieu of sending fellow members Christmas cards, members could donate the money they normally spent on cards to the fund. WOSL leaders urged members to participate and asserted that "the League has it in *its own power*, through a little self-sacrifice, to increase our National Disabled Fund very materially each year."[66] This same issue of *Carry On* also suggested that members could continue another tradition of taking out "Christmas Greeting" advertisements in the magazine in exchange for a donation to the fund as another way to send holiday wishes to distant friends.[67] The WOSL urged members to forgo the expenses of friendship and instead use their money to support the fund and their friends in need.

Even geographically distant units worked together to augment the fund. After the WOSL held its 1930 national convention in Paris, the Boston and

Detroit Units donated a movie about the convention to raise money for the fund. The movie could be lent to local units to screen for an admission fee that would be donated to the fund. The Boston and Detroit Units hoped the film would raise money for the fund, promote and advertise the WOSL, and "serve as a permanent record of great historic interest, not only to every member of the League, but to all who hold sacred the memories of what our service overseas stood for."[68] This fundraiser allowed units to publicly commemorate their own wartime service while they raised money for the fund. Such creative projects helped combine commemoration and service.

The fund also benefited from the philanthropy of Sallie McIntosh Clark, a WOSL member who served with the American Red Cross and who, in her 1932 will, created a trust to finance the WOSL's efforts to support disabled former overseas women.[69] Upon her death, this trust fund of $50,000 was to be transferred to the WOSL for this purpose for as long as the WOSL needed it, especially when members reached old age.[70] At some point, the WOSL might disband because of the age or death of most of its members. The trust would then be given to the American Red Cross; this transfer occurred in January 2001, shortly after the death of the last WOSL member from World War One.[71]

The WOSL also supported the few former overseas women who did receive some government aid as officially recognized veterans. It especially assisted the disabled women allowed into two government hospitals after its lobbying efforts succeeded in obtaining this benefit for them. Women who officially served in the Army Nurse Corps, the Navy Nurse Corps, the navy, or Marine Corps could reside at a home established at Danville, Illinois, and in a special wing of a tuberculosis hospital in Milwaukee, Wisconsin.[72] The national WOSL and many local units aided the Danville home from its inception, but the Danville facility did not sufficiently meet the needs of its female residents, and in March 1931 the women were moved to the Soldiers' Home in Dayton, Ohio.[73] At Dayton, those women who were in worse health lived in a hospital annex, while the healthier women stayed in a former hotel known as the Miller Cottage.[74] The move allowed each woman to have her own room and, if able, to travel into town by trolley car, something impossible at the more isolated Danville location. The WOSL president at the time, Mrs. G. H. Taubles, believed that the move was "encouraging . . . for it shows us that the Government is mindful of these women and a better, bigger Home will be found as the need arises."[75]

The WOSL appointed a chair to organize service projects to help the women at the Dayton home. These projects included subscribing to magazines for the residents, sending puzzles and amusements, and providing materials for them to make and sell hooked rugs and knitted items to earn pocket money.[76]

The WOSL also began an adoption program in which local units "adopted" women at the Dayton home who came from their geographic area and "by means of letters, remembrances, and personal interest re-establish[ed] the bonds of normal companionship which institutional life tends to destroy." Although the WOSL did not run the Dayton home, it supported it and aimed to "distribute the interest and activities of the League in a way that will bring a more personal touch into our relations with the Dayton Service Women."[77] The WOSL recognized that the government's inclusion of women at these institutions represented a victory in the fight to get overseas women some government benefits. By supporting the Dayton home, the WOSL showed its appreciation to the government even as it continued to advocate for further government benefits for former overseas women.

Through its support of these homes, the Fund for Disabled Overseas Women, and other initiatives to help the women it considered veterans, the WOSL created memorials constructed from human actions in place of stone. The service of the WOSL members at the veterans' homes transformed them into living memorials that commemorated the war by supporting the female veterans who lived there. The memory of the war became embodied in the war's survivors, both the veterans who needed help and those who provided it. By treating former overseas women as veterans no matter their official government status, the WOSL argued through its commemorative acts that these women should be defined and honored as veterans who earned benefits through their wartime service.

HELPING THEIR BOYS: WOSL SERVICE
TOWARD MALE VETERANS

The WOSL also devoted many of its commemorative activities to helping male veterans. Since so many former overseas women supported "the boys" during the war, they felt it remained their duty to continue helping them afterward. In 1922, National Service Committee chair Anne Hoyt wrote to the American Red Cross to determine how the WOSL could best assist its work. She told their chair Judge Payne that although the WOSL supported all of its initiatives, it felt that "our program should concentrate on the one line of service to the Ex-Service man, that being the thing for which by training, experience and understanding, the Overseas women are most especially fitted." Hoyt asked Judge Payne whether the ARC would accept the WOSL's offer to be its "especial—though of course not exclusive—agency to call on at need for any backing, supplementing or extending of its work for the Ex-Service man." The WOSL wanted to assist these men because it felt that "we have something that no other worker for him can have—that our grounded knowledge of him, our underlying admiration makes for a patience that cannot tire,—

and that the bond of common memories, or his sense of our understanding, enables us to help him without his experiencing any sting or feeling of demoralization."[78] Having intimately aided them during the war, the WOSL understood its postwar service to veterans as a way to continue its wartime duties.

Local units took this mission to heart and constantly aided male veterans. In 1927, the New England and Boston WOSL Units contributed a donation to the US Blind Veterans' Musicale Company, an orchestra composed of blind veterans who performed concerts to raise money for their fellow blind veterans.[79] During Christmas in 1924, a group of women from the New York WOSL units visited the US Veterans' Hospital No. 98 at Castle Point, New York. They spent time with the patients, observed the hospital's work, and celebrated Christmas. They also sent Christmas boxes to the patients at Castle Point and two other hospitals in the region.[80] WOSL units across the country conducted similar service work to help male veterans, especially disabled veterans or those who remained hospitalized.

The WOSL's female veterans also pursued service projects that helped the "welfare of the Army and Navy," as denoted in its mission.[81] The WOSL actively supported the summer Citizens' Military Training Camps (CMTC) run by the War Department to provide voluntary military training to young civilian men.[82] They encouraged members to volunteer as army hostesses who provided and staffed facilities for men to visit with their mothers and other women in a chaste environment. These hostess houses were modeled after similar facilities constructed at stateside bases during the war.[83] This hostess service allowed the WOSL to continue its dedication to military service and national preparedness. It also enabled it to create space for women in these male-dominated military landscapes, even if it was only through female occupations like hostess work.

The WOSL's support also extended to the male veterans who served as cemetery superintendents at the overseas American cemeteries established by the American Battle Monuments Commission (ABMC). The unit in Toledo, Ohio, sent the superintendents of the Meuse-Argonne and Oise-Aisne American Cemeteries subscriptions to the *Saturday Evening Post*.[84] By supporting these cemetery superintendents, the WOSL used acts of service to honor the Americans buried in these cemeteries, as well as the veterans who cared for their graves.

ADVOCACY FOR FORMER OVERSEAS WOMEN

Another main tenet of the WOSL's veteranist platform focused on advocacy on behalf of former overseas women. While many male veterans benefited from the political power of the American Legion and Veterans of Foreign

Wars, the WOSL quickly realized that it would have to advocate for itself, especially since many overseas women could not join those groups and lacked official veteran status. The WOSL served as the voice of former overseas women and tried to secure government benefits based on their wartime service and the belief that they deserved to be recognized as veterans by the government and the public.

The WOSL believed that these women's overseas wartime service entitled them to the benefits of "martial citizenship," the idea that a special type of citizenship could be earned through military service and entitled veterans to certain government benefits.[85] By conducting work that the WOSL defined as military service, members asserted that they deserved the same special rights and benefits given to male military veterans, even if they served as civilians and not officially in the military. They claimed that they earned these rights by fulfilling the duties of martial citizenship through their overseas service, and they returned home "with the conviction that they had by it been set apart."[86]

The government did not completely agree, and the WOSL grappled with the government's refusal to grant veteran status to many women who served overseas. Only women who officially served as members of the military could be considered for veterans' benefits.[87] This limited group of women included those who served in the Army Nurse Corps, the Navy Nurse Corps, in the navy as Yeoman (F), or in the Marine Corps. Women who served in one of the many voluntary organizations overseas were considered civilians ineligible for veterans' benefits, even though they often worked for, with, and among the military, frequently in uniform and often under oath.[88] They could not officially serve in the military because the government did not permit them to. As a result, many members of the WOSL received no benefits from the government after the war, despite any injuries, ailments, or mental afflictions they suffered as a result of their wartime service.

Even the women who officially served in the military struggled to gain recognition for their service and obtain veterans' benefits. During the war, army and navy nurses served in an undefined status without official rank: they were neither enlisted nor officers and they could not exercise authority over men under their care.[89] Army nurses succeeded in gaining relative rank from Congress in June 1920, but navy nurses did not receive this status because the navy deemed it superfluous.[90] The Yeoman (F) and the women marines, the first American women to serve as enlisted members of the US armed forces, became the only women to be most clearly considered veterans. However, they often struggled to receive care, and the Naval Reserve Act of 1925 barred women from future enlistment.[91] Although the small group of women who did officially serve in the military were in a better position than most former overseas women, they still faced challenges in receiving their benefits, especially when it came to health care and hospitals that were not equipped to care for women.[92]

The WOSL formed a National Legislative Committee to formally advocate for legislation to benefit former overseas women, especially those who did not officially serve in the military. This committee collected information about relevant legislation, suggested bills to support, and recommended proposals for legislation that would further its interests.[93] During her term as legislative committee chair, Faustine Dennis updated the WOSL about her committee's work in the April 1932 issue of *Carry On*. She described their efforts to persuade Congressman James Fitzpatrick (D-NY) of the Military Affairs Committee in the House of Representatives and World War One veteran Senator Hiram Bingham III (R-CT) to consider the proposed bills to give government hospitalization benefits to all women who served overseas with the army but were not in military service.[94] Dennis intended to advocate for these women and testify before congressional committees, if needed. She described how she had been asked whether the WOSL should continue to press for this legislation during the Great Depression. Unequivocally she answered yes and argued that "illness and death wait on no man and on no depression. If these sick women are to be cared for and returned to health, or helped until the day when all human efforts cease to matter, we must keep on unwaveringly until government hospitalization is gained for them." Even though she would not benefit herself since she served with the American Red Cross, she and her committee continued to be "happy to do our utmost to help these sisters of ours."[95]

Despite the WOSL's annual efforts to promote this legislation and Dennis's pronouncement, in that same year, 1932, Dennis and the WOSL reversed course and withdrew this legislation and other bills that sought benefits for overseas women.[96] They decided to comply with "the pleas of the US President for an economy program" in an act of patriotic cooperation during the Great Depression.[97] In 1933, after FDR took office, they even went "on record as approving the President's economy program" in the New Deal, and they did not reactivate the efforts of this committee until 1939, after the worst of the Depression ended.[98] These decisions demonstrated that the WOSL supported FDR and agreed with his conception of the New Deal as a type of emergency war measure that necessitated sacrifices from the citizenry.[99]

The WOSL took similar actions in line with the New Deal regarding the Bonus, the retroactive financial compensation originally planned to be given to First World War veterans in 1945.[100] In her 1932 report about the legislative committee's efforts to lobby for hospitalization benefits, Dennis expressed her opposition to the immediate payment of the Bonus. She explained that "were it a matter of a bonus, your chairman personally would feel that we should wait until a later time."[101] At the 1933 national convention when the WOSL elected Dennis as its national president, the league publicly announced its opposition to the immediate payment of the Bonus to overseas women. The *New York Times* reported on July 6, 1933, that the WOSL "closed its convention today with a declaration against payment of any bonus to women who served abroad during the World War. Leaders said several attempts had been made to have Congress provide compensation for nurses, welfare workers and others who saw overseas service."[102]

These decisions placed the WOSL squarely in support of FDR's New Deal economic recovery efforts, which prioritized national needs and the "war" against the Great Depression over veterans' demands, especially the immediate payment of the Bonus.[103] As early as his 1932 presidential campaign, Roosevelt opposed the immediate payment of the Bonus when there remained so many other pressing economic issues to solve. He viewed veterans as a minority group no more entitled to such relief than other struggling Americans.[104] Once elected president, FDR continued to oppose the immediate payment of the Bonus and enacted legislation that reduced existing veterans' benefits.[105] As part of his "Hundred Days" legislation early in his first term, the "Bill to Maintain the Credit of the United States Government," known as the Economy Act, reduced veterans' benefits and pensions by $460 million and sparked a political backlash against the New Deal by veterans who felt under attack.[106] By supporting the president's "economy program" in 1933, the WOSL endorsed the Economy Act and its reductions of veterans' benefits. It supported FDR and his New Deal effort to combat the Great Depression, just as it did in 1932 even before his election when it paused its legislative efforts.

The WOSL's cooperation with FDR's administration makes sense given its close ties with the American Legion. During the early years of the New Deal, the American Legion attempted to cooperate with FDR, while the Veterans of Foreign Wars (VFW) took a more confrontational stance and continued the fight for immediate payment of the Bonus and expanded veterans' benefits.[107] The WOSL's closer alignment with the American Legion might have influenced its decision to support FDR and his New Deal efforts to stabilize the economy, even if some of these measures reduced veterans' benefits.[108] The WOSL opted to temporarily sacrifice several of its goals in order to support the president's emergency measures to restore the American economy.

The WOSL's ties with the American Legion and its later support of the New Deal could also help explain its relative silence about the Bonus March. In the spring and summer of 1932, thousands of World War One veterans and their families descended on Washington, DC, in an attempt to persuade Congress to distribute the Bonus early as part of an effort that became known as the Bonus March.[109] During the 1932 WOSL national convention in Los Angeles, held from July 4 to 7 during the Bonus March, the WOSL adopted a resolution to address the events happening in Washington, DC. This reaffirmed the WOSL's obligation and allegiance to the government, resolving that the WOSL would "recommend to the several Units the desirability of forming a plan to work through the coming year with veterans and to encourage their full cooperation with the Government during its difficult period of financial adjustment."[110] As the Bonus March divided veterans' organizations, this moderate statement suggested that the WOSL may have tried to remain neutral about the issue, much like the American Legion, which, for the most part, tried to be somewhat impartial.[111] This may account for the absence of a discussion about the Bonus March or the immediate payment of the Bonus in *Carry On*. Taking sides might have hindered the WOSL's service projects and its advocacy for women veterans. Instead, it stayed focused on its mission and asserted its willingness to cooperate productively with both veterans and the government. Although it seemed to support the Bonus in theory, it did not believe immediate payment was the right course at that early point in the Depression.[112]

The WOSL aimed for neutrality during the Bonus March and stayed focused on its mission of serving veterans, a message it sent out loud and clear from the White House on June 16, 1932, during the height of the Bonus March.[113] That day, President Herbert Hoover and WOSL member First Lady Lou Henry Hoover hosted their annual White House garden party for one thousand disabled veterans. Assisted by the First Lady's fellow WOSL members Mabel Boardman, Lena Hitchcock, and Representative Edith Nourse Rogers, along with numerous uniformed nurses and other women, the veterans enjoyed sandwiches and sweets with the president and First Lady. Even while veterans protested, Mrs. Hoover and these prominent WOSL members tried to stay above politics by demonstrating their commitment to serving veterans.[114] Evidence indicates that other WOSL members and female veteranists likely took to the streets to aid the needy veterans in town for the Bonus March.[115]

The WOSL did not publicly support the immediate payment of the Bonus because the Bonus would not solve many of the issues the WOSL cared most about. It would provide only temporary assistance to male veterans and a few female veterans. The WOSL wanted long-term benefits and recognition for all veterans, especially women, not just a temporary influx of cash as a short-term solution. It worried more about the lasting problems that affected veterans, especially women veterans and those women denied veteran status. Faustine Dennis emphasized this difference in her 1932 article when she clarified why she supported the bill for hospitalization benefits but not immediate payment of the Bonus. She explained that "the whole emphasis of this bill, in my mind, is the physical suffering of women, who deserve this care from the government they served."[116] Indeed, First Lady Lou Henry Hoover and President Hoover, in office during the 1932 march, privately donated food, clothing, and other necessities to veterans who participated in the Bonus March, even as they publicly opposed the immediate payment of the Bonus and the Bonus March.[117] The Bonus served as the easy solution to veterans' problems, while the WOSL's commemorative service platform pushed for a harder but more comprehensive plan that gave all who served the care they deserved and the veteran status they earned. The WOSL believed such a course represented the best way to commemorate the Americans who served in the war—both men and women, both official veterans and unrecognized veterans.

PRESERVING THE HISTORY OF OVERSEAS WOMEN

Alongside its focus on service, and in accordance with the object of its organization, the WOSL worked to "to keep alive and develop the spirit that prompted overseas service."[118] This part of its mission constituted a key part of its veteranist agenda. By attempting to continue the spirit of their overseas service, WOSL members both commemorated women's overseas service and staked their claim in the commemorative narrative of the war as veterans.

The WOSL instituted a history project to document its war work, which consisted of questionnaire forms sent to WOSL members that each member would return along with an informal narrative about her service. The questionnaires asked for standard biographical data such as the organization the members worked with, the location of their overseas work, and any decorations they earned.[119] By May 1930, WOSL national historian Shirley Farr had received questionnaires from 1,115 women, narratives from 365 women, and both a questionnaire and a narrative from 1,228 women. She urged members to submit their questionnaires, especially their narratives, which she explained were necessary "if anyone is to ever turn these bits of personal experience into a mosaic which will picture what American women did overseas during the Great War."[120]

Farr emphasized the importance of including every WOSL member's story in the collective history of their wartime experiences. "May I urge anew," she wrote, "that no one will think: 'Oh, what I did wasn't important.' Please write and send in the account of what you did, and let someone else without personal bias judge what its value is for the general picture."[121] Farr wrote with impressive foresight about the importance of collecting the stories of women's overseas service before they were lost. She recognized that these records would be valuable to future historians and would help their stories become part of the narrative of American participation in the war. By spearheading this history project, the WOSL performed an act of service that helped to recognize, honor, and commemorate women as veterans alongside men.

Over the years, the WOSL maintained its promise to document the history of its members' service even when most of the World War One generation had passed on. In the early 1980s, younger WOSL members conducted oral histories of the few remaining World War One women. Longtime Detroit Unit member Estelle Davis's remarks in her 1982 oral history summed up the importance of recording that history. She also touched on her generation's long-standing belief in the importance of their service. After discussing her time in the Army Nurse Corps in France, she told her interviewer that "I've been very fortunate in being able, I think it's been the biggest thing in my life that I've been able to, see the kind of service that I did see."[122] Through this oral history, the WOSL preserved evidence of the deep meaning that service in World War One held for the pioneering women who went overseas.

Another oral history, by army nurse Laura Smith, documented the pain that overseas women experienced because of the lack of recognition of their service as veterans. In this 1983 recording made at the behest of the Santa Clara WOSL Unit, Smith read from part of a memoir she wrote for her grandchildren. She explained how "saying goodbye to all the friends we had made in service was very sobering. On the train and the streetcar home, I never felt so depressed and forlorn in all my life. No one knew me or noticed that I was a returning veteran. I do have empathy for the Vietnam Veterans, but the war was over and that was all that mattered."[123] By encouraging Smith to make this recording, the Santa Clara WOSL Unit preserved firsthand evidence of the feelings of the forgotten female veterans of World War One. This 1980s oral history project represented a major effort to record the history of the World War One women and demonstrated the WOSL's long-standing commitment to this part of its mission, even when the membership had shifted to the women of the next wars.

The WOSL also staked its claim in the commemorative narrative by encouraging members to wear their wartime uniforms when they publicly represented the league, especially at its national conventions. An announcement in the May 1931 issue of *Carry On* reminded readers that "everyone is urged to make an effort to take her uniform to convention. The wearing of the uniform adds very much to the impressiveness of the Memorial Service."[124] At the 1933 national convention, the WOSL unanimously adopted a resolution "that the regulation uniforms prescribed and worn during active service be adopted as the official uniforms" of the WOSL since they were "the only ones which could possibly carry any significance to the League."[125] Wearing uniforms visually demonstrated the diverse ways that women participated in the war effort overseas and connected women's service to the military. Even though many women served in civilian organizations, by wearing a uniform they interpreted their work as military service and defined themselves as veterans, albeit outside the official military apparatus. Uniforms formed an important way that American women commemorated their wartime service and sought inclusion in military culture and memorialization.[126] By choosing to continue wearing their uniforms, WOSL members reminded the public of their service to the military from within and outside its ranks and visually commemorated their wartime contributions. This visual representation of their service continued even into the 1980s, when so few of the World War One women remained alive. In her 1982 WOSL oral history, former Red Cross worker Edna Scott told her interviewers that the year before, she had put on her old uniform again at the WOSL's request because it wanted publicity. Linking her use of her uniform and her participation in the oral history program, she explained that "it doesn't matter about me, but . . . to the organization."[127] All those years later, Scott understood that even if showcasing her military service did not seem critically important to her, it was important to the WOSL and the longevity of the overall memory of women's World War One service.

Despite the WOSL's best efforts, the history of women's overseas service in World War One began to fade from public memory by World War Two. In August 1942, former WOSL national president Lena Hitchcock published a heated letter in the *Washington Post* that criticized the newspaper for inaccurately stating that the Women's Army Auxiliary Corps (WAAC) was the first group of uniformed American military women to serve overseas. Hitchcock's letter corrected this mistake, provided a brief history of women's overseas service in the Great War, and outlined their postwar efforts to gain government benefits. She concluded by saying that she and her comrades wanted to "pass the torch we once held to the keeping of the young women of today. We wish them God speed, honor in their great endeavor, and when their work is done, a safe return."[128] Through WOSL member Representative Edith Nourse Rogers's legislation that created the WAAC, the earlier WOSL members helped this next generation of American women in military service to gain better recognition and more benefits than they had themselves.

THE WORLD WAR TWO YEARS

The start of World War Two prompted the WOSL to refocus some of its veteranist agenda on service projects that supported the current war. Even before the US entered the conflict, it began leading aluminum drives for the defense effort and raised $1,500 to purchase a fully equipped mobile kitchen that it sent to help feed civilians in England.[129]

True to its organizational mission, the WOSL made itself available to serve in whatever capacity it could after Pearl Harbor. On December 10, 1941, the

New York City WOSL Unit sent a telegram to President Roosevelt informing him that the women of the WOSL "are ready to be of service again in this emergency, as we were in the last war when we served in the A.E.F."[130] Units and members across the country took this pledge seriously and engaged in a multitude of different service projects throughout World War Two.

The WOSL's wartime projects ranged in size and complexity. The work of the New York Unit provides an apt example. For one project, the unit collected gloves to donate to women working in chemical factories who needed them to protect their hands.[131] They then tackled a much larger endeavor: the outfitting of a dayroom at Grand Central Palace exhibition hall in New York City for members of the Women's Army Corps (WAC) to use for relaxation and recreation.[132] Individual members also devoted themselves to wartime service however they could. Elizabeth Phillips recalled in her 1984 oral history that "when World War II came along I tried to get in some branch of service. I ran up against the statement, oh yes, we'll take you but not just yet," so instead she created and led a successful project to send Red Cross parcels to men in prisoner of war camps.[133]

On the national scale, the WOSL chose to downgrade its plans for its 1942, 1943, and 1944 annual conventions and meetings because of wartime conditions.[134] The WOSL even gained recognition for its wartime work in the national press, when the *Chicago Daily Tribune* reported in June 1944 that the league was "actively engaged in war work today" and "eager to extend its benefits to women in uniform in the present conflict."[135] As this book's conclusion discusses, the WOSL's World War Two service platform went far beyond just opening membership to World War Two servicewomen. The WOSL also fought for women's right to serve in a more official capacity than they could in World War One. They argued passionately for women to obtain official veteran status.

CONCLUSION

The Women's Overseas Service League defined community service and advocacy as a form of commemoration to which it remained devoted throughout the interwar period. Through its veteranist commemoration projects, it supported, aided, and advocated for former overseas female and male veterans. Simultaneously, it attempted to include the story of overseas women in the historical and commemorative narrative of the war so that their wartime contributions would not be forgotten. It reminded the nation that these women too had served and fulfilled the duties of martial citizenship and should also be considered veterans. Although their service quickly faded from public memory, the WOSL hoped that their pioneering work overseas and their postwar commitment to the nation would create more opportunities for women to officially serve in the military. In the meantime, they used the WOSL to maintain a foothold in veterans' affairs, national defense, and military commemoration.

By eschewing most traditional memorial projects and focusing on service, the WOSL commemorated the past by looking toward the future. Having experienced the war firsthand, these women returned home with a different perspective about commemoration. They believed that service constituted the most appropriate memorial to the war. As the organization matured, the WOSL became even more devoted to this belief and declined to participate in the American Red Cross's Memorial Building to the Women of the World War, perhaps the biggest interwar memorial project to honor American women's World War One service. Even though the building combined service with traditional commemoration, this compromise did not focus enough on service for the WOSL, which by the 1930s formed the core of the avant-garde group of women who promoted veteranism through commemoration.

2

Service Inscribed in Stone

*Compromise at the American Red Cross's Memorial
Building to the Women of the World War*

IN DOWNTOWN Washington, DC, just blocks from the White House, an elegant neoclassical marble building occupies 1755 E Street Northwest. Set back from the street and flanked by overgrown shrubbery, at first glance it appears to be just another grand building adorned with columns. But those who pause for a closer look will see the inscription "In Memory of the Heroic Women of the World War" (fig. 2.1).

Named the Memorial Building to the Women of the World War, this structure characterized the intersection between women's pursuit of veteranism and their adherence to the traditions of statuary memorials. Built by an influential group of female leaders at the headquarters of the American National Red Cross (ARC), this building embodies the interwar debates between female veteranists about the best way to memorialize World War One and women's contributions to it.[1] Through this structure, the women of the ARC tried to strike a compromise between a traditional physical memorial and service to the living. Their choice underscored how veteranism did not completely dispense with traditional memorials. At the same time, the WOSL believed that the ARC's attempted compromise with the building did not focus enough on service.

By specifically memorializing women's wartime services, this building pushed for the inclusion of women in the narrative of the American memory of the Great War and their acceptance as veterans. By designating individual elements of the building to commemorate specific people and groups, the Memorial Building became a conglomerate commemorative site that encom-

Figure 2.1. Front facade of the Memorial Building to the Women of the World War, Washington, DC. The inscription above the columns reads "In Memory of the Heroic Women of the World War." September 27, 2019. Photograph by Allison S. Finkelstein.

passed the scope of women's wartime contributions. Its creators aspired for the building to form the epicenter of the female memory of the war, a location where women's wartime participation received first-class status in the commemorative landscape. As a structure that also aimed to facilitate women's postwar volunteer service within its walls, the building publicly affirmed that women's service did not stop when the guns of war were silenced.

Led by the women of the ARC and joined by other women connected to the war effort, this group memorialized the significant contributions of American women, defined broadly to include all types of service and sacrifice.[2] These inclusive definitions of service and sacrifice allowed the many official and unofficial ways that women aided the war effort to be commemorated at the building.

By trying to compromise, these women pursued two simultaneous goals. First, they argued that because of American women's traditional commitment to volunteer work, service-based commemorations were the most appropriate types of memorialization projects for women to sponsor. They asserted that these projects could be combined with elements of statuary memorials. Their attempted compromise failed to gain the support of the WOSL and revealed the disagreements among overlapping groups of female veteranists. Second, by dedicating a memorial to women's wartime contributions defined so inclusively, they attempted to legitimize all forms of female wartime service and insisted that women should be honored as veterans just like men. By combining a memorial to women's services and sacrifices with a building devoted to community service, the project constituted tangible evidence of women's contributions to the military, the nation, and local communities, in spite of gender-based restrictions on women's citizenship that excluded them from many types of national service. As women worked to gain the full rights of enfranchised citizens after the 1920 ratification of the Nineteenth Amendment, this building sent an important message in the nation's capital: despite the limitations imposed on them, women contributed to the war effort and continued to serve their nation.

THE ORIGINS OF THE MEMORIAL BUILDING
TO THE WOMEN OF THE WORLD WAR

A group of influential women within the ARC spearheaded the effort to create the Memorial Building to the Women of the World War. Mabel T. Boardman, a wealthy Washington, DC, philanthropist and a prominent, longtime leader of the ARC who served as its national secretary from 1921 to 1944, acted as their leader. With Boardman at the helm, this group crafted a powerful argument for a memorial that honored American women's wartime service.[3] They successfully gained permission from Congress to construct the building on government property at the American Red Cross's national headquarters in Washington, DC.

When they chose the type of memorial to build, the women of the ARC initiated a heated debate about the proper way to commemorate the war; this debate reflected the larger postwar national conversation about memorialization. Their arguments, and those of their opponents, illuminate the contentious nature of interwar commemorative culture and the divisions that existed within the female veteranist community. The ARC's final decision to construct a living memorial building underscored women's commitment to serving the nation and their interpretation of service as a form of commemoration, despite their differing views about how to execute these ideas.

The leaders of the Memorial Building came of age during the Progressive era; before the war, they had already devoted themselves to serving their local communities, states, and the nation.[4] Because of women's tradition of supporting the nation during wartime, by the time the US entered the war in 1917, it seemed natural for women to contribute to the war effort; this service continued after the war through veteranism.[5] Even before the war, many Progressive women already supported the American Red Cross. Founded in 1881 by the famous Civil War nurse Clara Barton, the ARC acted as the United States' chapter of the International Committee of the Red Cross.[6] Like all Red

Cross chapters, the ARC served as a neutral organization that provided aid to soldiers in wartime. The ARC also took on the unique task of assisting civilians during natural disasters and other peacetime crises under the "American Amendment" to the Geneva Convention.[7] In 1900, Barton solidified the ARC when the organization received a congressional charter that incorporated it into the federal government and designated it as the official organization to carry out the Geneva Convention in the US and act as the official US voluntary aid association. A few years later, organizational infighting led by Mabel Boardman forced Barton to resign as president. Now in control of the ARC, Boardman strengthened its connections to the federal government and increased the government's authority over the organization while she simultaneously gained considerable personal power over the ARC.[8]

After the US entered the World War in April 1917, President Woodrow Wilson designated the ARC as the official US organization to coordinate humanitarian assistance. General John J. Pershing, commander of the AEF, also selected it as one of the four official AEF welfare agencies.[9] Equally important, the ARC expanded its ranks and supplied over eighteen thousand professional uniformed Red Cross nurses to the military. Overall, around twenty-four thousand ARC nurses served during the war, both in the US and in Europe.[10] After the war, these nurses constituted one of the principal groups of women commemorated by the Memorial Building.

MEMORIALIZATION TRENDS AFTER THE FIRST WORLD WAR

The aftermath of World War One sparked a memorial building boom as Americans commemorated the recent victory.[11] Memorial projects became a popular cultural trend that resulted in diverse memorials still visible across America today.[12] The ARC bought into this fad and planned two major memorial projects: a statuary memorial to the deceased ARC leader Jane A. Delano and the American nurses who lost their lives, and a living memorial building dedicated to American women who supported the war effort.

Physical memorials to the First World War varied in material, form, shape, size, location, and other factors. Americans constructed memorials throughout the nation in big cities and small towns, as well as on the overseas battlefields in Europe. Some memorials took the form of unobtrusive markers that did not significantly alter the physical landscape, such as the bronze memorial plaques often placed on government buildings to honor employees who died in the war.[13] Memorial trees also became popular, especially in cities and parks and along roadways.[14] The most common commemorative works consisted of statuary monuments and utilitarian memorials that made a bigger impact on the landscape.[15] Statuary memorials represented the most traditional monument form used after the war. Extremely popular, they functioned as aesthetically pleasing pieces of art and often depicted the average doughboy or included a "roll of honor" with names of the local war dead.[16]

However, some Americans came to believe that the most fitting memorials served a purpose beyond simple commemoration through art. Such memorials still aimed for aesthetic beauty, but they could also serve the communities in which they were built. Interchangeably called utilitarian memorials, living memorials, memorial buildings, and liberty buildings, these structures often took the form of a building that housed a community service or civic organization.[17] They could also be structures designed for recreational purposes such as stadiums, bandstands, or towers with city views.[18]

These utilitarian memorials prompted lively debate among commentators. Those who supported them often cited the ideals of the war as their justification. An article in the December 1918 edition of *American City* called for the construction of liberty buildings as victory monuments. It argued that because the World War, more than any other, had been fought for liberty and democracy, it could best be commemorated with a living memorial focused on those principles.[19] The author admitted that nonutilitarian memorials could depict those principles but also argued that those memorials would "not have life," and that a monument that symbolized the recent war and its dead must immortalize "the principles for which they made the supreme sacrifice . . . by giving service rather than a statue or a shaft in which there could not pulse the life blood of a new day."[20] Such strong connections to the Allies' ideals convinced many Americans, including some in the ARC, that living memorial buildings represented a fitting form of commemoration. Living memorials also attracted some support because they embodied the principles of the Progressive movement by concretely giving back to the community.[21]

Others opposed living memorials and favored statuary monuments. In April 1920, the famous sculptor and art patron Gertrude Vanderbilt Whitney, a designer of statuary memorials who served overseas during the war, published an article in *Arts and Decoration* that denounced utilitarian living memorials.[22] Whitney believed that art should give pleasure to people and did not need to fulfill additional purposes. She saw utilitarian memorials as a misunderstanding of the purpose of artistic war memorials and thought that they took glory away from those being honored. She did not deny that the hospitals, stadiums, and other buildings created as living memorials were important and necessary, but she believed that they "have nothing to do with war memorials." Whitney denounced utilitarian memorials and, employing sarcasm in her criticism, urged Americans to build what she called "useless memorials" unable to be mistaken for anything other than a memorial. According to Whitney, such "useless" memorials would not get lost in the landscape of a city or have their memorial purposes forgotten; they would stand as permanent reminders of the war and fulfill what Whitney saw as the true goal of a memorial.[23] Even though she served and sacrificed in the war and was a WOSL member, Whitney opposed some aspects of veteranism.[24] Her opinion shows that female veteranists often disagreed with each other and that veteranism did not completely overtake "useless" statuary memorials. The debate between traditional forms of commemoration and more modernist approaches played out among WOSL members and never truly reached a resolution.

Some important officials in the art world shared some of Whitney's critiques of utilitarian memorials. The Commission of Fine Arts (CFA), the official advisory board that presides over artistic and architectural development in Washington, DC, published a pamphlet about war memorials that indicated a preference for statuary memorials.[25] The CFA believed memorials should be "devoid of practical utility, but . . . minister to a much higher use; they compel contemplation of the great men and ideals which they commemorate." Despite this statement, which indicated some opposition to utilitarian memorials— and also ignored the possibility that memorials could commemorate great women as well as great men—the CFA remained somewhat undecided about utilitarian memorials. In the same pamphlet, it conceded that living memorials did have some value. It described memorial buildings as "devoted to high purposes, educational or humanitarian, that whether large or small, costly or inexpensive, would through excellence of design be an example and inspiration to present and future generations." But the CFA cautioned that a memorial building must "impress the beholder by beauty of design, the permanent nature of the material used, and the fitness of the setting."[26] As might be expected, the CFA valued artistic achievement above all else, especially utilitarian goals. Perhaps as a form of appeasement, the CFA included utilitarian memorials in its suggestions with the disclaimer that artistic beauty must still take precedence. The CFA's own preferences, though certainly tilted toward more traditional monument styles, still allowed some room for more modernist approaches to commemoration that incorporated aspects of veteranist ideology, especially if they adhered to high artistic standards.

The ARC's decision to construct a living memorial building dedicated to women's roles in the war placed it in the center of this debate between traditional monuments and living memorial buildings. While its memorial building confirmed its support for living memorials, after its opening, the ARC also erected a traditional statuary memorial to honor Jane A. Delano and other deceased nurses. It located this memorial on the grounds of its headquarters, just behind the Memorial Building to the Women of the World War. That de-

Figure 2.2. Front facade of the Memorial to the Heroic Women of the Civil War, Washington, DC. September 27, 2019. Photograph by Allison S. Finkelstein.

cision, along with the choice to designate architectural details of the memorial building as individual memorials, demonstrates that the ARC still clung to some aspects of more traditional memorials and tried to find a middle ground that embraced parts of veteranism without completely rejecting traditional statuary memorials. These concessions eventually prompted the WOSL to assert that the project did not fully succeed as a living memorial.

Furthermore, the Memorial Building to the Women of the World War was not the first living memorial building constructed at the ARC's headquarters in Washington, DC. In 1917, the ARC completed its first headquarters building and dedicated it as the Memorial to the Heroic Women of the Civil War (fig. 2.2).[27] Authorized by Congress and built on the same parcel of government land where the World War One building would later be located, it commemorated the women of the North and South during the Civil War.[28] Just a few blocks from the ARC's former temporary headquarters inside the State, War, and Navy Building (today's Eisenhower Executive Office Building), the new headquarters positioned the ARC close to the federal agencies it collaborated with. This first memorial building created a precedent of honoring the wartime contributions of American women at the ARC Headquarters.

President Woodrow Wilson laid the cornerstone for the Memorial to the Heroic Women of the Civil War on March 27, 1915, as the Great War raged in Europe. Construction of the neoclassical, beaux arts marble building began shortly afterward.[29] Three stained-glass memorial windows by the Louis Comfort Tiffany Studio memorialized the women who lost relatives in the Civil War and those who cared for the sick and wounded combatants. As a joint gift from the Women's Relief Corps of the North and the United Daughters of the Confederacy, these windows symbolized the sectional reconciliation that the building encouraged.[30] They also added a spiritual element to the structure and featured Christian themes and images including St. Elizabeth of Hungary, St. Philomena, and figures who represented Mercy, Faith, Hope, and Charity.[31] This connection to Christianity differentiated the Civil War building from the more secular and modern World War One building, which lacked clear religious references and Christian undertones.

A little over a month after the US entered the World War, President Wilson returned to the ARC headquarters on May 12, 1917, to dedicate the completed Memorial to the Heroic Women of the Civil War. Wilson used his speech at the dedication ceremony to defend the nation's entrance into the conflict and gain support for the war effort.[32] Afterward, he reviewed about one thousand members of the Women's Volunteer Aid Corps, an occasion that the *Washington Post* believed to be the first mobilization of uniformed women war workers in the US.[33] At the building's dedication, the Civil War and World War One collided. Americans celebrated the reunion of the North and South by honoring women from both sides, while a new generation of American women participated in the current war. Thirteen years later, in 1930, these women would be honored at the same site with a memorial building of their own that cemented their place in the landscape of memory at the Red Cross's National Headquarters.

THE *SPIRIT OF NURSING*: THE JANE DELANO MEMORIAL

Jane Arminda Delano created the American Red Cross Nursing Service and led the organization during the First World War. She previously served as the superintendent of the Army Nurse Corps before she stepped down to focus on the ARC. Under her direction, the American Red Cross Nursing Service provided the majority of the army and navy nurses during the war.[34] On April 15, 1919, while she surveyed the conditions of American nurses still stationed in France, Delano died suddenly from mastoiditis, an infection of the ear and skull that might have been a complication from influenza.[35] Her death shocked the ARC and it eventually decided to construct a permanent memorial in her honor.[36]

The ARC established the Delano Fund Committee to pursue this secondary memorial project at its headquarters, even while it chose to erect a living memorial building as its main monument to the war. It completed the memorial to Delano in 1933, three years after the Memorial Building to the Women

Figure 2.3. South (back) facade of the Memorial Building to the Women of the World War with the Jane Delano *Spirit of Nursing* Memorial in the foreground, Washington, DC. September 27, 2019. Photograph by Allison S. Finkelstein.

of the World War opened. Officially named *Spirit of Nursing*, this memorial honored the service and sacrifice of Delano as well as the other 296 American nurses estimated at that time to have died during World War One.[37] Many of these women succumbed to influenza during the 1918 pandemic, one of the leading causes of death for American women who served in the war.[38] In contrast to the Memorial Building to the Women of the World War, this statue included no service component or utilitarian purpose; the ARC intended it for purely commemorative purposes (fig. 2.3).

The decision to erect a statue emerged after years of debate about potential ways to memorialize Delano and the other deceased nurses. In December 1921, Lillian L. White wrote to Clara Noyes about how they needed to communicate with all Red Cross nurses and districts to get their opinions about what type of memorial they wanted to build with the money raised by the Delano Fund Committee. White suggested four possible choices, none of which included statuary memorials. These choices comprised a home for ailing nurses, a hospital for nurses, money to augment the National Relief Fund, and a pension fund for nurses.[39] A utilitarian memorial appealed to the Red Cross even before the later idea for the living memorial building had been fully formulated.

The Delano Fund also pursued the possibility of a traditional statue, which

it ultimately chose. In 1927, the CFA rejected a design by Gertrude Vanderbilt Whitney, which she provided to the ARC for free.[40] By this time, the process of choosing a memorial had become so mired in debate that the Delano
Fund Committee chair, Adda Eldredge, realized that ARC members were
confused about the fund's plans for the memorial. She attempted to clarify
the situation and offered stakeholders a choice between a statue and a utilitarian memorial.[41]

Mabel Boardman, however, proposed the creation of a memorial room
dedicated to Delano and the deceased nurses inside the Memorial Building
to the Women of the World War, her new project. She thought that using this
utilitarian memorial room for service projects "would inspire and help to
carry on the nursing services of the Red Cross." Although Boardman initially
favored a statuary memorial for the Delano Fund project, she later realized
that "the many monuments now in Washington are becoming a detriment
to the beauty of the city and tend to give it, as many think, the appearance of
a graveyard."[42] With her new memorial building project now underway, perhaps Boardman thought it best to consolidate the two projects and focus on
the building. Of course, Boardman's personal investment in the Memorial
Building project may also have influenced her opinion. In the end, Boardman
lost this fight and a traditional statuary monument was built on the grounds
of the Red Cross Headquarters.[43] The Delano Memorial Fund also used part
of its resources to dedicate an Ionic marble column on the Memorial Building in memory of Delano and the other deceased nurses.[44]

Canadian sculptor R. Tait McKenzie received the commission to design
the *Spirit of Nursing* memorial. A physician and physical therapist as well as
a sculptor, McKenzie served as a medical officer in England during the war,
and his wife, Ethel O'Neill McKenzie, served with the ARC in England and
belonged to the WOSL.[45] His *Spirit of Nursing* memorial consists of a central
bronze statue of a nurse who stands within a marble stele flanked on both
sides by curved marble benches (see fig. 2.3). The backs of these benches contain an inscription of lines from the ninety-first psalm: "Thou shalt not be
afraid for the terror by night. Nor for the arrow that walketh in darkness. Nor
for the destruction that wasteth at noonday."[46] Since the memorial honored
all nurses from the various nursing organizations who died during the war
and not just Delano and ARC nurses, McKenzie intentionally designed the
figure of the nurse as a general representation of female nurses.[47] She wears
no specific uniform and bears no resemblance to any particular nurse, despite initial criticisms of this choice from the CFA.[48]

The memorial's design and inscription infused it with Christian overtones
and connected it to wartime imagery of nurses. The figure of the nurse bears a
striking resemblance to Michelangelo's Madonna della Pietà in St. Peter's Ba-

Figure 2.4. American Red
Cross poster, "The Greatest
Mother in the World," circa
1918. Library of Congress.

silica in the Vatican.[49] This stylistic similarity depicted the American nurse as
a type of religious mother to the soldiers she treated. It compared the nurse
to the Mother Mary and imbued her with a Christian mission of caring for
America's sons. This pictorial comparison of the nurse to the Madonna dominated World War One–era Red Cross imagery and became an iconic part of
the ARC's wartime posters. These posters featured drawings of ARC nurses
that resembled the Madonna and the later *Spirit of Nursing* statue. One of
these posters, titled "The World's Greatest Mother," showed a nurse cradling
a wounded soldier on a stretcher in a pose similar to the Madonna cradling
Christ in Michelangelo's Pietà (fig. 2.4).[50] A poster for the Third Red Cross
Roll Call showed a young nurse holding out her hands in the same position
as the nurse in the later *Spirit of Nursing* memorial (fig. 2.5). Both nurses on
these posters featured flowing headpieces that looked like nun's habits and
mimicked the head covering on the Madonna; this visually connected the
nurses to religious symbolism, and the posters may have influenced McKenzie's design of the statue.

The CFA worried about the religious undertones of the memorial, and, like

THIRD RED CROSS ROLL CALL

Figure 2.5. American Red Cross poster, "Third Red Cross Roll Call," 1919. Library of Congress.

Boardman, it also worried about the proliferation of monuments in Washington, DC. It thought that the memorial "carried the suggestion of a cemetery memorial instead of a civic monument" and believed it seemed more religious than secular.[51] Although many World War One memorials constructed during the interwar period included religious symbolism, the Memorial Building to the Women of the World War remained secular, while the *Spirit of Nursing* statue just behind it contained religious elements.[52] Perhaps the more traditional statuary memorial seemed appropriate for Christian iconography, while the more modern Memorial Building seemed too secular to include religious references as in the earlier Civil War building.

The coexistence of the *Spirit of Nursing* memorial and the Memorial Building to the Women of the World War on the same site indicates that debates regarding statuary memorials versus living memorials occurred even within the same organization. A traditional memorial and a memorial building influenced by veteranism coexisted on the same campus. Despite their decision to collectively commemorate women through a more modern memorial building, the ARC community still wanted to honor the individual memories of the deceased nurses in a more traditional manner. Like some other veteranists, they did not completely reject all forms of traditional statuary memorials.

CHOOSING A MEMORIAL BUILDING

The memorial building that ultimately became the ARC's main World War One memorial at its headquarters honored the services and sacrifices of all American women in the war. It constituted a *lieu de mémoire*—a site of memory that derives meaning from the landscape—that honored American women's contributions to the war while it facilitated their continued service work.[53] The building would operate as a living memorial because the ARC intended it to accommodate service activities. With this new memorial building, the ARC tried to embrace the concept of a memorial that could improve the present and the future while it commemorated the past.

Fundraising efforts for the project asserted that women's contributions to the war needed to be commemorated. A 1926 *New York Tribune* article urged readers to donate through an appeal to include women in the pantheon of memory. The article noted how "one of the aftermaths of war is the desire to express in stone, bronze or marble the affection of the people for those who gave their lives for their country." It asked, "What of the women who loved and lost? What memorial rises to commemorate their sacrifices?"[54] The new ARC memorial building would pay tribute to these American women.

The other Allied nations had already begun to honor their women, and Boardman called for the US to follow their lead. She described how Great Britain had restored the Five Sisters Window in York Minster to commemorate the 583 women who died while serving Great Britain during the war. A home for disabled male soldiers had been created in Richmond, England, as a living memorial to women's service, and a statue of the martyred nurse Edith Cavell had been erected in London. Canada laid the cornerstone for a Women's War Memorial Building in Ottawa, and in Florence, Italy, a monument to Italian mothers who lost their sons had been unveiled at the Duomo.[55]

Boardman envisioned that, like these memorials in Europe and Canada, the Memorial Building was "an expression in visual form of a great and tender gratitude to our American mothers who gave their sons and to our women who, like the soldiers, lost their lives in their country's cause."[56] To declare its eternal commemorative purpose, plans called for the building to contain the following inscription to emphasize its dual commemorative and service mission: "A Memorial built by the government and the People of the United States in loving gratitude for the sacrifices and services of the Women of America in the World War. That their labors to lessen suffering may be carried on, the Building is dedicated to the Chapter Service of the American Red Cross." A very similar inscription did make it into the completed building.[57] As the *New York Tribune* article asserted, this building would work "not only to commemorate sacrifice and service, but to help carry on the type of service that is commemorated . . . so that the humanitarian deeds of the Red Cross will themselves be part of the Memorial." By trying to interweave service and commemoration, the ARC hoped that the building would lessen the "suffering of mankind throughout the world now and for the years to come" while it honored American women.[58]

Specifically, the Memorial Building commemorated all types of American women's sacrifices and services during the war. A pamphlet that promoted the project explained that the sacrifice category included not just the nurses who died during the war but also "those other self-sacrificing women who died because of their war labors at home and overseas," and "the heartbreaking sacrifices made by American women who lost their sons or others dear to them for our country's sake." The pamphlet defined the service category as commemorating "all those who served faithfully, loyally, and tirelessly for the Government," as well as organizations such as the Red Cross, the YWCA, and the Salvation Army.[59] These broad categories recognized that women aided the war effort within and beyond official military, government, and civilian organizations. Women's work on the home front received equal recognition, as did the sacrifices made by women who lost their relatives and suffered personal tragedies. Their hardships and patriotism were just as important as those of the women who donned a uniform for overseas work or even the men who joined the military. The Memorial Building testified to women's contributions to the military long before they were officially able to enter all of its branches and insinuated that these women should be honored as veterans.[60]

The building's construction needed government authorization since the government owned the Red Cross Headquarters property in Washington, DC. Authorized by the Seventy-First Congress through Public Resolution No. 39, S. J. 98 on March 4, 1927, the ARC received a $350,000 government appropriation to support construction, as long as it matched that sum through its own fundraising efforts.[61] The resolution stated that the building would remain the property of the US government but be administered by the ARC and used by the District of Columbia Chapter of the ARC.[62]

This provision enabled the ARC to devote the Memorial Building to service activities. The District of Columbia Chapter intended to use the building as a model chapter house where it would conduct research on service activities from which the national organization could benefit. It would utilize the building as a place to study problems and programs before it submitted its conclusions to chapters nationwide.[63] Establishing this building as the Washington, DC, Chapter House gave it a specific service mission.

Blueprints of the building demarcated how each floor would be devoted to specific service activities and showed the breadth of the service work that would occupy it. The basement stored the practical necessities of the ARC's community service projects. It contained a room for cutting, assembling, and packing; rooms designated for storing emergency supplies, canteen supplies, a motor corps ambulance, and other materials; and a kitchen for canteen and nutrition classes. The first-floor rooms focused on the major community service areas to be studied by the DC Chapter. These included rooms for hospital service, home service, home hygiene and care of the sick, and the Junior Red Cross, as well as a braille room, a first aid classroom, and an office for the issuing of receipts and supplies. It also contained a staff office and the office of the chair and executive committee.[64]

A large room that resembled a ballroom occupied the second and third floors of the building. Interchangeably called the Hall of Service, the Service Hall, and the Community Workroom, this large, formal open space was decorated with fluted columns, pilasters, and the ARC emblem. It included a stage, above which hung a stone sign carved with gold text reading "to commemorate service."[65] This sign served as a reminder that the building commemorated women's wartime service work and facilitated their continued service. Blueprints for this hall also included plans for three small rooms that different versions demarcated as branch work rooms, branch classrooms, and a room for the nursing committee and health aids or for the production of garment supplies; a surgical dressing and cutting room; and a dressing room.[66] Although it is unclear from the building today whether these work rooms were ever created, according to these plans, at least, even this most formal floor of the building would be used for particular types of service work.[67] The DC Chapter also hoped to include facilities at the building to support disaster relief and home services for disabled ex-servicemen.[68]

Racial segregation norms of the time meant that the ARC needed to consider segregating the building, especially because of its public purpose. Blueprints of the basement show separate toilets specifically reserved for "male help" and "female help," which were probably used as segregated bathrooms.[69] Segregation seems to have been quietly discussed during the planning phase. In a letter to the ARC chair, Judge Payne, in March 1926, Mr. James L. Fieser, the ARC vice chair, described the current plan for accommodating African Americans at the building.[70] He had learned from Boardman that "there is definite space for two rooms assigned to negroes on the second floor. I question the wisdom of any notice of segregation of this sort."[71] Fieser did not suggest eliminating the plans for segregation but implied that this policy should not be publicly advertised. He adhered to common social practices and racial prejudices but hoped to conceal these choices.[72] Perhaps Fieser saw segregation as incompatible with the building's service goals, or perhaps he merely wanted to avoid controversy from either a lack of segregation or a backlash against it; his motivations are not clear in the correspondence. Veteranists were not immune to racial prejudice and they rarely strayed from the norms of Jim Crow, especially in the segregated city of Washington, DC. As a result, African Americans did not have an equal place at the Memorial Building, despite their contributions to the war effort and the wartime sacrifices they made.

The endorsement of several prominent public figures legitimized the importance of the building and its mission to continue women's service work. Upon accepting the role of honorary chair of the Memorial Fund Committee, General Pershing proclaimed that "no cause appears more worthy than this effort to commemorate the services of our women." Pershing highlighted women's diverse wartime contributions, from mothers of soldiers to nurses who served overseas. But he also subscribed to contemporary gender norms and lauded American women for their gentle, soothing natures, which comforted soldiers. Pershing viewed women as simultaneously brave and patriotic as well as nurturing and feminine, like the quasi-religious image of the ARC nurse depicted as the "world's greatest mother." He also emphasized women's postwar service and highlighted how "even in this Memorial of services and sacrifices they seek to make it a means of inspiring future generations."[73] He characterized women's commemorative efforts with this building as national service because it created a place for them to continue their wartime work. Pershing was the former commander of the AEF and a national hero at the time, and his endorsement established women as key players in the war effort and praised them as civic leaders and model citizens committed to serving their communities.

The campaign for the Memorial Building also received the support of chief justice of the Supreme Court and former president William Howard Taft, a close friend of Boardman's and an ARC supporter who served at separate times as its chair and president.[74] Taft endorsed the project and noted that "war memorials to the men are prominent throughout the country and shall our people be less grateful to the women who labored at home, on the battlefield, and in the hospitals with a patriotic devotion unexcelled and who, in giving those they loved, made even a greater sacrifice?" Taft believed a utilitarian memorial to be an appropriate choice because "the loyal and patriotic spirit of the women to whom this Memorial is built will be forever perpetuated in the humane work of the Red Cross." He understood veteranism's key tenet that commemoration should include continued service. Taft also thought it was fitting to locate the building so close to the government and military departments the ARC supported, perhaps to remind them of the ARC's contributions.[75]

Adding to the list of important public figures who supported the project,

Rear Admiral W. S. Benson, chief of naval operations during the war, provided his testimonial in 1923. He recalled how he was able to see "the actual work and to know of the sacrifices that were made by the women of the country, not only at home but abroad," and how he "was greatly impressed with the splendid work that was being done by the women of our country."[76] He described many ways that women supported the navy during the war, but he did not mention that the navy and Marine Corps were the first and only services to officially include women in their ranks, albeit temporarily.[77] Benson focused more on women's contributions that better fit into the category of voluntary activities, showing again how, despite advancements such as the Nineteenth Amendment and the women who served in the Yeoman (F) and the Marine Corps, gender roles still precluded women from being recognized for their military service or considered veterans, even when they did meet the government's criteria.

Despite these strong endorsements, the project encountered criticism from those who questioned its appropriateness and necessity. The Rockefeller Memorial, a charitable foundation that previously donated to the ARC's Civil War building, expressed doubts about the project when Boardman asked for a donation.[78] Arthur Woods, the foundation's acting president, suspected that the project's female leaders were overexcited about their mission, accused them of not thinking clearly about whether such a building was actually needed, and asked whether it was just a frivolous amusement to keep the "good ladies" of the ARC occupied. By calling them "good ladies," Woods made gender a defining factor in his opinion of the project and dismissively portrayed these women as amateurs who should not be trusted with such a big project.[79]

The project also encountered opposition from within the ARC. In 1925, Marquis Eaton, a prominent full-time volunteer from the Chicago Chapter, sent Boardman a heated letter that voiced his opposition to the building. He believed it was an unnecessary expense that would be especially detrimental to local ARC chapters. Eaton criticized the earlier Civil War memorial building for being overextravagant. He told Boardman it was "primarily a monument to your own courage, zeal, and wisdom." He feared that another memorial building would be a similarly selfish enterprise and doubted its proposed utilitarian service mission. Eaton contended that if the national ARC solicited donations for a memorial building, philanthropists would be less willing to donate to struggling local chapters and their service projects.[80]

Boardman quickly responded to Eaton's letter with a fierce defense of the new Memorial Building. To counter Eaton's accusations of unnecessary extravagance, she invoked ideas of patriotism and compared the situation to that of the Capitol Building. "We might house Congress in a building that cost a fraction of what the capitol cost in which they could have had as much space as they have in that building," she quipped, "but I wonder if any patriotic United States citizen would like to see Congress in a cheaply constructed building." She also doubted that the building would really deflect significant amounts of money from local chapters, especially since it housed projects to support the service work of those local chapters.[81]

Boardman also defended the project because it commemorated women's service, something Eaton ignored in his criticism. She argued that "many people have a feeling that they would like to show some appreciation for all that the women suffered and all they have done during the war."[82] Eaton's opposition showed how Boardman had to justify a women's memorial to those who did not seem to accept that women had earned a place in American military memory or roles as commemorative leaders. As a result, the building's service mission and the women it commemorated sometimes became overshadowed by the controversies and challenges commonly encountered by memorial projects, as well as the gender bias faced by female veteranists.

THE ARCHITECTURE OF THE MEMORIAL BUILDING
TO THE WOMEN OF THE WORLD WAR

Built of white Vermont marble in the neoclassical beaux arts tradition, the exterior of the Memorial Building to the Women of the World War mirrored the aesthetics of turn-of-the-century civic architecture in Washington, DC. This style mimicked that of nearby buildings such as the Daughters of the American Revolution's Memorial Continental Hall and the Pan American Union Building.[83] Architecturally, this choice incorporated the Memorial Building and its mission into the city's landscape and established the legitimacy of its mission.[84]

The design of the Memorial Building to the Women of the World War, and of the earlier Memorial to the Heroic Women of the Civil War, was directly influenced by the City Beautiful movement; the McMillan Plan that redeveloped Washington, DC, along the lines of L'Enfant's original designs; the beaux arts movement; and the requirements of the CFA.[85] The ARC Headquarters occupied a prime location near key elements of the city such as the White House and the emerging Federal Triangle. The site was surrounded by similar neoclassical beaux arts buildings as well as the new First Division Memorial, dedicated to that division's World War One service.[86] Any building on the site needed to fit into the surrounding aesthetics to assert its political importance in relation to this powerful neighborhood.

The prestigious New York architectural firm Trowbridge and Livingston designed both ARC memorial buildings to embody the aesthetics of the recently redesigned capital city.[87] Although known best for the Saint Regis Hotel in New York, Trowbridge and Livingston also designed public buildings and frequently worked in the beaux arts and neofederal styles.[88]

The exterior elements of the World War One building typify neoclassical beaux arts public buildings. Rectangular and with a flat roof, the building has a front facade facing north on E Street that contains the main entrance, accessed by a staircase flanked on each side by two memorial lamps (see fig. 2.1).[89] This staircase leads to a narrow porch that runs almost the entire length of the facade and is adorned with eight fluted columns topped with Ionic capitals, above which is engraved "In Memory of the Heroic Women of the World War."[90] A balustrade above the inscription also runs the length of the porch. The fenestration of the front facade comprises eight windows on the lower level and nine windows on the upper level. The sides of the building each contain basement entrances below a decorative four-columned porch, and each side includes the Red Cross symbol above the northernmost windows, although it is unclear whether these decorative symbols are original.[91] The rear facade, which faces south, features eight decorative pilasters that go from the second to the third story.

The placement of the World War One building behind the Civil War building on E Street, and its more simplistic design compared to the Civil War building, established a hierarchy of memorial buildings at the headquarters complex, with the Civil War building taking the highest place.[92] Symbolically, this indicated that although the ARC believed the World War and women's roles in it important enough to include in its commemorative compound, it did not intend for the World War to take precedence over the memory of the Civil War. It constructed the World War One building both literally and figuratively in the shadow of the Civil War building, an appropriate physical representation of the way that the female memory makers of World War One followed in the footsteps of the women who commemorated the Civil War. While the Civil War building housed the ARC headquarters and offices, the new World War One building took the utilitarian service aspect of living memorial buildings one step further by being used for more practical, hands-on service work. The two buildings were built only thirteen years apart by some of the same leaders, but the World War One building represented the ARC's continued effort to commemorate women at its headquarters through buildings that facilitated women's service, albeit with some new and more modern features.[93]

The World War One building served a dual memorial purpose with the inclusion of individual memorials, a feature not used in the Civil War building. Known for an imaginative use of architectural details, Trowbridge and Livingston suggested that the columns on various parts of the new building's

Figure 2.6. Detail of the column dedicated to the women of the YMCA and YWCA, east facade of the Memorial Building to the Women of the World War, Washington, DC. The inscription reads "To the Women with the Y.M.C.A. and Y.W.C.A." September 27, 2019. Photograph by Allison S. Finkelstein.

exterior and interior be dedicated to specific groups and individuals by engraving their names on the bases (fig. 2.6).[94] All but one of the columns on the building's front and side facades received such a dedication. These columns enabled the memorial fund to acquire more revenue to support the construction of the building and its service mission, since the committee required a monetary donation to dedicate a column. Each column became a memorial itself and transformed the building into a multilayered commemorative structure that served as the epicenter of the commemoration of women's wartime contributions and created a home for women's continued service work.[95]

The diversity of the column dedications demonstrated the range of ways that women took part in the war effort and reflected a cross section of American society. Organizations honored on columns included the women of the YMCA, the YWCA, the Catholic War Council, the Jewish Welfare Board, and the Women's Committee of the Council of National Defense, to name just a few. The columns of the religious organizations represented the only mention of anything religious in the building. Local tributes were popular and included a column given by the men of Houston, Texas, to commemorate the women of their city, a column dedicated to the women of the model workroom of the New York County Chapter of the ARC, and a column dedicated to the women of the District of Columbia Chapter of the ARC who ran the building's service projects.[96] Also represented were the Gray Ladies, who served as nurses at what was called the Walter Reed General Hospital during the war.[97]

As with most commemorations of women during the Great War, motherhood formed a prominent theme in the memorial, an appropriate choice for an organization advertised during the war as the "World's Greatest Mother."[98] The American Legion purchased a column in tribute to the American mothers who lost sons in the war, demonstrating its approval of the building.[99] By singling out mothers as worthy of commemoration, the American Legion helped to legitimize their losses as national sacrifices and supported a new generation of the republican motherhood ideology that revered American mothers for bearing sons for military service.

The mother of John Boyd Wolverton, an only son killed in the war, used her son's insurance money to dedicate a column on his behalf in honor of American women.[100] Instead of keeping the insurance money for herself, she used the money to donate this column in honor of her son's memory and her fellow American women, and to fund the service work housed in the structure. Because the column she dedicated was a type of physical memorial, her donation did not completely eschew traditional memorialization trends. It represented a compromise between creating a permanent physical memorial to her son, honoring American women, and adhering to the tenets of veteranism.

Mabel Boardman even received a column in her honor that inscribed her service to the ARC and the Memorial Building into its very stones.[101] Additionally, the two lamps that flanked the front staircase were dedicated to Boardman by the National Committee on Red Cross Volunteer Service. The inscriptions on these memorial lamps stated that they were intended to "carry on the light of her service for the sick and wounded of war and for those who suffer from disasters."[102] For better or worse, these lamps embodied the building's mission in the persona and achievements of Mabel Boardman, its most public spokeswoman.

The addition of these memorial columns and lamps established the World War One Building as a *lieu de mémoire* that included individual memorials as part of a collective attempt to create a living memorial building dedicated to women's service projects. The building constituted a multifaceted and multipurpose monument that consolidated what might otherwise have been geographically scattered individual memorials onto one site devoted to service. These personal tributes alluded to the custom of engraving the names of casualties on local or unit memorials, a memorial style popular at the time. Although the building as a whole eschewed the individuality of these casualty lists, the columns and lamps included an option for those who wanted to join the collective spirit and service mission of the building but still wanted to honor a specific individual or group.

The column dedications represented a visible halfway point between traditional statuary memorialization and veteranism. The funds raised through the donation of these memorial columns supported the building's construction and facilitated its service mission, transforming the donation of these aesthetically conservative columns into a philanthropic act attached to a more modern memorial building. The columns exemplified how the ARC's attempt to create a living memorial building devoted to service enabled it to avoid making a total commitment to strict veteranist commemorations.

Through this compromise, the ARC tried to redefine the parameters of commemoration in interwar America. It attempted to demonstrate that more traditional, permanent physical memorials could coexist and be combined with more modern and ephemeral acts of service. It argued that memorial buildings could be aesthetically pleasing and also incorporate important service work within their walls. Through its innovative memorial columns, the ARC contended that architectural elements of memorial buildings could be singled out as distinct memorials that honored individuals as part of a collective memorial. It professed that donating to a living memorial building dedicated to service could be considered an act of service itself. Through this endeavor, the ARC blurred the boundaries that separated service projects from statues and tried to show how these could be combined to create a meaningful, useful, and even beautiful memorial.

By centralizing and consolidating these memorials to women onto one site in the nation's capital, the organizers of the building also made another deliberate choice. They intended to convey to the nearby government officials the importance of women's wartime contributions and their continued national service.[103] They wanted women's war work to be recognized in a prominent place as they argued for the inclusion of women as veterans. Yet despite their intentions, some female veteranists viewed the project's attempted compromise as less than successful.

THE BLANK COLUMN AND THE
WOMEN'S OVERSEAS SERVICE LEAGUE

Although many organizations and individuals embraced the idea of the column dedications, one important women's organization did not: the Women's Overseas Service League (WOSL). When initially approached with the opportunity to donate money to dedicate a column, the WOSL sent a pamphlet to its members that described the offer and the likely $5,000 cost; this quickly generated debate within the league.[104] In June 1923, national president Louise Wells wrote to Boardman, herself a WOSL member, to explain why the WOSL had decided not to donate a column yet. Wells had listened to the WOSL chapters' opinions on the offer and learned that "there was overwhelming sentiment to the effect that for the present at least our best memorial to the dead would be our service to the living. The San Francisco Unit, backed up by others from California have brought us a most challenging appeal to help in caring for the many disabled ex-service women on the Pacific Coast and elsewhere." The WOSL believed the best way to commemorate the war was through direct service to its survivors. Even though the project was led by a WOSL member, involved WOSL members, and would be a living memorial building that housed ARC service activities, that was not enough for the league, since it cost so much to construct. That money could have been channeled directly into service activities that made a more immediate impact on those who needed help. Wells noted that this decision did not preclude future involvement with the project.[105]

The issue came up again four years later during the 1927 WOSL national convention. During this convention, the WOSL passed a resolution that more formally declined Boardman's standing invitation for the WOSL to participate in the Memorial Building.[106] The WOSL publicly declared its gratitude to the ARC and tried to maintain friendly ties with it, since many WOSL members had served with the ARC during the war and many of the project's leaders such as Boardman and Lucy Minnigerode were WOSL members.[107] The issue finally came to a head in February 1929 when WOSL national president Lena Hitchcock responded to yet another invitation from Boardman. This time, Boardman offered an indoor column dedicated to the WOSL women who died overseas, and once again the WOSL declined. Hitchcock cited organizational restraints that prevented the league from raising money from local units to pay for the column. The WOSL National Treasury had barely sufficient funds to cover its regular business needs, save money for the organization's disabled women, and help care for the women in the Soldiers' Home at Danville, Illinois, where it had started a new occupational therapy program for the female residents to sell handicrafts to help support themselves. With such expenses, Hitchcock did not have the funds to purchase the column, nor could she raise the dues that WOSL members paid to the national organization.[108]

In 1929, as in 1923 and 1927, the WOSL still considered its most important function to be service activities, especially those that helped former overseas women. Because the Memorial Building commemorated many women who were WOSL members, Hitchcock again emphasized their gratitude. She explained that they were not "inappreciative of your kindness and genuine interest in the League in giving us this opportunity. As it is, I feel that our own service work will have to be the only memorial which will ever be erected to these women."[109] Eager to maintain good relations with her sisters at the ARC, Hitchcock insinuated that both organizations had the same goal of commemorating women's wartime service but approached it differently. The WOSL's Washington, DC, Unit even sent ten members to the building's cornerstone dedication ceremony, and many WOSL members attended the building's 1930 dedication. The WOSL's magazine, *Carry On*, featured a lengthy article about the building's dedication ceremony that thanked Boardman for providing "the opportunity of having a share in this 'living memorial.'"[110] Although it respected the building's mission, the WOSL considered direct service toward veterans to be the only memorial it needed to commemorate women's roles in the war, while the ARC remained committed to its attempted compromise. By the end of the 1920s, the WOSL supported an almost entirely service-based approach to commemoration that contrasted with the ARC's endeavor to strike a balance between veteranism and statuary memorials.

These diverging opinions about the best way to commemorate women's service in the First World War exemplified the ongoing debate during the interwar period about the proper forms of commemoration, especially among female veteranists. The more modern and avant-garde WOSL leadership valued pure service over any type of physical memorial. Although the Memorial Building housed service activities, they could not be convinced to spare funds from their own service projects to support a plan that did not directly aid veterans and their members. By combining elements of traditional monuments with a building that lodged service activities, the ARC tried to compromise between the different memorial options being debated by Americans. The overlapping membership of the WOSL and the ARC demonstrated that even women who belonged to the same organizations and pursued veteranism disagreed about the best ways to conduct their work. This highlights the complicated layers of discourse that developed as American women reshaped commemorative practices. It also shows that there was no definitive end to traditional memorials, just an incomplete reconfiguring of commemoration.

The WOSL was one of the premier organizations that represented women who served overseas in the war, and its refusal to participate left the Memorial Building somewhat incomplete. This indicated that some female veteranists deemed its compromise to be unsatisfactory. Indeed, the southernmost column on the building's west facade remains blank today, perhaps intended to be used as the WOSL column. Although the ARC's compromise appeased many factions, Boardman's continued attempts to gain the WOSL's support classified its refusal to participate as a failure of the ARC's planning committee and an example of the fractured nature of veteranism.

The blank column may also indicate that some female veteranists, like many WOSL leaders, almost fully rejected traditional memorials in the aftermath of an untraditional war that altered humanity in unthinkably violent ways. Still facing the reality of the women and men whose lives were irrevocably damaged by the new mechanized warfare, some members of the WOSL seemed to view physical memorials of any kind as useless and preferred much more modernist projects. Even though living memorial buildings housed service activities, they still required vast construction funds that could have been used directly for service. Aesthetically, the building represented a very traditional neoclassical architectural style, and no component of it appeared to be more traditional than its columns. Perhaps the WOSL leadership felt that such a traditional architectural component could not embody the memory of a war that harmed so many people in new and horrible ways.[111]

Yet other WOSL women like Boardman and the ARC members who supported the Delano statue still clung to aspects of traditional commemorations even as they pursued and supported veteranism.[112] This disagreement and debate within the WOSL demonstrates the messy and impartial cultural transformation of commemoration after the First World War.[113] As a result, the ARC's living memorial building did not please all female veteranists.

CONCLUSION: PRESENTING THE BUILDING TO THE PUBLIC

The ceremony for the laying of the building's cornerstone on May 31, 1928, represented a milestone moment in the campaign to construct the Memorial Building. The Marine Band played to a crowd of over one thousand people as President Calvin Coolidge spread the first trowel of mortar for the cornerstone. Chief justice and former president Taft acted as the ceremony's presiding officer, and Secretary of War Dwight F. Davis accepted the building on behalf of the nation.[114] A time-capsule box was placed in the cornerstone and filled with memorabilia associated with the ARC, the ceremony, and the wartime organizations women served in.[115]

At the building's completion ceremony on March 19, 1930, General Pershing presented the building to President Herbert Hoover, who accepted it

Figure 2.7. General Pershing unveiling the American Legion column on the Memorial Building to the Women of the World War, 1930. Note the nurses behind him. Library of Congress. Additional caption information from NACP, RG 200.

on behalf of the nation along with First Lady Lou Henry Hoover, a WOSL member. The day was spent unveiling the various memorial columns and lamps that adorned the building (fig. 2.7).[116] Each dedication at these individual monuments added to the sense that the building served as the physical and aesthetic focal point of the commemoration of American women's roles in the Great War.

The architecture of the Memorial Building transformed it into a multipurpose living memorial. Trowbridge and Livingston, Architects combined elements of traditional monuments with utilitarian memorials to create a structure that contained layers of meaning and symbolism. The building took inspiration from the memorial buildings begun before World War One and included specifically designated spaces for service work in the building's floorplans. By continuing the ARC's foray into living memorials, this building demonstrated that many women in the ARC believed a hybrid service memorial to be an appropriate way to commemorate women's wartime contributions. Because the building did not focus enough on direct service, some veteranists questioned its effectiveness at fulfilling its service mission.

Although the Memorial Building did house service activities for many years, especially during the Second World War, WOSL leaders Louise Wells and Lena Hitchcock may have correctly foreseen that the building would not focus fully enough on service work in the long run.[117] In 1953, the District of Columbia Chapter vacated the structure and moved to a new office nearby on E Street, divorcing the building from its original service purpose.[118] As of early 2020, the building remains connected to community service because it houses American National Red Cross Headquarters conference rooms and a blood donation center.[119] However, the building in its entirety is not used for the specific, concrete community service projects and research originally intended for it, and the building's connection to World War One remains only partially clear. While paintings related to the ARC's World War One activities hang on the walls to help keep the story of the women it commemorated alive, the overgrown shrubs near the front facade obscure many of the memorial inscriptions on the columns. No interpretive signage near its exterior provides the public with information about the building's history. In the Hall of Service, a plaque with the name of donor Nancy Peery Marriott now hangs above the one that reads "To Commemorate Service." While the new plaque aesthetically matches the original one, Marriott could not have served in or supported World War One.[120] This new sign dilutes the building's original mission as a living memorial specifically dedicated to World War One women with the addition of the name of a modern philanthropist not associated with that war.

Nevertheless, by meticulously preserving this historic structure and continuing to use it for modern iterations of service, the ARC ensured that the building could continue much of its original purpose. While it may be little known, this memorial building still honors the legacy of American women's wartime services and sacrifices in the nation's capital and stands as a powerful, if overlooked, reminder of how women impacted the nation.

When it opened in 1930, such a reminder in the heart of Washington, DC, was needed as recently enfranchised women looked for novel ways to serve their country, fulfill the duties of citizenship, and gain the rights they felt they had earned. Indeed, another group of veteranist women originally recognized inside the Memorial Building, the World War Reconstruction Aides Association, dealt with this struggle as they tried to obtain veterans' benefits for their wartime service.

3

Commemoration through Rehabilitation

The World War Reconstruction Aides Association

IN SECTION 17 of Arlington National Cemetery, not far from the Argonne Cross memorial, rests the grave of Henry A. Pittman.[1] The front of Henry's grave identifies his service as a private in the Sixteenth Infantry during World War One. The back of his grave includes an inscription for his wife, buried with him. That inscription identifies her as only "His wife Rachel R. Sep 12 1893 Nov 2 1974."[2] Nothing in his wife's inscription indicates that she too served in the war as a uniformed Reconstruction Aide and became yet another unrecognized female veteran.

Rachel Pittman, known during the war by her maiden name, Rachel Ring, served as a physical therapist at Walter Reed Army Hospital from August 1918 to July 1920. She subsequently worked for the US Public Health Service and Veterans Administration hospitals until she resigned from full-time employment the day before her wedding.[3] To the casual observer, Rachel looks like any other wife buried with her husband and memorialized on the back of his headstone, as is customary at military cemeteries in the US. Rachel's own story of military service remains hidden on this headstone, unrecognized by the government in death just as she was unrecognized in life. Did the Pittmans choose to be buried in Arlington National Cemetery so that they could both be buried together in a way that recognized their military service? Or was this choice based only on Henry's service in the war? The full story may never be known.

The Pittmans' burial situation is not unique. Many of Rachel's fellow physical therapists, then called Reconstruction Aides, met their husbands while working with wounded veterans and were buried with them in military cemeteries without any indication on their headstones that they also served in the war. These graves form a striking visual representation of the challenges faced by female veteranists such as the Reconstruction Aides as they struggled to preserve their legacy and obtain veteran status.

Like their fellow female veteranists, the Reconstruction Aides viewed their wartime contributions as a form of military service, even though they later learned that they served outside the official ranks of the military and lacked veteran status. Inspired by their wartime work, they agreed that they could best commemorate the war by continuing to help male veterans, the military, and fellow women veterans. Through the creation of their own veterans' organization, the World War Reconstruction Aides Association (WWRAA), they devoted themselves to veteranism while they worked to preserve the memory of their wartime contributions. They rightly feared that their pioneering service would already be forgotten during their lifetime.

These attributes fit the Reconstruction Aides and the WWRAA squarely into the larger community of female veteranists. Its membership overlapped with the WOSL and they frequently interacted with other female veteranists. Through these connections, the story of the Reconstruction Aides further illuminates the innovative ideology promoted by female veteranists, the extent of their impact on American commemorative culture after World War One, and their arguments about who should be defined as a veteran.

THE ORIGINS OF THE WORLD WAR RECONSTRUCTION AIDES ASSOCIATION

Female Reconstruction Aides played an important new role in military medicine during World War One.[4] The term "Reconstruction Aides" referred to women employed in the fields of physical and occupational therapy, as they are known today. Reconstruction Aides helped to pioneer and professionalize these two medical fields, both still in their infancy before the war and often referred to during the war as rehabilitation, reconstruction, and physiotherapy.[5] The impetus for the development of rehabilitation programs for wounded service members emerged from the broader ideals of the Progressive era that valued medicine and science and encouraged recovery so citizens could contribute to society.[6]

During the war, Reconstruction Aides served as paid civilian employees under the American Red Cross or the American Expeditionary Forces.[7] An August 1917 executive order from Surgeon General William C. Gorgas directed the hiring of women to assist the Division of Special Hospitals with its wartime rehabilitation work.[8] Although these women supported the military, wore uniforms, and swore an oath of allegiance, unbeknown to them, they did not officially serve in the armed forces. This technicality later be-

came problematic since they could not receive veteran status and all the benefits that conveyed.

The women hired to rehabilitate wounded service members served as occupational therapy (OT) aides or physiotherapy (PT) aides in the US and
Europe.[9] They drew from their experiences in such fields as massage, physical education, gymnastics, and crafts.[10] Keenly aware of the professional nov-
elty of physical and occupational therapy and their roles as pioneers in these
medical fields, the female aides consistently professed their love for their
work. The soldiers they helped noticed it too, as indicated by an anonymous
poem from the July 1919 issue of *Carry On: A Magazine of the Reconstruction of Disabled Soldiers and Sailors*:

> The bluebirds who've come to Camp Lee
> To give it a taste of O.T.
> (If in doubt see above)
> Have fallen in love,
> Now who do you think it can be?
>
> Have they dared on a private to smile?
> Or the S.G.O.'s temper to rile?
> Oh no, for you see,
> It's been whispered to me,
> Heart and soul they love the work, all the while.[11]

As this poem shows, the aides passionately devoted themselves to their wartime work and the new professions they created in the process.

The Reconstruction Aides formed their own organization after the war.
This group originated in June 1920 when PT and OT aides at Fort Sheridan
created the Organization of Fort Sheridan Military Reconstruction Aides.
This group soon expanded and by December 1920 called itself the National
Association of Military Reconstruction Aides and boasted 323 members.[12] As
the organization evolved, it eventually settled on the World War Reconstruction Aides Association (WWRAA) as its name and received a Certificate of
Incorporation from the state of Indiana in 1933.[13] Because African Americans could not serve as Reconstruction Aides during the war, the WWRAA
remained an entirely White organization and never needed to consider including African American women.[14] This demonstrates once again how female veteranists represented the racial divide in wartime service and postwar
commemoration.

Although the main object of the association stated its intention "to augment
friendships and interests developed during period of service," the WWRAA

did much more than just serve as a way for the Reconstruction Aides to keep in touch.[15] As indicated by its organizational magazine, the *Re-Aides' Post*, the WWRAA served as an outlet for these women to organize their national conventions, advocate for benefits for themselves and subsequent Reconstruction Aides, further develop their profession, and pursue an agenda of veteranist commemorations. In one of the earliest issues of this publication, from July 28, 1920, Margaret McNamara, the chair of the Organizing Committee, outlined the group's initial aims. These included keeping "in touch with one another and with professional opportunities," creating a recognition pin for members, publishing a history of their wartime work, endeavoring to "submit certain types of Federal and State legislation," and gaining admission into the American Legion.[16]

Critically, the association helped its members maintain their connection to their wartime service and the meaning it held for them as women in the early twentieth century. Their wartime participation formed a pivotal moment in their lives when they stepped outside women's traditional roles and helped develop new fields of medicine. After the war, many of them looked back on this time fondly and understood its significance. Member Winifred Keith Pinto touched on this sentiment in the January 1928 edition of the *Re-Aides' Post*. She discussed the importance of the organization and asked her fellow aides, "Don't you realize with regret that you'll never again know the exhilaration of proffering such service or of knowing another group of such genuinely fine women or of making such precious friendships?"[17] The WWRAA provided an outlet to ensure that these reminiscences would not be forgotten and also used these memories to spur members on to further service.

RECONSTRUCTION WORK AS
A FORM OF MILITARY SERVICE

In the postwar years, the activities and beliefs of the female Reconstruction Aides demarcated them as veteranists. Proud of their role in the war, they viewed their work as an essential form of military service, despite having served outside the official ranks of the military. Like their fellow female veteranists, the Reconstruction Aides challenged the conventional notion that military service could be performed only by official members of the armed forces and that only those men could be considered veterans. They believed that they had conducted an important military service during wartime, that their skills remained essential to the postwar recovery of the nation and its wounded warriors, and that they too were veterans. They spread this message as they tried to claim their rights alongside male veterans.

From the start, WWRAA members knew that they had to distinguish their group from other women's organizations by emphasizing their service with the military and the pioneering techniques they helped develop. A 1920 article titled "Why They Organize" bluntly stated that "every woman who knitted a sock, rolled a bandage or did without a morsel of sugar during the emergency wants her organization. One feels the emphasis on the triviality of the service, coupled with the enlarged clamor to be recognized." But, the article asserted, the Reconstruction Aides were different, for the "same impulse that had sent the soldier to face death, now sent her to help him live again." The aides "all met on the common ground of service—impelled by the self same urge," and they grew "in experience together; they have discussed their failures and their successes together. . . . Above all, they have been pioneers together."[18]

The Reconstruction Aides consistently described their work as military service. In the November 1920 edition of the *Re-Aides' Post*, an article about Thanksgiving framed the aides as having served alongside America's fighting men. It told readers that "no volunteer in the service of the US during the war has more to be thankful for than the Reconstruction Aide. The opportunity to serve with the Nation's fighters was no mean privilege. It was given to the aide to serve heroes who wear the intangible badge of extraordinary heroism beneath the probe and the splint and the knife." It asserted that this "privilege brought development . . . she did not know her own capabilities until the service made her find herself," and "she sees the movement in which she was a pioneer now afoot all over her land henceforth to bring comfort to suffering humanity."[19] By speaking directly to the aides, this article compelled them to conceive of their wartime work as military service and to distinguish themselves as pioneers in their fields.

The skilled nature of the aides' groundbreaking work contributed to their belief that it should be classified as military service. In April 1919, Eleanor Rowland Wembridge, a supervisor of Reconstruction Aides in occupational therapy, published an article in *Carry On: A Magazine of the Reconstruction of Disabled Soldiers* that highlighted the valuable contributions of her accomplished female employees. She described the Reconstruction Aides' service as a "chance for skilled crafts women, and for women with academic and professional training to pay their final debt to the boys in the hospitals, who were so ready to sacrifice their all, when they turned from civilians into splendid soldiers. They must now face the harder task of changing again from soldiers and from hospital patients into healthy, efficient civilians."[20] Here, she characterized the aides as highly skilled professionals serving the nation even after the war's end.

The same issue of that magazine featured an unattributed article that also asserted the Reconstruction Aides' worth. It stated that "when the history of the physical reconstruction of disabled soldiers is finally written it will be found that the women of our country—in fact the women of all the allied countries—have played a very important role in reclaiming these men."[21] The Reconstruction Aides maintained this belief throughout the entire lifespan of the WWRAA and used it to justify their campaign for veteran status.

Longtime member Lena Hitchcock exemplified this conviction and devoted much of her life to defending it. During the war, she served in France in one of the first groups of Reconstruction Aides attached to the Army Medical Corps (fig. 3.1).[22] Afterward, she became a leader in the female veteran community and a president of the Women's Overseas Service League, in addition to her membership in the WWRAA. In her memoir about her wartime experiences, aptly titled "The Great Adventure," Hitchcock recounted how she visited her grandfather, a Union veteran and Republican politician, in 1918 before she left for France. He talked to her about her role upholding their family honor, for, he said, she was "the only one in the family whom the Army wants and will take." He told her to "hold the banner high, as the men and women" of her family had always done, and he sent her off by saying, "God bless you and keep you and help you to fulfill your duty."[23] Hitchcock framed this narrative of her departure for France in the shadow of the Civil War and the legacy of her family's military service, with no regard for her gender. This story could easily have been written by a man joining the army. It shows how she believed her work constituted military service even before she shipped overseas.

Lena framed the wartime experiences of the Reconstruction Aides as military service for the rest of her life. In a 1982 oral history, she said: "I served the army, or my country, and the men in it, in helping to restore their bodies to usefulness."[24] Keenly aware of the historical legacy of her experience as she recorded this interview for posterity, she defined her wartime work as service.

As the years passed, the Reconstruction Aides joined other female veterans in asserting their belief that they were veterans, even though they did not meet the government's official definition. Without official veteran status, they remained ineligible for government veterans' benefits. As they aged, this proved to be a major loss for them, just as it was for other women in the same situation. Many of the Reconstruction Aides who served overseas took part in the larger effort to obtain veterans' benefits led by the WOSL, and over the years they expressed their dismay that they lacked these benefits.

They began their long and ultimately unsuccessful fight to obtain veteran status during the early period of the WWRAA. They proclaimed in the July 28, 1920, edition of what later became the *Re-Aides' Post* that they would seek state and federal legislation as part of their mission.[25] Even just a few years after the war when most aides remained young and fairly healthy, they realized that their lack of veteran status and compensation could adversely affect

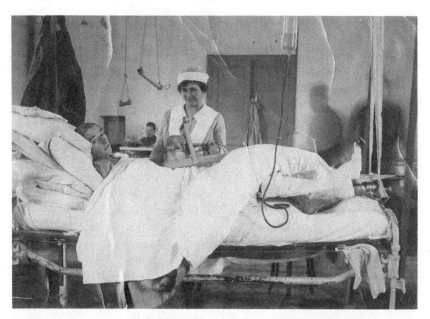

Figure 3.1. A Reconstruction Aide, Lena Hitchcock, helps patient Herbert Hahn use a loom in Châteauroux, France, December 1918 (Hitchcock 40). OHA 97 Angier and Hitchcock Collection, Otis Historical Archives, National Museum of Health and Medicine.

them. An article in the July 1922 edition of the *Re-Aides' Post* discussed the issue so members could be more aware of the risks they faced. The anonymous author explained that "there have been some silent tragedies among our sisters who have contracted T.B. or who have lost the use of an arm from overwork in the clinic, or who have sustained injuries through accident, and who did not know their rights under the Compensation Act because, perhaps, of the persistent bungle of the aide's status in the army and the consequent over wary attitude of some of the superior officers."[26] Even in 1922, they realized the uphill battle they faced and the risks of not fighting that battle.

Much of the problem stemmed from the confusion over the status of the Reconstruction Aides. Like the Hello Girls, many aides did not realize that their service did not give them veteran status, especially since they considered themselves to have completed military service. They soon learned they were ineligible for benefits, compensation, and even membership in the American Legion, all of which they tried to gain.[27]

In a further complication, some former aides received military honors at their burials, leading some members to believe they did have veteran status. Mrs. Charles L. Ireland received such a burial around November 1923. The

Re-Aides' Post reported that as a tribute to her faithful service, "military escort was given her body and Taps played by order of the Surgeon General."[28] To some of the aides, military honors at funerals indicated that they had earned veteran status.

Member Beulah Reimert took the question about the aides' veteran status and eligibility for membership in the American Legion straight to the top and wrote directly to General Pershing in 1924 or 1925; the *Re-Aides' Post* published his reply. Pershing declined to definitively answer whether the aides were eligible for membership in the American Legion, citing the War Department's lack of jurisdiction in the matter. However, he did note that "the Reconstruction Aides' were civilian employees of the medical department and as such were subject to the military laws and regulations of the United States Army while serving overseas." But, he continued, they "were never actually commissioned or enlisted in the United States Army and in consequence, though they served with our military forces, they have never been considered as a part thereof."[29]

Pershing then moved on to the question of whether Reconstruction Aides could receive military honors at their burials. He professed that "it would appear to be entirely appropriate in case of the death of a Reconstruction Aide for her casket to be draped with the American flag in recognition of her services to her country in time of war." Sensing that he needed to reassure Beulah of her nation's appreciation, Pershing ended his letter with a strong commendation of the Reconstruction Aides' wartime service. "I desire to take this opportunity," he wrote, "to express the appreciation of the War Department for the splendid service rendered by the Reconstruction Aides during the World War, as evidenced by the mutual spirit of cooperation and helpfulness which this personnel has at all times manifested in its relations with the military establishment."[30] While Pershing clearly valued the Reconstruction Aides and their contributions, he pointed out that their efforts did not technically constitute military service because they did not serve in the army. Of course, women could not fully serve in the army at the time except as nurses without rank, so the aides remained caught in the dilemma familiar to female veteranists.

By 1929, the WWRAA realized that it must try to obtain national legislation to secure veteran status. At its first national convention in June 1929, it debated the best approach, including whether to work through the American Legion. It also sought the advice of Congresswoman and WOSL member Edith Nourse Rogers. In her report about the convention, Mae Van Camp noted that "the Overseas League obtained the support of Mrs. Rogers Congresswoman from Massachusetts who says she antagonized everyone in Congress and also in the American Legion. She suggested that we work thru individual members and personal contacts."[31] To organize the effort, the WWRAA formed the Committee on Military Status, sometimes called the Committee on Attaining Military Status.

The status project was a focus of the second national convention in Washington, DC, in June 1931. The Committee on Attaining Military Status reported that the letters it sent to members asking for their opinions about the "advisability of acquiring military status . . . revealed that much confusion exists over the present status of the Aide relative to compensation and hospitalization. There was a general desire, however, to establish definitely military status." After the committee shared that it had been in touch with Faustine Dennis of the WOSL about that group's efforts to secure veteran status for women who served overseas, the convention voted to support the WOSL's bill. During the convention, the WWRAA also added language supporting the fight to secure compensation for current aides to the object of organization section in the WWRAA constitution.[32] The 1931 convention thus marked a turning point when the WWRAA felt empowered to take on the issue of veteran status as a defining goal of the association.

The WWRAA realized that it faced a tough battle and acknowledged that as a small organization it could do little by itself. Ethel Clements Dana admitted in the January 1933 issue of the *Re-Aides' Post* that although the Committee on Military Status had been working hard on this issue, it could not do it on its own. She explained that "the Women's Overseas Service League is a very strong and influential group of women, and when we discovered the difficulties they were having, we understood that as an organization we could do nothing by ourselves."[33] They teamed up with the WOSL, even though the WOSL focused only on overseas women, which excluded many members of the WWRAA who served in the US.

Sometimes, they sought the assistance of male veterans' groups and framed their request in terms of getting army nurse status for the World War Reconstruction Aides. Member Myrtle Thornton McLeod included an in-depth report in the October 1932 issue of the *Re-Aides' Post* that described her efforts to get the support of the Disabled Americans Veterans, the American Legion, and members of Congress. She included the full text of letters she received in response to her inquiries. Candid and emotional in her prose, she ended her article by directly referencing the Bonus March then taking place, something that other veteranists sometimes seemed wary of doing. She wrote that "observing the fifteen hundred Bonus Marchers leaving Los Angeles yesterday, June 9, 1932, for Washington, my heart went with them and I had to brush away a tear as they passed by. Again I say 'United We Stand, Divided we fall."[34] By openly showing her support for the Bonus March after writing so spiritedly about the effort to secure army nurse status for the Reconstruction Aides, McLeod correlated the WWRAA's struggles with those of the male veterans about to rally for their bonuses. She indicated that she may have viewed their effort as a similar campaign to simply get what the government owed them as veterans of the World War.

But unlike the Bonus Marchers, who felt that the Great Depression reinforced their need for the Bonus, the WWRAA stood in solidarity with the WOSL when it decided to pause its fight for veterans' benefits in the spirit of national unity during the economic crisis. Ethel C. Dana's "Report of the Committee on Military Status of the World War Reconstruction Aides" during the third national convention in Chicago in June 1933 explained that Faustine Dennis of the WOSL had informed them of its decision to suspend its effort to secure a bill giving hospitalization benefits to women who served overseas. Dana told the convention that "because of the current financial strain and stress under which our country is laboring the Overseas Service League has made no further effort to press their bill, neither can we be so selfish as to ask further consideration of the government, including added expense, when the Federal Treasury is at such a low ebb and when the whole country is trying to find ways and means to replenish it." She then made an impassioned plea for the WWRAA to put nation before self, just as it did during the war:

> Whether or not you agree that many of our present difficulties were caused by the World War the fact remains that the majority of our citizens believed that its veterans were receiving more from the public treasury than was their due and therefore have deprived them of many benefits previously enjoyed.
>
> Obviously this is no time to ask consideration for our group even though patriotic reasons did not forbid. Those in authority are struggling under heavy burdens and perplexing questions concerning our common good.
>
> It is our duty to serve as we did in 1917—not to ask for service, therefore your committee has made no further attempt to gain military status since the last convention in 1931.[35]

Dana's stirring speech, and the WWRAA's decision to align itself with the WOSL, created a unified front of female veteranists who placed the needs of the nation above their own. Ever committed to service, they sacrificed their own self-advocacy efforts in keeping with their veteranist ideology.

Of course, this decision did not mean that they completely gave up the fight, merely that they put it on hold during the crisis years of the Great Depression. As the Depression eased, the WWRAA broached the topic of veteran status again from time to time. In 1935, an article in the July issue of the *Re-Aides' Post* asked members to contact their representatives in Congress by sending their letters through Lena Hitchcock, then serving as chair of the Committee on Status of Aides.[36] An article from the *Re-Aides' Post* in April 1937 provided an update on the issue. Representative Donald McLean (R-NJ) had reportedly shown interest in their campaign and a willingness to support a bill to "regularize their position." However, as Ethel Clements Dana reported to the newsletter's editor, McLean wrote in a letter that

> even were a bill introduced it would have little or no chance of enactment. The difficulty is that similar bills in behalf of the Red Cross workers, Y.M. and Y.W.C.A. workers, the Russian Railway Corps, and many others who were not mustered into the regular armed forces, have been introduced but died in Committee. Knowing this, I do not feel that I should lend any encouragement to you and the many others who have so unselfishly given of your services during the World War.
>
> I believe there is much merit in your claim, and I sincerely wish I might be of some real service to the Reconstruction Aides, but I have serious doubt if any legislation, such as is being petitioned for, has any chance of enactment.[37]

Despite his support, McLean's honest assessment laid bare the reality the WWRAA faced. By publishing his opinions, the organization ensured that its members received his blunt prognosis coupled with his belief that they deserved veteran status. The same article also reported that Edith Nourse Rogers, whom Dana had interviewed about the topic, was "entirely frank and helpful."[38] These allies did them a favor by honestly explaining the challenges they faced. The WWRAA began to understand the reality of its situation, and while it did not give up, it moved forward with lower expectations.

As the organization entered the 1940s and Europe again went to war, members of the WWRAA experienced a deeper sense of disappointment. Dorothea Davis noted that her orders did not include the words "civilian employee" and that "the worst thing that happened to us was that we had no guardian angel as the nurses, yeomanettes, etc., had."[39] Aware of the situation of other women in the female veteran community, Davis saw the inequity in their struggle and how their lack of influential supporters could have impacted their success. In 1941, former physical therapist Bertha York Webb wrote to a fellow member named Daisy and echoed the frustration shared by her peers over their lack of military status. She told her that it "looks as if we might have another war on our hands. I hope the Convention took steps for military status for Aides now entering service. We were never good enough politicians to get it for ourselves and we waited too long before going after it."[40] Webb's resentment over their own lack of benefits made her want a better deal for the new aides.

Another member, Rachel Ring Pittman, wrote to WWRAA president Estelle Angier in May 1941 about their failed fight for status. She told Angier that although she felt it was too late to get full military status for themselves, "if an emergency again arises and calls for sudden expansion of the service, by all means get it for those entering or re-entering before they sign up, and if a 'rider' could be attached, get hospitalization privileges for all of us, as is accorded to nurses and yeomanettes at present."[41] Of course, an emergency did arise later in 1941, and the World War One women led the effort to obtain military benefits for the next generation of women.

As war seemed imminent, the Reconstruction Aides remained selflessly dedicated to serving their nation, despite bitterness over their treatment. In July 1941, Ruth Tibbals, the president of the San Diego Chapter of the WWRAA, wrote that at a recent chapter meeting, they decided "unanimously that the National Organization should offer the services of the Re-Aides to the government in whatever capacity we may be needed in defense work. We think that our services should be offered freely, without the proviso that we should be given military status."[42] Other members agreed with this approach, although not everyone believed they were owed benefits from the government. Gertrude Duncan Ross, for example, expressed her belief that "in common with the enlisted men, I counted my services as something more or less in the nature of a voluntary contribution, a part payment for the privilege of living under the best government on earth. I don't feel that the government owes me a brass farthing." She did, however, agree that they should help the aides who would come after them, for, she wrote, "the old order has changed. Army Aides should have military status."[43]

The WWRAA discussed the issue at its sixth biennial convention in July 1941. Instead of continuing to fight, a motion carried that stated the WWRAA "should cease to attempt to procure military status for its members"[44] In 1941, sensing that the US might soon be drawn into the new World War, the WWRAA decided to put service and nation before self yet again. It asserted its belief in its members' status as military veterans in the most appropriate way it could: by carrying on with the promise it had made to serve the country and fulfill the ideals of veteranism, even at the expense of its own needs.

THE WWRAA'S DEDICATION TO VETERANISM

As veteranists, the female Reconstruction Aides believed that one of the best ways to commemorate World War One was to continue their service by helping others, especially male and female veterans. Having served during wartime, they felt obligated to continue contributing to the nation in the postwar years. Like the WOSL, the WWRAA provided service opportunities for its members and helped the former aides organize a program of activities and publicly commit themselves to peacetime service.

From its formative days, the organization that became the WWRAA valued service as a central part of its mission. In the second issue of the publication later renamed the *Re-Aides' Post*, released on August 25, 1925, Alice Archer Rohns (Alice Watts) published a letter labeled "A Field for Service" that outlined why service should be a key component of this new association. She wrote that "pioneering stirs the soul and brings from the innermost depths the biggest things of which one is capable." She discussed how their roles as some of the first physical and occupational therapists broadened their confidence in their abilities and then addressed the need for an organization that would facilitate their continued service. "There are doubtless many aides," she wrote, "who, like myself are married—and would like to get from such an organization the information and inspiration necessary to carry into civic and social life the advantages of experience and insight gained in service— to make them valuable to every community and state."[45] In another early issue of the *Re-Aides' Post* from 1921, Mrs. E. C. Slagle compelled her fellow members not to "divorce the civilian needs from those of the disabled soldiers. The splendid commendation of our work in the past should inspire us to widen our range of thought and activity in our special field."[46] Slagle, like Rohns, felt inspired to continue and increase her work as a way to build on the legacy of her wartime service.

Having included veteranist service as a key part of its organizational ideology from its start in the 1920s, the WWRAA brought this commitment into even greater focus with its activities during the 1930s. Throughout the Great Depression, the former aides focused on helping veterans and fellow aides. In April 1932, WWRAA president Esther Macomber wrote a letter to her members in the *Re-Aides' Post* suggesting that they should all find ways to assist veterans during the Depression. She wrote: "In this day of great need, I am wondering if it would not be a fine thing for the different Units of our organization to provide in some way—work, food or clothes—for a worthy ex-service man or such a man and his family. Some of the Units are doing that very thing. We who have worked with these men are in a position to do a very intimate bit of service to them, for we are sure of being understood. Old clothing is so acceptable to these needy families. A Bridge Party given as a benefit with a charge of a can of corn, a pound of coffee, etc., works magic. Now is your chance to 'Carry On!'"[47] By invoking the constant veteranist refrain "Carry On" and describing the WWRAA's special connection to veterans, Macomber made a convincing case for why her members remained obligated to help veterans during the Depression.

In the months after Macomber's message, different units of the WWRAA reported the ways they heeded her call to service. Martha Moffett Bache of the Washington Unit described how they wove into their meeting "the expression of charitable intentions toward the veterans who are feeling extraordinarily the present need and it was decided that each aide bring articles of clothing to our June meeting as a means of carrying on in behalf of the men whom we once served."[48] In this way, the Washington Unit members made the needs of the former servicemen part of their normal operations, even when they themselves probably felt financially strained.

Macomber acknowledged that the Great Depression also impacted her members and lauded them for continuing to serve despite their own hardships. In her message in the January 1933 issue of the *Re-Aides' Post*, Macomber reflected on how "the year just ended held mingled joy and sorrow. For some of our members it held the greatest joy they have ever known, for others more sadness and trouble than it seemed possible to endure." Yet she wrote that "splendid reports have come to me from various Units, and it is inspiring to learn that their endeavors are so worthwhile. It is this spirit of helpfulness that will keep us banded together in true patriotic service."[49] To Macomber, serving others uplifted her members from the sorrow of the Great Depression by reminding them of their patriotic duty and value to the nation.

Even as the Depression continued, the WWRAA maintained its commitment to helping veterans, so much so that it reemphasized this as part of its organizational platform at its 1933 national convention in Chicago (fig. 3.2). At that convention, various units contributed verses to the "Re-Aides Song," sung to the tune of the song "Smiles." The verse by Abigail Bailey of Boston outlined their commitment to serving veterans:

There are men who need attention;
There are soldiers feeling blue;
There are buddies lying in the sunshine
Who would like a cheery word or two.
So we still must try to make them happy,
Make them feel that they are useful, too.
Just because we've done a little something
Don't just sit back and say, "We're through."[50]

By incorporating this mantra of service into the organizational song and the convention, Bailey provided yet another reminder of the WWRAA's central commitment to serving veterans.

The WWRAA also continued to help fellow female veterans. Beyond advocating for veterans' benefits, the WWRAA looked for other ways to assist.

Figure 3.2. World War Reconstruction Aides Association convention, Chicago, Illinois, 1933 (OHA371–001–00007–9). OHA 371 World War Reconstruction Aides Association Collection, Otis Historical Archives, National Museum of Health and Medicine.

As a small organization, it often supported and promoted the WOSL's larger efforts in this area. For example, in 1935 it publicized the cookbook produced by the St. Louis WOSL Unit to benefit the WOSL's National Disabled Women's Fund.[51] By using the *Re-Aides' Post* to encourage its members to support this cookbook and the fund, the WWRAA showed solidarity with female veteranists while helping its comrades.

During the months preceding the US entrance into World War Two, WWRAA members stepped up their veteranist activities and recommitted themselves to service. With war on the horizon, they began to prepare to do as much as they could in an emergency. In the *Re-Aides' Post* in January 1941, Hope Fullerton wrote, "Feeling that every civilian ought to be prepared in some way, these days, I have received the kind permission of the New York Chapter of the Red Cross to take the course leading to a 'nurses' assistant' volunteer job."[52] Estelle Angier, who served as the WWRAA's president in 1941, viewed the 1941 convention as an opportunity for the organization to refocus on service. She wrote in the April 1941 issue of the *Re-Aides' Post* that "these are troublous times. There is much that we, as former Aides, should do, and can do if we are all united." She urged her members to come to the convention so they could "'gird our aging loins,' so to speak, against an unpredictable future; where we raise once more a pledge of service to our country and flag."[53]

However, the WWRAA decided that instead of creating a program of service as a group, it would encourage members to help independently. It understood the challenges facing it and decided that "since our organization is a comparatively small group and widely scattered in its membership, we do nothing as an organization, but encourage our members to help as much as they can, as the need arises, through channels already established in their own communities."[54] This decision did not reduce or hamper its service activities; rather it seemed to have had the opposite effect as aides threw themselves into all types of service. By the start of the WWRAA's 1941 reunion in Chicago, the organization's intention to serve the nation in case of another war became well known publicly. The *Chicago Daily Tribune* even reported that the Reconstruction Aides were "now preparing to volunteer their services again 'for whatever use can be made of us in the national emergency.'"[55]

Once the US entered the war, the women of the WWRAA further heeded Angier's call and intensified their service in support of the war effort. Members Eva McLagan and Mary Watson Reid summed up the outlook of the former aides in the January–April 1942 edition of the *Re-Aides' Post*. McLagan wrote that "I'm surely behind our organization 100%!" and Reik quipped, "So we're in another war? Well, I guess we Aides will carry on and do our bit someway."[56] Christine Betholas wrote, "I never thought we'd see the day when our services would again be given to our country. I am head over heels in Red Cross work."[57] Betholas, like many other aides, wasted no time finding a worthy outlet to support the war effort.

The former Reconstruction Aides served the nation in a variety of ways during the Second World War. Some, like Emma Vogel, who became the director of the army's physical therapy aides, continued to work as army physical and occupational therapists and took on leadership roles in the current conflict. Others returned to work, such as Jane Feinman, who was reinstated in the Veterans Bureau.[58] Many threw themselves into volunteering. Individually or in conjunction with their local unit of the WWRAA, they volunteered with the Red Cross and the Walter Reed Gray Ladies, made "bundles for Britain," participated in salvage gathering, and did first aid and home nursing tasks.[59] Some, like Estelle Angier, tried unsuccessfully to serve overseas but were rejected because of their age. Angier ended up serving as commander of the women's first aid corps in Chicago during World War Two.[60]

As WWRAA members reflected on their actions, the amount of service they were performing astounded even themselves. In July 1942, the New York Unit reported that the scale of service by its "members since this war began is incalculable. I doubt that any women's group of equal number could re-port greater or more varied efforts to serve, but our members are so scattered that we find it too difficult to concentrate our efforts or centralize its organi-zation. Many are really too busy to come to meetings or even to report what they are doing."[61] Wartime service, in all its varied forms, quickly overtook the members of the WWRAA and prevented them from spending as much time on the organization as they had before the war.

Although members found their service in the new war meaningful, it made some nostalgic about their World War One experiences. Those women not serving in the armed forces, especially, missed the camaraderie they had felt as Reconstruction Aides. The ever-dedicated editor of the *Re-Aides' Post*, Laura Brackett Hoppin, explained that even though they were "serving our country now as proudly and loyally as we did during World War I," they missed "the excitement of working in a group in the thick of things, on the spot; yet each Aide, wherever she is, is doing her bit, and we are all eager to hear about it."[62] Anna G. Voris, who led what she called a "quiet existence" in Florida with "the rest of the aged and infirm," felt that for some former aides, "our hardest job now is to stay at home and knit sweaters and raise vegetables and let the next generation have their chance. We paved the way so they will not make the mistakes we made because we knew so little about what was ex-pected of us." She knew that "here will be new problems but never the same old A.E.F. We wouldn't have missed being there. More power to the girls who will help win this war."[63] Emily H. Huger, the WWRAA's president in 1943, shared some of Voris's nostalgia and desire to serve as she had before. She would have loved "just to be allowed a few hours each day in such curative work as we once did" but expressed that her "wish to our sister Aides is to keep up the work they are doing. Perhaps they may need us yet, and if so, we, one and all, will be ready."[64] Huger's wish alluded to the passing of the baton to the next generation and the WWRAA's hopes that they would con-tinue the veteranist ideology it had helped to develop.

During World War Two, the dedication of WWRAA members to vetera-nism led, in part, to the demise of their beloved organization. They were so focused on wartime service and sometimes too busy for the WWRAA, and the association lost some of its strength. Yet even as they faced the dissolu-tion of the association, they maintained their unselfish commitment to veter-anism. In advance of the association's 1949 reunion, members were requested to fill out questionnaires about their vision for the group's future and indicate whether they would attend the reunion. The leadership admitted that the or-ganization's strength was diminishing and they wanted to wrap up their affairs at the 1949 reunion, which they reluctantly decided would be their last. Ques-tions on the form asked what should be done with any remaining organizational funds and any historical materials. In many of the responses, an overwhelming number of women suggested ways that the funds could be used to support community service efforts aiding disabled veterans, their own members, other service organizations, and the younger generation of therapists.[65]

The responses on these questionnaires illuminate the depth of the former Reconstruction Aides' commitment to veteranism. Even as they faced the end of their cherished organization, they wanted to use their leftover funds to help others. For example, Winifred M. Keith (Mrs. René Wentworth Pinto) wrote that they could "give it to some Veteran's aide program, unless there is enough to justify a sinking fund for the use of 'over-taxed' Aides."[66] Margaret Lovell answered that "any remaining funds might go to the Red Cross," while Henrietta E. Failing asked whether there would be "enough to make a contribution to some research as the Cancer, Heart, arthritis or similar matter?"[67]

The topic of ending the WWRAA aroused bittersweet emotions for some members, even as they focused on charitable ways to use their funds. Abigail Roxanna Bailey (Mrs. Olo Galen Temple) suggested that "perhaps we have needy W.W.R.A. who might be helped" and added that she hoped "that the younger generation has better luck than we did," a reference to their failure to obtain veteran status.[68] Harriet Joor suggested that the funds "could go to some form of healing work for disabled veterans; to help the living in some way; perhaps for psychiatry. Or towards the training of younger women for such work as ours; for a rest fund for such workers." However, she continued, "probably these suggestions are 'no good.' I am too far away from the currents of such activity to form any suggestions that would be 'workable.'"[69]

Throughout its truncated lifespan, the WWRAA made veteranism a central tenet of its mission. It included service-based activities as a significant part of its agenda from its earliest days through the very end. It focused on serving former service members, female veterans, and other charitable causes. Yet while it passionately believed in community service, it also incorporated living memorials into its work, specifically through its participation in the American Red Cross's Memorial Building to the Women of the World War in Washington, DC.

THE WWRAA'S INTERIOR COLUMN AT THE MEMORIAL BUILDING TO THE WOMEN OF THE WORLD WAR

As in other groups of female veteranists, living memorial buildings became a matter of debate and disagreement within the WWRAA. The story of the WWRAA's involvement with the American Red Cross's Memorial Building to the Women of the World War expands the story of the building's creation and its impact on the female veteranist community, who remained divided in their support. Membership often overlapped between female veteranist organizations, and this building project reached some female veteranists who belonged to organizations that took different approaches to participating in it. Lena Hitchcock, for example, led the WOSL's opposition to the Memorial Building as its president and yet remained a devoted member of the WWRAA. As Hitchcock's membership in both organizations demonstrates, the members of the WWRAA and the larger female veteranist community disagreed about the best way to conduct veteranist commemorations. However, unlike the WOSL, the former Reconstruction Aides followed the lead of Mabel Boardman and the women of the Red Cross and eventually reached a compromise that included them in the building.

The WWRAA first broached the subject of living memorials as part of its conversations about its Endowment Fund, which later became central to its participation in the Memorial Building. It began discussing the Endowment Fund around 1925. President Alice Ueland envisioned it as a fund that each member would pay into and that could be used for a variety of purposes, such as supporting the organization and creating a living memorial, although the fund's purpose changed over the years. She wrote in the *Re-Aides' Post* that "the question has arisen: 'What kind of memorial would the Fund be used for?'" and suggested that "I am sure all aides would want a living memorial. Furthermore, I can only say that with women of intellect, understanding and experience, such as made up the personnel of the World War Reconstruction Aides, we can surely trust that a fitting use would be made of the fund."[70] Ueland indicated that a group so focused on service could want only a living memorial that would benefit others, instead of a traditional statuary monument.

Other former aides saw it differently and wanted the fund to be used in a more purely service-oriented manner, a perspective that set up the subsequent debate about the Red Cross Memorial Building. In a June 1926 article in the *Re-Aides' Post* titled "Endowment Fund Suggestions," Emma Dyer Litzenberg made a strong appeal to use the fund only to assist WWRAA members, many of whom would need support in the future if their effort to obtain government status failed. She wrote that she would support the Endowment Fund only "so far as it will help the future of the Aides themselves. There are many organizations for the ex-service man but none so far as I know to help an indigent aide. We are not allowed in the American Legion, could not take out war insurance, find it almost impossible to get Federal Employees insurance, or anything but an accident policy."[71] With this passionate declaration, Litzenberg connected the fund to the ongoing fight for veteran status. Ultimately, the WWRAA decided to establish the fund through a fee paid by members and chose to use it to support the association, the publication of the *Re-Aides' Post*, and a later as yet undecided effort to create a living memorial to the Reconstruction Aides.[72]

By at least 1929, the WWRAA found another potential use for its Endowment Fund when Mabel Boardman offered it the opportunity to donate a column in its honor at the Red Cross's Memorial Building to the Women of the World War in Washington, DC. A letter from Boardman to WWRAA secretary-treasurer Daisy Doty Gallois published in January 1929 in the *Re-Aides' Post* explained the mission of the Memorial Building and the different column options the WWRAA could consider donating: an exterior column for $5,000 or an interior wooden-fluted column in the Hall of Service for $1,000. Boardman noted that, of course, their "organization and the fine services its members rendered would be commemorated in the general building, but should you desire a special memorial such as these columns, we would be very glad to include such a memorial, at the cost I have given."[73]

The association discussed this offer during its first national convention in June 1929, and Laura Hoppin, who had spoken with Boardman about it on several occasions, provided more information.[74] Some members wanted to focus on improving their struggling Endowment Fund, but others, dismayed by the fund's poor progress, pushed to end that project and instead use the fund to purchase a column in the Memorial Building.[75] At this suggestion, Mrs. Von Stein stated that she understood that "the endowment fund was for use of needy Aides or their children. She felt it should be left as such."[76] However, when they put the question about purchasing a column to the whole convention, they voted in favor of doing so, and in the next motion, they also voted to discontinue the Endowment Fund.[77] Although some dissenting voices within the WWRAA preferred to focus on more purely service-based projects like the WOSL, its members did not all support the same very modern approach to veteranism. This situation again demonstrates that female veteranists did not always agree with each other and that veteranism took various forms throughout the larger female veteranist community.

By the time of the publication of the July 1929 issue of the *Re-Aides' Post*, the WWRAA had formed a memorial fund committee and announced its plans in an article titled "Our Memorial." This article explained that they had voted to discontinue the Endowment Fund at the convention; since only nineteen aides had paid full life subscriptions and only five had partially paid, they concluded that their goal of "$20,000 was beyond our reach." All those who wanted a refund would receive it, but many members of the Life Fund intended to donate their contributions to the memorial project. The WWRAA chose to purchase one of the $1,000 interior wooden-fluted columns in the building's Hall of Service. Its memorial column would be one of twelve and would be identified with a metal plate. The article compelled members to donate and stated that "every aide will wish to contribute her share to this memorial, our first public recognition, and a permanent tribute to our war service." This issue also contained Mabel Boardman's article "The Columns," which she frequently used as part of the campaign to gain support for the building.[78]

The fundraising process turned out to be more difficult than originally anticipated as the WWRAA struggled to raise the $1,000. Much of the trouble probably stemmed from the October 1929 stock market crash and the onset of the Great Depression. Undeterred, the WWRAA began a concerted campaign to induce its members to donate. In October 1929, Zaidee Bonney reported that it had raised only $325 and she implored members to donate.[79] She asked them, "Is there an Aide who does not wish to see a public recognition of the professions of physio and occupational therapists? Send your checks now!"[80] In a January 1930 article titled "The New Campaign," president Louisa C. Lippett declared the column fundraising effort to be of "first importance" at the moment and asked for donations, for if the dedication had not been delayed, they would have missed the deadline.[81] Indeed, the Chicago and Buffalo Units reported in that issue that they were working to secure donations for the column, having understood that paying for the column required a concerted campaign, especially because many aides probably had trouble donating because of the economic crisis.[82]

The delayed deadline enabled the aides to raise the $1,000 to purchase their memorial column in the Hall of Service. The column included a metal plate with an identifying inscription: "Gift of the World War Reconstruction Aides."[83] The April 1930 edition of the *Re-Aides' Post* summarized the March 19, 1930, dedication of the Memorial Building with pride so that all members could rejoice in their successful fundraising effort, completed just days before the building's dedication. Mrs. Harold Travis Smith (Marguerite Sanderson) and Mrs. Helen Tanquary Smith unveiled the column; the former had been appointed the first Reconstruction Aide and became the director of both physiotherapy and occupational therapy in France. The latter was the first head aide appointed and established the first unit of occupational therapy at Walter Reed.[84] More than a dozen former aides attended the ceremony, including Emma Vogel, Louisa Lippett, Ethel Clements Dana, Roberta Montgomery, and others.

After the dedication, member Ethel Clements Dana explained that "the whole building is dedicated to service and it is intended that all rooms shall serve some useful purpose." She asked whether there could be a "more fitting place to have our national memorial than in a room dedicated to service and in use daily by women volunteers, as we did, to help those who need help." Referencing their struggle to raise the $1,000, she reassured members that if they "had been with me on the day of my visit, they would have come away as enthused as I was, and would feel as I do, that to fail to be represented among all the other service organizations, would admit of indifference and lack of cooperation, which can not really be true."[85] By emphasizing how meaningful it was for their column to be located in a space dedicated to service work alongside other women veterans, Dana viewed the column as a veteranist memorial that facilitated service. Her position represented a compromise between traditional commemorative practices and the more modernist, purely action-based veteranist projects. She recognized her organization's struggle to raise the money and reassured her fellow members that their column represented a dignified way to facilitate service work in their name within the Memorial Building.

The WWRAA's second national convention in Washington, DC, in June 1931 included a special ceremony at the pillar so members could see the memorial and celebrate its installation. Several aides who wore their old uniforms formed a color guard, and speeches reflected on the column's importance. In one speech, Lois Clifford reminded the audience of the veteranist goal pursued by the WWRAA through the purchase of this column. She spoke of how "we worked and worked hard, and are proud of our achievement, but, proud as we are of this pillar, more than pillars or buttons or badges, are we proud of our service to mankind which this pillar commemorates and grateful for the friendships and comradeships that this service brought to us. Let this achievement give us courage to carry on in any and all enterprises in the future."[86] As demonstrated in Clifford's words, the WWRAA, ever aware of its commitment to service and the obligation to carry on its mission, interpreted its column as a form of veteranism and did not want it to be a distraction from its veteranist agenda.

The saga of the Reconstruction Aides' column shows that even within the same organization, female veteranists did not always agree on how to execute veteranism. They debated, compromised, and found different ways to pursue service and commemorate their part in the World War. Veteranism constituted a flexible, changeable ideology, adapted to suit the needs of different women in various contexts. Some members of the WWRAA viewed their interior column in the Hall of Service as a compromise, a way to remain committed to service while also trying to gain proper recognition for their wartime work. Yet others saw it as a departure from the veteranist ideology at the core of their mission.

Although they hoped that their pillar would remain a permanent memorial to their work, the Hall of Service no longer contains the Reconstruction Aides' memorial column. All of the inscriptions on the room's columns are now missing, robbing the WWRAA's column of its ability to maintain its original purpose and erasing the commemorative legacy of the organization within this memorial building.[87] By striking a bargain between traditional commemoration and veteranism, they ended up with the same outcome that a purely veteranist memorial would have produced: an ephemeral monument, an absence from the permanent commemorative landscape, and evidence that their fear of being mostly forgotten came true.

THE WWRAA'S STRUGGLE TO PRESERVE ITS HISTORICAL LEGACY

Even though they did not know the eventual fate of their memorial column, the former Reconstruction Aides found good reason to worry about the historical legacy and longevity of their service, even immediately after the war's end. They feared that their pioneering contributions to World War One were already being forgotten in their lifetime, by both the younger generation of therapists and the nation as a whole. As the years passed, this fear became an almost all-consuming sentiment among the members of the WWRAA. It increased as World War Two overshadowed them and as they faced the disbandment of the WWRAA in 1949. This fear, combined with disappointment about their failure to gain veterans' benefits, led many members of the WWRAA to feel disillusioned, rejected, and forgotten as they saw the memory of their service further recede from public consciousness.

Early on, the WWRAA knew it would have to work hard to maintain its place in the historical narrative of the war. It expressed this clearly in its effort to establish the doomed Endowment Fund. In the October 1926 edition of the *Re-Aides' Post*, a short article urged members to donate to the Endowment Fund and justified the cost by arguing that it would help to preserve and promote the memory of their service. The article told readers that "now is the time for us to gather our forces and to become a recognized part of the army of patriots who served their country. It is also the time for us to take our place as the foundation of two growing professions. We are now the old-timers, and from us must come the inspiration, the deeper meaning of service that could be experienced only by those of our unique service."[88]

As the group matured, it maintained its effort to preserve its legacy and developed a concrete project to specifically record its history: the publication of a book. The WWRAA published the *History of the World War Reconstruction Aides* in 1933. Spearheaded and edited by Laura Brackett Hoppin, a devoted WWRAA leader and longtime editor of the *Re-Aides' Post*, it formed "an account of the activities and whereabouts of Physio Therapy and Occupational Therapy Aides who served in US Army Hospitals in the United States and in France during the World War."[89] Although intended to be a history, the book actually consists of an alphabetical listing of women who served as Reconstruction Aides and does not include a narrative history of their service. Aides submitted contributions to Hoppin, who organized them and added information from old copies of the Re-Aides' Post and other documents. This resulted in long entries for some women and short entries for others.[90] At minimum, most entries identified the woman as a PT or an OT and stated where she served during the war. Some entries included a woman's current address, married and maiden names, and varied descriptions of her wartime service, postwar activities, accomplishments, and present situation, with a few photos of the aides interspersed throughout. It read more like a directory or retroactive yearbook than a historical account.

Hoppin worked on the book for several years and the WWRAA proudly reported about the many illustrious institutions that it either sent copies to or that asked for a copy. As recorded in the Re-Aides' Post in 1934, these included the Imperial War Museum, the New York Public Library, the Library of the College of Physicians in Philadelphia, the Library of Congress, and other institutions.[91] The WWRAA felt proud of the book and its value as historical documentation of its members' wartime work. Even while the book remained in draft form, the WWRAA knew it would be a valuable way to record its history. In a 1929 update about the project, it urged members to submit their stories and told them that "we feel sure that every aide will agree that the History is worth every cent that it costs, and that we did the right thing to not cut it down to a bare list of addresses."[92] Indeed, the book remains an extremely beneficial source today, even without the narrative that would have made it more useful to scholars. It represented a tangible way for the WWRAA to preserve its memory. While it did succeed in recording some of its history, it did not do enough to prevent the memory of the Reconstruction Aides' service from fading, even within their lifetimes.

World War Two proved to be the turning point that hindered the longevity of the WWRAA. As discussed earlier, many members found themselves so busy with wartime service activities that they did not have much time to devote to the WWRAA. This also meant reduced submissions to the Re-Aides' Post and less regular issues. In many ways, the Re-Aides' Post had acted as the main organ keeping the scattered WWRAA together, so the reduction in regularity loosened the ties that bound the members together and impacted the whole organization. In 1944, the members agreed that there should be "no convention at the present time," another blow to the main event that united the organization and its future.[93] Ironically, the members' dedication to veteranism during World War Two led to the WWRAA's eventual demise, and in turn, the fading memory of their own service.

Beyond the relative organizational inactivity of the WWRAA during World War Two, the war and its new generation of aides overshadowed the memory of the aides of World War One. The World War One aides were keenly aware of this and felt sensitive about being overlooked. In the *Re-Aides' Post* from the summer of 1943, Hoppin included a copy of a letter that member Eunice M. Coates sent to the editor of *Life* magazine in which she corrected errors in an article's representation of occupational therapy. She believed that the article gave the impression that occupational therapy in army hospitals was new during World War Two, and she found the article's "false statements" offensive and misleading. She told the editor that "my resentment of these false statements is shared by five hundred young women who served in the Army as Reconstruction Aides in Occupational Therapy during and following World War I—also by hundreds of ex-service men who owe their rehabilitation to occupational therapy treatments administered in Army, Public Health and Veterans Hospitals."[94]

As World War Two continued, the public amnesia about the first Reconstruction Aides continued and worsened. In the summer 1944 issue of the *Re-Aides' Post*, member Helene Hartley Anderson sarcastically asked, "Isn't it interesting to read of the 'new' discoveries being made these days in therapy?" She lamented that "it has taken American people twenty years to learn even the meaning of the words, 'Occupational Therapy.' We were a 'lost' generation. We are glad to be 'discovered.'"[95] Anderson understood with bitter clarity that the work of the World War One Reconstruction Aides had been all but forgotten by the public in the short time between the two conflicts. By calling the group a "lost generation," she ironically repurposed the term usually associated with the writers and artists scarred by the First World War into a term that described how the memory of their own wartime service had been lost.

The members of the WWRAA did not let their resentment over the attention now being given to the new aides turn them against these younger women. In fact, they repeatedly mentioned their joy that their previous wartime service and failed effort to gain military status had at least paved the way for the new aides and enabled them to get the status and benefits they could not. In the *Re-Aides' Post* published in the autumn of 1945, just after the end of World War Two, president Dora I. Dysart explained that the return of peace meant that the World War One aides must for the most part relinquish their reconstruction work to the "more nimble fingers" of the younger aides. She explained that "we do this a bit unwillingly, but in the knowledge that we were pioneers. It is because of us and the results we accomplished that now our successors enjoy the honor and prestige of actual rank in the armed forces. We are happy for them and wish them well. Pioneers there must always be, and we take credit in our two respective careers."[96] Dysart's positive message encapsulated the joy that the first aides felt in seeing the younger women continue their legacy and gain the veterans' benefits they lacked.

The WWRAA also wanted to bring the World War Two aides into the organization as members. In the summer of 1944, president Emily H. Huger wrote in the *Re-Aides' Post* about the importance of welcoming the new aides into the association. With regard to the new generation of aides, Huger told the WWRAA, "Remember this: Your organization, into which we wish to bring the younger women who are now on the job, must be very much alive, so that there will be no need for a second association of the same sort and interests."[97] Like the leaders of the WOSL, Huger realized that they must embrace the new aides and entice them to become active members to keep their group alive. Huger found support for this idea, but the association folded in 1949 before it could be implemented.[98]

With its momentum slowed by World War Two, the years immediately afterward brought new challenges to the WWRAA. The busy lives of the members, their advancing age, and the increase in member deaths further slowed the organization's activity. After the death of Esther Macomber, a very active member and leader from St. Paul, Minnesota, Gracia Loehl (Mrs. G. J. Maloney) wrote in the autumn 1945 issue of the *Re-Aides' Post* that she feared Macomber's death was "the end of our unit also. These are such busy days that it is hard for us who live outside of Minneapolis and St. Paul to attend meetings."[99] Similarly, in December 1946, Ruth Early wrote to announce her resignation from the WWRAA. "Since Alton Vary passed away," she explained, "I have realized that with one single exception I know no one in the New York unit enough to be familiar with in terms of service or connection. The shock of Alton's death knocked every desire to finish the article we planned." Laura Brackett Hoppin added an editor's note stating that "Ruth may not need us, but we do need her!"[100]

Despite Hoppin's plea for Ruth to remain a member, she too realized that the organization faced mounting challenges. In the summer 1946 issue of the *Re-Aides' Post*, she reminded readers that "any organization, that has survived practically by correspondence alone for twenty-five years, with a membership larger today than it was in 1924 (when I became editor), is something for which to be proud in a great way." Yet despite succeeding against the odds for so long, she told them how she had been "thinking about that 'something' that holds us together . . . we of the World War Reconstruction Aides Association are bound together by ties that we cannot break, even if we decide to resign." She added that "one of these days, I will not be your editor. I, too, am growing old."[101] Although her words were meant to inspire readers, she honestly admitted that her work as editor might soon conclude.

Hoppin's intuition about the end of the WWRAA became reality in 1949 when the upcoming reunion prompted the leadership to ask for members' thoughts on the group's future as they began to draw down their activities and contemplate the end of the organization. The questionnaires they sent to members before this reunion asked them to respond to several difficult questions about how they should proceed. As discussed earlier, these forms asked members whether they would attend the 1949 reunion, encouraged them to share ideas for how to use the WWRAA's leftover funds, and asked what they should do with their historical and archival materials. These questionnaires and the decision to end the association provoked emotional responses from members, who saw the fragility of the fraying ties that bound their sisterhood together. In a letter to Estelle Angier in which she explained that she could not attend the 1949 reunion, member and former national treasurer Madeleine Ashley Carter told Angier of her hope that "a number of Re-Aides all over this country will find some way to keep in touch with one another and keep the torch of friendship and remembrance burning."[102] Carter feared that the dissolution of the WWRAA might mean that their friendships would end and their service would be forgotten. Many other aides shared Carter's fears and expressed them on the questionnaires.

In addition to suggesting how to use the WWRAA's leftover money in ways that supported veteranism, some members wanted to use the money to help preserve the memory of their service. Mildred Lincoln Pierce wrote that as someone still employed in teaching occupational therapy, she held a unique position that involved studying and working along with the "new, younger generation of Occupational Therapists, whose training is so scientific and functional that they have no interest in the diversional work that you and I did in World War I." So, she suggested, "let's rest on our laurels and offer our historical material to the National Occupational Therapy Association or the Congressional Library in Washington and if we have money left turn it into the scholarship fund that every O.T. school maintains."[103] Pierce wanted to use the money to help younger women in their field while commemorating their own service. She hoped that by funding a scholarship, the leftover money could help the younger therapists learn about and perhaps appreciate the pioneering work of the World War One women who supported their education.

The topic of the younger generation of therapists came up frequently around this time; some members felt sad that the Second World War aides achieved more recognition, and others hoped that these younger women would fare better than they had. Unable to attend the 1949 reunion, Abigail Roxanna Bailey wrote on her questionnaire that "I shall be with you in spirit . . . I hope the younger generation has better luck than we did."[104] Bailey put her hopes in the younger generation's ability to succeed where hers had failed.

Like Bailey, Ethel C. Dana also felt a sense of disillusionment and failure in 1949 as the WWRAA disbanded. Having devoted herself so passionately over the years to leadership in the WWRAA, especially to the fight for veteran status, Dana remained angry about their situation. In a long 1949 letter to Mrs. Adrogna, president of the WWRAA, Dana shared her feelings about the organization's end, its failures, and the impact of World War Two on its memory.[105] She wrote that "I feel too that this may be the last reunion of the W.W. Re Aides. In fact there seems little use in continuing the organization. No one seems to remember the first world war Aides and our mark as pioneers is forgotten. Only we who went through it know or care about our struggles to make 'a go' of occupational therapy." She felt that "the aides of the second World War were advertised and dramatized until the public became familiar with these and with their work, whereas there are very few among the general public who even know that there were O.T.'s in the first world war. We were not recognized then and we are not now—not even as to benefits that Congress has bestowed on the Aides of the recent war. We have not been able to change this although some of us have made strenuous efforts. We are comparatively few in numbers and of course growing fewer."[106] Dana tied the aides' lack of recognition directly to World War Two. She felt that it overshadowed the memory of their service and obscured their place as pioneers. Having played such a big part in the fight for veteran status, she resented their failure, even though they had laid the groundwork for the World War Two aides to receive the benefits they were denied.

While many members echoed Dana's disillusionment, others remained somewhat optimistic. On the back of her questionnaire, Hope Fullerton added a "personal note" saying that she wanted to keep the organization going "in any fashion available—even 'Daughters of.'" She took a different view than Dana and explained how during World War Two, "as a WAC on duty with Air Force at Mitchel Base, I had the opportunity and privilege of cutting the tape of sending the message of acceptance of commission of our first Mitchel therapist (O.T.) The years were not wasted then, you bet! The outfits I served with all learned a bit about OT's & PT's of War I & deeply respected all of you just because one was now with them. We have a proud heritage." Fullerton also commented that the association's historical material should be "available for use in case matter of War I status was again brought up in Congress," and she added that a note should be sent to women representatives to that effect.[107]

Positive as she was, Fullerton seemed to be in the minority among her fellow members. The question about the disposition of the historical materials seemed to have hit a particular nerve with many members who submitted questionnaires. On the back of her questionnaire, Harriet Joor wrote that "such material is precious; but I fear it would be tucked away, covered with dust and forgotten, wherever we bequeathe it. It belongs, with the medical records of WWI; but it would be thrown away, I know."[108] By 1949, Joor felt that the Reconstruction Aides had been so forgotten by the public and abandoned by the government that their precious historical materials would not be valued enough to be saved.

Even Lena Hitchcock shared some of this sense of hopelessness about the legacy of their service. In an undated letter to a Colonel MacDaniel about donating her personal effects to a museum exhibit, she wrote that "when I go, no one will be interested—I'm gradually clearing out my possessions . . . I am truly thrilled to think these very sentimental memorials will have a home."[109] Hitchcock understood that the preservation of her wartime possessions could function as a memorial to her service. But she felt disillusioned as she made these arrangements. After she had devoted so much of her life to advocating on behalf of World War One women and preserving their memory, her cynicism in her later years reflects the sense of frustration shared by so many former aides. Even during their own lifetimes, they could see that their pioneering service had started to fade from historical memory. Harriet Lee Johnson, on the back of her questionnaire, raised the question that so many aides might have been thinking as the WWRAA ended its tenure. In her elegant cursive, she wrote, "Surely historical material of the WWRAA should not be destroyed. Is there no WWI historian who might use it?"[110]

After agonizing over the dissolution of the WWRAA for many months, the organization officially disbanded at the July 1949 reunion in Chicago, its final convention. At the time, only about four units remained active at the local level, and members of those units appointed a Terminal Committee composed of longtime WWRAA leaders to close out the association and its business.[111] Louise Robinson, recording secretary, wrote a letter for the terminal issue of the *Re-Aides' Post* that summarized the reasons for the organization's dissolution. "It is with deep regret and mixed emotions," she wrote, "that we reluctantly lay to rest that publication which, through the past thirty years, has brought us news of our buddies of World War I. However, we have to realize that age, infirmities and increasing cares, the intrusion of World War II, and various other considerations have made the struggle for survival of such an organization as ours a losing one." She explained that in the next year, the Terminal Committee hoped to find a suitable repository in Washington, DC, for the WWRAA's records, "to prove to future generations that we once existed and contributed a vital share in the development of Army medical practice." She asked for contributions of artifacts, photos, and issues of the *Re-Aides' Post* to complete the collection and mentioned an idea to publish a supplemental history to explain the items, since the Surgeon General's office claimed that the records of the Reconstruction Aides had been lost in a fire. We are, she lamented, "a vanished and forgotten service!!" The Terminal Committee also planned a year-long test of a plan proffered by Laura Brackett Hoppin to keep members in touch with each through an abbreviated newsletter that would be called "The Mail Bag."[112]

The final convention touched on many of the issues that had been central to the WWRAA during its years of operation. It included a "Status Committee Report" from Mable Hahn that reminded members of the decision to abandon the fight for military status at the 1941 convention, but still provided an update about inquiries made since. Hahn had hoped that the establishment of military status for current occupational and physical therapists would help their case, but it had not.[113] The preservation of their historical materials also featured as a key topic of discussion. They recognized that they wanted to do something, "while the sunset glow is yet in the skies, to preserve the fruit of our efforts for future generations, to make provision that some time, perhaps, some body will read the records of our pioneering and recognize the worth of what we did." Colonel Emma Vogel took up this charge and became "the nucleus of a committee to decide where the materials should be sent." She explored an offer from the chief of the Historical Department of the Surgeon General's Office to accept the WWRAA's historical material and decide whether it best belonged with that department, the Medical Museum, or the Library of Congress. Vogel also looked into whether the Smithsonian Institution already had a Reconstruction Aide uniform in its collection of women's World War One uniforms.[114]

Throughout the reunion, those present expressed a profound sense of regret and disappointment that the association had ended prematurely. Though they remained proud of their achievements, they hoped that "the Reconstruction Aides of World War II should know that they have the benefits they have as Reconstruction Aides because of the struggles of the pioneer organization." They saw all too clearly their own failures. Yet they never doubted their commitment to veteranism. They closed the reunion with expressions of regret for disbanding, but also "with the wish that local Units would carry on as long as possible."[115]

CONCLUSION

Although the WWRAA ended its formal operations as an organization in 1949, some of its most dedicated members did carry on and try to preserve its legacy. In particular, Colonel Emma Vogel spent several years toward the end of her life acting as the steward of the memory of the Reconstruction Aides and some of their precious historical materials. She donated many of her personal papers to the Armed Forces Medical Museum, now known as the National Museum of Health and Medicine, where most of the historical materials of the WWRAA ended up, thanks to her efforts.[116] Throughout her retirement, Vogel kept in close touch with the staff of the museum regarding these donations, often with questions about their safekeeping and preservation. In April 1979, she wrote to Dr. Edward R. White, the museum's associate director, about these concerns. She explained that "I am one of very few surviving physical therapists who served in WWI and I am the only one who had continuous serv[ic]e in the Army Medical Department from 1919 until my retirement in 1951. I feel strongly that I have an obligation to contribute in any way I can."[117] Despite Vogel's worries, her perseverance paid off, and these materials now safely reside at the National Museum of Health and Medicine, where they help to preserve the legacy of the Reconstruction Aides.

Although the story of the Reconstruction Aides and the WWRAA includes some major losses and disappointments, it is not a story of complete failure. These women fit squarely within the larger community of female veterans of World War One and they worked hard to defend their belief that they were military veterans. Their dedication to veteranism through constant service only further substantiated these claims. As the epilogue of this book will show, they eventually did gain some partial recognition from the government regarding their wartime service, although this occurred much too late for most of the women to benefit.[118] The continued preservation of their materials at the National Museum of Health and Medicine laid to rest their fears that their wartime service would be completely forgotten. But their experiences also show that veteranism itself was, by its nature, an ideology somewhat limited by the ephemeral nature of commemorative acts of service. In the case of the WWRAA, even the identification of its interior pillar at the Memorial Building to the Women of the World War, which it intended to be a permanent fixture, has disappeared, preventing the organization from being recognized within the building.

Yet despite these challenges, the memory of the Reconstruction Aides lives on because of their records. As written in the July–October 1941 edition of the *Re-Aides' Post*, likely by editor Laura Brackett Hoppin, the WWRAA's members were "the pioneers of two wonderful professions that will carry on and on, long after all of us have ceased to exist, yet we will not be forgotten. Someone, a long time from now, will think about writing a history of these professions, and it can not be done without mention of the Reconstruction Aides."[119] Hoppin understood that the memory of a veteranist organization like theirs would last only through the organizational records that could one day be used to reconstruct its activities. This same concept held true for other female veteranists, such as the American War Mothers, who also focused their commemorative practices on intangible service.

4

"Let Us Take Up the Torch
Individually and Collectively"

The American War Mothers and Veteranist Commemorations

In 1935 or 1936, a headline in a Mobile, Alabama, area newspaper resurrected the memory of the First World War by highlighting the mothers of the doughboys. The headline read "U.S. Doughboys Did the Fighting but Mothers Really Won the War, Says Soldier Who Came Back." The article covered a recent event in Mobile's Lyons Park during which the Mobile Chapter of the American War Mothers planted a live oak tree to commemorate their children who served in the war. At the ceremony, World War One veteran and Mobile mayor Cecil F. Bates praised American mothers for their wartime service. He exclaimed that "it was the heroic mother who furnished the inspiration and really won the war—it was the thought of them that encouraged and strengthened our soldiers."[1] Instead of idealizing battle or his fellow veterans, Bates honored mothers, a sensible choice in the 1930s when the World War constituted a source of disillusionment and remained under public scrutiny.

This public celebration of the services and sacrifices of American mothers during World War One, capped by the planting of a memorial tree, epitomized the veteranist mission of the American War Mothers (AWM). Founded in 1917 to unite mothers of service members in support of the war effort, the AWM embraced the ideals of veteranism. Because these mothers asserted that they had served the nation during the war, their approach to postwar commemoration emphasized the importance of continuing that service. They believed that their roles as mothers required them to focus their commemorative efforts on serving the nation by helping veterans and other war mothers, rather than only by building monuments. The AWM championed the platform of veteranist commemorations promoted by other women's groups such as the WOSL, the ARC, and the WWRAA. In pursuit of their veteranist agenda, the group grappled with race, the peace movement, and the economic struggles of the Great Depression.

A BRIEF HISTORY OF THE AMERICAN WAR MOTHERS

Alice Moore French of Indiana organized the AWM during World War One. After her only child, Donald, left to serve in 1917, she responded to the request of the Indiana section of appointees to the US Food Administration for the mother of an Indiana soldier to help collect signatures for a Food Pledge Campaign.[2] A widow active in women's clubs and civic life, French used her new position to form the Indiana War Mothers, an organization that united mothers of service members to support the war effort and to advocate for their children's welfare. The Indiana War Mothers created a constitution in April 1918 and that fall wrote a national constitution that expanded the state organization into the national American War Mothers.[3] Article VII of this national constitution defined the group as a "non-political" organization that would not "promote the candidacy of any person seeking public office."[4] This clause helped the organization try to remain apolitical and inclusive so that its work would benefit the military and veterans instead of one particular political party.[5]

Incorporated by Congress on February 24, 1925, the AWM evolved into a patriotic association focused on supporting veterans and commemorating the war.[6] Similar in structure to the WOSL, the AWM consisted of national, state, and local chapters; the national-level organization and national officers presided over the other chapters.[7] It held a national convention every two years and published a magazine titled *American War Mother*.[8] Over the years, committees at the national and lower levels of the organization included the Legislative Committee, the Hospitalization Committee, the Americanization Committee, the Memory Tree Committee, the Gold Star Committee, the Welfare Committee, the Emblem and Memorial Markers Committee, the Child Welfare Committee, and the American War Mothers Memorial Home Committee, to name a few.[9]

After the war, the AWM shifted its focus to supporting veterans. It recognized that it could still play an important role in the nation. At the 1923 national convention, national president Mrs. H. H. McCluer reminded the assembled members that they had come "to this convention to help mold the future. And the boys and the friends who are gone, we know they see us this morning assembled to carry on what they have given us."[10] McCluer believed that the AWM members had a duty to continue their wartime work by supporting veterans and honoring their children's wartime service.

Even though they attempted to remain apolitical, the AWM became involved in debates over issues such as disarmament and international affairs. It considered itself a partner of the American Legion and supported the legion's Americanization effort and opposition to the recognition of Soviet Russia (fig. 4.1).[11] Although members of the AWM did not always agree with each other, overall, the organization strongly supported efforts to promote world peace and Americanization, the movement to acculturate immigrants to American customs.[12] Founder Alice French particularly championed internationalism, supported the establishment of a "World Court" to prevent future conflicts, and became outspoken in support of the peace movement.[13] She hoped that the AWM could help "find a way whereby our national and international differences would be settled other than by the blood of our precious sons."[14] French advocated for peace for the rest of her life and incorporated her beliefs into the AWM.

The AWM's constitution delineated its mission of community service and patriotic support of the nation, the armed forces, and veterans. Its mission committed it to "keep alive and develop the spirit that prompted world service; to maintain the ties of fellowship of that service and to assist and further any patriotic work; to inculcate a sense of individual obligation to the State, and Nation; to work for the welfare of the Army and Navy; to assist in any way in their power men and women who served and were wounded or incapacitated in the World War; to foster and promote friendship and understanding between America and the Allies in the World War."[15] This mission statement indicated the commemorative aspects of these objectives. By starting the statement with the objectives of keeping alive and developing "the spirit that prompted world service" and maintaining "the ties of fellowship" from the war, the constitution delineated how the AWM would memorialize the war through its projects.

According to the constitution, members had to be female citizens of the United States who had a son or daughter of their own blood who served in the armed forces of the US or its allies during the Great War between April 6, 1917, and November 11, 1918, and who received an honorable discharge or remained in the service.[16] By limiting members to blood mothers, the AWM restricted stepmothers and adoptive mothers from membership and privileged birth mothers as the only true war mothers. In concert with its support of Americanization, the exclusion of noncitizen mothers prevented many immigrant mothers from joining, even if their children served in the military

Figure 4.1. Back cover of *The Indianan* 1, no. 10 (July 1921). The caption aligns the American War Mothers with the American Legion and its auxiliary. John J. Pershing Papers, Manuscript Division, Library of Congress.

during the war. This kept the organization dominated by mostly middle- and upper-class White Christian mothers. It is also significant that a child's dishonorable discharge prevented the mother from becoming a member; this demonstrated that children had to conform to the military's definition of honorable service for their mother to join. The AWM did recognize that women had served in the war, and it allowed mothers of the few daughters who met the requirements to become members, signifying that the AWM valued women's military service as equal to that of men, at least for the purposes of becoming a member. However, by forbidding immigrant mothers from becoming members, the AWM did not aim to be an ethnically inclusive organization. Nor did it intend to be racially inclusive: racial prejudice and the norms of Jim Crow America placed restrictions on the membership of Black women in the organization.

SEGREGATION AND THE "COLORED" AMERICAN WAR MOTHERS CHAPTERS

Although other organizations of female veteranists excluded African American women mostly because wartime restrictions on Black women's service opportunities made them ineligible for membership, the widespread wartime military service of African American men created hundreds of thousands of African American women who met the criteria to become members of the American War Mothers.[17] While the organization as a whole did not view African American mothers as equal to White mothers and the constitution did not mention segregation, some chapters did eventually allow African American women to join, but only in separate, segregated "colored chapters."[18] The issue of whether to include African American mothers emerged at least by the 1921 convention. During an open discussion at the convention, an unnamed delegate asked president Alice French whether "a colored woman is eligible to become a war mother. We had colored boys in the war. It has been asked me, and I wondered if they would be allowed in, or if they would have a chapter of their own?"[19] With her question, this delegate referred to how some Americans, especially minorities, viewed wartime military service as a way to attain full citizenship rights.

This question sparked a heated debate at the convention as members spoke up and revealed their differing views on the admission of African American members. Mrs. Longbotham from Sacramento announced that her chapter had two Black women as members, after which Mrs. Huffman, most likely from Kentucky, voiced her opposition to that policy.[20] Mrs. Huffman reminded the group that she had previously taken a message to the Washington convention stating that they should use the term "white war mothers" in their constitution. She had urged that convention to "let the colored war mothers have a chapter of their own, and they voted down my motion. And of course, we do not want them in the same organization, but you people can, unless you have your own State by-laws,—You can refuse the colored mothers, or you can admit them, if you want them in. That is part of our constitution." Although she failed to officially inscribe segregation into the AWM constitution, by disagreeing with the chapters who welcomed African American members, Mrs. Huffman still tried to deny African American war mothers the same opportunities as White war mothers. Mrs. Digney, the incoming national president from White Plains, New York, agreed that at the Washington convention it had been accepted that each state would be "governed by its own conditions, and we tabled the discussion of that question."[21] In doing so, the AWM avoided a difficult and divisive decision. It allowed each state's chapters to be directed by local racial conditions, which likely meant that any chapters able to form in the South would be segregated.

Dissatisfied with this situation, some members rekindled the debate and argued that by excluding African Americans, the AWM denied them their status as American citizens. At the 1921 convention, Mrs. Murray exclaimed, "I don't think we should exclude them. The Government accepted the black soldiers, but they should be permitted to organize in their own way. But I don't think we should draw the line. I don't think it is a secular organization; it is a patriotic organization, and we should take every mother that has sent a boy." Mrs. Donald added that her chapter also had African American members and noted that "they don't conflict with us at all," although they had never actually affiliated with the AWM but still considered themselves members. Sensing the tensions created by this discussion, Mrs. Norton from Sacramento asked the attendees at the convention "to please not discuss this question. Our colored mothers gave as we gave. We have gold star mothers among them. Let each state care for its own people. We Sacramento War Mothers are not afraid to stand upon our feet and say that we welcome the colored mother of any American man who served." Even though she lauded her own chapter's inclusion of African American mothers, Mrs. Norton, like many of the other women who spoke up, did not want this to become a national policy. She wanted to avoid the issue since she seemed to think it divided the convention and distracted members from their mission. She might have been somewhat more racially inclusive than other members, but not enough to persuade them to treat African American mothers equally. Taking her cue, president French explained that someone had suggested that they have a question box available for attendees to submit questions about "knotty problems" rather than asking them on the floor and sidetracking the convention's proceedings.[22] Putting aside the issue of segregation and ending the discussion demonstrated that female memory makers did not always agree, even as they pursued the same goals within the same organization. This decision to leave the choice about the inclusion of African American mothers to the individual units maintained the status quo and sanctioned segregation. Despite their goals to be inclusive and patriotic, as people of their time, the AWM members did not push for racial or ethnic equality within their organization.

With the issue handled in this way, some African American women were allowed to join the AWM and form their own segregated chapters, and others may have been allowed to join integrated chapters, such as in Sacramento. Traces of some of the segregated chapters can be found within the scattered records of the American War Mothers. During the interwar period, African American chapters included the Lincoln Chapter in Washington, DC, the Colonel Charles Young Chapter in Chicago (named for the third African American graduate of the US Military Academy, who went on to become the first African American colonel), and the Golden Chapter of the Colored American War Mothers in Kentucky.[23] Kentucky in particular hosted an active community of segregated chapters, especially after the start of World War Two, and additional segregated chapters may have existed in other states and cities.

Kentucky's segregated chapters provide a glimpse of how they operated within the structure of the statewide organization, especially during World War Two when African American women organized more segregated chapters in Kentucky (fig. 4.2). Initially, at least one segregated chapter composed of mothers of World War One service members existed in Kentucky. Named the Golden Chapter of the Colored American War Mothers, it appears to have been based in the Louisville area. The chapter even included several mothers of men who served with the 369th Infantry Regiment, the famed Harlem Hellfighters. Membership applications for the chapter in 1933 specifically listed each mother as having applied to the Golden Chapter of the Colored American War Mothers, a distinction that demarcated them as African American.[24]

While records of the activities of the segregated Kentucky chapters remain scarce for the interwar period, more records survived from World War Two. These records show the growth of African American participation in the organization in Kentucky. Sometime between 1933 and January 10, 1944, the Golden Chapter disbanded and then reorganized because of the new war.[25] African American women also organized several new segregated chapters in Kentucky during World War Two, and by 1944, Kentucky's various AWM chapters included 582 White members and 185 "colored" members.[26] During World War Two, state president Mrs. Mary Moran took an active interest in the "colored" chapters and even attended their group meetings, which involved several chapters. Impressed, she suggested that the "Colored Chapters

Figure 4.2. Undated photo of African American members of the American War Mothers at a convention at the First Baptist Church on Clinton Street in Frankfort, Kentucky. Kentucky Historical Society.

continue their group meetings and that the White Chapters take up group meetings."[27] Despite the continued segregation of the Kentucky state chapter, the expansion of African American chapters during World War Two and the interest shown in them by the White Kentucky state president suggest that the segregated chapters played a key role in the state organization and received at least some respect and support from the White leaders and members.

At the national level, some African American members did attend the national conventions and navigated the tricky situation of being included in the organization but not fully integrated or allowed to participate equally. The proceedings of the 1935 convention in Washington, DC, recorded the attendance of Mrs. Louise A. Pinckney from the Lincoln Chapter in Washington, DC. She addressed the convention and invited all the attendees to a banquet the next night hosted by her chapter in honor of past and present state and national presidents and "visiting colored delegates."[28] Held at the Whitelaw Hotel, the convention headquarters for the African American members segregated from the main convention's headquarters at the Wardman Park Hotel, this banquet featured as its guest speaker Dr. Emmett J. Scott, a well-known

African American leader who served as the special assistant to the secretary of war during World War One.[29] It also included national president Mrs. Ochiltree and state president Mrs. Mary T. Shanahan.[30] This announcement indicated that African American women gained some inclusion in the national conventions and that the Lincoln Chapter in Washington, DC, was large enough to host a major banquet with such a renowned speaker. The attendance of Mrs. Ochiltree and Mrs. Shanahan lent legitimacy to the banquet and signified some appreciation for the African American members' work with the organization.

Nevertheless, the African American women did not let the segregation of the convention's main headquarters go unprotested. To highlight the racism at the convention, the *Baltimore Afro-American* published a photograph of four members of the Colonel Charles Young Chapter who were refused admission to the general convention banquet at the Wardman Park Hotel. The caption read "Their Sons Died, but They Were Turned Down."[31] The segregation of the banquet caused an outcry among the African American convention delegates and members. In response, the African American delegates did not invite the White delegates to their memorial services at Colonel Charles Young's grave in Arlington National Cemetery. When they learned of this, White delegates were reported to have "expressed regret that they were not notified."[32] The African American delegates also brought the incident to the attention of the AWM's leadership. The *Chicago Defender* reported that the members of the Colonel Charles Young Chapter discussed the convention's segregation at their next meeting and received assurance from state officials that "such an un-American action would not occur again."[33] By protesting their unfair treatment at the convention, these African American women asserted their desire for equal treatment and refused to accept the status quo.

African American convention delegates exposed the disagreements among White AWM members regarding segregation. While some White members refused to grant African American members the opportunity to participate fully in the convention, the state officials from Illinois, presumably White, recognized this choice as "un-American."[34] They hoped to prevent such treatment in the future, and some even wanted to honor an African American war hero alongside the segregated chapters.

While the African American delegates protested the discrimination at the convention, they also recognized the opportunities the AWM gave them that other organizations did not. As a 1934 article in the *Baltimore Afro-American* reported the year before the 1935 convention incident, the American Gold Star Mothers organization did not include any African American members. In an interview for the article, Mrs. Louise Pinkney (without a "c") noted that the AWM included African American members in separate "colored chapters" and commented that "the colored groups receive every courtesy and attention accorded the whites. They have participated in all the affairs of the national organization, both national and local." She added that an African American member from her own chapter "was the fifth in line to place a wreath on the Unknown Soldier's grave at Arlington on Mother's Day" and that Mrs. George Seibold, the White founder of the American Gold Star Mothers, "always invited the members of the Lincoln chapter to attend its affairs." According to Mrs. Pinkney, the current president of that group had not yet invited these African American women to an event, an indication that she might not have been as racially progressive as her predecessor.[35] This situation typified the discord over race within the larger community of female veteranists: some organizations' chapters allowed African American members, while others did not. In fact, Alice French granted a charter to an AWM chapter composed of Native American women at Fort Yates, North Dakota, another indication that the AWM's racial policies varied widely.[36]

The AWM's struggle to define its racial policies indicates an increasing awareness of race among female veteranists, even though the AWM continued to allow segregation. Similar to other women's service organizations in the interwar period such as the WOSL, the ARC, and the YWCA, the AWM could not ignore racial issues.[37] The dissenting opinions about race within the AWM and the open arguments about segregation demonstrate that although bound together by the same mission, female veteranists subscribed to a variety of different attitudes and often disagreed about the best way to execute their mission. In keeping with the social norms of the day, the AWM's focus on community service and patriotism did not prevent it from frequently excluding African American women from the veteranist community.

MOTHERHOOD AS WARTIME SERVICE

The AWM pursued veteranism because it defined the role of mothers of military members as a form of wartime service that should continue even after the war's end. Veteranist commemorations provided members with a way to honor their children's participation in the war while they continued to support the military and veterans. Veteranism enabled the AWM to create more space for women to collaborate with the armed forces and to act as civic leaders in their communities.

The ideologies of republican motherhood, maternalism, and contemporary cultural conceptions of motherhood formed a central part of the mission and beliefs of the AWM. From the time of the early republic, American women had been encouraged to support the nation through republican motherhood by raising their children to become patriotic American citizens and sending their sons to the military.[38] In this way, women could contribute to the nation while they remained in the domestic sphere.[39] During the First World War, republican motherhood played a large role in American women's contributions to the war effort, as well as the public's perception of their participation. Mothers became a symbol of American patriotism, especially as depicted in the imagery of the American Red Cross propaganda posters that featured the "world's greatest mother."[40] Similarly, the ideology of maternalism asserted that a mother's domestic role of raising her children and running her home played an essential function in society, and that mothers had special qualities that made them well suited to reform work.[41] By accepting this idea during and after the war, the AWM furthered women's position in society without challenging established gender norms.[42]

Unlike auxiliary organizations such as the American Legion Auxiliary and the Veterans of Foreign Wars Auxiliary, the AWM did not consider itself to be an auxiliary predicated on its familial association with members of the military. The organization was based on members' own wartime service. Like the members of the WOSL and the WWRAA, and the women honored by the Memorial Building to the Women of the World War, AWM members believed they had served and sacrificed during the war. The script for the ceremony held when they accepted new members included dialogue that clearly defined motherhood as a wartime service. This 1928 text stated that "these women formed the second line of defense; with clear heads and brave hearts they made carrying on successful in the great war." It then mentioned Molly Pitcher and Betsy Ross and reminded the assembled chapter that "they have fought a good fight and kept the faith. Their service so unsparingly given in our organization will be an inspiration to every member of all tomorrows."[43] Members continued to hold this belief over the years. In 1934, Mrs. Ochiltree reminisced about the World War and opined that "the success of this struggle of our people was greatly forwarded by the help of the Mothers who, in united effort, stood firm for conservation of resources and for the necessary economies and sacrifices that won the World War."[44] Referring to the AWM's origins in Indiana's food conservation efforts, Mrs. Ochiltree reminded members of their wartime contributions.

Prominent public figures agreed with Mrs. Ochiltree—most significantly, President Herbert Hoover. In a message released on March 2, 1933, and sent to *American War Mother* magazine, Hoover wrote to Mrs. Virgil McClure that "probably more than any other man in public life, I have had reason to know at first hand the magnificent response made by American mothers during the war period. Their courage, fortitude, energy, and cooperation, were of decisive inspiration and practical helpfulness. Theirs was an indispensable service, nobly rendered, and deserving of the undying gratitude of the nation."[45] As head of the US Food Administration during World War One, the

AWM directly supported Hoover's mission, something he did not forget even in his last days as president.[46] His message in the AWM's magazine demonstrated that he viewed the organization's contributions as a wartime service and that he remained aware of its continued service work in support of the nation, many years after the war's end.

Other people outside the organization agreed with the AWM's definition of its activities as wartime service and echoed President Hoover's gratitude. Early on, at the 1921 convention in Sacramento, the opening speaker, General J. J. Borree, the adjutant general of California, praised the AWM for its important wartime contributions. He told the AWM that

> to you belong the credit of many victories won, you who so freely gave your loved ones to Humanity's cause. It is true that the sorrows and sacrifices of mothers for a Nation are soon forgotten, and are little known by it. Men earn glory and distinction, but the thousand watchful nights and sacrifices by which a mother develops a hero are soon forgotten. No one counts, for the mothers, themselves, did not count. The strength of an army is judged by its morale, by the morale of the individual soldier. . . . The mother is, to the Army, what she is to the Nation, in her resting the divine duty of guiding and teaching her child so he may grow to manhood, a God-fearing, self-governed, law abiding citizen. You, the mothers, have rendered a splendid service; with your sacrifices you brought victory to our armies and peace to a war-torn world. This was indeed a sacrifice.[47]

By invoking the importance of motherhood, General Borree defined a mother's role of raising her children and sending them to the military as a service to the nation, one that he viewed as partially responsible for the Allied victory.

The next speaker, Bishop William Hall Morland, agreed with Borree's praise for the wartime services of American mothers and urged them to focus their postwar energies toward pursuing peace. His visit to the battle-scarred Western Front convinced him that war must never happen again. He believed the AWM could play an important role in the pursuit of world peace. He entreated its members to help peace come "out of destruction" and to work for justice for "those boys who have come back, broken or maimed or gassed or weak or diseased or blinded or crippled or unemployed,—that they should receive immediate attention and relief."[48] Bishop Morland understood that mothers' service did not end with the Armistice because they often remained responsible for the care of veterans. As the traditional caregivers in society, mothers occupied a unique position to pursue peace since they dealt with the physical and mental wounds of war.

The veteranist commemorations pursued by the AWM honored the martial contributions of war mothers alongside the military. At the 1921 convention, speaker Mr. S. J. Lubin reminded the AWM to commemorate its own wartime service. He told the convention that "sometimes, it is more difficult to live than to die," and that "the final burden of war is not carried by the soldiers, but, rather, by the parents, who, through struggle and loving sacrifice, raises the soldier for far different end and purpose." Although he admitted that fathers also suffered, he believed that because fathers had other interests to distract them, they suffered less than mothers. He told the audience that "the mother, in the very beginning, makes the greatest sacrifice, which is typical of the larger service she renders throughout her son's life, to the end. Therefore, it is fitting that we pay reverence, not alone, to the soldier, but to the war mother as well."[49] He believed mothers should be commemorated just as much as soldiers, for they bore that final burden of war. As an organization, the AWM shouldered this burden collectively and believed it remained its postwar duty to support America's veterans.

SERVICE TOWARD VETERANS

Helping veterans formed the foundation of the AWM's veteranist agenda. As "mothers of the nation," members considered themselves to be mothers to all veterans and military members. Each level of the organization prioritized service to veterans as one of its most important activities.

Although the AWM focused on service as its main form of memorialization, this did not mean that it rejected all forms of more traditional commemoration such as monuments and ceremonies in favor of more modern veteranist memorials. People and traditions do not change overnight, and most female veteranists augmented their service work with other activities. For example, the AWM held annual Mother's Day ceremonies at the Tomb of the Unknown Soldier, raised the flag on the US Capitol on Armistice Day in 1934, participated in other Armistice Day ceremonies, and issued a commemorative stamp in 1934; some local chapters even built statuary memorials (fig. 4.3).[50] The AWM printed a ritual book that outlined its operational rules, traditions, mission, and rituals for local chapters to use that included sections titled "Ceremony for Dedication of Boulders, Tablets or Other World War Memorials" and "Planting and Dedicating of Memory Trees."[51] The Kentucky Chapter conceived of and helped create the War Mothers Memorial Bridge in Frankfort, Kentucky, and remained involved with the living memorial movement for years; in 1945, Kentucky president Mary Moran received and accepted an appointment to the Committee for the American Commission for Living Memorials.[52] However, the national organization as a whole did not create a national, permanent statuary memorial to commemorate the war.

The AWM justified its decision to pursue veteranism as a form of com-

Figure 4.3. The American War Mothers conducted their annual Mother's Day ceremony at the Tomb of the Unknown Soldier on May 12, 1929, with the participation
of bugler Sergeant Frank Witchey, who sounded "Taps" at the burial of the Unknown
Soldier in 1921. Library of Congress.

memoration by connecting its service mission to the memory of the American service members buried overseas. Alice French reminded the 1923 convention that its mission began during the war when members of the AWM
supported the men in the armed forces "just as mothers would."[53] During
her 1921 trip abroad, she visited the overseas cemeteries and saw the flag-
draped caskets that held the bodies of American dead who awaited repatriation. Afterward, she came to believe that the AWM had a duty to honor the
dead by assisting those who survived and by promoting peace.[54] She felt that
"those boys who are resting under the sod of France are here. There isn't any
end and they, you know, can be counted on. They can count on we Mothers
also every time." She made an emotional appeal to the convention to listen
to these "boys," for "ever since the Armistice was signed we have been looking for an individual to pick up the torch. We have picked this one, we have
picked that one. Each time a new leader has come on the scene we have
thought: 'That is the person now,' but you know I believe, Mothers, the boys
were talking to us. Let us take up the torch individually and collectively. . . .

Now I believe the boys are here. I believe they are speaking. I believe they are counting on you, Mothers, to pick up the torch. We rocked these boys to sleep and I believe we should help them to rest in their last resting place. They say, 'We shall not sleep if you do not take up the torch.'" French metaphorically insinuated that these dead bodies had power and voices they used to speak to the living. She implied that they urged her and the AWM to memorialize their lives by dedicating their organization's postwar mission to service.[55] The AWM thus heeded the call of these soldier dead and devoted itself to serving veterans through service projects conducted by all levels of the organization.

State and local chapters pursued a variety of large and small projects to support veterans. The 1928 yearbook of the Kansas City Chapter proclaimed that six of the thirteen activities the chapter supported in 1928 helped veterans; a total of ten activities involved some form of community service. These activities included the sale of carnations to support hospital relief and entertainment programs, projects that brought Christmas cheer to hospitals, and activities that aided soldiers' loan funds.[56] In 1936, Indiana's Clinton County Chapter adopted two hospitalized ex-servicemen and provided them with gifts, sent fruit baskets to ill veterans at Christmas, delivered groceries and blankets to the widow and children of a deceased serviceman, and mailed books and magazines to the Soldiers' Home at Lafayette.[57]

At the national level, the organization's National Hospitalization Committee advocated for and supported veterans' hospitals, soldiers' homes, and other institutions.[58] The Prison Committee helped ex-servicemen and women in prison by providing them with care packages, writing them letters and holiday cards, and helping with their rehabilitation.[59] Many of these prisoners went to jail as "victims of the drug habit," perhaps after being wounded.[60] The National Legislative Committee and the state legislative committees supported and lobbied for bills in Congress that affected the welfare of veterans and disabled veterans.[61] In 1923, the national AWM formally endorsed the Bonus to provide retroactive payment to World War veterans in 1945, an issue that became contentious during the Great Depression.[62] The AWM's initial support of the Bonus demonstrated its dedication to political advocacy on behalf of veterans.

One of the biggest and most well-known national service initiatives the AWM conducted to aid veterans centered on its national annual sale of carnations each May just before Mother's Day.[63] The AWM sold carnations because they served as its national flower and organizational symbol. The campaign mirrored the VFW's "Buddy Poppy" program and the British Legion's "Poppy Appeal."[64] World War One veterans and their families made paper carnations, and the proceeds from their sale funded welfare work for needy veterans and their families. In Washington, DC, for example, the AWM sold carnations at the American Red Cross Headquarters, the site of the Memorial Building to the Women of the World War.[65] The campaign even received official endorsements from President Calvin Coolidge and General Pershing in 1924; Pershing supported the project for many years.[66]

The AWM achieved two goals by combining commemoration with community service in the carnation campaigns. First, it honored and commemorated service members, their families, and war mothers. One newspaper described the carnation campaign as having the "double significance of tribute to the mothers of the country and the possible means with which to provide comfort and pleasure to the heroes of this country in the persons of disabled ex-service men."[67] Second, the AWM supported needy veterans and their families. Another article detailed how the funds raised from the sale helped the families of needy veterans by providing coal, bedding, food, and shoes for their children, which would help these children remain in school. It explained that "carnations, many of which are made by disabled vets, are a symbol. They are even more than that. They are a means of preserving and fostering the courage, self-respect and faith of many men, who, in giving the best of themselves for the sake of their country, are unable now to give the best they wish they could to their families."[68] As mothers, AWM members recognized they must do more than help only veterans; veterans' families also needed support. They understood that the wounds of war affected entire families and that they could honor veterans by aiding their loved ones.

During the Great Depression, the AWM's support for veterans proved even more important. Although it often became more difficult to sustain, the AWM did its best to continue assisting veterans. At the AWM executive board meeting in September 1933, president Virgil Stone discussed a proposal to increase dues to finance the creation of a relief fund for the national headquarters in Washington, DC. She admitted that many people objected to the increase, but she defended it since it would support the men and women who sought help at the headquarters. The VFW and the American Legion even sent destitute veterans to their headquarters for aid. President Stone wanted every chapter to contribute to the fund so it could provide relief to these veterans, some of whom may have arrived as part of the 1932 or 1933 Bonus Marches.[69] The AWM had established such a strong reputation for helping veterans that many people assumed the AWM to be the best place to go for help.

To illustrate the seriousness of the situation, Mrs. Stone spoke about one veteran who came to the headquarters at the behest of the VFW and needed to be hospitalized. When he arrived, he told them that "I was weary, hungry, cold and discouraged, and I saw the sign on the door, 'American War Mothers,' and I said to myself, 'I will find a friend in here.'" Stone and her colleagues helped him as much as they could, and although they could not get him into a hospital, they gave him clothes. Mrs. Stone told the executive board that "Mrs. Huntington and Mrs. Faries and I are known as beggars. I want you to know that, that some of your National Officers are known in Washington as beggars."[70] Unable to provide clothes, Mrs. Stone and her colleagues presumably resorted to some sort of begging to acquire some clothing. In this and countless other ways, the AWM did not let the difficulties of the Great Depression derail its dedication to providing immediate, tangible relief to needy veterans.

After surviving the Great Depression, the AWM maintained its dedication to service during the Second World War. It supported the war effort both as individuals and as a group through a variety of different activities. For example, Mrs. Eva M. Price, vice president of the Roanoke, Virginia, chapter, acted as chair for the Women's Land Army and served as an air-raid warden, following her previous time with the Red Cross and the Gray Ladies, likely before World War Two.[71]

Most importantly, in 1942, the AWM opened membership in the organization to the citizen mothers of service members serving in World War Two. President Roosevelt even approved the bill to make this critical change, which welcomed a new generation of women eager to support the veteranist mission.[72] Doing so greatly expanded their ranks and their capacity to aid the war effort and commemorative service projects after its conclusion.

African American war mothers in Kentucky, especially, took up the call to arms created by this membership change. On January 10, 1944, the Golden Chapter received its reinstatement, after presumably being dormant. Kentucky African American war mothers organized at least two other segregated chapters in 1943 and at least three in 1944.[73] During World War Two, these segregated Kentucky chapters joined their White sisters to pursue wartime service projects and support veterans. By April 1944, the fifty-eight members of the African American Dorie Miller Chapter in Lexington, Kentucky—named after the African American recipient of the Navy Cross for heroism at Pearl Harbor—raised $375 for the fourth War Bond Drive and $14.24 for the Red Cross; they also made dressings for the Red Cross every Friday night, among other service activities.[74] Later in 1944 the chapter president, Mrs. Mattie Madden, reported that they were "now engaged in collecting games of all kinds for Veterans General Hospital at Tuskegee Institute, Tuskegee, Alabama which has 1,600 returned colored soldiers from overseas." She explained that "as mothers, we are striving to do our best to help bring victory to the noble cause, for which our sons and daughters are fighting and dying."[75] Madden's statement exemplified the veteranist mission that all members of the AWM, Black and White, felt committed to during World War Two: supporting the war effort and the men and women of the armed forces.

By 1947, the ranks of the AWM numbered over forty thousand mothers of service members from both World Wars, and the organization gained a spot on the Veterans Administration Advisory Committee.[76] This new position allowed it to directly influence veterans' care and spread its veteranist ideology at the highest levels of the federal government. The AWM also helped the new generation of wounded service members through the continued success of its biggest veteranist commemoration project: the American War Mothers Memorial Home. Though it was created well before World War Two and was originally intended for World War One veterans, it ended up providing a key service to World War Two veterans and their female relations—including war mothers—during and after World War Two.

THE AMERICAN WAR MOTHERS MEMORIAL HOME

The AWM demonstrated its commitment to veteranism with the successful creation and support of a memorial home to lodge female visitors of the patients at the army's Fitzsimons General Hospital.[77] Located in Aurora, Colorado, about nine miles from Denver, Fitzsimons General Hospital was a living memorial hospital complex opened in 1918 and renamed in 1920 to honor Lieutenant W. T. Fitzsimons, believed to be the first American officer to have died in the war.[78] Even though it was one of the largest veterans' hospitals, with almost three thousand patients, extensive facilities, and a focus on tuberculosis treatment, its hard-to-reach location made it expensive and difficult for mothers and wives to visit and find suitable, affordable accommodations.[79] The AWM decided to establish a home near the hospital "where these visiting mothers and wives could have a pleasant home like place to stop while there and at a very modest price, and if they did not have the price, might make their visit any way."[80] The home served veterans by aiding their female relatives who needed assistance; these women could stay at the home for a nominal fee or for free (fig. 4.4).[81]

The AWM independently created and ran the home as its major national service project. In 1925, it formed a corporation organized under Colorado law called the War Mothers National Memorial Home Association, of which shares of one hundred dollars were sold only to members and chapters of the AWM.[82] This corporation purchased five acres of land adjacent to the hospital and construction work began as fundraising continued. The craftsman-style home was completed in October 1925, and the corporation granted the AWM a twenty-year lease without any rent payments.[83] The AWM continuously raised money over the years to fully support the home and formed the Home Operating Committee to oversee its operation.[84] The Home Operating Committee selected a matron to run the facility and supplied it with furnishings before it opened on November 1, 1925. The AWM believed it to be "the

Figure 4.4. Reverse side of the "Wear a Carnation" flier. The imagery on this flier juxta-posed the war with the comforts of the distinctively American, "homey," craftsman-style memorial home. Framed by drawings of carnations—the American War Mothers' organizational flower—the flier promoted the calming atmosphere of the memorial home. John J. Pershing Papers, Manuscript Division, Library of Congress.

first home of its kind to be established in the United States, and we feel [it] is filling a great mission. It is also the first home to be established by mothers provided entirely by themselves."[85] The AWM took pride in the Memorial Home's demonstrated success as an endeavor independently executed by a women's organization to help fellow women, including many mothers like themselves.

The AWM dedicated the home as a living memorial in honor of the organization's Gold Star mothers.[86] Rather than erect a national memorial to these women, the AWM built a home to help veterans and their families cope with the war's consequences. As a living memorial in the truest sense of the word, the Memorial Home fulfilled its purpose when inhabited by living bodies. The home represented the AWM's commitment to veteranism through the creation of a utilitarian living memorial that supported veterans, war mothers, and other women.

Other female veteranist groups supported the mission of the Memorial Home. The WOSL's magazine *Carry On* published a celebratory article about the home's dedication on July 11, 1926. The article lauded the AWM for "the intangible gift to the nation's invalid service men" at Fitzsimons General Hospital, many of whom suffered from tuberculosis. It emphasized that funds for the home had been raised through the AWM's annual carnation sale, making this site of community service one built through other acts of service. Mrs. H. H. McCluer, the AWM national president, told *Carry On* that "we felt that the greatest gift we could give our hospital veterans was to make it possible for them to have their loved ones come and visit them . . . many a man is cheered on in his struggle for health by having some relative visit him. And of course it means so much to the wives and mothers for even a few days at the bedside of those who do not recover."[87] The WOSL and the AWM agreed that creating a community service–based memorial to help people heal from the war represented the proper way to honor Gold Star mothers. In fact, the Denver Unit of the WOSL regularly volunteered at the hospital.[88] The WOSL supported this utilitarian living memorial building because unlike the Memorial Building to the Women of the World War, it provided direct support to veterans and their families and did not waste money on architectural flourishes.

The AWM successfully executed its veteranist agenda through the Memorial Home. The organization's 1926 report noted that the home represented "a great asset in service." The home's matron reported that more than 150 mothers and wives of patients had been lodged at the home, 27 of whom received free accommodations since they did not have adequate funds. The home hosted almost 100 patients, husbands, and guests for entertainment, as well as parties for the hospital's Disabled American Veterans post and the Red Cross. The AWM kept strict financial reports about the home's opera-

Figure 4.5. The 1944 dedication ceremony for the presentation of the Margaret N. McCluer Annex and the Missouri Cottage to the American War Mothers at their Memorial Home in Aurora, Colorado. American War Mothers National Headquarters Collection, Military Women's Memorial Collection.

tion in an attempt to use its sparse funds wisely, but it never sought a profit. As president Mrs. Thomas Spence stated at the 1929 convention, in terms of finances, the memorial home would be run at "a loss probably, but we are not running the Home for profit, we are running it for service." The audience responded with loud applause and demonstrated their support for the home's mission and its status as a veteranist memorial.[89]

The 1926 dedication of the Memorial Home represented only the beginning of the AWM's long-term service work at this facility. *Carry On* reported that several state AWM chapters planned to construct additional buildings at the Memorial Home, and the AWM continued its support of the Memorial Home and the hospital's patients for many years.[90] It also expanded and improved the Memorial Home. On September 27, 1944, in the midst of World War Two, the AWM dedicated a new building at the Memorial Home.[91] Called the Margaret N. McCluer Annex, this living memorial building honored McCluer, a senior national president of the AWM who held office from 1923 to 1927 (fig. 4.5).[92] At the dedication ceremony, Major General Omar H. Quade, the commanding general of Fitzsimons General Hospital, gave a speech and thanked the AWM for its constant support of the hospital since its establishment in 1918.

He pointed out that in addition to its other noble work, the AWM saw the hospital's need for such a facility and took it on as a national project. In doing so, he said, AWM members were "perpetuating for time immorial [*sic*], the memories of their own loved ones who so gallantly gave their lives in World War I, that others who follow, and their loved ones, might partake of periods of rest and relaxation, and have a comfortable place of temporary abode, close to their sick."[93] General Quade acknowledged that the AWM had created a complex of living memorials that commemorated World War One by serving ill or disabled veterans.

By 1944, World War One veterans and their families were benefiting from the Memorial Home complex alongside World War Two veterans. Newly disabled veterans had already begun to arrive at the hospital, ushering in a new generation of patients and families at the Memorial Home. General Quade recognized this and emphasized how the timing of this new annex would help these incoming veterans. He told the AWM that he was "glad to know that your organization has seen fit to expand the work of this project, to coincide with the expansion of our hospital under the trying conditions we are experiencing in this second world war."[94] General Quade's remarks showed how the AWM broadened its work to assist any and all veterans in need, no matter the war they served in. At the Memorial Home complex, the First World War intersected with the Second World War. These living memorial buildings epitomized the ideology of veteranist commemorations, linked the two World Wars, supported women, and kept alive the memory of the First World War and the sacrifices of its Gold Star mothers.

SUPPORTING FELLOW WAR MOTHERS

In addition to supporting and advocating for veterans, the AWM devoted time and resources to supporting its own members. Like the WOSL, the AWM developed social welfare programs to help its members. In an era when limited social welfare was only just starting to be provided by the federal government, these women took it upon themselves to provide for each other. Because they believed that they had served and sacrificed for the nation, they felt it to be their patriotic duty to help fellow members and understood this as a way to commemorate these mothers' wartime service. While they did not argue that their members should be formally considered military veterans, as did other veteranist women in the WOSL or the WWRAA, they believed they should be recognized for their wartime service.

National officers led the effort to support members and set an example for others to follow. In 1929, the fourth vice president, Mrs. Peter Campbell, assisted one Gold Star mother in getting her dependency claims, helped another obtain her son's Bonus, and helped a widow get her claims heard before the Veterans Bureau.[95] Efforts like this demonstrated the AWM's recognition that its fellow members deserved assistance just as much as official military veterans.

During the Great Depression, the AWM increased its efforts to support fellow members and other war mothers. As part of the 1933 discussion about the proposed increase in dues, Mrs. Stone included stories about destitute mothers who also sought help at the AWM's headquarters in Washington, DC. One night, the headquarters received a phone call indicating that a woman with an AWM membership card had been picked up on the highway, "alone and destitute." After this woman arrived at the headquarters, they learned that she had been a member of the AWM but had been unable to pay her dues for two years. The woman had traveled to Washington, DC, to find her estranged son, a "cripple" whose government pension had been cut, leaving him unable to help his mother. The staff at the headquarters did their best to assist the woman; they took her to the emergency room when she became ill and even moved her back to Norfolk to seek better help. Stone told the executive board that "I could stand here for hours and tell you of the cases that have come to us. Yet we have not one cent to do this relief work with except as we beg or go into our own pockets. Therefore, I say, there should be some provision whereby every chapter in the United States should contribute something of a relief fund to be used at National Headquarters."[96] Without a relief fund raised through a small increase in dues, Stone and the other AWM leaders at the headquarters could not adequately help the mothers and veterans who sought help there. Stone even proposed the creation of a penny fund to help indigent war mothers. As reported by the *Indianapolis News* on September 26, 1933, she wanted to establish an endowment fund to support indigent war mothers by having each AWM member save one penny per day for several years.[97] Like the WOSL, the AWM asked its members to invest in the organization as a way to help their comrades and themselves.

The AWM also supported legislation that would benefit war mothers. In 1935, it announced its support for the "Forgotten Mothers Bill," which would have given dependent parents of wartime casualties an extra twenty dollars a month from the government, just as the government already gave to widows and orphans.[98] The name of this bill played on the popular Great Depression term the "Forgotten Man," sometimes used to refer to World War One veterans abandoned by the government, and included mothers in the concept.[99] By supporting this bill, AWM members advocated for mothers and posited that to properly memorialize the war, they must help the mothers who also suffered in its aftermath.

AWM members also aided their fellow war mothers through their steadfast support of the Gold Star mothers and widows pilgrimage. As discussed in the next chapter, this government-funded trip took women to visit the graves of their relatives buried in the American cemeteries in Europe. Many members of the AWM were Gold Star mothers eligible for the trip, so they formed a national Gold Star Committee to focus on their particular issues.[100] They lobbied for the passage of the Gold Star pilgrimage bill and passed official resolutions that stated their support.[101] Member Ethel Stratton Nock, a Gold Star mother very active in the cause, served as the AWM's liaison officer for the Gold Star pilgrimage in 1929. She reported that although "the mothers eligible for the pilgrimage to the cemeteries overseas form only a small part of the membership of the American War Mothers, the organization as a whole took an active part in furthering the legislation in Congress" to benefit not just AWM members but "all eligible widows and mothers." Mrs. Nock helped the War Department notify all eligible widows and mothers, assisted its efforts however she could, and served as a resource for eligible AWM members.[102]

As a Gold Star mother who had visited her son's grave at the Meuse-Argonne American Cemetery in France at her own expense, Mrs. Nock believed in the importance of extending this chance to all Gold Star mothers and widows.[103] She appreciated "this opportunity for service" and told the AWM's fifth national convention that, since her own trip, "my greatest object in life was to bring the comfort I had received to all other mothers of our glorious sons whose bodies are guarded by the Stars and Stripes in the beautiful fields of honor overseas."[104] As an alternative to building a traditional monument in memory of her son, Mrs. Nock commemorated him by helping other women heal.

The AWM's strong support of the Gold Star pilgrimage indicated its belief that a government-sponsored trip to the overseas cemeteries constituted a form of veteranist commemoration on behalf of Gold Star women. Its support of the pilgrimage characterized its overall commitment to veteranism in place of a national monument.

CONCLUSION

After "The War to End All Wars," the AWM hoped there would be no more wars. Its members realized that the existence of their organization would be limited to their lifetime, since they wanted no subsequent generations of war mothers. Thus, they initially incorporated their group for just twenty years and planned to revisit the issue in 1937.[105] As members grew older, they worried more about their organization's longevity and their ability to pursue veteranist projects. In 1940, Mrs. Eleanor Cresswell Wagner of the Admiral R. E. Coontz Chapter wrote to the American Red Cross in thanks for its continued support of the carnation sale. She explained that "we mothers are getting old and can no longer earn the money we once did to supply the comforts that our disabled 'World War' Veterans need and seem to expect from the Mothers. While life lasts we hope not to disappoint these boys of ours and with the kind friends who year after year help us in our annual drive for funds we plan to carry on."[106] Without knowing that another war would soon create a new generation of war mothers, they realized that their organization's legacy might die with them. Yet even as they grew older and needed more assistance themselves, they worried about their boys and tried to help them.

To their dismay, the outbreak of World War Two created new war mothers. The AWM welcomed them into the organization as it continued its veteranist mission.[107] It kept up its commemorative service activities through World War Two and its aftermath. By 1947, it had increased its influence so much that it gained representation on the Veterans Administration Advisory Committee. The *New York Times* reported that it had "800 members working on a voluntary basis in veterans hospitals" in addition to donating supplies to the hospitals and caring for the families of needy veterans.[108] It maintained a focus on veteranist commemorations and still did not erect a large, permanent national memorial to the First World War. Rather, it wanted its deeds of service in the present to constitute its memorial to the past.

But memorials in the form of community service are intangible and ephemeral, something that the AWM seemed to realize. When AWM members died and could no longer perform acts of commemorative service, their war memorials died with them, removing the evidence of their commemorative contributions from the collective memory of the United States. Even the physical manifestations of their community service efforts proved insecure. The American War Mothers Memorial Home at Fitzsimons General Hospital in Colorado flourished in the years after World War Two but closed in 1960. Fitzsimons General Hospital closed in 1996, becoming part of the University of Colorado Anschutz Medical Campus and also home to a medical research park named the Fitzsimons Innovation Community. This further obscured the memory of the First World War on the landscape, although it retains some elements of its living memorial status through the continued use of the Fitzsimons name.[109] Although the American War Mothers Memorial Home remains today and was designated a Local Historic Landmark by the city of Aurora's Historic Preservation Commission in 1988, because of its 1960 closure and the hospital's demise, it no longer serves its intended community service purpose.[110] The home is now dilapidated and neglected, and the power of its memorial status has been diminished.[111] In Europe, craftsman buildings strikingly similar in their purpose to the Memorial Home, and also connected to honoring Gold Star mothers, suffered a similar fate, but in this case, the government completely erased them from the landscape.

5

"A Great Living and Moving Monument"

The Gold Star Pilgrimages as Veteranist Memorials

AN OCEAN away from Aurora, Colorado, other craftsman-style buildings also commemorated Gold Star women during the early 1930s. Built to accommodate the needs of the Gold Star mothers and widows who traveled to the American cemeteries in France as part of the official government pilgrimages, these temporary rest houses resembled the American War Mothers Memorial Home more closely than the formal cemeteries and monuments that surrounded them. By combining monuments and cemeteries with veteranism, the Gold Star pilgrimages embodied the concept of a hybrid, living memorial focused on service. Senator Robert Wagner of New York even defined the pilgrimage program as a memorial when he asserted in 1929 that "such a holy pilgrimage to the American shrines in Europe would be a great living and moving monument to peace."[1]

Similar to other living memorials and veteranist commemoration projects, the Gold Star pilgrimages assisted Americans who sacrificed during the war. Gold Star women believed that as mothers and wives who had lost their children or husbands in war, they had served and sacrificed for the nation. Those Gold Star women who chose to bury their loved ones in the overseas American cemeteries further served the nation when they relinquished their relatives' bodies and graves to the American government. These women lobbied Congress to send them on a pilgrimage to the overseas cemeteries to help alleviate their grief. As an official government initiative, the Gold Star pilgrimages demonstrated that the government agreed with their request to be recognized for their sacrifices through service rather than a statue. The government agreed that it had an obligation to honor and help Gold Star women in this manner.

When they requested the pilgrimage, Gold Star mothers and widows told the government that this type of veteranist commemoration represented the best way to recognize their losses. The government's acquiescence to their request demonstrated its acceptance of service as a form of commemoration, one uniquely appropriate for American women. Nevertheless, the pilgrimages did not completely reject more traditional forms of memorialization. The memorial landscapes being created by the American Battle Monuments Commission (ABMC) formed the backdrop of the pilgrimages and constituted the *lieux de mémoire* believed to assuage the Gold Star women's grief, especially through the graves, memorial tablets, and monuments that formed the locus of their visit. The pilgrimages combined these traditional monuments with the more personal and ephemeral veteranist memorialization program requested by the pilgrims. Yet as the rest houses demonstrate, at the same time that the pilgrimages included women and veteranism in the landscape of military memory, they also separated women from the main commemorative narrative and granted them only a temporary place at the overseas cemeteries.

THE AMERICAN BATTLE MONUMENTS COMMISSION: GUARDIAN OF AMERICA'S OVERSEAS MILITARY MEMORY

The origins of the Gold Star pilgrimages began during World War One as the US grappled with the question of what to do with the remains of US service members who died in Europe. In September 1918, Secretary of War Newton D. Baker publicly pledged that the government would repatriate the war dead to the US for burial, as it had done during the Spanish-American War.[2] This promise ignited controversy since no task of this size had ever been attempted overseas; over 116,000 Americans had died in World War One, and America's Allies did not immediately support the repatriation plan.[3] Eventually, the War Department decided to send a questionnaire to the next of kin to ask whether they wanted their loved ones' remains returned home or buried in an overseas American military cemetery.[4]

When they received the questionnaire, many next of kin struggled to choose a final resting place for their loved ones as they grieved. At the same time, they had to negotiate the government bureaucratization and collectivization of their mourning process. Families worried about the handling of the deceased and the process of military interment. As they had been during the Civil War, Americans remained deeply concerned with the treatment and burial of the dead, something they described during the Civil War as the "work" of death.[5] While dealing with the immense death toll of the Civil War, the military struggled and often failed to properly bury Civil War casualties. In an attempt to improve the process, the US created a system of burying and handling the dead that accorded honor to the fallen. After the establishment of a national cemetery system and a standardized process for military burial during the Civil War and its aftermath, the treatment of the war dead continued to evolve during World War One as Americans contemplated their earlier struggles with military burial.[6] This issue even became politicized when former president Theodore Roosevelt, who lost his son Quentin in 1918, publicly declared his intention to leave Quentin's body in France because he believed that "where the tree falls, there let it lie."[7]

Despite Roosevelt's statement, many families remained torn about their burial choice.[8] Some, like Mrs. Elizabeth Conley of Philadelphia, seemed unable to decide between repatriation and an overseas burial. Mrs. Conley lost both her sons William and Francis in the war. The army buried Francis in a temporary grave in France but never found or identified William's remains. While deciding what to do with Francis's remains, Mrs. Conley changed her mind at least five times. She first told the army she wanted Francis's body back, then she decided to leave it in France, and later she changed her mind several more times. In a letter to the Quartermaster Corps in 1921, she wrote that after "seeing so many others being brought back to the United States, I want mine back too."[9] When she learned that William's remains could not be identified and repatriated, she requested that Francis be buried in France, because, she wrote, "if I can't get both back, I will let them stay there."[10] Mrs. Conley's final request came too late to be cancelled, as the army had already shipped Francis's remains to the US. In 1931, with her friend and fellow Gold Star mother Mrs. Katherine M. Gallagher, Mrs. Conley traveled to the Meuse-Argonne American Cemetery as part of the Gold Star pilgrimage to visit the Tablets of the Missing that memorialized William.[11] Mrs. Conley's tortured decision-making process demonstrates the anguished choices faced by Gold Star families.

Although many next of kin decided to repatriate their loved ones, the families of 30,973 deceased service members chose an overseas burial, numbers that justified the creation of permanent American military cemeteries overseas.[12] Another situation also factored into the decision to create these cemeteries: the thousands of unidentifiable remains and missing service members lost in this first fully mechanized, total war. These men could not be sent home for burial by their families, so the establishment of overseas cemeteries and memorial sites provided a dignified solution for the burial and memorialization of those who could not be identified.[13]

The creation of overseas American military cemeteries and memorials also served diplomatic goals by representing the US overseas and physically reminding Europeans about the American contribution to the Allied victory by glorifying the AEF. The cemeteries and memorials helped the US claim a place in the postwar international order as they symbolically projected American power overseas alongside the cemeteries being established by the British, French, Germans, and other combatants.[14] Without similar American cemeteries, American participation in the critical ending phase of the war might be forgotten or overlooked. The corresponding American monuments near the cemeteries also helped ensure that America's contributions to the war would be remembered. For example, the Montfaucon American Monument, which commemorates the American victory in the Meuse-Argonne Offensive, towers over the countryside from atop a hill, asserting the US military's perception that the AEF turned the tide of the war.[15] However, the diplomatic goals of the cemeteries and memorials also meant that the cemeteries subsumed the individuality of those buried there within the larger purposes of these national shrines.[16]

The American effort to create overseas cemeteries began out of necessity during the war in 1917, when the army established the Graves Registration Service (GRS) under the Quartermaster Corps to identify and bury American casualties in temporary cemeteries in Europe.[17] After the war, these scattered graves needed to be consolidated into the permanent American cemeteries now promised by the government. To accomplish this mission, Congress enacted legislation on March 4, 1923, to establish the American Battle Monuments Commission (ABMC).[18] Congress entrusted the ABMC, an independent federal agency of the executive branch, to be the "guardian of America's overseas commemorative cemeteries and memorials."[19] First led by General John J. Pershing, the ABMC established eight permanent cemeteries for the World War One dead and fourteen monuments to honor the achievements of the AEF.[20] The cemeteries, which remain under the care of the ABMC today, also contain Tablets of the Missing that honor by name the missing and unaccounted-for service members; the ABMC later established further cemeteries and memorials to honor those in World War Two.[21]

The establishment of the American cemeteries required the permission of the countries where they were located. The French government initially banned the exhumation and transport of bodies from 1919 to 1921, fearful of hygienic risks and the gruesomeness of transporting so many bodies in the already war-torn country. For some of these reasons, Great Britain prohibited the repatriation of its dead and created its own foreign cemeteries managed by what became the Commonwealth War Graves Commission (CWGC).[22] In this climate, the US eventually resolved most of the issues with France concerning the creation of overseas US cemeteries and repatriation and received permission to move forward.[23]

The decision to create the overseas military cemeteries and their design also emerged from the military cemeteries of the Civil War era that utilized standardized rows of identical headstones and created a collective landscape of the war dead.[24] These vast cemeteries gave the Civil War dead a visual power that shaped American society and culture for the next century. This

Figure 5.1. View of the Meuse-Argonne American Cemetery and Memorial in France, looking toward the chapel. Note the parklike landscape; the uniform, symmetrical grave plots separated by rows of trees; and the expertly manicured landscape. July 2012. Photograph by Allison S. Finkelstein.

same sacrificial landscape can be seen in the meticulous rows of identical headstones in the shape of crosses and Stars of David at the ABMC cemeteries.[25] Likewise, the Civil War created an expectation that a systematic accounting of the dead and their honorable burial constituted an obligation of the government.[26]

Civil War cemeteries, the private cemeteries established in nineteenth-century America, and the Allies' First World War cemeteries all influenced the designs of the ABMC cemeteries.[27] The resulting cemeteries and memorials displayed the aesthetic sensibilities of high-style modern classicism, the French Romanesque Revival, and the French eclectic style, all popular architectural styles at the time that embraced modernist aesthetics yet still referenced historical precedents.[28] While each cemetery received a unique design, they were all highly controlled, formal spaces designed to be symmetrical and precisely landscaped with formal entrances, long walkways with intersecting axes, stone memorials, and chapels (fig. 5.1).[29] The orderliness of the cemeteries helped to mitigate the violent chaos still visible on the surrounding battlefields and provided mourners with a controlled space to grieve.

The memorial landscapes of the ABMC played a central role in the Gold Star pilgrimages. The main premise of the pilgrimages asserted that visiting these cemeteries could help ease the pain of the Gold Star pilgrims. Gold Star mother Ethel Stratton Nock, an ardent advocate for the pilgrimage and an active member of the American War Mothers, often recounted the life-changing effect of her independent visit to her son's grave at the Meuse-Argonne American Cemetery before the pilgrimages.[30] During a 1929 congressional hearing about the pilgrimage legislation, Nock described how after her son's death, she was "a broken, grief-stricken woman, avoiding all contacts outside my home and wrapped in a great sorrow that seems to me now as completely selfish." Only visiting her son's grave ended her depression. She explained that "in the year and a half that has elapsed since I saw the white crosses overseas, I have devoted my life to service to veterans and gold-star mothers."[31] The visit enabled her to find solace in veteranist service work that commemorated her son, especially with the American War Mothers. Nock demonstrated the healing power a visit to the ABMC cemeteries could provide to other Gold Star women and how her visit inspired her commitment to veteranism as a way to commemorate her son.

THE GOLD STAR PILGRIMAGE PROGRAM

The Gold Star pilgrimages formed an important part of the national collective mourning process after World War One.[32] The Gold Star emerged as an emblem for American casualties during World War One and became a substitute for traditional black mourning clothes.[33] By wearing a gold star on their clothing, much like a wartime medal, Gold Star families used their bodies as memorials and adopted a corporeal, living embodiment of the memory of the dead that also signaled the sacrifice they had made for the nation through their personal loss.

To create communities for collective mourning and support, the Gold Star mothers and widows established various organizations such as the Gold Star Association and the Gold Star Mothers, Inc.; they also actively participated in the American War Mothers.[34] The idea for the government-sponsored pilgrimage program began because of the difficulties in visiting the overseas cemeteries. Visits to the isolated cemeteries proved expensive and challenging for many Gold Star women to make independently.[35] Their associations lobbied Congress in the 1920s for an official government-sponsored pilgrimage. They convinced the government of its necessity through an appeal to their sacrifices as mothers and widows, the goodwill it would foster with the former Allies, and the endorsement of the politically powerful American Legion.[36]

These various groups lobbied so passionately for the government-sponsored pilgrimage because they believed that mothers and widows could gain some closure by visiting the cemeteries. Ethel Stratton Nock wrote to General Pershing after her visit to her son's grave to share this very sentiment. "I feel uplifted mentally and physically because of this pilgrimage," she told Pershing, "and will be able, I am sure, to bring peace to many troubled hearts of Gold Star Mothers."[37]

Victory came on March 2, 1929, when, after much debate in Congress and an endorsement from President Coolidge, Public Law 70–952 authorized "an act to enable the mothers and widows of the deceased soldiers, sailors, and marines, of the American forces now interred in the cemeteries of Europe to make a pilgrimage to these cemeteries."[38] The mothers and widows who accepted the invitation represented a cross section of American society at the time. They came from all across the US, from urban and rural locations, varying economic and social classes, and different religious, ethnic, and racial backgrounds.

Despite the diversity of the pilgrims and the inclusion of African American women, the army racially segregated the groups of pilgrims who went on the trip. This decision resulted in widespread backlash against the program from the African American community and their supporters, including a letter-writing campaign and petitions.[39] For example, on February 21, 1930, Massachusetts governor Frank G. Allen wrote to President Hoover after learning of the planned segregation that "some of the Gold Star Mothers thus affected are citizens of Massachusetts." He told Hoover that "our honored dead of both races made the supreme sacrifice and Gold Star Mothers, whether white or colored, suffered the same loss, I believe the proposed action of the War Department, in causing an arbitrary separation of the races, is ill-advised, unfair and contrary to the ideals of our American government." He implored Hoover to "rescind all orders which in any way establish a color line in connection with the coming pilgrimages of Gold Star Mothers."[40] Allen's letter reflected many of the arguments made by those opposed to the segregation of the trips and exposed the hypocrisy of a supposedly democratic nation segregating a veteranist memorialization project intended to help the mothers and widows of fallen service members. The secretary of war responded to Allen's letter with a defense similar to the others being proffered by the government in response to the outcry. He cited the large numbers of pilgrims and explained that the requirement to provide suitable accommodations meant they must be split into groups. "The composition of the groups was determined," he wrote, "after the most careful consideration of the interests of the pilgrims themselves. No discrimination whatever will be made as between the various groups. Each group will receive equal accommodations, care and consideration."[41]

However, the treatment of African American pilgrims was not exactly the same as or equal to that of the White pilgrims. In New York, they stayed at the Harlem YMCA instead of the hotels used by the White pilgrims, and some of them traveled to Europe on ships of a different class than the White pilgrims, such as former freighter vessels refitted for passengers.[42] Accompanied by African American officers, including the army's highest-ranking Black officer, Colonel Benjamin O. Davis, these segregated groups had itineraries closely resembling those of the White pilgrims, but with the addition of special entertainment from World War One Harlem Hellfighters Band veteran Noble Sissle and his jazz musicians.[43]

Many eligible African American women felt conflicted about whether to accept their invitations or to protest the segregation by refusing to participate.[44] Nonetheless, at least 168 African American mothers and widows accepted their pilgrimage invitations and traveled in separate, segregated parties during the summers of 1930 and 1931; others likely went during later summers.[45] For some of the women, the once-in-a-lifetime opportunity to visit the grave of their loved one outweighed the desire to protest their unequal treatment, particularly when the government did include African Americans, something that could not be assumed in American society at the time.

The segregation of the pilgrimages reflected the restricted inclusion of African American women into American commemorative culture and especially the female veteranist community. Although African American women could participate in the pilgrimages, like the WOSL, the ARC, and the AWM, the government adhered to prejudiced, Jim Crow era policies that treated them differently from White women. Based on the government's action, if not its words, African American Gold Star women's services and sacrifices did not equate to those of White women. This veteranist commemoration project could include Black women only if it adhered to the norms of segregation. The segregation of the pilgrimages mirrored the segregation of African American servicemen in the AEF and the highly restricted opportunities for African American women to serve in formal ways during the war, particularly overseas. The pilgrimages became one more way to consign African American women in the postwar years to segregated veteranist commemoration activities.

One group of Gold Star relatives excluded from the pilgrimages were Gold Star fathers. The exclusion of men from the final pilgrimage legislation resulted from more than just a lack of strong male advocacy; it had to do with the historical connections between women and the mourning process, especially in the context of wartime deaths, motherhood, and maternalism.[46] While the Gold Star could be worn by any family member of a wartime casualty, and while earlier versions of the pilgrimage bill included fathers and husbands, men did not receive the same special status and inclusion as mothers and widows.[47] Deep-seated popular sentiment rooted in republican mother-hood and maternalism privileged women's roles in mourning military casu-alties and defined motherhood as a form of wartime service to the nation.[48] At the same time, it also relegated women to more traditional social roles, even as women gained new political power with the vote.[49]

The memory of the Civil War also influenced women's privileged role above men in the commemoration of the World War One dead. Women's public participation in Civil War mourning; the establishment and maintenance of military cemeteries, memorials, and battlefields; and pilgrimages to those sites carved out a unique role for women in memorialization.[50] Especially in the South, women led the movements to establish military cemeteries, and women created mourning traditions that honored fallen soldiers.[51] As the daughters and granddaughters of the generation who memorialized the Civil War, the women of the First World War grew up observing their elders' roles in commemoration.

The Civil War's legacy, republican motherhood, and maternalism helped justify the Gold Star pilgrimage and at times elevated the mothers above the widows.[52] Although the government included widows in the final pilgrim-age legislation and many widows went on the trip, widows did not lobby as persistently for the legislation as mothers, and only widows who did not re-marry remained eligible.[53] Influenced by the heightened importance given to motherhood, some mothers felt themselves to be more deserving of inclu-sion than widows, and mothers outnumbered widows on the pilgrimages.[54] This may have been partly because mothers might have had more time than widows to lobby for the pilgrimage and participate in the trip. By the 1930s, these mothers' other children were probably grown, while the widows might still have had children at home, might have been working to support their families, or might have chosen to marry again, thus disqualifying them from participation. These situations could have prevented some widows from be-ing as active in the lobbying effort or as readily able to travel as the mothers, who might still have had a husband's support and income.

The Gold Star pilgrimages drew inspiration from earlier and contempo-raneous pilgrimages to military sites. Pilgrimages to battlefields, cemeteries, and memorials became popular after the Civil War, especially as part of com-memorative traditions.[55] Likewise, after World War One, pilgrimages to battle sites became popular among most of the combatant nations. People traveled to the battlefields independently and as part of organized trips such as the American Legion's 1927 "Second AEF" trip to its convention in Paris.[56] The ABMC even assigned Major Dwight D. Eisenhower, an officer in its Histori-cal Section, to lead the production of an accurate guidebook to the Ameri-can battle sites in Europe, titled *A Guide to the American Battle Fields in Eu-*

rope, published in 1927.[57] The ABMC viewed this product as important and popular enough to later bring Eisenhower back to its staff in 1928 for almost seventeen months to help prepare an expanded and revised edition, renamed *American Armies and Battlefields in Europe*, published in 1938.[58]

While military pilgrimages gained popularity, the religious connotations of the word "pilgrimage" remained significant in the context of these new iterations of battlefield tourism and the Gold Star program. The terms "pilgrimage" and "pilgrim" carried religious meaning, connected the trips to spiritual rituals of grief, and imbued them with a sense of the sacred that distinguished them from normal tourism.[59] The ABMC cemeteries contained overtly religious symbolism and spaces; each cemetery included a chapel and all the headstones took the form of either crosses or Stars of David. Despite being government programs, neither the cemeteries nor the pilgrimage remained completely secular.

At the heart of the meaning of a pilgrimage is the sense that pilgrims can capture a part of the past and experience an event even if they did not participate themselves.[60] Pilgrims try to distinguish themselves from regular tourists through the connections that bring them on their pilgrimage; they want their journey to be viewed as a public ritual linked to ideas of national or religious identity.[61] These descriptions aptly characterize the Gold Star pilgrimages since the army distinguished the pilgrims from normal tourists as part of an elaborate, public, and somewhat spiritual rite of national remembrance staged by the US government.

The army's Quartermaster Corps meticulously planned and organized the Gold Star pilgrimages. It accounted for every detail of each pilgrim's journey, such as their transportation from their homes to the point of embarkation in New York City, their identification badges, and their medical histories.[62] The Quartermaster Corps split the pilgrims who accepted the invitation into groups that traveled in a "party" during the summers of 1930 to 1933.[63] In total, 6,654 women who represented the social, economic, ethnic, religious, geographic, and racial diversity of the AEF participated in the Gold Star pilgrimages.[64] The army arranged and paid for the entirety of every woman's trip.[65] Each party's overseas itinerary varied based on the location of the main cemetery to be visited, but most trips to France included stops at the major sights in Paris such as the Arc de Triomphe, Napoleon's tomb, the Eiffel Tower, and Notre Dame.[66]

Throughout the trip, the pilgrims' military officer escorts, nurses, and even European officials treated them with respect and honor. Each group that went to Paris laid a wreath on the French Tomb of the Unknown Soldier under the Arc de Triomphe during a special ceremony.[67] The officers gave cemetery visits careful consideration since they realized they could be upsetting. In keeping with gender stereotypes of the day that portrayed women as weaker and more emotionally fragile, they forbade formal ceremonies at the cemeteries or other activities that might agitate the pilgrims' emotions. Trip planners wanted to "keep the emotional reaction at a minimum" to protect the pilgrims' physical and mental health.[68] This preoccupation with maintaining the public composure, dignity, and well-being of the pilgrims during the cemetery visits triggered the construction of rest houses to provide the pilgrims with some privacy at the cemeteries even as they publicly mourned throughout the trip.

At the same time that the Gold Star pilgrimages demonstrated the government's commitment to the families of the war dead, the program attracted a lot of publicity that promoted the ABMC and the military during a period of increasing isolationism and pacifism. Colonel Richard T. Ellis, the main officer in charge of the pilgrimage, created a scrapbook in which he saved newspaper articles and other publicity materials related to the pilgrimage. Over one hundred pages long, this scrapbook documented the high level of public interest in the program and contained articles that both praised and criticized it.[69] The pilgrimages also gained national exposure in popular culture through John Ford's film *Pilgrimage* (1933). The film told the fictional story of a Gold Star mother from Arkansas who struggled with regrets about her relationship with her son during the trip.[70] With so much public interest in the program from the media and even Hollywood, the army carefully crafted the official image of the pilgrimage.[71]

American women's success in convincing the US government to sponsor and pay for the entire pilgrimage demonstrated the growing power of women at the national level and their increasingly important place in the commemorative culture surrounding World War One. Even after winning the franchise, these women remained on the political stage and framed their civic identities in terms of uniquely female issues such as motherhood and marriage.[72] Just as they did after the Civil War and the Spanish-American War, women made significant contributions to the memorialization of World War One. But as the temporary rest houses constructed at the cemeteries demonstrate, this inclusion remained gender restricted, racially segregated, and ephemeral; it left no permanent, tangible evidence of women's importance to overseas commemoration on the landscape.

GOLD STAR PILGRIMS SERVED
AND SACRIFICED FOR THE NATION

Gold Star mothers and widows defined the loss of their child or husband as a wartime service and sacrifice that included them in the larger community of women supported by female veteranists, and they were often veteranists themselves. Though they did not define themselves as female veterans like the women who served overseas or worked as Reconstruction Aides, they believed they contributed to the war effort in a critical, personal, and deeply tragic way. Because of their losses, they received a place of distinction in the interwar commemorative culture. For example, the Memorial Building to the Women of the World War specifically honored them through the memorial columns on its facade. Those Gold Star women who chose an overseas burial for their loved one performed a further act of service and sacrifice by presenting his or her bodily remains to the country to use as part of the symbolic diplomatic and political messages embodied by the cemeteries. Because the families of the missing and unaccounted-for service members had no choice about what to do with their loved ones' bodies, their mothers and widows also received invitations to the pilgrimage so they could view their relatives' names on the Tablets of the Missing and stand by an unknown soldier's grave.

Newspaper coverage of the pilgrimages reiterated that the Gold Star pilgrims served and sacrificed for the nation. A May 1931 article in the *National Tribune* stated that "this tribute to motherhood was offered by Congress in order that these women who made such glorious sacrifices in the World War might visit the scenes of their sons' great heroism." By indicating that the pilgrimage was "offered" by Congress, the article highlighted how the government intended the trip to honor the pilgrims. The article invoked the rhetoric of republican motherhood—but omitted the widows and any daughters who might have died—and described the mothers' service as encapsulated in raising their sons into men they sent to battle. The *National Tribune* believed that this made it "peculiarly fitting that a nation should pay tribute to its motherhood," for, as Milton said, "they also serve who only stand and wait."[73]

Dignitaries involved with the pilgrimage agreed that the Gold Star women served and sacrificed. At the "tea-reception" held at the Restaurant Laurent in Paris for Party "A" of the pilgrimage on May 26, 1932, the American ambassador to France, Walter E. Edge, echoed these sentiments. He declared that 1932 inaugurated "the third year that the American Government has given the opportunity for the representatives of American womanhood who made greater sacrifices than those who actually laid down their lives, to visit France and the shrines of your immortal loved ones." General Pershing agreed and proclaimed to the attendees that "no group of Americans knows more deeply, more completely what war means than a Gold Star Mother or Widow. It is she who makes the real sacrifice, she who knows how to lay the most precious gift upon the altar of freedom more than any other." He even told them that "I feel very greatly, and I want to thank you in my own name for what you did for the victory of the American army, which of course means the victory of the Allies."[74]

Whether they intended it or were conscious of it, Gold Star families who chose to bury their loved ones in an overseas military cemetery further served the US by enabling these cemeteries to fulfill various political purposes. Memorials alone could not achieve the diplomatic goals of the US. Hundreds of military cemeteries from the different combatant nations already peppered the fields of France and Belgium.[75] The US needed overseas cemeteries to position the nation equally alongside the other combatants, something it could not do without the bodies of American service members. No matter their motivation, Gold Star women served the nation by relinquishing the bodies of their loved ones.[76]

In the eyes of the government, this service and sacrifice elevated these Gold Star women above others who chose repatriation. The government publicly recognized the Gold Star pilgrims' assistance in promoting a powerful international image and fostering ties of friendship and peace with Europe. In a letter included in a congressional hearing about the proposed pilgrimages, Senator Robert Wagner explained this belief when he remarked that "the ranks of mothers and sweethearts would constitute a new expeditionary force and a first line of defense for peace. Europe would see us in a new light—not as fighting doughboys, nor as gallant legionnaires, but as a nation of homes and families whose members are capable of the most pious sentiments."[77]

The French military specifically praised the pilgrims for their service in fostering a positive Franco-American diplomatic relationship. At a reception for the pilgrims on August 18, 1932, French General Pagezy lauded the assembled women. He told them that "it is a great honor to us to have you maintain their tombs in France. It is a deed of which we understand the full meaning and which we feel profoundly . . . we keep very piously this sacred trust. It is to us a proof of the eternal friendship that has always existed and will always exist between our two nations."[78]

Throughout the pilgrimages, French citizens emphasized the importance of the cemeteries that bound the Gold Star women to France. The Société Bienvenue Française, a French organization committed to promoting intellectual and moral exchanges between nations, presented each pilgrim with French soil in a small bag made from conjoined pieces of the American and French flags.[79] At a 1932 tea reception, a representative of this society told the pilgrims that they thought "you should keep with you something of the remembrance of the places where you have been, and of the soil of France where your beloved have so gloriously lain down their lives. Therefore we have asked you to accept from our society a little bag, and in that bag earth of France which is sacred to you."[80] A letter that accompanied the bags explained that it was "a little memorial present, from your pious pilgrimage to France," filled with "the earth of France, which is sacred to you, as it is to

Figure 5.2. The official War Department badge worn by Julia C. Underwood during her pilgrimage. Julia C. Underwood Pilgrimage Collection, National WWI Museum and Memorial Archives, Kansas City, Missouri, USA.

us, because of all the young heroes who rest in our soil."[81] The Société Bienvenue Française regarded the Gold Star pilgrimages as sacred commemorative journeys rooted in the land where Americans had fought and died. It wanted these souvenirs to serve as a memorial of the trip and the French *lieux de mémoire* so that the women could bring the battlefield home with them in the form of this small memorial.

Without technically defining the pilgrims as military veterans, the army treated the pilgrims like civilian participants of the war and presented them with an official armband and badge to distinguish them from normal American tourists (fig. 5.2). During a separate shipboard ceremony, the United States Lines shipping company presented each pilgrim with another medal to be worn around their necks while on the ocean liners.[82] Aesthetically, the army badges resembled military medals. They aligned the pilgrims with male veterans and symbolically equated their sacrifices with military service.[83] Authorized by the War Department and issued by the Quartermaster Corps, the army badges served as pseudomilitary medals that honored the pilgrims and marked them as having served their country, just like military veterans of the war received the World War One Victory Medal.[84] While the Gold Star women did not advocate for veterans' benefits for themselves in the same way as other female veteranists, by lobbying for the pilgrimage program from the government, they succeeded in receiving the one benefit they desired and the recognition they believed they deserved. Distinguished by the army as separate from ordinary civilians, the Gold Star pilgrims occupied an intermediate position between veterans and civilians, fitting them into the eclectic group of veteranist women who participated in the First World War outside the traditional and official confines of military service.

THE GOLD STAR PILGRIMAGES AS VETERANISM

Although the Gold Star pilgrimages were not specifically referred to as community service, analysis demonstrates that they constituted a form of veteranist commemoration. Every Gold Star woman who chose an overseas burial for her relative, or whose loved one remained missing, received an invitation to participate in the pilgrimage, free of charge. By paying for the pilgrimage, the government performed an act of service at the request of these women, who saw it as the government's obligation. With its compliance, the government admitted that no physical memorial or tangible offering such as money or certificates could fully honor and commemorate the Americans buried overseas and their mothers or widows. The government agreed that it could properly memorialize the sacrifice of these women and their soldier dead only by sending them on this pilgrimage.

The ABMC's cooperation indicated that the agency in charge of traditional commemoration overseas also understood the value of veteranist commemorations. General Pershing, the ABMC's chair, told a group of pilgrims at a 1932 tea reception that "no monument can sufficiently honor these fallen dead too greatly, nor can be erected in any material form anything that will express completely the feelings of gratitude that are in our hearts for what they did for us."[85] Even though he devoted his postwar life to building physical monuments to the AEF in Europe with the ABMC, Pershing recognized their limits. As Americans continued to debate the best way to memorialize the war, Pershing seemed to value both traditional physical memorials and veteranist projects. Similar to some female veteranists, he embraced aspects of more modernist forms of commemorations while he promoted traditional statuary memorials, blurring the divisions between modernist and statuary commemoration.

Testimony from the pilgrims indicated that the pilgrimage comforted them and that they understood the trip as a type of veteranist memorial. One pilgrim believed the experience to be "a great comfort to every pilgrim mother I'm sure, to have had this rare privilege." She recognized that the government provided an experience that might otherwise have been impossible for many of these women. She returned feeling patriotic and explained that if she were a man she would get an eagle tattooed upon her chest. She exclaimed that "I went over 100% American, and returned 200%," for "gratitude burns deeply in my heart and never will be forgotten, and while I shout 'Vive la France,' I also exclaim 'Vive la America,' my beloved country."[86] In July 1930, Maud L. Reives wrote a letter of thanks for the pilgrimage and requested that she be remembered "to Capt. Earnest who had charge of our bunch while in France and who was untiring in his efforts to serve the Gold Star Mothers."[87] By using the phrase "to serve," Mrs. Reives indicated that she understood the pilgrimage as a service to the Gold Star women performed by the government.

The pilgrimages profoundly affected the participants and they spoke of its positive influence on their emotional recovery. On July 21, 1930, Mrs. Callie M. Laird of Little Rock, Arkansas, thanked the War Department for the trip, which she understood "was made possible by the generosity of the government." She described how "while it was especially sad at the cemeteries, at the same time, our burden was made lighter when we saw with our own eyes, the wonderful manner in which the cemeteries were kept and of which previously we had only our vague imagination. I am so glad now after this visit that I decided to leave the remains where they are buried . . . I am at home now, thoroughly satisfied that even tho we sacrificed so much for Democracy, yet the Government had done so much for us that our burden is made lighter."[88] Mrs. Laird's pilgrimage eased some of her heartbreak and allowed her to see firsthand how honorably the overseas cemeteries commemorated the American dead. Visiting these sites convinced her that she made the right decision when she chose an overseas burial. Hilde A. Meystre, the mother of Private Emile F. Meystre, buried at Aisne-Marne American Cemetery, penned the poem "Our Hearts O'erflow" upon her return from her 1930 pilgrimage. The poem described how both Gold Star mothers and their sons sacrificed for freedom, and ended with two verses that described the pilgrimage as a government service to the pilgrims:

> We are the Gold Star mothers,
>   Back from La Belle France.
> Back to our own loved country,
>   That gave us this wondrous chance,
> Gave us a time of pleasure
> To ease our saddened hearts,

Things we never dreamed of
We saw in those treasured marts.

We thank the Congress of USA.
    And all others that helped the way
To give us mothers a perfect day.[89]

Meystre's repetition of the word "gave" emphasized that the pilgrimage formed a type of veteranist commemoration given to them through a service. By using "pleasure" and "saddened hearts" back to back, she showed the contrasting elements of the pilgrimage that made it successful. Meystre understood that by passing the legislation for the trip, Congress successfully honored the pilgrims through an intangible veteranist memorial.

THE GOLD STAR PILGRIMAGE REST HOUSES AS A PHYSICAL MANIFESTATION OF VETERANISM

The temporary rest houses constructed at the ABMC cemeteries for the use of the pilgrims represented the physical manifestation of the government's veteranist agenda. Built specifically to accommodate women's needs and to provide them with a private place for comfort and rest, they created a distinctly female space on the predominantly male military landscape at the cemeteries. Despite the gendered stereotypes they adhered to, the rest houses showed the army's dedication to the program's success and to making the women comfortable. The segregation of the pilgrimages meant that separate rest houses for African American pilgrims did not need to be built, as the African American women would travel apart from the White pilgrims and could have the rest houses to themselves during their time at the cemeteries.

The Quartermaster Corps constructed these rest houses at several ABMC cemeteries because of the isolated locations of some of the cemeteries and their lack of adequate toilet, refreshment, and rest facilities.[90] Although most of the widows were middle aged or slightly younger, the mothers were often older and in poorer health.[91] The trip proved physically demanding and the officers wanted to provide appropriate facilities throughout the journey as health and safety were of paramount importance.

Since the army used the pilgrimages to try to bolster the military's reputation, the national press coverage of the pilgrimages might have influenced its decision to build the rest houses.[92] It could face a potential public relations disaster if the trip compromised the pilgrims' health.[93] If successful, the pilgrimages could positively publicize the army during a time of public cynicism about the Great War.[94] By protecting the pilgrims' well-being, the rest

Figure 5.3. The rest house at Aisne-Marne American Cemetery and Memorial in France, undated. Note the "private" sign that indicated the rest house should not be entered by regular cemetery visitors. Record Group 92, National Archives, College Park.

houses demonstrated the army's concern for their welfare and helped prevent potential criticisms or controversies.

The rest houses originated in several similar American building types common in the decades around the 1930s: ladies' rest rooms, military base hostess houses, and country clubs. Recognized parts of the American landscape, these structures accommodated women and families in public spaces and in predominantly male environments.[95] Because the rest houses were vernacular structures—buildings that emerged from the everyday, commonplace landscape—their design, function, and distinctly feminine nature would have been familiar to the pilgrims and the army. By imitating these buildings, the army included the pilgrims at the cemeteries, although the rest houses simultaneously separated the women from the main commemorative narrative at the cemeteries and relegated them to the traditional roles of mourning mothers and widows. Nonetheless, the pilgrims still actively influenced the early memorialization activities at the cemeteries.[96]

The architecture of the rest houses indicated their purpose as familiar places of comfort to the pilgrims.[97] Similar to bungalows common in the US

Figure 5.4. The rest house at St. Mihiel American Cemetery and Memorial in France, undated. Positioned near a grave plot, this rest house must have been visible to the cemetery's visitors. The nearby graves provided a stark reminder of the purpose of the pilgrimage. This image encapsulates the pilgrimage's combination of permanent statuary memorials and veteranist commemorations. Record Group 92, National Archives, College Park.

at the time, these one-story structures were designed in the craftsman style popular in the early twentieth century.[98] In 1930, Colonel Ellis described the rest houses as "attractive wooden one-story houses laid out and furnished something along the lines which one would expect to find in an attractive country-club," with "a comfortable, shady porch and a large open fire-place."[99] Photographs show that Ellis accurately described the rest houses; those at the Meuse-Argonne, Oise-Aisne, Aisne-Marne, and St. Mihiel Cemeteries matched his description and looked very similar to each other, if not exactly alike (figs. 5.3 and 5.4). The rest houses each had a hipped roof with a central projecting cross gable on the front facade and a Palladian window centered in the gable. The structures included decorative projecting false beams in the gables and exposed rafters under the eaves, classic elements of craftsman houses.[100] According to Ellis's description, it can be inferred that the horizontal exterior siding was wood.

Many photographs show furniture on the porches and plants climbing up the porch supports, suggesting that the pilgrims utilized these outdoor

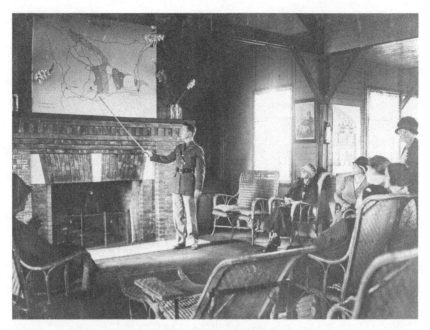

Figure 5.5. Lieutenant Lucas giving an illustrated talk to pilgrims inside the St. Mihiel rest house, undated. This image shows the contrast between the military and the domestic atmosphere of the rest houses. Note the exposed beams in the ceiling, a common feature in craftsman-style architecture. Record Group 92, National Archives, College Park.

spaces. The rest houses themselves were surrounded by plants, although the landscape features near them were more informal than the highly formalized cemetery horticulture. Evidence of the exact location of the rest houses at the cemeteries does not survive, so their relation to the other elements of the cemetery cannot be determined.[101]

The interiors of the rest houses contained, according to Colonel Ellis, "tables, comfortable chairs and a rest room for the use of the nurses and the hostess," and there was also a kitchen equipped with a stove, water heater, and coffee percolator.[102] The large military maps on the walls provided the only indication that these rooms were not in a typical American home or country club. These maps almost seem like a male, military intrusion into the homelike environment at the rest houses. An interior image of the St. Mihiel rest house even showed a lieutenant giving an illustrated talk to the pilgrims using the map over the fireplace, possibly an account of the St. Mihiel Offensive (fig. 5.5). While intended to be female-oriented areas of relaxation, the rest houses also served educational purposes and facilitated such presentations by officers on the trips.

The rest houses and the hostesses who ran them succeeded in providing comfort and privacy to the pilgrims. Colonel Ellis reported that their construction "undoubtedly was for the good of the pilgrimage and received favorable commendation not only from official visitors but from the Pilgrims themselves."[103] In a 1930 letter of thanks to Colonel Ellis, pilgrims Mrs. Hattie B. Bisbee and Mrs. Sarah Parker reminisced about "the Hostess Mrs. Abbott and Madam Juliette who in their sweet sympathetic manner made each visit to the cemetery much easier to bear."[104] WOSL member Eleanor Barnes visited the St. Mihiel rest house in 1930 after the WOSL convention in Paris. She reported in *Carry On* that it "did much towards bracing up the mothers after their difficult visit. They all voiced the same sentiments—they were quite satisfied to go back home leaving their boys in this lovely spot so carefully tended, and they were more than happy because of all the Government had done for them."[105] The battle-scarred landscape might have been traumatic for the pilgrims to visit, but the rest houses tempered that trauma by evoking the comforts of home and providing a female place of respite.

The stark visual contrast between the small, vernacular rest houses and the formal, monumental architecture of the ABMC cemeteries and monuments visually displayed the debate between veteranist commemorations and physical monuments. In comparison to the ABMC's monumental architecture, the rest houses must have seemed quaint and out of place. As true living memorials to the pilgrims, the rest houses fulfilled their commemorative purpose only when inhabited with the bodies of the pilgrims. Built specifically to be used by women as they memorialized their loved ones, these vernacular rest houses embodied the concept of veteranism at a site dominated by traditional memorials. Located on the same memorial landscape as the ABMC sites, the rest houses demonstrated how different forms of memorialization coexisted during the interwar period as commemorative practices underwent an incomplete transformation that partially embraced modernist ideas but never fully rejected traditional statuary commemoration.

As a type of veteranist memorial project created by the government, the Gold Star pilgrimages lacked any permanent memorial structure and thus demonstrated the tenets of more modernist iterations of veteranism as promulgated by female veteranists themselves, such as the WOSL. Instead of erecting a memorial to the Gold Star women, the government heeded their request and created a living memorial to them in the form of the trips. While some veteranist women disagreed with the government funding such costly trips during the Great Depression, most supported them and understood them as a useful type of commemoration that helped the Gold Star women.[106] The fervent support of the AWM and the laudatory remarks of WOSL member Eleanor Barnes attest to the general support of the female veteranist community for the pilgrimages and their belief in the program's veteranist nature.

The demolition of the rest houses after the pilgrimages erased the visible evidence of women's commemorative roles at the cemeteries during the Gold Star program and destroyed the closest thing to a physical memorial to the Gold Star women constructed as part of the pilgrimage program. The government never intended for women to become a permanent part of the cemetery narratives. Although the rest houses were built to serve and commemorate women, their destruction showed that women's roles in official military commemorations often remained limited and momentary. Furthermore, the paradox of veteranism meant that even when the military did include women, much of their involvement occurred through intangible projects formed from people's actions instead of marble. Though effective at the time, these veteranist memorials by nature could not survive to teach future generations about women's profound impact on and involvement with military memorialization, especially at the ABMC cemeteries.

CONCLUSION

The Gold Star pilgrimages demonstrated three crucial points about American women's participation in the commemoration of World War One. First, despite being prohibited from serving in most branches of the armed forces, women influenced the military in terms of policy making and commemoration both during and after the war, and they often occupied an intermediate position between civilians and veterans. Second, the physical evidence of women's influential roles in the postwar commemorative culture, such as the rest houses, is often absent from the commemorative landscape today. And third, some of the most important evidence of women's roles in military commemoration was intangible from the start. Conceived of as a living memorial program to serve the Gold Star pilgrims, the pilgrimages never fully constituted a brick-and-mortar memorial able to stand in perpetuity and attest to women's importance in the commemorative discourse. As a type of veteranism implemented by the government, the Gold Star pilgrimages existed only for a certain moment in time through the lived experiences of the pilgrims. The memory of these women's influence diminished with the removal of the rest houses and the deaths of the pilgrims.

Conclusion

Beyond the Great War

AS THE YEARS passed after World War One, female veteranists did not go quietly into the night. Rather, the Second World War remobilized these women activists as they supported the nation and the military on both the home front and the war front. While this book has focused mainly on their activities during the interwar period, their story cannot be concluded without acknowledging the profound impact of their contributions during World War Two. Although the new conflict partially overshadowed their own wartime legacy, the fruits of their activism and leadership during World War Two produced some of their biggest policy victories at the national level: the creation of the Women's Army Corps (WAC) and the GI Bill. For decades, their role in these successes remained understudied, especially because the younger generations benefited from them much more than most of the World War One women.

When the United States went to war again in 1941, female veteranists dedicated themselves to supporting the war effort. Of course, during the intervening years of peace, they had never abandoned serving their country. With the start of the new war, they simply shifted their focus toward the victory effort, even while they remained committed to memorializing the First World War and helping its female and male veterans. As the previous chapters have shown, the female veteranists of World War One threw themselves into countless types of service projects to support the Second World War. They worked independently and as part of organizations such as the WOSL, the WWRAA, the AWM, the ARC, and other groups.

The scale of their contributions reached such an intensity that they even received recognition from President Truman in 1946 when he sent a message of praise to the twenty-fifth annual WOSL convention. He told them that "America is justly proud of the splendid work that was done overseas

"A short refresher course and she was ready for action again"

GEORGE PRICE

Figure C.1. This cartoon by George Price depicts a World War One "Donut Dolly" going back to work during World War Two. Women's Overseas Service League Collection, National WWI Museum and Memorial Archives, Kansas City, Missouri, USA.

by American women, both in World War I and World War II. Your patriotic determination 'to keep alive and to develop the spirit that prompted overseas service' is at once a challenge and an inspiration to your fellow Americans."[1] Although Truman wrote this message for the WOSL, it demonstrated the overall impact made by the larger female veteranist community during this period. Truman recognized that their commitment to supporting their nation continued throughout their lifetimes and inspired other Americans. Even though they did not always succeed in obtaining veteran status from the government or full recognition in the commemorative narrative of the Great War, female veteranists maintained their devotion to serving their nation.

A cartoon drawn by George Price and collected by the WOSL comically summed up the World War One women's commitment to supporting the new war effort (fig. C.1). It shows an old woman, presumably a former Salvation Army "Donut Dolly," in a battered World War One uniform coat serving doughnuts to a group of eager young servicemen as two bewildered young servicewomen watch them. The caption reads "A short refresher course and she was ready for action again."[2] Though humorous, the cartoon made a significant point: it demonstrated the dedication of the World War One women to national service even when the general public seemed to forget about their past contributions, including the confused young women in the cartoon, for whom they paved the way.

PASSING THE TORCH: UNRECOGNIZED FEMALE VETERANS AND THE CREATION OF THE WOMEN'S ARMY CORPS

During World War Two, the female veteranists of World War One also reached out to the next generation of women who supported the armed forces and continued their campaign to obtain veteran status for them. The female veteranist community viewed these women as continuing their legacy. They hoped they would not become unrecognized veterans like many of their own cohort. Their wartime experiences and postwar struggles provided them with critical insights about how to improve women's relationship with the military. As they reflected on their own past, they tried to create conditions and policies for women during World War Two that gave them the benefits denied to many women during the First World War.

WOSL member Representative Edith Nourse Rogers made the plight of servicewomen in World War Two one of her personal missions and tried to prevent another generation of women from being denied veteran status.[3] To do so, she introduced the Women's Army Auxiliary Corps (WAAC) Act in Congress on May 28, 1941, before the US entered World War Two.[4] In a later congressional hearing about the act in January 1942, after the start of the war, Rogers cited her service in World War One and that of other women like her in the US and England as her inspiration for the bill. She justified the creation of the WAAC by explaining that many women wanted to serve their country but, she said, "could not serve without compensation, no matter how much they wanted to give their services." She specifically noted that during the last war, "there were women in our own services, the dietitians, the telegraph operators, physiotherapists . . . who served with our armed forces in the hospitals, and sometimes nearer the front, who when injured or ill could not receive any compensation," for they lacked official military rank or veteran status.[5] She hoped to rectify these problems with her bill. In defending the need for the WAAC and her hope for women to gain veteran status, Rogers referred to the WOSL's work and its endorsement of the bill. She told the Senate Committee on Military Affairs: "I have seen women who have been overseas, who have been injured over there, and they are not allowed even hospitalization by the Government. It is very tragic."[6] On another occasion in the House of Representatives in March 1942, she spoke to her colleagues about the travails of the unrecognized women veterans of World War One and explained that "the knowledge of these heart-breaking cases, the bitterness which some of these loyal, patriotic women felt, was one of the prime factors in my plan for a Women's Army Auxiliary Corps."[7] However, Rogers also noted that while she had originally "wanted very much to have these women taken in as a part of the Army, just as are the nurses," she had been "nursing this measure along through the years, as you see, and realized that I could not secure that."[8] This meant that while the WAAC would provide more benefits and security for women in the army, it would not achieve Rogers's original goal to make them fully part of the army and thus full veterans.

Helen Douglas Mankin, another WOSL member who held public office as a member of the Georgia legislature, testified to the House Committee on Military Affairs in May 1942 about the WAAC and the original plan to make it part of the army.[9] She argued for including women in a Women's Army Corps rather than an auxiliary and explained why women needed veterans' benefits.[10] Like Rogers, she recounted the interwar struggles of the women who served in World War One without veteran status and shared how the WOSL had helped them. She told them that "I made up my mind at that time that, if we ever had another world war, I would do everything I could so that that would not happen again." Through her testimony, she explained that without fully allowing a woman into the army, the government would be "making her part military and part civilian" and explained the risks that entailed. However, like Rogers, she seemed to understand she might not win this fight, and given the circumstances of the war, she conceded that "as for the Women's Overseas Service League, we would rather have this bill with the word 'auxiliary,' than to have no bill at all."[11]

Despite the efforts of Rogers, Mankin, and the WOSL, Congress did not make the WAAC part of the army, nor did it grant women in the WAAC military status on an equal basis to men or provide them with veteran status. Although Rogers wanted the WAAC Act to give veteran status to women, she encountered resistance from some male members of Congress who initially prevented her from succeeding.[12] For example, Congressman Clare Eugene Hoffman (R-MI) opposed the very idea of women working with the military, and in a long tirade, he argued that the WAAC would actually hurt the war effort. He believed that if the nation took women into the military, "who then will maintain the home fires; who will do the cooking, the washing, the mending, the humble, homey tasks to which every woman has devoted herself . . . to me this bill seems to strike at and destroy the very foundation—the base— which supports and maintains the fighting men."[13] The WOSL remained undeterred by comments such as Hoffman's, and the *New York Times* reported that it vocally protested the WAAC's auxiliary status and continued to lobby for "protection and privileges for the Women's Auxiliary Army Corps to equal those extended to men in armed services." WOSL president Mrs. Herman Bakker explained that they adopted a resolution to specifically seek "war risk insurance, bonuses, hospitalization and monthly wages equal to those of the soldiers." Bakker said that copies "had been forwarded to Secretary Stimson and General Marshall."[14] Having spent so long fighting for their own benefits without much progress, WOSL members refused to accept that the new servicewomen would suffer the same fate.

Nevertheless, the WAAC Act did open up more opportunities for women's military service when it finally became law on May 14, 1942.[15] Rogers had also been speaking to leaders in the navy, and soon after the passage of the WAAC Act, Public Law 689 created the Women's Naval Reserve, known as the WAVES (Women Accepted for Volunteer Emergency Service) on July 30, 1942.[16] During World War Two, women also gained opportunities to serve in the Marine Corps as part of its women's reserve and in the women's reserve of the Coast Guard, called the SPARs.[17] Yet other women, such as the Women Airforce Service Pilots, known as the WASPs, served as civilian pilots and later endured struggles similar to those of the World War One women as unrecognized veterans.[18]

Rogers remained unyielding in her efforts and true to her veteranist beliefs, and even after the creation of the WAAC she continued to argue that women in the army should hold official military rank and receive veterans' benefits. In 1943, she introduced the Women's Army Corps (WAC) Act into Congress.[19] This act created a Women's Army Corps as part of the regular army instead of as an auxiliary like the WAAC, just as Helen Douglas Mankin had described in her 1942 congressional testimony.[20] The passage of the WAC Act finally granted women military rank in the army, and veteran status. Rogers directly cited her service in the Great War and her community of unrecognized women veterans as the inspiration for the creation of both the WAAC and the WAC. In a December 1945 interview with Mattie A. Treadwell, a historian and veteran of the WAAC and WAC who later wrote the official US Army history of the WAC, Rogers explained her motives.[21] "My motives?" she asked. "In the first World War, I was there and *saw*. I saw the women in France, and how they had no suitable quarters and no Army discipline. Many dieticians and physiotherapists who served then are still sick in the hospital, and I was never able to get any veterans' compensation for them, although I secured passage of one bill aiding telephone operators. I was resolved that our women would not again serve with the Army without the protection men got."[22] After years of struggle, Rogers finally enabled many opportunities for women's military service and veterans' benefits that female veteranists had been fighting to obtain for two decades. She and her compatriots opened the door for more American women to officially serve in the armed forces during and after World War Two, although most of her cohort continued to lack such benefits for themselves.

After the creation of the WAAC and the WAC, female veteranists from

World War One also supported the women who joined the military. The Treasury Unit of the District Red Cross in Washington, DC, donated a fully furnished recreation room to the WAAC Operations Committee at Bolling Field, and Mabel Boardman attended the opening.[23] Another prominent veteranist leader, WOSL president Mrs. Herman Bakker, spoke at the graduation ceremony for the third group of women commissioned as WAAC officers on September 26, 1942, at Fort Des Moines, Iowa. She told the new officers that they fulfilled "a reality that we had foreseen as a need thru these intervening 22 years—a highly trained, effective unit ready to give full service to their country." She drew on her experiences as a Red Cross nurse in France to inspire them. She told them that "we were an untrained group of volunteers. You in turn serve your country, but fully equipped to give the best in service, to help win this war and maintain the peace that follows."[24]

Some eligible World War One women even joined the WAC. Nada Elerie, a WOSL member who served in France with the Red Cross during World War One, joined the WAC in 1944 after some of the age limitations were relaxed. She urged other women to join and told them that there was "such a definite need for them to do important jobs."[25] Emma Vogel, however, never left her position as an army physical therapist after her appointment in 1919. She was active in the WWRAA, and when active-duty army physical therapists finally gained military status in 1943, she became the first military director of physical therapy aides and received a commission as a major. She eventually served as the first chief of the Women's Medical Specialist Corps and was promoted to colonel in 1947.[26] During World War Two, she represented the World War One women from within the ranks of the army and helped connect them to the current war effort.

Yet even after Edith Nourse Rogers secured these victories for the World War Two servicewomen, the unrecognized female veterans of World War One continued to fight for the acknowledgment and benefits they believed they deserved. Most famously, the telephone operators who served with the Army Signal Corps in France, informally called the Hello Girls, pursued a prolonged battle to obtain veterans' benefits.[27] Led by former telephone operator Merle Egan Anderson and assisted by volunteer attorney Mark Hough, the Hello Girls finally achieved veteran status in 1979.[28] By that time, most of those still alive were in their eighties or nineties; many had passed away and did not live to see their work officially recognized as military service. Likewise, the former Reconstruction Aides did not receive any government recognition that their wartime experiences constituted a type of active military service until 1981, when most were elderly and many already deceased. This small victory came about after the GI Bill Improvement Act of 1977 provided for the Department of Defense to determine whether certain groups of civilians or contractors could be considered for active service regarding some benefits from the Veterans Administration (VA).[29] The task of investigating additional groups fell to the secretary of the air force, who determined in 1981 that "the service of the members of the group known as the Reconstruction Aides and Dietitians in World War I, be considered active military service in the Armed Forces of the United States for all laws administered by the Veterans' Administration."[30] This gave any Reconstruction Aides and dietitians who remained alive access to certain VA benefits but not did not grant them full veteran status.[31] While this determination certainly provided some satisfaction to the few remaining Reconstruction Aides and proved the strength of their argument all along, it occurred too late for most of these women to benefit from it, and it still did not retroactively fully define either group as members of the military.

FEMALE VETERANIST LEADERS
AND THE DEVELOPMENT OF THE GI BILL

Perhaps the most significant legacy of the female veteranists of World War One, and their biggest impact on World War Two veterans, occurred even before the end of the war. It came in the form of the Servicemen's Readjustment Act of 1944, commonly known as the GI Bill. As the ranking minority member of the House of Representatives' World War Veterans Legislation Committee, WOSL member Representative Edith Nourse Rogers played a key role in sponsoring the GI Bill. Male World War One veterans joined her, including Representative John Rankin (D-MS), chair of the World War Veterans Legislation Committee, and Senator J. Bennett "Champ" Clark (D-MO), chair of the Senate Finance Committee's Subcommittee on World War Veterans Legislation and a founder of the American Legion.[32]

Although Rogers's role in creating the GI Bill and her own First World War service remain somewhat underemphasized in many discussions of the GI Bill, her status as a nationally prominent veteranist deeply impacted her involvement with this legislation.[33] After her World War One service as a nurse in France and England with the YMCA and the Red Cross, Rogers worked at the army's Walter Reed General Hospital with the Red Cross for several years. In 1922, President Harding appointed her as his personal representative to supervise the care given to disabled veterans. She maintained this position through reappointments from President Coolidge and President Hoover, even after her election to the House of Representatives in 1925 when she won her late husband's seat.[34] As a member of Congress, she made veterans' issues one of her key priorities, and she became known as an unfaltering advocate for veterans and their families. She worked so hard on veterans' issues that many service members recognized her as their champion and wrote to express their thanks. In 1947, for example, one such veteran named Captain Joseph Piggott wrote to tell her that "its about time we send a Women to the White House as President. Yes I mean you. I am sure that every Veterans for 98–1917–1941 will go out for you. Your splendid Record in Congress and your work for Veterans can not be Beaten by any other Member of Congress."[35] Piggott saw Rogers as a champion for all living veterans and did not think her gender precluded her from leadership on veterans' issues or even the presidency. Indeed, viewed within the long tradition of women's support for veterans, it seems to have bolstered her role.

Because Rogers was a publicly recognized female veteranist, her leadership in the development of the GI Bill indicates that this legislation can be considered a form of memorialization in line with the veteranist commemoration projects pioneered by her community of women veteranists. The GI Bill provided unprecedented benefits to male and female veterans of the Second World War, although in practice it did not always apply equally to women, African Americans, and other minorities.[36] Overall, the GI Bill aimed to create an effective and fair system to assist veterans as they reintegrated into society. Among other things, it provided veterans with hospitalization and rehabilitation benefits; educational benefits; loans to purchase homes, farms, and businesses; job counseling and help finding employment; and readjustment allowances for unemployed veterans.[37] Intimately involved with its development, Representative Rogers watched as President Roosevelt signed the bill into law on June 22, 1944, and formed a central figure in a photograph of that event (fig. C.2).

Conceived of by World War One veterans, this legislation tried to prevent the government from repeating its often disastrous interactions with World War One veterans during the interwar years. The GI Bill can be considered a direct result of World War One and the struggles of its veterans.[38] Having learned from their own experiences, the men and women of the World War One generation chose to memorialize the new generation of veterans through legislation that required the government to take responsibility for their welfare.

The passage of this bill suggests that female veteranists and their allies, often male veterans, had fueled a moderate distaste for statuary memorials that increased during and after the Second World War. As more Americans turned away from traditional monuments and toward living memorials in the wake of the Holocaust, the atomic bomb, and new urban development, their veteranist ideology gained a renewed appeal.[39] Perhaps the GI Bill can be understood as the first national memorial to the Second World War and can explain why it took until 2004 to erect the National World War II Memorial in Washington, DC. Many World War Two veterans may have been so focused

Figure C.2. FDR signing the GI Bill in the Oval Office, June 22, 1944, with (left to right) Bennett "Champ" Clark, J. Hardin Peterson, John Rankin, Paul Cunningham, Edith N. Rogers, J. M. Sullivan, Walter George, John Stelle, Robert Wagner, unknown, and Alben Barkley. Note that Rogers is the only woman in this image. Courtesy of the Franklin D. Roosevelt Presidential Library and Museum.

on rebuilding their lives using the benefits from the GI Bill that they did not pay attention to the lack of a memorial in their honor until their later years.[40] The GI Bill publicly sanctioned female veteranists' belief that Americans who return from war require government support that should take precedence over the creation of statuary memorials. The bill provided veterans with some of the services that female veteranists deemed essential to their welfare during the interwar period and often lacked themselves, such as hospitalization and rehabilitation benefits. When the government failed to provide these benefits to veterans in the past, especially to women, female veteranists took it upon themselves to deliver these services. It is no coincidence that a well-known WOSL member like Edith Nourse Rogers spearheaded the GI Bill. This legislation adhered to the WOSL's veteranist ideology and justified the activities it had pursued since its inception. Influenced by her participation in the WOSL, Rogers achieved the nationalization of the veteranist ideology pioneered by the WOSL and other female veteranists through the passage of the GI Bill, although its veteranist origins remained mostly out of sight.

By passing the GI Bill, Congress publicly declared that the government would try to prevent another generation of forgotten American veterans. Although female veteranists did not achieve a clear victory over statuary memorials amid the complicated commemorative culture, the 1944 GI Bill, helmed by a WOSL member, demonstrated that they exerted a strong influence on American society, politics, and culture. The voices of these female activists continue to resonate today through later iterations of the GI Bill that have helped subsequent generations of American veterans. These bills have identified veterans as a special class of citizens who earned specific rights and benefits because of their military service.[41] The GI Bill benefits represent a gift from the lost generation to the greatest generation, which continues to impact American veterans even so many decades after the First and Second World Wars.

THE COMMEMORATION OF FEMALE VETERANISTS AFTER WORLD WAR TWO

After World War Two, the World War One women persisted in their effort to include their contributions in historical and commemorative narratives, even when they faced setbacks in their fight for veteran status. They achieved two notable victories, one in Kansas City, Missouri, and the other at the entrance to Arlington National Cemetery. During the 1956 WOSL national convention held in Kansas City, Missouri, the Liberty Memorial (now known as the National WWI Museum and Memorial) dedicated a three-part mural by artist Daniel MacMorris.[42] This mural decorates the south wall of Memory Hall, a structure at the memorial intended as a meeting room for patriotic organizations. Memory Hall also contains memorial plaques that honor men and women from Kansas City who died in World War One.[43]

Titled *Women in War*, this triptych mural depicts the various ways that American women supported World War One. Although it focuses on just that conflict, MacMorris intended it to be universal in its depictions of women's war work; he wanted it to also be applicable to women's World War Two service.[44] The largest section of the mural in the center includes the caption "Steadfast beside us women of World War I, God's gentle angels who bound our wounds and healed our troubled spirits."[45] In the middle of this painting, near the top, MacMorris depicted the "Angel of Mercy," a veiled woman with massive golden wings whose outstretched arms hold a lit torch and a caduceus, the symbol of medicine. Her pose alludes to St. Mary as she looks down on a group composed mostly of nurses and other women who tend to injured soldiers (fig. C.3).

The right portion of the mural honors Blue Star mothers whose children survived the war. Captioned "Hope like a Blue Star kept mother's faith alive," it depicts the return of service members to their mothers and families, as

Figure C.3. Center section of the *Women in War* mural by Daniel MacMorris, located inside Memory Hall at the National WWI Museum and Memorial. Image courtesy of the National WWI Museum and Memorial, Kansas City, Missouri, USA.

an angel watches from above (fig. C.4). The left portion of the mural honors Gold Star mothers with the caption "Blood and mother's tears given for a star of gold." It shows a grieving Gold Star mother being comforted by a priest as an angel hovers in the background above a large headstone and the figure of death. Although Gold Star widows are not mentioned in the caption, the painting includes a younger woman with her two children who may represent them (fig. C.5).

During the dedication ceremony for the mural, WOSL women marched in their wartime uniforms, a visual reminder of their service. The procession also included female World War Two veterans, an honor guard from the Marine Corps Reserve, and First World War Medal of Honor recipients John Barkley and M. Waldo Hatler. In his speech at the ceremony, Kansas City mayor William E. Kemp professed that "the hall would not be complete . . . without something to call to mind through the years to come the part that women played in the great wars to preserve freedom in the world."[46] Thirty-eight years after the Armistice, women finally gained a permanent place in one of the most prominent stateside memorials to American participation in the First World War. Though certainly a more traditional type of commemo-

Figure C.4. "Blue Star Mothers," the right section of the *Women in War* mural by Daniel MacMorris. Image courtesy of the National WWI Museum and Memorial, Kansas City, Missouri, USA.

Figure C.5. "Gold Star Mothers," the left section of the *Women in War* mural by Daniel MacMorris. Image courtesy of the National WWI Museum and Memorial, Kansas City, Missouri, USA.

rative object located within a memorial building, this mural operates as an educational tool that fits it within the broad parameters of veteranist commemorations. It also serves as another reminder that veteranists did not completely discard traditional memorialization trends in favor of more modern ones, but experimented with and supported both.

At the entrance to Arlington National Cemetery on October 20, 1997, another memorial opened that paid tribute to America's World War One women as part of its larger mission. The Women In Military Service For America Memorial (WIMSA) "recognizes all women who have served in or with the United States Armed Forces—past present and future." Created by the nonprofit Women In Military Service For America Memorial Foundation, Inc., WIMSA functions as a living memorial and includes exhibits and spaces for ceremonies; an archive and artifact collection are located off-site. To support the utilitarian aspect of its mission, and in line with the ideals of veteranism, the foundation collects, preserves, documents, and interprets the history of America's military women, including those who served outside the official armed forces.[47]

At the memorial's 1997 dedication ceremony, Frieda Hardin, a veteran of the navy Yeoman (F), wore her World War One uniform as she delivered one of the keynote speeches.[48] She told the audience that in her 101 years of life, she had "observed many wonderful achievements—but none as important or as meaningful to the progress of women in taking their rightful place in society." She proclaimed that "for my part, I have always been very proud of my Navy service."[49] Hardin even invoked "carry on," the unofficial mantra of female veteranists, when she exclaimed, "To those women now in military service, I say, 'Carry on.' To those women who may be thinking about a career in the military service, I say, 'Go for it.'"[50] Alongside several generations of military women, Hardin inscribed her service and the service of her World War One sisters into the landscape of military memory at Arlington National Cemetery (fig. C.6).

Although many female veteranists objected to erecting traditional statuary monuments in their honor and preferred community service and veterans' advocacy, their inclusion in the hybrid living memorials at the National WWI Museum and Memorial and the Women In Military Service For America Memorial proved critical for the long-term preservation of their memory. Today, both organizations, among several others, preserve records and artifacts that document the history of the female veteranist community. The impact of their pioneering contributions to World War One and their subsequent leadership in the commemorative culture that developed in its aftermath would be lost had these records not survived. Without specific prominent monuments in their honor clearly visible on the landscape, the scope of their national in-

Figure C.6. Former Yeoman (F) Third Class Frieda Hardin (center) waves to the crowd after her speech at the dedication ceremony for the Women In Military Service For America Memorial on October 18, 1997, at Arlington National Cemetery, Virginia. Her son, Captain Jerald Kirsten, USNR (Ret.), stands on her left and Brigadier General Wilma L. Vaught, USAF (Ret.), the president of the Women In Military Service For America Memorial Foundation, stands on her right. Image courtesy of the Military Women's Memorial Collection.

fluence remains somewhat diminished. Their archival records enable their multifaceted, avant-garde approach to commemoration to be exposed and understood. Most importantly, such items demonstrate how these female activists' commemorative work led them to an even more critical mission that impacted the US military and veterans' policy for years to come: their unceasing advocacy on behalf of unrecognized female veterans and their refusal to accept that women could not serve equally in the armed forces.

The eclectic group of American women who believed that they served and sacrificed in World War One developed and pursued veteranism as a way to help male and female veterans, their local communities, and their nation. They believed that their wartime services and sacrifices endowed them with a duty to carry on their wartime work. As a result, they defined community service and advocacy as forms of commemoration. They sometimes preferred these more modernist methods to traditional commemorations such as stone statues and monuments. While all female veteranists did not completely reject traditional statuary memorials, they often saw veteranist commemorations as more useful and they frequently combined them with statuary memorials as they experimented with hybrid memorial projects.

Although these women did not secure a decisive victory for veteranism over statuary memorials, they impacted and shifted the commemorative discourse of the interwar period. They suggested that stone monuments should not always be the de facto way to memorialize wars. By proposing action-based alternatives to physical monuments, they crafted a cultural legacy that persists today, even though it remains mostly overlooked and forgotten.

By continuing their wartime service through commemorative service activities, female veteranists reminded the nation that they too contributed to the war effort and asserted that they should be considered veterans. They argued that they fulfilled the duties of martial citizenship even before they could all vote, equally enter the military, or be eligible for veteran status. Through their commemorative projects and their campaign to include their stories in the historical record, they pushed for women to gain the full rights of citizenship beyond the vote, especially in terms of military service and benefits. Even when they failed, they hoped that the next generation of women would have more-equal opportunities to contribute to national defense and would officially be considered veterans.

Because women's veteranist commemorations often took the form of acts of service, much of the evidence of women's intensive memorialization of the Great War was intangible and ephemeral from the start. Most of this evidence no longer exists on the landscape and often remains absent from the history of American commemorative culture in the interwar period. By uncovering the history of women's veteranist ideology, this book has restored the legacy of these women's innovative contributions to commemoration and veterans' advocacy.

Although the ephemeral nature of female veteranists' activities diminished their visible impact on the commemorative landscape, their pioneering memorialization methods and their fight for recognition still exert a strong, though often invisible impact on the US. Through their decades of struggle and their unceasing hope for a better future, their activism created change. In the longer trajectory of American women's military service, the activities and ideology of the female veteranists of World War One served as a stepping-stone that opened up better military opportunities for future generations of women. Their leadership guided the creation of important legislation that expanded veterans' benefits for both men and women and created a legacy that continues today. Despite the challenges they faced, these pioneering women remained determined to try to prevent the repetition of their hard-learned lessons. They maintained their commitment to commemoration through service, and their veteranist ideology became embedded into American culture, even if its connection to the unrecognized women veterans of the Great War stayed in the shadows.

Notes

Abbreviations Used in Notes
ARC Archives—American Red Cross Archives, National Headquarters, Washington, DC
LOC—Library of Congress, Washington, DC
MWMC—Military Women's Memorial Collection, Women In Military Service For America Memorial Foundation, Inc., Arlington, VA
NAB—National Archives Building, Washington, DC
NACP—National Archives II, College Park, MD
NHHC—Naval History and Heritage Command, Archives Branch, Washington, DC
NMAH—National Museum of American History—Washington, DC
NMHM—National Museum of Health and Medicine—Silver Spring, MD
UTSA—University of Texas at San Antonio Libraries Special Collections

Introduction

1. *Carry On* 3, no. 2 (May 1924): 12, box 1922–1932, folder 1924, Women's Overseas Service League *Carry On* Periodical Collection, Gift of Carolyn Habgood, Military Women's Memorial Collection, hereafter abbreviated MWMC; *Carry On* 4, no. 1 (February 1927): 42, box 1922–1932, folder 1927, Women's Overseas Service League *Carry On* Periodical Collection, Gift of Carolyn Habgood, MWMC; *Carry On* 15, no. 1 (February 1936): 7, box 1933–1939, folder 1936, Women's Overseas Service League *Carry On* Periodical Collection, Gift of Carolyn Habgood, MWMC.

2. Andrew M. Shanken, "Planning Memory: Living Memorials in the United States during World War II," *Art Bulletin* 84, no. 1 (March 2002): 130–47; Kristin L. Britanik, "Where Are the Ladies' Rest Rooms?: The Evolution of Women-Only Resting Rooms amid Social Changes of the Early Twentieth-Century" (master's thesis, University of Maryland, College Park, 2012), 69.

3. For more on the history of the WAAC and WAC, see Mattie E. Treadwell, *United States Army in World War II, Special Studies: The Women's Army Corps* (Washington, DC: Center of Military History, 1995).

4. This argument contrasts with Francesca Morgan's contention that many women's patriotic groups, especially those active before World War One, reinforced women's exclusion from military service and supported "men-centered nationalism" even as they

championed women's political activism. However, during World War One, as Morgan notes, some of these groups did begin to support measures that gave women political standing. Francesca Morgan, *Women and Patriotism in Jim Crow America* (Chapel Hill: University of North Carolina Press, 2005), 4, 101, 105.

5. Christopher Capozzola, *Uncle Sam Wants You: World War I and the Making of the Modern American Citizen* (New York: Oxford University Press, 2008), 92–93.

6. For more on republican motherhood, see Rebecca Jo Plant, *Mom: The Transformation of Motherhood in Modern America* (Chicago: University of Chicago Press, 2010), 56–58; Linda K. Kerber, *Women of the Republic: Intellect and Ideology in Revolutionary America* (Chapel Hill: University of North Carolina Press, 1980).

7. Because the Hello Girls did not form their own separate organization, they are not examined independently in this book. Rather, their story is told as part of the story of the WOSL and the larger community of female veteranists. Additionally, the saga of the telephone operators' fight for veteran status has already been well explored in great detail by Elizabeth Cobbs in *The Hello Girls: America's First Women Soldiers* (Cambridge, MA: Harvard University Press, 2017). For more on the Hello Girls, see also Jill Frahm, "The Hello Girls: Women Telephone Operators with the American Expeditionary Forces during World War I," *Journal of the Gilded Age and Progressive Era* 3, no. 3 (July 2004): 272–93; Jill Frahm, "Advance to the 'Fighting Lines': The Changing Role of Women Telephone Operators in France during the First World War," *Federal History* 8 (2016): 95–108.

8. William Pencak, *For God & Country: The American Legion, 1919–1941* (Boston: Northeastern University Press, 1989), 296–301; Mrs. Jos. H. Thompson, *History: National American Legion Auxiliary* (Pittsburgh, PA: Jackson-Remlinger Printing, 1926), 1:34, 36–41; Frank Ernest Hill, *The American Legion Auxiliary, A History: 1924–1934* (Indianapolis: American Legion Auxiliary, 1935), 5–8.

9. Pencak, *For God & Country*, 297.

10. "Membership Application Form," Veterans of Foreign Wars Auxiliary, 2011, https://vfwauxiliary.org; Herbert Molloy Mason Jr., *VFW: Our First Century* (Lenexa, KS: Addax, 1999), 23, 149, 170–73. Women who served overseas while officially in military service were allowed to join the VFW after WWI, but membership was barred to them starting in 1944 and did not reopen until 1978.

11. Pencak, *For God & Country*, 298.

12. Janie Blankenship, ed., *VFW Magazine: Women at War, from the Revolutionary War to the Present*, special publication, July 2011, 57, 59; "History of Post 50 American Legion 1919–1951," Rita R. McDonald Collection (WWI–WWII, Yeoman (F)), document collection #1216, MWMC; George W. Orton, "On Your Mark, Legion, Get Set, Go!," *American Legion Weekly* 4, no. 20 (May 19, 1922): 8, https://hdl.handle.net; Jessica L. Adler, *Burdens of War: Creating the United States Veterans Health System* (Baltimore: Johns Hopkins University Press, 2017), 204–5.

13. Information about the National Yeoman (F) organization was found at the Naval History and Heritage Command, Archives Branch (NNHC), and the National Museum of American History (NMAH). Collections used at the NHHC included the Papers of Helen G. O'Neill (collection 236) and Papers of Eunice C. Dessez (collection 226); and at the NMAH, the Yeoman (F) Archive Files in the Armed Forces History Division.

14. Susan Zeiger, *In Uncle Sam's Service: Women Workers with the American Expeditionary Force, 1917–1919* (Ithaca, NY: Cornell University Press, 1999), 3.

15. See, for example, Robyn Muncy, *Creating a Female Dominion in American Reform, 1890–1935* (New York: Oxford University Press, 1991).

16. Zeiger provides a detailed explanation of these different meanings of women's World War One service. *In Uncle Sam's Service*, 51, 69,141.

17. Capozzola, *Uncle Sam Wants You*, 6–20, 83–116.

18. For more about the professionalization of women's wartime service, specifically in the field of rehabilitation, now called physical therapy and occupational therapy, see Beth Linker, *War's Waste: Rehabilitation in World War I America* (Chicago: University of Chicago Press, 2011); Adler, *Burdens of War*.

19. While many female veteranists had connections to the suffrage movement, their number did include a few women opposed to suffrage. For example, Alice H. Chittenden, a vocal antisuffragist, was a member of the WOSL. "Alice Chittenden of Red Cross Dead," *New York Times*, October 3, 1945, 19; Susan Goodier, "Anti-Suffragists as Politicians," *New York Archives* 7, no. 2 (Fall 2007), https://www.nysarchivestrust.org.

20. For example, the Women's Relief Corps helped needy Union veterans. Morgan, *Women and Patriotism*, 12. Likewise, Patrick J. Kelly described women's extensive philanthropic and volunteer work helping returning Union soldiers after the Civil War. Patrick J. Kelly, *Creating a National Home: Building the Veteran's Welfare State, 1860–1900* (Cambridge, MA: Harvard University Press, 1997).

21. Lena Hitchcock, "The Great Adventure," box 240, WOSL Records, MS 22, UTSA; Lena Hitchcock, oral history (03), July 14, 1982, recorded by the WOSL, UC–MS022/7, box 182, WOSL Records, MS 22, UTSA; Jessi Ash Arndt, "Family Home of Mrs. Speel Historic Spot," *Washington Post*, July 27, 1937, 13, ProQuest Historical Newspapers; "Mrs. Virginia W. Speel: Republican Committeewoman for Many Years Dies in Capital," *New York Times*, April 14, 1945, 15, ProQuest Historical Newspapers; "Suffragists at Work Here: Congressional Union Selects Committees in All Police Precincts," *Washington Post*, September 3, 1916, A5, ProQuest Historical Newspapers; Nancy F. Cott, *The Grounding of Modern Feminism* (New Haven, CT: Yale University Press, 1987), 53–81.

22. Zeiger, *In Uncle Sam's Service*, 2; Sharon A. Gutman, "Influence of the U.S. Military and Occupational Therapy Reconstruction Aides in World War I on the Development of Occupational Therapy," *American Journal of Occupational Therapy* 49, no. 3 (March 1995): 258; Frahm, "Hello Girls," 275–77.

23. "WWI 'Hello Girl' Merle Egan Anderson Is Dead," *Seattle Post-Intelligencer*, June 3, 1986, D2; Sally Gene Mahoney, "1918 Operator Still Seeks Justice after 50 Years," *Seattle Times*, July 20, 1975, H6; news clippings of Signal Corps telephone operator Merle Egan Anderson, WOSL Seattle Unit, no box, WOSL Collection, National WWI Museum and Memorial Archives. For more on Anderson, the Hello Girls, and their fight for veteran status, see Cobbs, *Hello Girls*, 272–303.

24. Zeiger, *In Uncle Sam's Service*, 27–32. For more about African American women's wartime service, see Nancy Marie Robertson, *Christian Sisterhood, Race Relations, and the YWCA, 1906–46* (Urbana: University of Illinois Press, 2007); Adele Logan Alexander, introduction to *Two Colored Women with the American Expeditionary Forces*, by Addie

W. Hunton and Kathryn M. Johnson (New York: G. K. Hall, 1997); Addie W. Hunton and Kathryn M. Johnson, *Two Colored Women with the American Expeditionary Forces* (Brooklyn, New York: Brooklyn Eagle Press, n.d., ca. 1920), https://archive.org; Mark Whalan, *The Great War and the Culture of the New Negro* (Gainesville: University Press of Florida, 2008); Morgan, *Women and Patriotism*. For more on the history of African American female nurses, see Darlene Clark Hine, *Black Women in White: Racial Conflict and Cooperation in the Nursing Profession, 1890–1950* (Bloomington: Indiana University Press, 1989).

25. Zeiger, *In Uncle Sam's Service*, 27–28.

26. Morgan, *Women and Patriotism*, 120; Zeiger, *In Uncle Sam's Service*, 28; Alexander, introduction, xviii; Lisa Budreau, "War Service by African American Women at Home and Abroad," in *We Return Fighting: World War I and the Shaping of Modern Black Identity*, ed. Kinshasha Holman Conwill (Washington, DC: Smithsonian Books, 2019), 62; Regina T. Akers, *The Navy's First Enlisted Women: Patriotic Pioneers* (Washington, DC: Naval History and Heritage Command, 2019), 43–44; Richard E. Miller, "The Golden Fourteen, Plus: Black Navy Women in World War One," *Minerva* 13, no. 3 (December 31, 1995).

27. Morgan, *Women and Patriotism*, 120; Zeiger, *In Uncle Sam's Service*, 28; Alexander, introduction, xviii.

28. Zeiger, *In Uncle Sam's Service*, 28; Hine, *Black Women in White*; Morgan, *Women and Patriotism*, 120–21; Alice Dunbar-Nelson, "Negro Women in War Work," in *Scott's Official History of the American Negro in the World War*, by Emmett J. Scott (Chicago: Homewood Press, 1919), 377–79, https://archive.org; Budreau, "War Service," 61–62; Marian Moser Jones and Matilda Saines, "The Eighteen of 1918–1919: Black Nurses and the Great Flu Pandemic in the United States," *American Journal of Public Health* 109, no. 6 (June 2019).

29. No African American women went overseas as part of the US military; they went only as part of auxiliary organizations. The first Black woman to go overseas during the war is believed to be Mrs. James L. Curtis, followed by Hunton and Johnson. Zeiger, *In Uncle Sam's Service*, 28; Alexander, introduction, xxi; Budreau, "War Service," 60–62; Lettie Gavin, *American Women in World War One: They Also Served* (Niwot: University Press of Colorado, 2006), 138–39; Hunton and Johnson, *Two Colored Women*, 136–37.

30. Dunbar-Nelson, "Negro Women in War Work," 378; Brittany Cooper, "Mary Church Terrell and Ida B. Wells," in *We Return Fighting: World War I and the Shaping of Modern Black Identity*, ed. Kinshasha Holman Conwill (Washington, DC: Smithsonian Books, 2019), 102.

31. Budreau, "War Service," 60; Hunton and Johnson, *Two Colored Women*, 136–37; Susan Chandler, "Addie Hunton and the Construction of an African American Female Peace Perspective," *Affilia* 20, no. 3 (Fall 2005): 270–83; Gavin, *American Women*, 138–41; Robertson, *Christian Sisterhood*; Joyce Blackwell, *No Peace without Freedom: Race and the Women's International League for Peace and Freedom, 1915–1975* (Carbondale: Southern Illinois University Press, 2004); Maria Quintana, "Addie Waites Hunton (1866–1943)," *Black Past*, January 7, 2010, https://www.blackpast.org.

32. Hunton and Johnson, *Two Colored Women*; Nikki Brown, *Private Politics and*

Public Voices: Black Women's Activism from World War I to the New Deal (Bloomington: Indiana University Press, 2006), 84–100.

33. Hunton and Johnson, *Two Colored Women*, 3.

34. Hunton and Johnson, 6.

35. Alexander, introduction, xxii–xxiii; Blackwell, *No Peace without Freedom*; Chandler, "Addie Hunton," 270–71, 275–81.

36. I have not yet been able to find evidence of Hunton or Johnson having been members of any of the female veteranist organizations discussed in this book, particularly the WOSL. Likewise, Hunton's papers do not seem to exist in a cohesive unit, making her postwar life elusive.

37. African American women with the YWCA staffed segregated hostess houses for the African American troops stationed in the US so these men could have a space to engage in moral, military-approved, and regulated socialization and visits with female family members and acquaintances. Capozzola, *Uncle Sam Wants You*, 93; Robertson, *Christian Sisterhood*, 52–54; Budreau, "War Service," 60–62; Dunbar-Nelson, "Negro Women in War Work," 379; Morgan, *Women and Patriotism*, 54–55; Allison S. Finkelstein, "Carry On: American Women and the Veteranist-Commemoration of the First World War, 1917–1945" (PhD diss., University of Maryland, College Park, 2015), 69, 224–26.

38. Dunbar-Nelson, "Negro Women in War Work," 376–77; Cooper, "Mary Church Terrell," 102. Lisa Budreau noted that many African American women served with the American Red Cross Motor Service in the US. "War Service," 62.

39. Zeiger, *In Uncle Sam's Service*, 27–28; Capozzola, *Uncle Sam Wants You*, 93–94; Dunbar-Nelson, "Negro Women in War Work," 387–90; Budreau, "War Service," 60–62; Mary-Elizabeth B. Murphy, *Jim Crow Capital: Women and Black Freedom Struggles in Washington, D.C., 1920–1945* (Chapel Hill: University of North Carolina Press, 2018), 6–7, 48–51; Morgan, *Women and Patriotism*, 117–26. Morgan analyzed the complicated nature of Black women's support of the war effort, particularly through women's clubs and the larger umbrella organization the National Association of Colored Women.

40. Emmett J. Scott, *Scott's Official History of the American Negro in the World War* (Chicago: Homewood Press, 1919), 355–64, 381–82, 391–92, https://archive.org; Cooper, "Mary Church Terrell," 105.

41. Dunbar-Nelson, "Negro Women in War Work," 382–97; Budreau, "War Service," 60–62.

42. As an example, the YWCA, the Women's Relief Corps, and the Women's Christian Temperance Union were all segregated. For more about gender, race, and Progressive women, see Noralee Frankel and Nancy S. Dye, eds., *Gender, Class, Race, and Reform in the Progressive Era* (Lexington: University Press of Kentucky, 1991); Morgan, *Women and Patriotism*, 118.

43. For more about the segregation of the Gold Star pilgrimages, see Lisa M. Budreau, *Bodies of War: World War I and the Politics of Commemoration in America, 1919–1933* (New York: New York University Press, 2010); Lisa M. Budreau, "Gold Star Mothers," in *We Return Fighting: World War I and the Shaping of Modern Black Identity*, ed. Kinshasha Holman Conwill (Washington, DC: Smithsonian Books, 2019), 67–69; Rebecca Jo Plant

and Frances M. Clarke, "'The Crowning Insult': Federal Segregation and the Gold Star Mother and Widow Pilgrimages of the Early 1930s," *Journal of American History* 102, no. 2 (September 2015): 406–32.

44. Allan Teichroew, "Mary Church Terrell Papers: A Finding Aid to the Collection at the Library of Congress," August 2018, https://hdl.loc.gov; Joan Quigley, *Just Another Southern Town: Mary Church Terrell and the Struggle for Racial Justice in the Nation's Capital* (New York: Oxford University Press, 2016), 84–86, 90; Murphy, *Jim Crow Capital*; Cooper, "Mary Church Terrell," 102–5; Lonnie G. Bunch III, "On the Horizon—toward Civil Rights," epilogue to *We Return Fighting: World War I and the Shaping of Modern Black Identity*, ed. Kinshasha Holman Conwill (Washington, DC: Smithsonian Books, 2019), 140; Delaware Historical & Cultural Affairs, "Patriotism Despite Segregation: African-American Participation during World War I," https://history.delaware .gov/african-americans-ww1/.

45. Dunbar-Nelson, "Negro Women in War Work," 386–87; Cooper, "Mary Church Terrell," 102–5. For an in-depth study of the racial issues in another wartime recreational organization similar to the War Camp Community Service, called the Commission on Training Camp Activities, see Nancy K. Bristow, *Making Men Moral: Social Engineering during the Great War* (New York: New York University Press, 1996), 36–41, 137–78.

46. The National Memorial Association, the sponsor of the National Negro Memorial Building in Washington, DC, succeeded in getting its joint resolution for the project passed by Congress and signed into law by President Calvin Coolidge in 1929. Coolidge appointed Terrell as a member of the planning commission, but the Great Depression hindered the fundraising effort and the building was never constructed. Today, the Smithsonian Institution's National Museum of African American History and Culture traces its lineage back to this earlier failed project, which would have included museum elements as part of its status as a living memorial building, putting it in line with veteranism. Kathleen M. Kendrick, *Official Guide to the Smithsonian National Museum of African American History & Culture* (Washington, DC: Smithsonian Books, 2017), 10–11; Lonnie G. Bunch III, *A Fool's Errand: Creating the National Museum of African American History and Culture in the Age of Bush, Obama, and Trump* (Washington, DC: Smithsonian Books, 2019), 5–6; Mabel O. Wilson, *Begin with the Past: Building the National Museum of African American History and Culture* (Washington, DC: Smithsonian Books, 2016), 23, 26–28; Plant and Clarke, "'Crowning Insult,'" 417–18; Lonnie G. Bunch III, "The Definitive Story of How the National Museum of African American History and Culture Came to Be," *Smithsonian*, September 2016, https://www .smithsonianmag.com; Murphy, *Jim Crow Capital*, 39–44; Teichroew, "Mary Church Terrell Papers"; "Design of the Proposed National Memorial Building to Commemorate the Heroic Deeds of Negro Soldiers and Sailors Who Fought in All the Wars of Our Country, and the World War," subject file, 1884–1962, National Memorial Association to Honor Negro Soldiers and Sailors, 1924, 1928, 1939, box 24, reel 18, Mary Church Terrell Papers, Manuscript Division, LOC, Washington, DC, http://hdl.loc.gov.

47. "Statement of Mrs. Mary Church Terrell, First President of National Association of Colored Women," 22–23, in "Hearings Before the Committee on Public Buildings and Grounds, House of Representatives, Seventieth Congress, First Session, on H.J. Res. 60

to Create a Commission to Secure Plans and Designs for and to Erect a Memorial Building for the National Memorial Association, Incorporated in the City of Washington, as a Tribute to the Negro's Contribution to the Achievements of America," February 1, 1928, subject file, 1884–1962, National Memorial Association to Honor Negro Soldiers and Sailors, 1924, 1928, 1939, box 24, reel 18, Mary Church Terrell Papers, Manuscript Division, LOC, Washington, DC, http://hdl.loc.gov.

48. Dunbar-Nelson, "Negro Women in War Work," 389–90.

49. Special thanks to one of the anonymous readers of this manuscript who suggested I look into the work of Ora Brown Stokes.

50. A. B. Caldwell, ed., *History of the American Negro, Virginia Edition* (Atlanta: A. B. Caldwell, 1921), 5:137–39, https://archive.org.

51. Kimberly J. Lamay Licursi, *Remembering World War I in America* (Lincoln: University of Nebraska Press, 2018), 17–19, 24–27; Roger Christman, "A Guide to the Virginia War History Commission, 1915–1931" (Richmond: Library of Virginia, 2004), https://ead.lib.virginia.edu.

52. Licursi, *Remembering World War I*, 24.

53. "Ligue des Femmes Alliées de la Grande Guerre," Bibliothèque nationale de France, Gallica, June 1924, 1, https://gallica.bnf.fr.

54. "Ligue des Femmes Alliées," 1.

55. Gaynor Kavanagh, *Museums and the First World War: A Social History* (London: Leicester University Press, 1994), 138; Mary Wilkinson, "Patriotism and Duty: The Women's Work Collection at the Imperial War Museum," *Imperial War Museum Review* 6 (1991): 31–38.

56. I conducted research in the IWM Archives in 2012 that contributed to this summary of the work of the Women's Section. "Subject. Report of the Women's Section of the Imperial War Museum. May 1st, 1917–February 23rd, 1918," from "Report of Imperial War Museum 1917–1918," folder EN1/3/GEN/009, Women's Work Committee Report 1917–1918, Imperial War Museum (IWM) Archives, London; "Women's Work," in "Report of Imperial War Museum 1918–1919," 10, folder EN1/3/GEN/009, Women's Work Committee Report 1917–1918, IWM Archives, London.

57. Kavanagh, *Museums and the First World War*, 138.

58. Kavanagh, 70.

59. The historiography of American memory includes but is not limited to the following works that influenced this book: David Thelen, "Memory and American History," *Journal of American History* 75, no. 4 (March 1998): 1117–29; Michael Kammen, *A Season of Youth: The American Revolution and the Historical Imagination* (New York: Oxford University Press, 1978); Michael Kammen, *Mystic Chords of Memory: The Transformation of Tradition in American Culture* (New York: Alfred A. Knopf, 1991); John Bodnar, *Remaking America: Public Memory, Commemoration, and Patriotism in the Twentieth Century* (Princeton, NJ: Princeton University Press, 1992); Edward T. Linenthal and Tom Engelhardt, eds., *History Wars: The Enola Gay and Other Battles for the American Past* (New York: Henry Holt, 1996); Erika Doss, *Memorial Mania: Public Feeling in America* (Chicago: University of Chicago Press, 2010); G. Kurt Piehler, *Remembering War the American Way* (Washington, DC: Smithsonian Institution Press,

1995); Kirk Savage, *Standing Soldier, Kneeling Slave: Race, War and National Identity in Nineteenth-Century America* (Princeton, NJ: Princeton University Press, 1997); Kirk Savage, *Monument Wars: Washington, D.C., the National Mall, and the Transformation of the Memorial Landscape* (Berkeley: University of California Press, 2009); Kristin Ann Hass, *Sacrificing Soldiers on the National Mall* (Berkeley: University of California Press, 2013); David Blight, *Race and Reunion: The Civil War in American Memory* (Cambridge, MA: Belknap Press of Harvard University Press, 2001); Ari Kelman, *A Misplaced Massacre: Struggling over the Memory of Sand Creek* (Cambridge, MA: Harvard University Press, 2013); Alison Landsberg, *Prosthetic Memory: The Transformation of American Remembrance in the Age of Mass Culture* (New York: Columbia University Press, 2004); Michel-Rolph Trouillot, *Silencing the Past: Power and the Production of History* (Boston: Beacon Press, 1995); Steven Trout, *Memorial Fictions: Willa Cather and the First World War* (Lincoln: University of Nebraska Press, 2002); Charles Reagan Wilson, *Baptized in Blood: The Religion of the Lost Cause, 1865–1920* (Athens: University of Georgia Press, 1980); Gaines M. Foster, *Ghosts of the Confederacy: Defeat, the Lost Cause, and the Emergence of the New South* (New York: Oxford University Press, 1985); Carol Reardon, *Pickett's Charge in History and Memory* (Chapel Hill: University of North Carolina Press, 1997); Gary Gallagher, *Causes Won, Lost, & Forgotten: How Hollywood and Popular Art Shape What We Know about the Civil War* (Chapel Hill: University of North Carolina Press, 2008); William A. Blair, *Cities of the Dead: Contesting the Memory of the Civil War in the South, 1865–1914* (Chapel Hill: University of North Carolina Press, 2004); Jerry Lembcke, *The Spitting Image: Myth, Memory, and the Legacy of Vietnam* (New York: New York University Press, 2000); Marita Sturken, *Tangled Memories: The Vietnam War, the AIDS Epidemic, and the Politics of Remembering* (Berkeley: University of California Press, 1997); Kristin Ann Hass, *Carried to the Wall: American Memory and the Vietnam Veterans Memorial* (Berkeley: University of California Press, 1998); Patrick Hagopian, *The Vietnam War in American Memory: Veterans, Memorials, and the Politics of Healing* (Amherst: University of Massachusetts Press, 2009); Nina Silber, *The Romance of Reunion: Northerners and the South, 1865–1900* (Chapel Hill: University of North Carolina Press, 1993); Karen L. Cox, *Dixie's Daughters: The United Daughters of the Confederacy and the Preservation of Confederate Culture* (Gainesville: University Press of Florida, 2003); Cynthia Mills and Pamela H. Simpson, eds., *Monuments to the Lost Cause: Women, Art, and the Landscapes of Southern Memory* (Knoxville: University of Tennessee Press, 2003); Caroline E. Janney, *Burying the Dead but Not the Past: Ladies' Memorial Associations & the Lost Cause* (Chapel Hill: University of North Carolina Press, 2008); Morgan, *Women and Patriotism*.

60. Mark A. Snell, ed., *Unknown Soldiers: The American Expeditionary Forces in Memory and Remembrance* (Kent, OH: Kent State University Press, 2008); Steven Trout, *On the Battlefield of Memory: The First World War and American Remembrance, 1919–1941* (Tuscaloosa: University of Alabama Press, 2010), 1, 252; Budreau, *Bodies of War*; Lisa M. Budreau, "The Politics of Remembrance: The Gold Star Mothers' Pilgrimage and America's Fading Memory of the Great War," *Journal of Military History* 72, no. 2 (April 2008): 371–411; Michael Sledge, *Soldier Dead: How We Recover, Identify, Bury, & Honor Our Military Fallen* (New York: Columbia University Press, 2005); Ron Robin,

Enclaves of America: The Rhetoric of American Political Architecture Abroad, 1900–1965 (Princeton, NJ: Princeton University Press, 1992); John Graham, *The Gold Star Mother Pilgrimages of the 1930s: Overseas Grave Visitations by Mothers and Widows of Fallen U.S. World War I Soldiers* (Jefferson, NC: McFarland, 2005); Constance Potter, "World War I Gold Star Mothers Pilgrimages, Part I," *Prologue* 31, no. 2 (Summer 1999): 140–45; Constance Potter, "World War I Gold Star Mothers Pilgrimages, Part II," *Prologue* 31, no. 3 (Fall 1999): 210–15; Holly S. Fenelon, *That Knock on the Door: The History of Gold Star Mothers in America* (Bloomington, IN: iUniverse, 2012); Plant, *Mom*; Rebecca Jo Plant, "The Gold Star Mothers Pilgrimages: Patriotic Maternalists and Their Critics in Interwar America," in *Maternalism Reconsidered: Motherhood, Welfare, and Social Policy in the Twentieth Century*, ed. Marian van der Klein, Rebecca Jo Plant, Nicole Sanders, and Lori R. Weintrob (New York: Berghahn Books, 2012); Lotte Larsen Meyer, "Mourning in a Distant Land: Gold Star Pilgrimages to American Military Cemeteries in Europe, 1930–33," *Markers* 20 (2003): 31–75.

61. Perhaps the two most groundbreaking works in the study of the memory of the First World War in Europe and Great Britain are by Paul Fussell and Jay Winter. While Winter's arguments about traditional and modernist types of commemoration deeply influenced this book, Fussell's arguments about how the memory of the Great War has seeped into and shaped modern life were not as relevant. Thus, although Fussell's work is pivotal in the field and has certainly influenced my thinking, it was not a major focus of my historiographical analysis. Jay Winter, *Sites of Memory, Sites of Mourning: The Great War in European Cultural History* (Cambridge: Cambridge University Press, 1995); Paul Fussell, *The Great War and Modern Memory* (New York: Oxford University Press, 1975). Other examples of studies of the memory of the First World War outside the US include Mark David Sheftall, *Altered Memories of the Great War: Divergent Narratives of Britain, Australia, New Zealand and Canada* (London: I. B. Tauris, 2010); Mark Connelly, *The Great War, Memory and Ritual: Commemoration in the City and East London, 1916–1939* (Rochester, NY: Royal Historical Society, 2001); Nicholas J. Saunders, ed., *Matters of Conflict: Material Culture, Memory and the First World War* (Abingdon, Oxfordshire, UK: Routledge, 2004); Marilène Patten Henry, *Monumental Accusations: The monuments aux morts as Expressions of Popular Resentment* (New York: Peter Lang, 1996); Richard van Emden, *The Quick and the Dead: Fallen Soldiers and Their Families in the Great War* (London: Bloomsbury, 2011); George L. Mosse, *Fallen Soldiers: Reshaping the Memory of the World Wars* (New York: Oxford University Press, 1990); Annette Becker, *War and Faith: The Religious Imagination in France, 1914–1930*, trans. Helen McPhail (New York: Berg, 1998); Marina Larsson, *Shattered Anzacs: Living with the Scars of War* (Sydney, Australia: University of New South Wales Press, 2009); Jay Winter, *Remembering War: The Great War between Memory and History in the Twentieth Century* (New Haven, CT: Yale University Press, 2006).

62. Winter, *Sites of Memory*, 3.

63. Jennifer Wingate, *Sculpting Doughboys: Memory, Gender, and Taste in America's World War I Memorials* (Farnham, UK: Ashgate, 2013); Jennifer Wingate, "Doughboys, Art Worlds, and Identities: Sculpted Memories of World War I in the United States" (PhD diss., Stony Brook University, 2002), 39–52; Jennifer Wingate, "Motherhood, Me-

morials, and Anti-Militarism: Bashka Paeff's 'Sacrifices of War,'" *Woman's Art Journal* 29, no. 2 (Fall–Winter 2008): 31–40; Jennifer Wingate, "Real Art, War Art and the Politics of Peace Memorials in the United States after World War I," *Public Art Dialogue* 2, no. 2 (September 2012): 162–89; Jennifer Wingate, "Over the Top: The Doughboy in World War I Memorials and Visual Culture," *American Art* 19, no. 2 (Summer 2005): 26–47; Shanken, "Planning Memory," 130–47. Shanken asserted that living memorials probably dated back to Reconstruction but were considered a new type of memorial after World War One. He argued that living memorials did not become a preferred type of memorial until World War Two, something I contest.

64. The topic of women's participation in the war has already been ably covered by many scholars, including Zeiger, *In Uncle Sam's Service*; Margaret Randolph Higonnet, Jane Jenson, Sonya Michel, and Margaret Collins Weitz, eds., *Behind the Lines: Gender and the Two World Wars* (New Haven, CT: Yale University Press, 1987); Linker, *War's Waste*; and Dorothy Schneider and Carl J. Schneider, *Into the Breach: American Women Overseas in World War I* (New York: Viking Adult, 1991). The WOSL is mentioned briefly and tangentially in the following: Kirsten Marie Delegard, *Battling Miss Bolsheviki: The Origins of Female Conservatism in the United States* (Philadelphia: University of Pennsylvania Press, 2012); Lynn Dumenil, *The Second Line of Defense: American Women and World War I* (Chapel Hill: University of North Carolina Press, 2017). I briefly discussed the WOSL in Allison S. Finkelstein, "American Women in the War," in *World War I Remembered*, ed. Robert J. Dalessandro and Robert K. Sutton (n.p., Eastern National, 2017), 97–107.

65. Schneider and Schneider, *Into the Breach*, 59–62; Susan Ware, *Partner and I: Molly Dewson, Feminism, and New Deal Politics* (New Haven, CT: Yale University Press, 1987), 73–85.

66. For more about women involved with variants of the suffrage movement, social reform, and Progressivism, see Muncy, *Creating a Female Dominion*; Ellen Carol DuBois, *Harriot Stanton Blatch and the Winning of Woman Suffrage* (New Haven, CT: Yale University Press, 1997); Elisabeth Israels Perry, *Belle Moskowitz: Feminine Politics and the Exercise of Power in the Age of Alfred E. Smith* (New York: Oxford University Press, 1987); Ware, *Partner and I*; Frankel and Dye, *Gender, Class, Race, and Reform*; Cott, *Grounding of Modern Feminism*; Kathryn Kish Sklar, "Hull House: A Community of Women Reformers," *Signs* 10, no. 4 (Summer 1985): 658–77; Linda Gordon, "Social Insurance and Public Assistance: The Influence of Gender in Welfare Thought in the United States, 1890–1935," *American Historical Review* 97, no. 1 (February 1992): 19–54; Maureen A. Flanagan, *Seeing with Their Hearts: Chicago Women and the Vision of the Good City, 1871–1933* (Princeton, NJ: Princeton University Press, 2002).

67. Molly Ladd-Taylor, *Mother-Work: Women, Child Welfare, and the State, 1890–1930* (Urbana: University of Illinois Press, 1994); Linda Gordon, *Pitied but Not Entitled: Single Mothers and the History of Welfare, 1890–1935* (New York: Free Press, 1994); Kerber, *Women of the Republic*; Theda Skocpol, *Protecting Soldiers and Mothers: The Political Origins of the Social Policy in the United States* (Cambridge, MA: Harvard University Press, 1992); Seth Koven and Sonya Michel, eds., *Mothers of a New World: Maternalist Politics and the Origins of Welfare States* (New York: Routledge, 1993); S. J. Kleinberg,

Widows and Orphans First: The Family Economy and Social Welfare Policy, 1880–1939 (Urbana: University of Illinois Press, 2006); Sonya Michel, *Children's Interests/Mothers' Rights: The Shaping of America's Child Care Policy* (New Haven, CT: Yale University Press, 1999); Rebecca Jo Plant, "Anti-Maternalism: A New Perspective on the Transformation of Gender Ideology in the Twentieth-Century United States," *Social Politics* 22, no. 3 (Fall 2015): 283–88; Rebecca Jo Plant, "Gold Star Mothers Pilgrimages."

68. Karen J. Blair, *The Clubwoman as Feminist: True Womanhood Redefined, 1868–1914* (New York: Holmes & Meier, 1980); Anne Fior Scott, *Natural Allies: Women's Associations in American History* (Urbana: University of Illinois Press, 1991); Karen J. Blair, *The Torchbearers: Women and Their Amateur Arts Associations in America, 1890–1930* (Bloomington: Indiana University Press, 1994); Karen J. Blair, *Joining In: Exploring the History of Voluntary Organizations* (Malabar, FL: Krieger, 2006). Many organizations of female veteranists can be classified as patriotic associations, war organizations, or hereditary societies, according to Blair's typology of American voluntary organizations.

69. Capozzola, *Uncle Sam Wants You.*

70. Stephen R. Ortiz, *Beyond the Bonus March and GI Bill: How Veteran Politics Shaped the New Deal Era* (New York: New York University Press, 2010); Julia Eichenberg and John Paul Newman, eds., *The Great War and Veterans' Internationalism* (Basingstoke, UK: Palgrave Macmillan, 2013); Kelly, *Creating a National Home.*

71. Pierre Nora, "Between Memory and History: Les Lieux de Mémoire," *Representations* 26 (Spring 1999): 7–24; Pierre Nora, ed., *Rethinking France: Les Lieux de Mémoire*, trans. David P. Jordan (Chicago: University of Chicago Press, 2009); Maurice Halbwachs, *On Collective Memory*, trans. Lewis A. Coser (Chicago: University of Chicago Press, 1992); Benedict Anderson, *Imagined Communities: Reflections on the Origin and Spread of Nationalism* (New York: Verso, 1991).

72. Halbwachs, *On Collective Memory*, 144.

73. Anderson, *Imagined Communities*, 9–10.

74. "Cullum Hall History," United States Military Academy, West Point, n.d., https://www.westpoint.edu.

75. Alice L. F. Fitzgerald, *The Edith Cavell Nurse from Massachusetts* (Boston: W. A. Butterfield, 1917), https://archive.org. Special thanks to Dr. Marian Moser Jones for alerting me to this source and suggesting I use it.

76. "Women in World War One: Anna Coleman Ladd," Smithsonian National Museum of American History, n.d., https://www.si.edu.

77. "How Wounded Soldiers Have Faced the World Again with 'Portrait Masks,'" *St. Louis Post-Dispatch Sunday Magazine*, March 26, 1933 (supplement to the newspaper), box 2 of 7, letters (1920–1937), folder 4 of 11, 1914–1925, American Red Cross Studio for Portrait-Masks File, scrapbook (1914–1923), folder 2 of 7, B2.68, Anna Coleman Ladd Papers, ca. 1881–1950, Archives of American Art, Smithsonian Institution. I conducted extensive in-person research in this collection at the Archives of American Art in 2013 before it was made available online. It is now available at https://www.aaa.si.edu.

78. "How Wounded Soldiers Have Faced the World Again with 'Portrait Masks,'" *St. Louis Post-Dispatch Sunday Magazine*; Wingate, *Sculpting Doughboys*, 119, 163–67, 180; Jean Fitzgerald, revised by Jayna Josefson, "A Finding Aid to the Anna Coleman

Ladd Papers, 1881–1950, in the Archives of American Art," July 20, 2012, http://www
.aaa.si.edu. During the war, other people pursued similar work with facial wounds, facial masks, and soldiers with disfigured faces, such as Harold Gillies and Francis Derwent Wood in Great Britain. See Suzannah Biernoff, "The Rhetoric of Disfigurement in
First World War Britain," *Social History of Medicine* 24, no. 3 (December 2011), https://
doi.org/10.1093/shm/hkq095; Suzannah Biernoff, "Flesh Poems: Henry Tonks and the
Art of Surgery," *Visual Culture in Britain* 11, no. 1 (March 2010): 25–47; Suzannah Biernoff and Jane Tynan, "Making and Remaking the Civilian Soldier: The First World War
Photographs of Horace Nicholls," *Journal of War and Culture Studies* 5, no. 3 (September 2012): 277–95, https://doi.org/10.1386/jwcs.5.3.277_1; Suzannah Biernoff, "The Face
of War," in *Ugliness: The Non-beautiful in Art and Theory*, ed. Andrei Pop and Mechtild
Widrich (New York: I. B. Tauris, 2014).

79. Wingate, *Sculpting Doughboys*, 163–67, 180.

80. *Carry On* 1, no. 1 (January 1922): 4, box 1922–1932, folder 1922, Women's Overseas Service League *Carry On* Periodical Collection, Gift of Carolyn Habgood, MWMC.

Chapter 1

1. *Carry On* 5, no. 4 (November 1926): front cover, box 1922–1932, folder 1926,
Women's Overseas Service League *Carry On* Periodical Collection, Gift of Carolyn Habgood, MWMC.

2. As an ARC searcher, M' Edna Corbet's wartime volunteer work overseas likely
could have involved helping service members at hospitals communicate with their families, informing families when a service member died at a hospital, photographing service
members' graves to send to their families, and researching the fate of missing service
members through a variety of means such as interviews with their comrades. Search-
ers saw the horrors of the war in an up close and often deeply personal way, an experience that might have influenced Corbet's perspective when she wrote this poem.
Gavin, *American Women*, 192–94.

3. "Incorporation of Women's Overseas Service League Hearing Before the Committee on the Judiciary House of Representatives Sixty-Seventh Congress Second Session
on H.R. 7299 Serial 23 January 12, 1922," 3, box 1, National Articles of Incorporation,
By-laws, Manuals, Minutes, Finances, Rules of Procedure, 80.19.19 +etc., folder Articles
of Incorporation 1922–29, WOSL Records, National WWI Museum and Memorial Archives; Helene M. Sillia, *Lest We Forget: A History of the Women's Overseas Service League*
(privately published, 1978), 5. Sillia was a WOSL member, served for many years as the
WOSL national historian, and wrote this history for the WOSL, which published it in
1978. This book chapter marks the first in-depth scholarly analysis of the WOSL. Thus
far, the WOSL has been included only very briefly in a few secondary sources, including Zeiger, *In Uncle Sam's Service*; Dumenil, *Second Line of Defense*; Cobbs, *Hello Girls*;
and Adler, *Burdens of War*.

4. "Mrs. Oswald Chew," *New York Times*, November 4, 1948, 29.

5. Sillia, *Lest We Forget*, 5, 72, 217.

6. "Incorporation of Women's Overseas Service League Hearing," 4.

7. "Articles of Incorporation of the Women's Overseas Service League: By-laws of the
Women's Overseas Service League," 6–7, box 1, National Articles of Incorporation, By-

laws, Manuals, Minutes, Finances, Rules of Procedure, 80.19.19 +etc., folder Articles of Incorporation 1922–29, WOSL Records, Women's Overseas Service League Collection, National WWI Museum and Memorial Archives.

8. "Articles of Incorporation, 1922–29," 4. Although the WOSL failed to get a congressional charter to nationally incorporate the organization, it was incorporated in the state of Indiana in 1924 and granted a charter by that state in 1926. Sillia, *Lest We Forget*, 5.

9. "Incorporation of Women's Overseas Service League Hearing," 8, 13–14.

10. Sillia, *Lest We Forget*, ii.

11. Sillia, *Lest We Forget*, 5; Alvin Owsley, "Comrades in Service—A Message from the American Legion," *Carry On* 2, no. 2 (May 1923): 1, 6, 24, box 36, WOSL Records, MS 22, UTSA.

12. "Incorporation of Women's Overseas Service League Hearing," 5–6.

13. "Incorporation of Women's Overseas Service League Hearing," 3.

14. "Incorporation of Women's Overseas Service League Hearing," 3.

15. "Incorporation of Women's Overseas Service League Hearing," 5.

16. "Incorporation of Women's Overseas Service League Hearing," 5. Mrs. Chew emphasized that the WOSL had a duty "to assist its own members and obtain recognition and memorials for the overseas women who died or were killed in service."

17. "Incorporation of Women's Overseas Service League Hearing," 15.

18. "Incorporation of Women's Overseas Service League Hearing," 16.

19. Zeiger, *In Uncle Sam's Service*, 2; Sillia, *Lest We Forget*, 1; Schneider and Schneider, *Into the Breach*, 287–89. Estimates of how many American women served overseas in World War One vary widely. Zeiger estimated there were at least sixteen thousand, while Sillia estimated about ninety thousand. Dorothy Schneider and Carl J. Schneider argued that twenty-five thousand seemed like a "realistic, conservative figure."

20. For example, the roster from November 1940 listed 140 different organizations. These included the American Committee for Devastated France, the American Library Association, the Army Nurse Corps, the American Red Cross, the Harvard Surgical Unit, the Jewish Welfare Board, the Knights of Columbus, the Navy Nurse Corps, the Salvation Army, the Signal Corps, the US Navy, the YMCA, and the YWCA, to name just a few. "Roster: Supplement to *Carry On*," *Carry On* 19, no. 4 (November 1940): 3, box 1940–1947, folder 1940, Women's Overseas Service League *Carry On* Periodical Collection, Gift of Carolyn Habgood, MWMC.

21. "Roster: Supplement to *Carry On*," *Carry On* 19, no. 4 (November 1940): 3, box 1940–1947, folder 1940, Women's Overseas Service League *Carry On* Periodical Collection, Gift of Carolyn Habgood, MWMC; Sillia, *Lest We Forget*, 300–301.

22. "Incorporation of Women's Overseas Service League Hearing," 6.

23. Sillia, *Lest We Forget*, 6.

24. "Incorporation of Women's Overseas Service League Hearing," 19.

25. "Incorporation of Women's Overseas Service League Hearing," 6

26. For a detailed analysis of the economic, social, racial, and religious backgrounds of overseas women workers in World War One, see Zeiger, *In Uncle Sam's Service*, 26–50. She asserts that "despite the popular image of women at the front as 'heiresses' using their wealth and influence to aid the cause, the majority of women who served with the AEF were in fact from the lower middle class" (31).

27. "Articles of Incorporation, 1922–29," section 2, 6.

28. See the introduction of this book for a more in-depth discussion of the wartime service of African American women both overseas and in the US. Zeiger, *In Uncle Sam's Service*, 28.

29. Zeiger, *In Uncle Sam's Service*, 28.

30. Zeiger, *In Uncle Sam's Service*, 27–28; Hunton and Johnson, *Two Colored Women*.

31. For examples of women's service, reform, and welfare activities at the turn of the century, see Sklar, "Hull House"; Gordon, "Social Insurance and Public Assistance"; Muncy, *Creating a Female Dominion*.

32. *Seattle Times*, April 10, 1970, A6, "News Clippings and Information WOSL Seattle Unit," WOSL Collection, National WWI Museum and Memorial Archives.

33. Sillia, *Lest We Forget*, 9.

34. Sillia, 291–20.

35. "Anna Hitchcock, Former Therapist, Dies at Age 97," *Washington Post*, November 4, 1986, B4, ProQuest Historical Newspapers.

36. Lena Hitchcock oral history (03), July 14, 1982, recorded by the WOSL, UC-MS022/7, box 182, WOSL Records, MS 22, UTSA.

37. See Wingate, *Sculpting Doughboys*.

38. Sillia, *Lest We Forget*, 7–8.

39. Edgar Guest, "Memorial Day," *Carry On* 2, no. 2 (May 1923), box 36, WOSL Records, MS 22, UTSA.

40. "Overseas Unit of D.C. Women Attends Party," *Washington Post*, March 1, 1937, 12, ProQuest Historical Newspapers.

41. *Carry On* 11, no. 3 (August 1933): 23, box 1933–1939, folder 1933, Women's Overseas Service League *Carry On* Periodical Collection, Gift of Carolyn Habgood, MWMC.

42. *Carry On* 11, no. 3 (August 1933): 12–13, 23.

43. "Incorporation of Women's Overseas Service League Hearing," 14.

44. Sillia, *Lest We Forget*, 7.

45. For example, on Armistice Day in 1924, the Toledo WOSL Unit held a French dinner at a member's home that "was of a purely social nature, and was greatly enjoyed by all the members." Minute Book, Toledo Unit, c. 1920–1946, November 11, 1924, box W.O.S.L. RECORDS, Minute Books of Toledo, Ohio Unit, 2 vols., 84.150.2–.3, folder W.O.S.L. Records Minute Book, Toledo Unit c. 1920–1946, 84.150.2, WOSL Collection, National WWI Museum and Memorial Archives.

46. Minute Book, Toledo Unit, May 6, 1925, National WWI Museum and Memorial Archives.

47. "Minutes of the Ninth Annual Convention, July 8–11, 1929, Minneapolis, Minnesota," 5, folder Ann. Convention Agendas, 1930–61, WOSL Collection, National WWI Museum and Memorial Archives; "Memorial Service of the Thirty-Sixth National Convention Women's Overseas Service League," pamphlet in labeled binder, Liberty Memorial Association Minute Book Collection, National WWI Museum and Memorial Archives.

48. Eben Putnam to Irene M. Givenwilson, June 26, 1922, box WOSL: Correspondence, 1924–62; congressional bills, 1929–1951, box 4, folder Irene Givenwilson Cornell,

1921–3 Re: Women who died in service George Washington Memorial, WOSL Collection, National WWI Museum and Memorial Archives.

49. Mrs. Henry F. Dimock to Irene M. Givenwilson, May 22, 1922, box WOSL: Correspondence, 1924–62; congressional bills, 1929–1951, box 4, folder Irene Givenwilson Cornell, 1921–3 Re: Women who died in service George Washington Memorial, WOSL Collection, National WWI Museum and Memorial Archives.

50. Russell G. Creviston to Irene M. Givenwilson, June 23, 1922, box WOSL: Correspondence, 1924–62; congressional bills, 1929–1951, box 4, folder Irene Givenwilson Cornell, 1921–3 Re: Women who died in service George Washington Memorial, WOSL Collection, National WWI Museum and Memorial Archives.

51. "George Washington Memorial Association Records, 1890–1922," Smithsonian Institution Archives, record unit 7471, http://siarchives.si.edu.

52. "Report of the Chairman of the Memorial Committee, June 1st, 1923," box WOSL: Correspondence, 1924–62; congressional bills, 1929–1951, box 4, folder: Irene Givenwilson Cornell, 1921–3 Re: Women who died in service George Washington Memorial, WOSL Collection, National WWI Museum and Memorial Archives.

53. *Carry On* 3, no. 3 (August 1924): 5, box 36, WOSL Records, MS 22, UTSA.

54. *Carry On* 9, no. 3 (August 1930): 42, box 1922–1932, folder 1930, Women's Overseas Service League *Carry On* Periodical Collection, Gift of Carolyn Habgood, MWMC.

55. "Articles of Incorporation," 10–11, National WWI Museum and Memorial Archives.

56. For more information on the benefits World War veterans received, see Ortiz, *Beyond the Bonus March*, 13–31.

57. Undated typed history of the WOSL, box WOSL-National, History Projects, Service Projects, Rosters, 2, folder WOSL History Project, WOSL Collection, National WWI Museum and Memorial Archives.

58. Undated typed history of the WOSL, 97.

59. "Bulletin as Voted by the Eleventh Annual Convention of the Women's Overseas Service League," 2, unlabeled folder, WOSL Collection, National WWI Museum and Memorial Archives.

60. "Proceedings of Fourth Annual Convention of the Women's Overseas Service League held at San Francisco, California, July 14–16, 1924," 90–91, box Women's Overseas Service League: Reports, Ann. Natl. Conventions, 1921–25 (1st–5th), box 7, folder WOSL Transcript Fourth National Convention 1924, San Francisco, Part 1, 1–125, WOSL Collection, National WWI Museum and Memorial Archives.

61. "Proceedings of Fourth Annual Convention," 90–93.

62. "Proceedings of Fourth Annual Convention," 96–97.

63. *Carry On* 6, no. 2 (May 1927): 15, box 1922–1932, folder 1927, Women's Overseas Service League *Carry On* Periodical Collection, Gift of Carolyn Habgood, MWMC.

64. *Carry On* 3, no. 2 (May 1924): 23, box 1922–1932, folder 1924, Women's Overseas Service League *Carry On* Periodical Collection, Gift of Carolyn Habgood, MWMC.

65. *Carry On* 7, no. 1 (February 1928): back cover, box 1922–1932, folder 1928, Women's Overseas Service League *Carry On* Periodical Collection, Gift of Carolyn Habgood, MWMC.

66. *Carry On* 10, no. 1 (February 1931): 9, box 1922–1932, folder 1931, Women's

Overseas Service League *Carry On* Periodical Collection, Gift of Carolyn Habgood, MWMC.

67. *Carry On* 10, no. 1 (February 1931): 19.

68. *Carry On* 11, no. 3 (August 1930): 41, box 1922–1932, folder 1930, Women's Overseas Service League *Carry On* Periodical Collection, Gift of Carolyn Habgood, MWMC.

69. Sillia, *Lest We Forget*, 209–10.

70. W. J. Bardsley to Shirley Farr, October 17, 1932, box WOSL, Rosters of women who served & died, awards, ways and means reports, correspondence, box 3, folder Correspondence, 1931033 re: Sallie M. Clark Bequest (for disabled ex-service women) F 10, WOSL Collection, National WWI Museum and Memorial Archives; biography of Sallie McIntosh Clark, undated, box 5, WOSL Records, MS 22, UTSA; Sillia, *Lest We Forget*, 209–10.

71. Biography of Sallie McIntosh Clark, WOSL Records, MS 22, UTSA; Sillia, *Lest We Forget*, 209–10.

72. Zeiger, *In Uncle Sam's Service*, 170.

73. Mrs. G. H. Taubles to All Units, February 16, 1931, box WOSL Correspondence, 1924–62, congressional bills, 1929–1951, box 4, folder Shirley Farr Correspondence, 1924–55, WOSL Collection, National WWI Museum and Memorial Archives. For more about the Soldiers' Home in Dayton, see Kelly, *Creating a National Home*.

74. *Carry On* 12, no. 1 (February 1933): 13–15, box 1933–1939, folder 1933, Women's Overseas Service League *Carry On* Periodical Collection, Gift of Carolyn Habgood, MWMC. It seems that the women moved again to a different building in March 1938. *Carry On* 17, no. 4 (November 1938): 10, box 1933–1939, folder 1938, Women's Overseas Service League *Carry On* Periodical Collection, Gift of Carolyn Habgood, MWMC.

75. Mrs. G. H. Taubles to All Units, February 16, 1931.

76. *Carry On* 12, no. 1 (February 1933): 15, box 1933–1939, folder 1933, Women's Overseas Service League *Carry On* Periodical Collection, Gift of Carolyn Habgood, MWMC; *Carry On* 14, no. 4 (November 1935): 6–7, box 1933–1939, folder 1935, Women's Overseas Service League *Carry On* Periodical Collection, Gift of Carolyn Habgood, MWMC.

77. *Carry On* 13, no. 2 (May 1934): 21–22, box 1933–1939, folder 1934, Women's Overseas Service League *Carry On* Periodical Collection, Gift of Carolyn Habgood, MWMC.

78. Anne Hoyt to Judge Payne, October 6, 1922, box WOSL Correspondence, 1924–62; congressional bills, 1929–1951, box 4, folder Irene Givenwilson Cornell, 1921–3 Re: Women who died in service George Washington Memorial, WOSL Collection, National WWI Museum and Memorial Archives.

79. *Carry On* 6, no. 2 (May 1927): 39–40, box 1922–1932, folder 1927, Women's Overseas Service League *Carry On* Periodical Collection, Gift of Carolyn Habgood, MWMC.

80. *Carry On* 5, no. 1 (February 1925): 10–12, 53, box 1922–1932, folder 1925, Women's Overseas Service League *Carry On* Periodical Collection, Gift of Carolyn Habgood, MWMC.

81. "Articles of Incorporation, 1922–29," 4.

82. *Carry On* 3, no. 2 (May 1924): 10, box 1922–1932, folder 1924, Women's Overseas Service League *Carry On* Periodical Collection, Gift of Carolyn Habgood, MWMC.

83. "Report on the Ninth Annual Convention—Women's Overseas Service League Held at Minneapolis—July 6th–11th, 1929, Presented by Beatrice G. Lesser, Delegate, at the Annual Luncheon at the Union League Club, Sept. 28, 1929," 2, unlabeled folder, WOSL Collection, National WWI Museum and Memorial Archives; "Transcript Fourth National Convention 1924," 106–9, box Women's Overseas Service League: Reports, Ann. Natl. Conventions, 1921–25 (1st–5th), box 7, folder WOSL Transcript Fourth National Convention 1924, San Francisco, part 1, WOSL Collection, National WWI Museum and Memorial Archives. For more on World War One hostess houses, see Cynthia Brandimarte, "Women on the Home Front: Hostess Houses during World War I," *Winterthur Portfolio* 42, no. 4 (Winter 2008): 201–22. For more on the Citizens' Military Training Camps, see Donald M. Kington, *Forgotten Summers: The Story of the Citizens' Military Training Camps, 1921–1940* (San Francisco: Two Decades Publishing, 1995).

84. Minute Book, Toledo Unit, February 9, 1927, National WWI Museum and Memorial Archives.

85. For more about the term "martial citizenship," see the work of historian Patrick J. Kelly. Kelly, *Creating a National Home*, 2–5; Zeiger, *In Uncle Sam's Service*, 171.

86. Sillia, *Lest We Forget*, 2.

87. Jean Ebbert and Marie-Beth Hall, *The First, the Few, the Forgotten: Navy and Marine Corps Women in World War I* (Annapolis, MD: Naval Institute Press, 2002), 97.

88. Zeiger, *In Uncle Sam's Service*, 170–71.

89. Susan H. Godson, *Serving Proudly: A History of Women in the U.S. Navy* (Annapolis, MD: Naval Institute Press, 2001), 70–71, 76–77; Zeiger, *In Uncle Sam's Service*, 109–15.

90. Godson, *Serving Proudly*, 77; Zeiger, *In Uncle Sam's Service*, 168–69. According to Godson, the navy surgeon general Edward R. Stitt asserted that navy nurses were already treated as officers administratively, and he believed their "noble calling" already placed them on a higher plane than rank would.

91. Ebbert and Hall, *The First, the Few*, 97–109; Zeiger, *In Uncle Sam's Service*, 169.

92. Ebbert and Hall, 103–8.

93. "Articles of Incorporation," 10–11, National WWI Museum and Memorial Archives.

94. Zeiger, *In Uncle Sam's Service*, 170; *Carry On* 11, no. 2 (May 1932): 14–15, box 1922–1932, folder 1932, Women's Overseas Service League *Carry On* Periodical Collection, Gift of Carolyn Habgood, MWMC; "Fitzpatrick, James Martin," *Biographical Directory of the United States Congress: 1774 to Present*, n.d., http://bioguide.congress.gov; "Bingham, Hiram," *Biographical Directory of the United States Congress: 1774 to Present*, n.d., http://bioguide.congress.gov.

95. *Carry On* 11, no. 2 (May 1932): 14–15, box 1922–1932, folder 1932, Women's Overseas Service League *Carry On* Periodical Collection, Gift of Carolyn Habgood, MWMC.

96. Zeiger, *In Uncle Sam's Service*, 170–71; Sillia, *Lest We Forget*, 10.

97. Sillia, *Lest We Forget*, 10; Zeiger, *In Uncle Sam's Service*, 171.

98. Sillia, *Lest We Forget*, 10.

99. For more on how FDR used the analogy of war to promote the New Deal, see Michael G. Sherry, *In the Shadow of War: The United States since the 1930s* (New Haven, CT: Yale University Press, 1995), 15–26.

100. Ortiz, *Beyond the Bonus March*, 24–25.

101. *Carry On* 11, no. 2 (May 1932): 14–15, box 1922–1932, folder 1932, Women's Overseas Service League *Carry On* Periodical Collection, Gift of Carolyn Habgood, MWMC.

102. "A.E.F. Women Oppose Taking Bonus," *New York Times*, July 7, 1933, 9.

103. Sherry, *In the Shadow of War*, 15–26.

104. Ortiz, *Beyond the Bonus March*, 58–59.

105. Ortiz, 66.

106. Stephen Ortiz argues that the Economy Act sparked "a rapid political mobilization by military veterans against New Deal policy." *Beyond the Bonus March*, 66.

107. Ortiz, *Beyond the Bonus March*, 66–67, 98.

108. The WOSL did cooperate with the VFW but seemed to have had a stronger alliance with the American Legion.

109. Donald J. Lisio, *The President and Protest: Hoover, MacArthur, and the Bonus Riot* (New York: Fordham University Press, 1994), x; Ortiz, *Beyond the Bonus March*, 2. For more on the Bonus March, see Paul Dickson and Thomas B. Allen, *The Bonus Army: An American Epic* (New York: Walker, 2004), 4–5; Roger Daniels, *The Bonus March: An Episode of the Great Depression* (Westport, CT: Greenwood, 1971); W. W. Waters, with William C. White, *B.E.F.: The Whole Story of the Bonus Army* (New York: Arno Press and the New York Times, 1969); Harris Gaylord Warren, *Herbert Hoover and the Great Depression* (New York: Oxford University Press, 1959).

110. *Carry On* 11, no. 2 (May 1932): 26, box 1922–1932, folder 1932, Women's Overseas Service League *Carry On* Periodical Collection, Gift of Carolyn Habgood, MWMC.

111. Ortiz, *Beyond the Bonus March*, 32–33, 60–63. Ortiz provides an in-depth discussion and timeline of the VFW's and American Legion's involvement with and reactions to the Bonus March.

112. For more about women's involvement with the New Deal, see Muncy, *Creating a Female Dominion*; Susan Ware, *Holding Their Own: American Women in the 1930s* (Boston: Twayne, 1982); and Susan Ware, *Beyond Suffrage: Women in the New Deal* (Cambridge, MA: Harvard University Press, 1981).

113. For more about the WOSL and the Bonus March, see Allison S. Finkelstein, "Remember My Forgotten Man (and Woman): Popular Culture, Politics, and Female Veteranists in the 1920s and 1930s," chap. 6 in "Carry On," 284–333.

114. "1,000 Disabled Veterans at White House Garden Fete; Nurses and Ladies in Colorful Outfits," *Washington Post*, June 16, 1932, 8, ProQuest Historical Newspapers; Matthew A. Wasniewski, ed., *Women in Congress, 1917–2006* (Washington, DC: Government Printing Office, 2006), 70–75.

115. For example, WOSL member Emma C. Steed, known as "Mother Steed," helped veterans by providing them with food, clothing, and housing during the Bonus March.

Other members may have assisted her. "'Mother' Steed, Soldiers' Friend through Two Wars, Dead at 85," *Washington Post*, December 18, 1949, M22.

116. *Carry On* 11, no. 2 (May 1932): 14–15, box 1922–1932, folder 1932, Women's Overseas Service League *Carry On* Periodical Collection, Gift of Carolyn Habgood, MWMC.

117. Nancy Beck Young, *Lou Henry Hoover: Activist First Lady* (Lawrence: University Press of Kansas, 2004), 157.

118. "Articles of Incorporation," 4, National WWI Museum and Memorial Archives.

119. Questionnaires of Lucile K. Moore and Ellen Sterling Bacorn, box WOSL Correspondence, 1924–62, congressional bills, 1929–1951, box 4, folder Zada Daniels Papers autobiographical information on WWI women veterans, inc. citation, WOSL Collection, National WWI Museum and Memorial Archives.

120. "Report of National President Women's Overseas Service League July 1929– May 1930, Report of the National Historian," unlabeled folder of WOSL documents, WOSL Collection, National WWI Museum and Memorial Archives. The WOSL's efforts to preserve its history did have some limited success. In 1978, the WOSL published an official organizational history, *Lest We Forget: A History of the Women's Overseas Service League*, written by its historian Helene M. Sillia. The WOSL also conducted an oral history project, especially active in the 1980s. "Women's Overseas Service League Oral Histories," Michigan State University Libraries Digital Repository, https://d.lib.msu .edu. The WOSL donated much of its original material to the University of Texas, San Antonio, where it forms the Women's Overseas Service League Records today; a substantial number of records also reside at the Women's Memorial Foundation Archives in Arlington, Virginia, and some at the National WWI Museum and Memorial Archives in Kansas City, Missouri.

121. "Report of National President Women's Overseas Service League July 1929– May 1930, Report of the National Historian," National WWI Museum and Memorial Archives.

122. Estelle M. Davis, interview by Lois Collet, October 23, 1982, Women's Overseas Service League Oral Histories, Michigan State University Libraries Digital Repository, https://n2t.net/ark:/85335/m5rx36.

123. Laura Smith, recording of herself, 1983, Women's Overseas Service League Oral Histories, Michigan State University Libraries Digital Repository, https://n2t.net/ark :/85335/m54d8b.

124. *Carry On* 10, no. 2 (May 1931): 42, box 1922–1932, folder 1931, Women's Overseas Service League *Carry On* Periodical Collection, Gift of Carolyn Habgood, MWMC.

125. *Carry On* 12, no. 3 (August 1933): 13, box 1933–1939, folder 1933, Women's Overseas Service League *Carry On* Periodical Collection, Gift of Carolyn Habgood, MWMC.

126. For a more detailed analysis of the meaning of American women's World War One uniforms, see Allison S. Finkelstein, "Exhibiting Veteranist-Commemorations: American Women's First World War Uniforms at the Smithsonian's National Museum," chap. 5 in "Carry On," 237–83. For more on women's World War One uniforms in the US and overseas, see Barton C. Hacker and Margaret Vining, eds., *Cutting a New Pat-*

tern: Uniformed Women in the Great War (Washington, DC: Smithsonian Institution Scholarly Press, 2020).

127. Edna Scott, interview by Evelyn McHiggins, Jane Piatt, and Geneva K. Wiske-mann, July 14, 1982, Women's Overseas Service League Oral Histories, Michigan State University Libraries Digital Repository, https://n2t.net/ark:/85335/m5hq5q.

128. Lena Hitchcock, "Before We Had the WAACS," *Washington Post*, August 31, 1942, 8, ProQuest Historical Newspapers.

129. "Mrs. Cruger Heads Aluminum Drive in Eighth Precinct," *Washington Post*, July 19, 1941, 8; "Overseas League Raises $1,500 for Mobile Kitchen," *Washington Post*, March 15, 1941, 13.

130. "AEF Women Await Call: Local Unit of Overseas League Tells Roosevelt It Is Ready," *New York Times*, December 11, 1941, 37.

131. "It's a Woman's War," *New York Times*, October 4, 1942, D4.

132. "Dayroom for WACs Dedicated," *New York Times*, January 22, 1944, 10.

133. Elizabeth Margaret Phillips, unknown interviewer, April 28, 1982, Women's Overseas Service League Oral Histories, Michigan State University Libraries Digital Repository, https://n2t.net/ark:/85335/m5xd73.

134. "Overseas League to Meet," *New York Times*, July 11, 1943, 36; Dorothy Jacobson, "Women in War Work," *Chicago Daily Tribune*, June 28, 1944, 17; Kate Massee, "Women in War Work," *Chicago Daily Tribune*, July 13, 1943, 19.

135. Dorothy Jacobson, "Women in War Work," *Chicago Daily Tribune*, June 28, 1944, 17.

Chapter 2

1. The American Red Cross has undergone several name and acronym changes throughout its existence. Whitney Hopkins and Susan Watson at the American Red Cross Archives, National Headquarters, Washington, DC, advised me to refer to the organization using the acronym ARC. I am grateful for their insight on this and other topics related to ARC history.

2. The ARC wartime publicity campaign advertised nursing with posters that announced, "Nursing is Military Service." Marian Moser Jones, *The American Red Cross from Clara Barton to the New Deal* (Baltimore: Johns Hopkins University Press, 2013), 168.

3. Julia F. Irwin, *Making the World Safe: The American Red Cross and a Nation's Humanitarian Awakening* (New York: Oxford University Press, 2013), 28; Thomas Martin, Elizabeth G. McPherson, and David Mathisen, revised by Brian McGuire, "Mabel Thorp Boardman: A Register of Her Papers in the Library of Congress" (Washington, DC: Manuscript Division, LOC, 2006), 3, http://hdl.loc.gov.

4. See Sklar, "Hull House"; Muncy, *Creating a Female Dominion*; Irwin, *Making the World Safe*, 28.

5. Marian Moser Jones discusses how within the ARC, the Progressive professionalism of men often conflicted with the female culture of voluntarism. *American Red Cross*, xiii.

6. Irwin, *Making the World Safe*, 15.

7. Irwin, *Making the World Safe*, 5; American Red Cross, "Who Are We: Our History," n.d., http://www.redcross.org.

8. Irwin, *Making the World Safe*, 27–30.

9. Irwin, *Making the World Safe*, 73, 109. The other organizations were the YMCA, the Salvation Army, and the Knights of Columbus.

10. "American Women: Health and Medicine: Red Cross and World War I," Library of Congress: American Memory, n.d., http://memory.loc.gov; "The Army Nurse Corps," Women in the US Army, n.d., https://www.loc.gov; Jones, *American Red Cross*, 157. The ARC estimated that about ten thousand American nurses served overseas. Schneider and Schneider, *Into the Breach*, 287.

11. Trout, *On the Battlefield of Memory*, 1; Winter, *Remembering War*, 1.

12. For an examination of statuary trends in US World War One memorials, see Wingate, "Doughboys, Art Worlds," 39–52; Wingate, *Sculpting Doughboys*.

13. Examples of these plaques were found in project files 1910–1952, Records Relating Primarily to Projects, World War I Memorials, Records of the Commission of Fine Arts, Record Group 66 (RG 66), National Archives Building, Washington, DC (NAB). Boxes consulted within these records include box 211, Interstate Commerce Commission, Library of Congress Memorial; box 210, Forest Service; box 209, Agriculture Department.

14. Wingate, *Sculpting Doughboys*, 8, 75, 79.

15. Several authors provide short overviews of the debates occurring in the US over the best way to commemorate the war, centered on whether a memorial should be utilitarian or a traditional stone structure: G. Kurt Piehler, "Remembering the War to End All Wars," in *Unknown Soldiers: The American Expeditionary Forces in Memory and Remembrance*, ed. Mark Snell (Kent, OH: Kent State University Press, 2008), 29, 41–44; Wingate, "Doughboys, Art Worlds," 39–52; Wingate, *Sculpting Doughboys*.

16. For an in-depth analysis of World War One statues, see Wingate, "Doughboys, Art Worlds"; and Wingate, *Sculpting Doughboys*.

17. For an analysis of the origins of living memorials, see Shanken, "Planning Memory; Wingate, *Sculpting Doughboys*, 70–84, 190–91; Mosse, *Fallen Soldiers*, 220–21; Michele H. Bogart, *Public Sculpture and the Civic Ideal in New York City, 1890–1930* (Chicago: University of Chicago Press, 1989), 284. For information on liberty buildings, see Britanik, "Where Are the Ladies' Rest Rooms?," 69.

18. Examples of this type of memorial include the Washington, DC, World War One Memorial (a bandstand) and the Liberty Memorial in Kansas City, Missouri (a tower and tourist attraction now known as the National WWI Museum and Memorial).

19. "Liberty Buildings as Victory Monuments," *American City*, December 1918, folder Project Files World War I Memorials (General), box 208, RG 66, NAB; "About Us," American City and County, http://americancityandcounty.com; Wingate, *Sculpting Doughboys*, 79; Blair, *Torchbearers*, 103–6.

20. "Liberty Buildings as Victory Monuments," box 208, RG 66, NAB.

21. Piehler, *Remembering War*, 41–43; Shanken, "Planning Memory," 132.

22. Whitney designed several World War One memorials such as the St. Nazaire Memorial in France as well as the small sculpture *The Spirit of the Red Cross*, which resides

in the Civil War Building at the ARC Headquarters today. Jennifer Meehan, "A Finding Aid to the Gertrude Vanderbilt Whitney Papers, 1851–1975, Bulk 1888–1942, in the Archives of American Art," Archives of American Art, n.d., http://www.aaa.si.edu; Gertrude Vanderbilt Whitney, "The Useless Memorial," *Arts and Decoration* 12, no. 6 (April 25, 1920): 421. For more on Whitney, see Wingate, *Sculpting Doughboys*, 84–85, 115–16, 129–34.

23. Whitney, "Useless Memorial."

24. Whitney's name appears in several membership rosters of the WOSL. Box 1922–1932 and box 1933–1939, *Carry On* Periodical Collection, MWMC.

25. For a history of the CFA, see Sally Kress Tompkins, *A Quest for Grandeur: Charles Moore and the Federal Triangle* (Washington, DC: Smithsonian Institution Press, 1993), 1–9.

26. "War Memorials: Suggestions as to the Forms of Memorials and the Methods of Obtaining Designers," folder Project Files World War I Memorials (General), box 207, RG 66, NAB.

27. American Red Cross, *American Red Cross National Headquarters Visitor's Guide* (American Red Cross, June 2007), informational pamphlet; Shane MacDonald, guided tour of American Red Cross National Headquarters, August 16, 2013.

28. *American Red Cross National Headquarters Visitor's Guide*; "Urgent Deficiencies Appropriations," Pub. L. No. 32, "Women of the Civil War," 38 Stat. 233 (1913); Mr. Hughes to Miss Butler, November 13, 1920, box 22, American Red Cross Historical and WWI Nurse Files, folder 301, Delano, Jane, September–December 1920, Records of the American National Red Cross, National Archives Gift Collection, Record Group 200 (RG 200), National Archives, College Park, MD (NACP). Since I conducted research in this collection within Record Group 200 at the NACP in 2013, the name of the Record Group has changed to "American National Red Cross (ANRC)." Record Group 200 is now the overall record group for donated records at the NACP. For the sake of clarity and with the permission of the NACP, RG 200 will be used throughout this book. Thanks to Tom McAnear, archivist at the NACP, for his guidance with this citation.

29. *American Red Cross National Headquarters Visitor's Guide*.

30. *American Red Cross National Headquarters Visitor's Guide* and guided tour of American Red Cross National Headquarters. For more about the Women's Relief Corps, see Morgan, *Women and Patriotism*.

31. Undated postcards of the memorial windows, box ARC Buildings and Memorials, Civil War Memorial, Women of World War, DC Chapter, Old Georgetown Road, Ballroom Open House 6/16/2006, ARC New National Headquarters, folder ARC Buildings-Memorial Windows, Stained Glass, American Red Cross Archives, National Headquarters, Washington, DC. Hereafter, the collection will be abbreviated as ARC Archives.

32. "New Marble Home of the American Red Cross Dedicated," *St. Louis Post-Dispatch*, May 13, 1917, 1, ProQuest Historical Newspapers; "Wilson Eulogizes Our Principles," *Los Angeles Times*, May 13, 1917, 15, ProQuest Historical Newspapers; "Red Cross Home Dedication May 12," *Washington Post*, April 16, 1917, 7, ProQuest Historical Newspapers.

33. "Red Cross Home Dedication May 12," *Washington Post*, April 16, 1917, 7; "New

Marble Home of the American Red Cross Dedicated," *St. Louis Post-Dispatch*, May 13, 1917, 1.

34. Jones, *American Red Cross*, 167–68; American Red Cross, "Jane Delano Founder of the American Red Cross Nursing Service," https://www.redcross.org.

35. "Noted R. C. Worker Is Dead in Paris," *Miami Herald*, April 19, 1919, 5, America's Historical Newspapers; "Jane A. Delano Memorial Pamphlet," box 22, folder 301, RG 200, NACP; Kathleen Burger Johnson, "Delano, Jane Arminda (1862–1919)," in *An Encyclopedia of American Women at War: From the Home Front to the Battlefields*, ed. Lisa Tendrich Frank (Santa Barbara, CA: ABC-CLIO, 2013), 186–88; Gavin, *American Women*, 62–63.

36. F. C. Munrow, Red Cross General Manager to all department and bureau heads of HQ, April 18, 1919, box 21, folder 301, RG 200, NACP. Numerous examples of memorial ceremonies for Delano were found in box 21 and box 22, American Red Cross Historical and WWI Nurse Files, RG 200, NACP. A committee was formed in April 1920 to organize efforts for a memorial to Delano. Clara D. Noyes, "Unveiling of Memorial to Our Heroic Nurses," *Red Cross Courier*, 358–59, box 1, Nurses Memorial, folder 005, Nurses Memorial, RG 200, 1917–1934, NACP.

37. "Jane A. Delano Memorial," Smithsonian American Art Museum Inventory of American Sculpture, https://siris-artinventories.si.edu.

38. Gavin, *American Women*, 11–12, 63–64, 75, 157, 252–56. The number of American nurses who died during their wartime service varies in different sources; a definitive number is hard to verify. *Spirit of Nursing* used the number available at the time, and it may not be accurate.

39. Lillian L. White to Clara Noyes, box 22, folder 301, RG 200, NACP.

40. "Report of the Delano Committee to the State Nurse's Association, July 9, 1927," Mabel Thorp Boardman Papers, Manuscript Division, LOC, Washington, DC.

41. Letter from Adda Eldredge, box 1, folder 005, RG 200, NACP.

42. Mabel Boardman to Lucy Minnigerode, July 18, 1927, 1–2, box 1, folder 005, RG 200, NACP.

43. Noyes, "Unveiling of Memorial to Our Heroic Nurses," 358.

44. "Abstract of Report of the Delano Memorial Fund, January 17, 1921," box 1, folder 005, RG 200, NACP.

45. Noyes, "Unveiling of Memorial to Our Heroic Nurses," 358. Mrs. R. Tait McKenzie was a member of the Philadelphia WOSL Unit. "Presented at Court," *Carry On* 6, no. 3 (August 1927): 21, box 37, WOSL Records, MS 22, UTSA; Theresa R. Snyder, revised by Nicole Topich, "R. Tait McKenzie Papers, 1880–1940," University of Pennsylvania, University Archives & Records Center, 2012, https://archives.upenn.edu; "McKenzie, Ethel O'Neil," *Canada's Early Women Writers*, 1980–2014, Simon Fraser University Library Digital Collections, https://cwrc.ca.

46. Noyes, "Unveiling of Memorial to Our Heroic Nurses," 358–59.

47. Letter to Mr. Cammerer, January 26, 1933, box 43, PI 79-Entry 17, Delano, Jane A. Memorial to District of Columbia-Armory (box 43), folder Project Files, Jane A. Delano Memorial, RG 66, NAB.

48. Letters from several members of the CFA to McKenzie criticized the design of

the memorial. These letters can be found in box 43, folder Project Files, Jane A. Delano Memorial, RG 66, NAB.

49. Peter Spring, trans. and ed., *Guide to the Vatican: Museums and City* (Vatican City: Edizioni Musei Vaticani, 2007), 215–16.

50. Irwin, *Making the World Safe*, 86; Wingate, *Sculpting Doughboys*, 175–76; John M. Kinder, "Iconography of Injury: Encountering the Wounded Soldier's Body in American Poster Art and Photography of World War I," in *Picture This: World War I Posters and Visual Culture*, ed. Pearl James (Lincoln: University of Nebraska Press, 2009), 345–47.

51. Letter to Mr. Cammerer.

52. Many memorials to the First World War were created in the shape of a cross, such as the Memorial Peace Cross in Bladensburg, Maryland, and the Argonne Cross at Arlington National Cemetery. All of the overseas American World War One cemeteries run by the American Battle Monuments Commission used headstones in the shape of crosses or Stars of David instead of the rectangular headstones used in military cemeteries in the US. These religious headstones and the chapels at each ABMC cemetery give the cemeteries a distinctly religious tone.

53. Nora, "Between Memory and History"; Nora, *Rethinking France*.

54. Transcript of text of *New York Tribune* article from February 11, 1926, sent from Mabel Boardman to Mr. Augustus K. Oliver on March 27, 1926, 1, box 429, specifications for erection and completion of World War memorial, folder 481.7, RG 200, NACP.

55. Mabel T. Boardman, "American Women's War Memorial," December 1926, box 428, 481.13 Main Building & Grounds-Alterations Rebuilding & Relocating, folder 481.73, Memorials-Inscriptions, RG 200, NACP. This article was most likely published in the *Red Cross Courier*.

56. Boardman, "American Women's War Memorial."

57. Transcript of text of *New York Tribune* article from February 11, 1926, sent from Mabel Boardman to Mr. Augustus K. Oliver on March 27, 1926, 2. I could not find this exact inscription as it was written in the *New York Tribune* article on the building. However, a similarly worded inscription does exist inside the front foyer above the central door. It reads "A living memorial given by the government and the people of the United States in loving memory of the sacrifices and services of America's heroic women in the World War dedicated to the service of suffering humanity through the American Red Cross."

58. Transcript of text of *New York Tribune* article from February 11, 1926, sent from Mabel Boardman to Mr. Augustus K. Oliver on March 27, 1926, 2, 4.

59. Undated pamphlet, box 429, folder 481.7, RG 200, NACP.

60. At the start of World War One, women already served in the army and navy as uniformed nurses but lacked any official rank. On March 21, 1917, the navy announced that women could officially join the navy and Marine Corps as Yeoman (F) and female marines. Ebbert and Hall, *The First, the Few*, ix, 1.

61. The plans for the building required approval from the CFA, the director of Public Buildings and Public Parks of the National Capital, the American National Red Cross Committee, the secretary of war, the chair of the Senate Committee on the Library, and

the chair of the House Committee on the Library. Public Resolution No. 39, S. J. 98, box 429, folder 481.7, RG 200, NACP.

62. Public Resolution No. 39, S. J. 98.

63. Public Resolution No. 39, S. J. 98; pamphlet about WOSL dedicating column, 1, scrapbook of Toledo Unit kept by Julia Norton, 84.150.1, WOSL Collection, National WWI Museum and Memorial Archives.

64. "First Floor Plan, Memorial Building to the Women of the World War," box ARC Buildings and Memorials, Civil War Memorial, Women of World War, DC Chapter, Old Georgetown Road, Ballroom Open House 6/16/2006, ARC New National Headquarters, ARC Archives; unlabeled blueprint, box 428, folder 481.7, DC Chapter House, RG 200, NACP.

65. I gathered this information while on a tour of American Red Cross National Headquarters on August 16, 2013.

66. "First Floor Plan, Memorial Building to the Women of the World War"; unlabeled blueprint.

67. In several visits to the building, I could not find evidence of these workrooms. It is unclear whether they were ever added to the Hall of Service, or whether they were there initially but were removed in later years.

68. Pamphlet about the Memorial Building (no date), box 429, folder 481.7, World War Memorial General, RG 200, NACP.

69. Unlabeled blueprint.

70. I learned of Fieser's official title in the ARC from Jones, *American Red Cross*, viii.

71. Mr. James L. Fieser to Judge Payne, box 428, folder 481.73, Memorials-Inscriptions, RG 200, 1917–1934, NACP.

72. Julia Irwin notes that during World War One at least, the ARC had no national segregation policy in place and allowed local chapters to conform to practices of segregation and discrimination. *Making the World Safe*, 102.

73. Undated pamphlet, box 429, folder 481.7, World War Memorial General, RG 200, NACP.

74. Irwin, *Making the World Safe*, 49.

75. Undated pamphlet, box 429, folder 481.7, World War Memorial General, RG 200, NACP.

76. Rear Admiral W. S. Benson to Boardman, April 26, 1923, box 429, folder 481.7, World War Memorial General, RG 200, NACP.

77. Ebbert and Hall, *The First, the Few*; Godson, *Serving Proudly*.

78. Irwin, *Making the World Safe*, 35, 57–58.

79. Arthur Woods to Hon. Eliot Wadsworth, July 24, 1923, box 429, folder 481.7, World War Memorial General, RG 200, NACP.

80. Marquis Eaton to Boardman, June 9, 1925, box 429, folder 481.7, World War Memorial General, RG 200, NACP.

81. Mabel Boardman to Marquis Eaton, June 11, 1925, 1–2, box 429, folder 481.7, World War Memorial General, RG 200, NACP.

82. Mabel Boardman to Marquis Eaton, June 11, 1925, 1.

83. The Pan American Union Building (1910), barely one block from the ARC Headquarters, is an excellent example of a neoclassical-inspired beaux arts civic building. For a detailed analysis of the neoclassical and beaux arts influences on architect Paul Cret's design for the Pan American Union Building, see Elizabeth Grossman, *The Civic Architecture of Paul Cret* (New York: Cambridge University Press, 1996), 26–64. The Headquarters of the Daughters of the American Revolution at Memorial Continental Hall (1905), located directly next to the ARC Headquarters, is also a great example of beaux arts neoclassicism. "About DAR: National Headquarters Washington DC," National Society of the Daughters of the American Revolution, http://www.dar.org.

84. Virginia McAlester and Lee McAlester, *A Field Guide to American Houses* (New York: Alfred A. Knopf, 1996), 6–7, 378–83.

85. For a more detailed discussion of the origins of the architectural style of the Memorial Building to the Women of the World War, see Finkelstein, "Carry On," 121–25.

86. The creation of the Federal Triangle, not far from the ARC Headquarters, represented a concerted effort to incorporate the ideals of the City Beautiful movement into new federal buildings in DC. See Tompkins, *Quest for Grandeur*.

87. Adolf F. Placzek, *Macmillan Encyclopedia of Architects* (London: Free Press, 1982), 228–30.

88. Placzek, *Macmillan Encyclopedia of Architects*. Partner Breck Trowbridge studied at the École des Beaux-Arts in Paris in addition to founding and serving twice as president of the Society of Beaux-Arts Architects in New York

89. McAlester and McAlester, *Field Guide*, 378–79.

90. McAlester and McAlester, *Field Guide*, 180–85; fieldwork by the author, May 31, 2013.

91. Guided tour of American Red Cross National Headquarters, Washington, DC.

92. For a discussion of how hierarchies of memorials are used in a cultural landscape, see Grossman, *Civic Architecture*, 119–43.

93. For studies of women's commemorations of the Civil War, see Silber, *Romance of Reunion*; Cox, *Dixie's Daughters*; Mills and Simpson, *Monuments to the Lost Cause*; Janney, *Burying the Dead*.

94. Mabel Boardman, "The Columns," *Red Cross Courier*, February 1, 1928, box 428, folder 481.73, Memorials-Inscriptions, RG 200, NACP; Placzek, "Trowbridge and Livingston," in *Macmillan Encyclopedia of Architects*, 228–30.

95. In addition to the exterior columns, two interior columns in the foyer served as memorials, and columns in the Hall of Service were also used as individual memorials.

96. Boardman, "The Columns."

97. Pamphlet about WOSL dedicating column, 2, WOSL Collection, National WWI Museum and Memorial Archives.

98. Wartime propaganda posters depicted the ARC as the "World's Greatest Mother." Irwin, *Making the World Safe*, 86.

99. Boardman, "The Columns."

100. Boardman, "The Columns."

101. Boardman, "The Columns."

102. Fieldwork by the author, May 31, 2013.

103. Wingate, "Doughboys, Art Worlds"; Wingate, *Sculpting Doughboys*.

104. Pamphlet about WOSL dedicating column, 1, scrapbook of Toledo Unit kept by Julia Norton, 84.150.1, WOSL Collection, National WWI Museum and Memorial Archives.

105. Louise Wells to Mabel Boardman, box 428, folder 481.73, Memorials-Inscriptions, RG 200, NACP.

106. Copy of WOSL resolution from July 17–20, 1927, convention sent to Mabel Boardman, box 428, folder 481.73, Memorials-Inscriptions, RG 200, NACP.

107. Boardman and Minnigerode's names appear in several membership rosters of the WOSL. Box 1922–1932 and box 1933–1939, *Carry On* Periodical Collection, MWMC; copy of WOSL resolution from July 17–20, 1927, convention sent to Mabel Boardman.

108. Lena Hitchcock to Mabel Boardman, February 16, 1929, box 428, folder 481.73, Memorials-Inscriptions, RG 200, NACP.

109. Lena Hitchcock to Mabel Boardman, February 16, 1929.

110. *Carry On* 7, no. 3 (August 1928): 30; *Carry On* 9, no. 2 (May 1930): 7–8, box 37, WOSL Records, MS 22, UTSA.

111. This was especially true for many artists after the war, especially in Europe, who lashed out against traditional aesthetics and created art that reflected the war's destruction. For a description of the war's influence on art, see chap. 6 in Winter, *Sites of Memory*.

112. Although Boardman did travel to France and Italy in 1918, it is not likely that she witnessed the horrors of the war to the same extent as the rank and file ARC workers closer to the battle lines. She described sensing the horrors of war upon her arrival in France, but her letters to her mother from Europe depicted activities focused on inspection tours, meetings, and social events with other prominent Americans helping in Europe. She only occasionally left Paris and Rome and did not venture anywhere near the embattled areas of either country. Box 8, Mabel Thorp Boardman Papers, Manuscript Division, LOC, Washington, DC; letters from Mabel Boardman to her mother, April 9, 1918–May 9, 1918, Mabel Thorp Boardman Collection, American Red Cross Historical Biography, Boardman, Mabel: Miscellaneous Material, American Women's War Relief 1914, ARC Archives; Irwin, *Making the World Safe*, 137.

113. Winter, *Sites of Memory*, 2–5.

114. "Cornerstone Laid for Women's World War Memorial," box 429, folder 481.73, Laying of Cornerstone Dedication Ceremony General Correspondence, RG 200, NACP.

115. "List of Articles to Go in Corner Stone Box of Red Cross Memorial Building to the Women of the World War," box 429, folder 481.73, Laying of Cornerstone Dedication Ceremony, RG 200 1917–1934, NACP.

116. "Press Release March 19, 1930: President Hoover Accepts World War Memorial to Women from General Pershing," box 429, folder 481.73, Laying of Cornerstone Dedication Ceremony, RG 200, NACP; "Press Release March 15, 1930: Memorial to Women of World War to be Dedicated Wednesday," 1, box 429, folder 481.73, Laying of Cornerstone Dedication Ceremony, RG 200, NACP.

117. In her "Report on the Collections of Uniforms of Women Worn during the Great War, 1914–1918," presented to the National Society of the Colonial Dames of America in

1941, Mrs. Marcus Mitchell Benjamin explained that their collection of women's World War One uniforms could not be stored at the Red Cross Headquarters because "every bit of space . . . has been turned over to War Relief work." Minutes of the Twenty-Fifth Biennial Council of the National Society of the Colonial Dames of America, "Report on the Collections of Uniforms of Women Worn during the Great War, 1914–1918," 60, folder NSCDA Report, Smithsonian Institution Archives, Colonial Dames Collection Documents, NMAH, Division of Armed Forces History.

118. "American Red Cross Headquarters Designated Historical Landmark," June 15, 1966, 2, box ARC Buildings and Memorials, folder ARC Buildings-Civil War Memorial, ARC Archives.

119. Susan Watson, archivist at ARC Archives, email message to author, November 12, 2019.

120. As of 2020, Nancy Peery Marriott appears to be alive, making it highly unlikely that she could have served in or supported World War One during the conflict. "Meet the Founders," Nancy Peery Marriott Foundation, https://npmfoundation.org.

Chapter 3

1. The Argonne Cross memorial at Arlington National Cemetery was dedicated by the Argonne Unit of the American Women's Legion to the men who died in France. "Argonne Cross (WWI)," Arlington National Cemetery Explorer, n.d., https://ancexplorer .army.mil.

2. I obtained the information on these graves from my fieldwork at the cemetery and from Find a Grave.com.

3. "Obituaries," *Physical Therapy* 55, no. 3 (March 1975): 286, https://doi.org/10.1093 /ptj/55.3.286; Laura Brackett Hoppin, ed., *History of the World War Reconstruction Aides* (Millbrook, NY: Williams Tyldsley, 1933), 86.

4. Linker, *War's Waste*, 61. The wartime experiences of the Reconstruction Aides have already been analyzed in great depth by Linker. This chapter builds on her scholarship by uncovering what these women did *after* the war. For more on the history of Reconstruction Aides, see Beth Linker, "Strength and Science: Gender, Physiotherapy, and Medicine in Early-Twentieth-Century America," *Journal of Women's History* 17, no. 3 (Fall 2005); Jaclyn Faglie Lowe, "The Reconstruction Aides," *American Journal of Occupational Therapy* 46, no. 1 (January 1992): 38–43; Judith Pettigrew, Katie Robinson, and Stephanie Moloney, "The Bluebirds: World War I Soldiers' Experiences of Occupational Therapy," *American Journal of Occupational Therapy* 71, no. 1 (January/February 2017): 1–9; Gutman, "Influence of the U.S. Military," 256–62.

5. Linker, *War's Waste*, 74–75.

6. Linker, *War's Waste*, 2; Gutman, "Influence of the U.S. Military," 259.

7. Emma E. Vogel, "Physical Therapists before World War II (1917–1949)," in *Army Medical Specialist Corps*, ed. Robert S. Anderson (Washington, DC: Office of the Surgeon General, Department of the Army, 1968), 57, https://history.amedd.army.mil; Ann M. Ritchie Hartwick, *The Army Medical Specialist Corps: The 45th Anniversary* (Washington, DC: Center of Military History, 1993), 9, https://history.army.mil.

8. Linker, *War's Waste*, 61.

9. Linker, *War's Waste*, 71.

10. Linker, *War's Waste*, 63–70.

11. Anonymous untitled poem in *Carry On: A Magazine of the Reconstruction of Disabled Soldiers and Sailors* 1, no. 10 (July 1919): 32, box 001, folder 009, OHA 97, Otis Historical Archives, National Museum of Health and Medicine (NMHM). According to Jaclyn Faglie Lowe, this magazine was published by the Red Cross for the Office of the Surgeon General from June 1918 to July 1919. Lowe, "Reconstruction Aides," 40–41.

12. Eric W. Boyle, OHA 371, World War Reconstruction Aides Association Collection, Finding Aid, NMHM, 2012, 1.

13. To reach a consensus about the organization's name, members were polled and findings reported in the *Re-Aides' Post*. "Personal Opinion," *Re-Aides' Post* 7, no. 1 (July 1927): 7, box 002, folder 002, OHA 371, Otis Historical Archives, NMHM; Esther Macomber, "Farewell," *Re-Aides' Post* 12, no. 1 (July 1933): 6, box 002, folder 002, OHA 371, Otis Historical Archives, NMHM.

14. African American women did not get the opportunity to serve as army physical therapists until 1943, when a segregated physical therapy training course was briefly established at Fort Huachuca and terminated in 1944 after "the requirement for Negro physical therapists was met with the commissioning of the trainees in December 1944." Emma E. Vogel, Katherine E. Manchester, Helen B. Gearin, and Wilma L. West, "Training in World War II" in *Army Medical Specialist Corps*, ed. Robert S. Anderson (Washington, DC: Office of the Surgeon General Department of the Army, 1968), 154–55, https://history.amedd.army.mil; American Physical Therapy Association, "1943: The Special Women's Medical Service Corps Program for African-Americans Launches," 100 Milestones of Physical Therapy: APTA 100 Years, 1921–2021 https://centennial.apta.org; Steven D. Smith, *The African American Soldier At Fort Huachuca, Arizona, 1892–1946* (Fort Huachuca, AZ, and Seattle: US Army Fort Huachuca, AZ, and Center of Expertise for Preservation of Historic Structures & Buildings, US Army Corps of Engineers, Seattle District, 2001), 110–11.

15. "The Constitution of the Re-Aides' Association," *Re-Aides' Post* 6, no. 4 (April 1927): 10, box 002, folder 002, OHA 371, Otis Historical Archives, NMHM.

16. *????* 1, no. 1 (July 28, 1920) 1, box 003, OHA 371, Otis Historical Archives, NMHM. The very early editions of the publication that later became the *Re-Aides' Post* did not yet have a title and were labeled with just *????* to demonstrate that the nascent newsletter still needed a title.

17. Winifred Keith Pinto, "Who Are, What Are, Why Are We?," *Re-Aides' Post* 7, no. 2 (January 1928): 5, box 002, folder 003, OHA 371, Otis Historical Archives, NMHM.

18. "Why They Organize," *????* 1, no. 1 (July 28, 1920): 2, box 003, OHA 371, Otis Historical Archives, NMHM.

19. "Thanksgiving," *Re-Aides' Post* 1, no. 5 (November 24, 1920): 2, box 003, OHA 371, Otis Historical Archives, NMHM.

20. Eleanor Rowland Wembridge, "How the Reconstruction Aides Have Proved What They Are For," *Carry On: A Magazine of the Reconstruction of Disabled Soldiers and*

Sailors 1, no. 7 (April 1919): 10–11, box 001, folder 009, OHA 97, Otis Historical Archives, NMHM.

21. "Physio-Therapy's Part in Reconstruction," *Carry On: A Magazine of the Reconstruction of Disabled Soldiers and Sailors* 1, no. 7 (April 1919): 7–9, box 001, folder 009, OHA 97, Otis Historical Archives, NMHM.

22. Hoppin, *History of the World War.*

23. Lena Hitchcock, *Great Adventure*, xi–xii, box 240, WOSL Records, MS 22, UTSA.

24. Lena Hitchcock oral history (03), July 14, 1982, recorded by the WOSL, UC–MS022/7 Lena Hitchcock, box 182, WOSL Records, MS 22, UTSA.

25. ???? 1, no. 1 (July 28, 1920): 1, box 003, OHA 371, Otis Historical Archives, NMHM.

26. "A Bit of Service," *Re-Aides' Post* 3, no. 1 (July 1922): 3, box 003, OHA 371, Otis Historical Archives, NMHM.

27. "American Legion Draws Re-Aides' to Convention," *Re-Aides' Post* 4, no. 2 (October 1923): 1, box 003, OHA 371, Otis Historical Archives, NMHM.

28. "Devoted Member Buried with Military Honors," *Re-Aides' Post* 3, no. 3 (January 1923): 1, box 003, OHA 371, Otis Historical Archives, NMHM.

29. "Letter from General Pershing to Beulah Reimert O.T.," *Re-Aides' Post* 4, no. 5 (April, 1925): 4, box 003, OHA 371, Otis Historical Archives, NMHM.

30. "Letter from General Pershing to Beulah Reimert O.T.," 4.

31. Mae Van Camp, "The First National Convention of the World War Reconstruction Aides," *Re-Aides' Post* 9, no. 1 (July 1929): 4–5, box 002, folder 004, OHA 371, Otis Historical Archives, NMHM.

32. "Treasurer's Report," *Re-Aides' Post* 11, no. 1 (July 1931): 2–5, box 002, folder 006, OHA 371, Otis Historical Archives, NMHM.

33. Ethel Clements Dana, "The Committee on Military Status," *Re-Aides' Post* 12, no. 3 (January 1933): 4, box 002, folder 008, Otis Historical Archives, NMHM.

34. Myrtle Thornton McLeod, "Ninth Corps Area," *Re-Aides' Post* 12, no. 2 (October 1932): 3–6, box 002, folder 007, Otis Historical Archives, NMHM.

35. Ethel C. Dana, "Report of the Committee on Military Status of the World War Reconstruction Aides," *Re-Aides' Post* 12, no. 2 (October 1933): 5, box 002, folder 008, OHA 371, Otis Historical Archives, NMHM.

36. "To Former Reconstruction Aides," *Re-Aides' Post* 15, no. 1 (July 1935): 6, box 002, folder 0010, OHA 371, Otis Historical Archives, NMHM.

37. "Veterans' Status," *Re-Aides' Post* 16, no. 4 (April 1937): 4, box 002, folder 012, OHA 371, Otis Historical Archives, NMHM.

38. "Veterans' Status," *Re-Aides' Post* 16, no. 4 (April 1937): 4, box 002, folder 012, OHA 371, Otis Historical Archives, NMHM.

39. "Dorothea David (Mrs. Charles Dwight Custiss)," *Re-Aides' Post* 20, no. 3 (January 1941): 7, box 002, folder 016, OHA 371, Otis Historical Archives, NMHM.

40. Bertha York Webb to Daisy, n.d., box 001, folder 011, OHA 97, Otis Historical Archives, NMHM. Daisy was probably Daisy Doty Gallois, but no last name was included in the letter.

41. Rachel Ring Pittman to Estelle Angier, May 12, 1941, box 001, folder 011, OHA 97, Otis Historical Archives, NMHM.

42. Ruth B. Tibbals to Estelle Angier, July 2, 1941, box 001, folder 011, OHA 97, Otis Historical Archives, NMHM.

43. "Opinions on Military Status," *Re-Aides' Post* 20, no. 3 (January 1941): 16, box 002, folder 016, OHA 371, Otis Historical Archives, NMHM.

44. "Second Business Meeting," *Re-Aides' Post* 21, no. 1–2 (July–October 1941): 4–5, box 002, folder 016, OHA 371, Otis Historical Archives, NMHM.

45. Alice Archer Rohns (Alice Watts), "A Field for Service," *????* 1, no. 3 (August 25, 1920): 2, box 003, OHA 371, Otis Historical Archives, NMHM.

46. As quoted in Sidney Helen Boteler, "Occupational Therapy with Visiting Nurse Cases," *Re-Aides' Post* 7, no. 1 (July 1927): 5, box 002, folder 002, OHA 371, Otis Historical Archives, NMHM.

47. Esther Macomber, "I Salute You," *Re-Aides' Post* 2, no. 4 (April 1932): 3, box 002, folder 007, OHA 371, Otis Historical Archives, NMHM.

48. Martha Moffett Bache, "Washington Unit," *Re-Aides' Post* 12, no. 1 (July 1932): 4, box 002, folder 007, OHA 371, Otis Historical Archives, NMHM.

49. Esther Macomber, "W.W.R.A. Convention—1933," *Re-Aides' Post* 12, no. 3 (January 1933): 3, box 002, folder The Re-Aides' Post, 1933 OHA371/002, OHA 371, Otis Historical Archives, NMHM.

50. "Re-Aides' Song 1933 Convention—Chicago (Tune—'Smiles')," *Re-Aides' Post* 12, no. 2 (October 1933): 5, box 002, folder 008, OHA 371, Otis Historical Archives, NMHM.

51. "Reporters for April," *Re-Aides' Post* 14, no. 3 (January 1935): 5, box 003, folder 010, OHA 371, Otis Historical Archives, NMHM.

52. "Hope Fullerton (Mrs. Arthur B. Tuttle)," *Re-Aides' Post* 20, no. 3 (January 1941): 11, box 002, folder 016, OHA 371, Otis Historical Archives, NMHM.

53. Estelle Angier, "The Sixth Biennial Convention," *Re-Aides' Post* 20, no. 4 (April 1941): 3, box 002, folder 016, OHA 371, Otis Historical Archives, NMHM.

54. "Attention!," *Re-Aides' Post*, 20, no. 4 (April 1941): 5, box 002, folder 016, OHA 371, Otis Historical Archives, NMHM.

55. Marcia Winn, "'Real Angels' of World War Convene Here," *Chicago Daily Tribune*, July 10, 1941, 13, ProQuest.

56. "Out of the Mail Bag," *Re-Aides' Post* 21, no. 3–4 (January–April 1942): 8, box 002, folder 017, OHA 371, Otis Historical Archives, NMHM.

57. "Out of the Mail Bag," 5.

58. "Out of the Mail Bag," 7.

59. "Out of the Mail Bag," 6; *Re-Aides' Post* 22, no. 2 (January 1943): 6, box 002, folder 018, OHA 317, Otis Historical Archives, NMHM.

60. *Re-Aides' Post* 22, no. 4 (April 1943): 3–4, box 002, folder 018, OHA 371, Otis Historical Archives, NMHM; "Red Cross First Aid Station Set Up at War Show," *Chicago Daily Tribune*, June 22, 1943, 3.

61. *Re-Aides' Post* 22, no. 1 (July 1942): 8, box 002, folder 017, OHA 371, Otis Historical Archives, NMHM.

62. Laura Brackett Hoppin, "Reporters for January 1943," *Re-Aides' Post* 22, no. 2 (October 1942): 7, box 003, folder 017, OHA 371, Otis Historical Archives, NMHM.

63. "Anna G. Voris," *Re-Aides' Post* 21, no. 3–4 (January–April 1942): 10, box 002, folder 017, OHA 371, Otis Historical Archives, NMHM.

64. Emily H. Huger, "Greetings from the President," *Re-Aides' Post* 23, no. 1 (Summer 1943): 3, box 002, folder 018, OHA 371, Otis Historical Archives, NMHM.

65. These questionnaires were found in box 001, folder 009, OHA 371, Otis Historical Archives, NMHM.

66. Questionnaire from Winifred M. Keith, box 001, folder 009, OHA 371, Otis Historical Archives, NMHM.

67. Questionnaires from Margaret Lovell and Henrietta E. Failing, box 001, folder 009, OHA 371, Otis Historical Archives, NMHM.

68. Questionnaire from Abigail Roxanna Bailey, box 001, folder 009, OHA 371, Otis Historical Archives, NMHM.

69. Questionnaire from Harriet Joor, box 001, folder 009, OHA 371, Otis Historical Archives, NMHM.

70. Alice Ueland, "Re-Aides Endowment Fund to Be Raised," *Re-Aides' Post* 5, no. 7 (December 1925): 1, box 003, OHA 371, Otis Historical Archives, NMHM.

71. "Endowment Fund Suggestions," *Re-Aides' Post* 6, no. 1 (June 1926): 1, box 003, OHA 371, Otis Historical Archives, NMHM.

72. Alice Ueland, "Reconstruction Aides Endowment Fund," *Re-Aides' Post* 6, no. 2 (October 1926): 7, box 002, folder 001, OHA 371, Otis Historical Archives, NMHM.

73. "Memorial," *Re-Aides' Post* 8, no. 3 (January 1929): 6, box 002, folder 004, OHA 371, Otis Historical Archives, NMHM.

74. Mae Van Camp, "The First National Convention of the World War Reconstruction Aides," *Re-Aides' Post* 9, no. 1 (July 1929): 3, box 002, folder 004, OHA 371, Otis Historical Archives, NMHM.

75. Van Camp, "The First National Convention," 3–7; Winifred Keith Pinto, "Our First National Convention," *Re-Aides' Post* 8, no. 4 (April 1929): 5, box 002, folder 004, OHA 371, Otis Historical Archives, NMHM.

76. Van Camp, "The First National Convention," 4.

77. Van Camp, 3.

78. "Our Memorial," *Re-Aides' Post* 9, no. 1 (July 1929): 6–7, box 002, folder 004, OHA 371, Otis Historical Archives, NMHM.

79. "Our Memorial," 7.

80. "The Memorial Fund," *Re-Aides' Post* 9, no. 2 (October 1929): 4, box 002, folder 004, OHA 371, Otis Historical Archives, NMHM.

81. Louisa C. Lippett, "The New Campaign," *Re-Aides' Post* 9, no. 3 (January 1930): 3, box 002, folder 005, OHA 371, Otis Historical Archives, NMHM.

82. "Chicago Unit No. 1," *Re-Aides' Post* 9, no. 3 (January 1930): 4, box 002, folder 005, OHA 371, Otis Historical Archives, NMHM; "Buffalo Unit No. 6," *Re-Aides' Post* 9, no. 3 (January 1930): 4, box 002, folder 005, OHA 371, Otis Historical Archives, NMHM.

83. Margaret Lovell, "The Memorial Inscription," *Re-Aides' Post* 9, no. 3 (January 1930): 5, box 002, folder 005, OHA 371, Otis Historical Archives, NMHM.

84. "Gift of the World War Reconstruction Aides," *Re-Aides' Post* 9, no. 4 (April 1930): 3, box 002, folder 005, OHA 371, Otis Historical Archives, NMHM.

85. "Gift of the World War Reconstruction Aides," 3.

86. "Social Activities," *Re-Aides' Post* 11, no. 1 (July 1931): 8–9, box 002, folder 006, OHA 371, Otis Historical Archives, NMHM.

87. I could not find any plaques on the columns inside the Hall of Service in a visit to the building on January 13, 2020. Asked that day, staff members could not recall seeing plaques on those columns during at least the past twenty years. According to the staff, while their collection does contain a few memorial plaques from various parts of the building's interior, they do not have one from the Reconstruction Aides' memorial column in the Hall of Service, nor did they know about this column.

88. "Twenty Thousand Dollars," *Re-Aides' Post* 6, no. 2 (October 1926): 8, box 002, folder 001, OHA 371, Otis Historical Archives, NMHM.

89. Hoppin, *History of the World War*, 3.

90. "Where Is the History?," *Re-Aides' Post* 8, no. 3 (January 1929): 9, box 002, folder 004, OHA 371, Otis Historical Archives, NMHM.

91. "Recognition for the History," *Re-Aides' Post* 12, no. 4 (April 1934): 4, box 003, folder 009, OHA 371, Otis Historical Archives, NMHM.

92. "Where Is the History?," *Re-Aides' Post* 8, no. 3 (January 1929): 9, box 002, folder 004, OHA 371, Otis Historical Archives, NMHM.

93. Emily H. Huger, "To the Members," *Re-Aides' Post* 24, no. 1 (Summer 1944): 3, box 002, folder 018, OHA 371, Otis Historical Archives, NMHM.

94. "The Fight is On!," *Re-Aides' Post* 23, no. 1 (Summer 1943): 11, box 002, folder 018, OHA 371, Otis Historical Archives, NMHM.

95. "Helene Hartley Anderson," *Re-Aides' Post* 24, no. 1 (Summer 1944): 7, box 002, folder 018, OHA 371, Otis Historical Archives, NMHM.

96. Dora I. Dysart, "Greetings," *Re-Aides' Post* 24, no. 2 (Autumn 1945): 3, box 002, folder 020, OHA 371, Otis Historical Archives, NMHM.

97. Emily H. Huger, "To the Members," *Re-Aides' Post* 24, no. 1 (Summer 1944): 3, box 002, folder 018, OHA 371, Otis Historical Archives, NMHM.

98. Elizabeth Weir Wright, "Chicago Unit," *Re-Aides' Post* 24, no. 1 (Summer 1944): 6, box 002, folder 018, OHA 371, Otis Historical Archives, NMHM.

99. "Gracia Loehl (Mrs. G. J. Maloney)," *Re-Aides' Post* 24, no. 2 (Autumn 1945): 9, box 002, folder 020, OHA 371, Otis Historical Archives, NMHM.

100. "Ruth Earle (Mrs. George J. Schreiber)," *Re-Aides' Post* 25, no. 2 (December 1946): 4, box 002, folder 022, OHA 371, Otis Historical Archives, NMHM.

101. Laura Brackett Hoppin, "Roundabout," *Re-Aides' Post* 25, no. 1 (Summer 1946): 4, 16, box 002, folder 021, OHA 371, Otis Historical Archives, NMHM.

102. Madeleine Ashley Carter to Estelle Angier, July 14, 1949, box 001, folder 009, OHA 371, Otis Historical Archives, NMHM.

103. Questionnaire from Mildred Lincoln Pierce, box 001, folder 009, OHA 371, Otis Historical Archives, NMHM.

104. Questionnaire from Abigail Roxanna Bailey, box 001, folder 009, OHA 371, Otis Historical Archives, NMHM.

105. "Mrs. Adrogna Elected Head of W.R.A.A.," *Chicago Daily Tribune*, July 27, 1947, F1.

106. Ethel C. Dana to Mrs. Adrogna, April 22, 1949, box 001, folder 009, OHA 371, Otis Historical Archives, NMHM.

107. Questionnaire from Hope Fullerton, box 001, folder 009, OHA 371, Otis Historical Archives, NMHM.

108. Questionnaire from Harriet Joor, box 001, folder 009, OHA 371, Otis Historical Archives, NMHM.

109. Lena Hitchcock to COL McDaniel, n.d., box 003, folder 001, OHA 97, Otis Historical Archives, NMHM.

110. Questionnaire from Harriet Lee Johnson, box 001, folder 009, OHA 371, Otis Historical Archives, NMHM.

111. *Re-Aides' Post* 27, no. 1–4 (Convention Number 1949–50): 1–2, box 002, folder 022, OHA 371, Otis Historical Archives, NMHM.

112. Louise C. Robinson, "Dear Fellow Aides," *Re-Aides' Post* 27, no. 1–4 (Convention Number 1949–50): 1–3, 6, 9, box 002, folder 022, OHA 371, Otis Historical Archives, NMHM.

113. Louise C. Robinson, "Dear Fellow Aides," *Re-Aides' Post* 27, no. 1–4 (Convention Number 1949–50): 5, box 002, folder 022, OHA 371, Otis Historical Archives, NMHM.

114. Louise C. Robinson, "Dear Fellow Aides," *Re-Aides' Post* 27, no. 1–4 (Convention Number 1949–50): 5, 8, 9, box 002, folder 022, OHA 371, Otis Historical Archives, NMHM. For the history of the Smithsonian's collection of women's World War One uniforms that was created starting in 1919 by the National Society of the Colonial Dames of America, see Finkelstein, "Exhibiting Veteranist-Commemorations," chap. 5 in "Carry On," 237–83.

115. Louise C. Robinson, "Dear Fellow Aides," *Re-Aides' Post* 27, no. 1–4 (Convention Number 1949–50): 9, 10, box 002, folder 022, OHA 371, Otis Historical Archives, NMHM.

116. "Our Story," National Museum of Health and Medicine, May 1, 2012, https://www.medicalmuseum.mil.

117. Emma Vogel to Dr. Edward R. White, April 7, 1979, box 001, folder Correspondence with Museum OHA 353/001 001:00005, OHA 353, Otis Historical Archives, NMHM.

118. "Remembering the Reconstruction Aides," *PT Transforms* (blog), American Physical Therapy Association, March 9, 2018, http://www.apta.org/; Department of Defense, Office of the Secretary of the Air Force, "Determinations of Active Military Service and Discharge; Civilian or Contractual Personnel," *Federal Register* 46, no. 138 (July 20, 1981): 37306, https://cdn.loc.gov.

119. "Out of the Mail Bag," *Re-Aides' Post*, 21, no. 1–2 (July–October 1941): 8, box 002, folder The Re-Aides' Post, 1941, OHA 371/002 002:00016, OHA 371, Otis Historical Archives, NMHM.

Chapter 4

1. "US Doughboys Did the Fighting but Mothers Really Won the War, Says Soldier Who Came Back," n.d., no newspaper name, in scrapbook "History of American War Mothers from October 1933 to September 1935, assembled by National Historian Mrs.

J. E. Wilcox of Bancroft, Kansas," no box, no folder, American War Mothers National Headquarters Collection, MWMC.

2. Elizabeth Cafer du Plessis, "Alice French, Indiana War Mothers: From World War I 'Kitchen Soldiers' to Postwar Immigrant Reformers," in *Feminist Frontiers: Women Who Shaped the Midwest*, ed. Yvonne J. Johnson (Kirksville, MO: Truman State University Press, 2010), 101–3.

3. du Plessis, "Alice French," 102–3, 107.

4. "Constitution and By-Laws, American War Mothers, Amended September 23, 1929," 6, in "American War Mothers First Annual Report Philadelphia, Pennsylvania, Acceptance of Act of Incorporation 1925," American War Mothers National Headquarters Collection, MWMC.

5. du Plessis, "Alice French," 106–9.

6. *Indiana Chapter of American War Mothers* (pamphlet), title page, box A-78, 76.268, folder American War Mothers 1951 Constitution & By-Laws, Indiana Chapter, C. 1951, American War Mothers Collection, National WWI Museum and Memorial Archives.

7. "Constitution and By-Laws, American War Mothers," 7.

8. "Constitution and By-Laws, American War Mothers," 11, 23–24.

9. "Constitution and By-Laws, American War Mothers," 3, 12.

10. "National American War Mothers Fourth Annual Convention, Kansas City, Missouri, October 1–4, 1923," 2–3, no box, no folder, MWMC.

11. "Three Objectives for Indiana War Mothers," unlabeled newspaper, box 1, Alice Moore French Papers, folder 8, AWM Indiana Chapter Scrapbook 1921–26, M458, Indiana Historical Society.

12. du Plessis, "Alice French," 113–16.

13. du Plessis, "Alice French," 116.

14. "History of American War Mothers," 22, box 1, Alice Moore French Papers, folder 7, History of American War Mothers, M458, Indiana Historical Society.

15. "Constitution and By-Laws, American War Mothers," 5.

16. "Constitution and By-Laws, American War Mothers," 6. Mothers of children who did not serve during the dates of official American participation were excluded from membership.

17. While the exact number of African Americans who served in World War One remains hard to verify, most estimates put the number at between 350,000 and 400,000. "World War I and Postwar Society," *African American Odyssey: A Quest for Full Citizenship*, LOC, March 21, 2008, published online in conjunction with an exhibit of the same title, organized by and presented at the Library of Congress, https://memory.loc.gov; Capozzola, *Uncle Sam Wants You*, 33; Scott, *Scott's Official History*, 149; Krewasky A. Salter, "From Civil War to World War: African American Soldiers and the Roots of the Civil Rights Movement," in *We Return Fighting: World War I and the Shaping of Modern Black Identity*, ed. Kinshasha Holman Conwill (Washington, DC: Smithsonian Books, 2019), 71.

18. "Proceedings Tenth National Convention American War Mothers, September 30–October 3, 1935, Wardman Park Hotel, Washington, D.C.," 82, no box, no folder, MWMC.

19. "Transcript of Proceedings: Second Biennial Convention of American War Mothers, 1921," 118–19, unlabeled box of American War Mothers material, MWMC.

20. "Transcript of Proceedings: Second Biennial Convention of American War Mothers, 1921," 118; "Yearbook 1925–1927, Kentucky Chapter American War Mothers," 3, Kentucky Historical Society Digital Collections, http://www.kyhistory.com. This document lists a Mrs. Huffman as the Kentucky Chapter's fourth vice president from 1926 to 1927 and a member of the Constitution Committee for the convention, indicating this is likely the same Mrs. Huffman.

21. "Transcript of Proceedings: Second Biennial Convention of American War Mothers, 1921," 118–19; Program "Dedication of Memory Trees," box 67, folder 1460-50–80-50, Memorial Trees 8/1925 to 3/1932, Records of the National Park Service, Record Group 79 (RG 79), National Capital Region, Subject Files, 1924–1951, NACP.

22. "Transcript of Proceedings: Second Biennial Convention of American War Mothers, 1921," 119.

23. "Army-Navy Union Groups Give Ball," *Washington Post*, May 26, 1935, ST8, ProQuest Historical Newspapers; Bertie L. Roberts, "Quincy Club Pays Honor to Officers," *Chicago Defender*, August 27, 1938, 17, ProQuest Historical Newspapers; "Chas. Young War Mothers Fete Friends," *Chicago Defender*, October 26, 1940, 4, ProQuest Historical Newspapers; "Gold Star Mothers Given Unique Reminiscent Tea," *Chicago Defender*, October 16, 1937, 15, ProQuest Historical Newspapers; George Franklin Proctor, "An Old Lady (Dedicated to Col. Charles Young Chapter American War Mothers)," *Chicago Defender*, March 12, 1938, 16, ProQuest Historical Newspapers; "War Mothers Receive Reports on Convention," *Washington Post*, November 12, 1933, F9, ProQuest Historical Newspapers. Colonel Young became a famous military figure and it is widely believed that discrimination prevented him from being sent to France during World War I. Jeffrey T. Sammons and John H. Morrow Jr., *Harlem's Rattlers and the Great War: The Undaunted 369th Regiment & the African American Quest for Equality* (Lawrence: University Press of Kansas, 2014), 54–56, 142–45. Golden Chapter of the Colored American War Mothers applications, 1933, box 4, folder 1, American War Mothers Collection, MSS 127, Kentucky Historical Society.

24. Golden Chapter of the Colored American War Mothers applications, 1933, box 4, folder 1, American War Mothers Collection, MSS 127, Kentucky Historical Society.

25. "Chapters Organized—1944–1945," box 17, scrapbook 1, American War Mothers Collection, MSS 127, Kentucky Historical Society.

26. "State President Report, October 14, 1943, to October 15, 1944," 2, box 17, scrapbook 1, American War Mothers Collection, MSS 127, Kentucky Historical Society.

27. Mrs. Mary Moran, "Recommendations," circa 1944–1945, box 17, scrapbook 1, American War Mothers Collection, MSS 127, Kentucky Historical Society.

28. "Proceedings Tenth National Convention, American War Mothers, September 30–October 3, 1935, Wardman Park Hotel, Washington, D.C.," 82, unlabeled box, American War Mothers National Headquarters Collection, MWMC.

29. In 1919, Scott published *Scott's Official History of the American Negro in the World War*. He also served for many years as the private secretary to Booker T. Washington.

30. "War Mothers Detail Events of Conclave," *Washington Post*, September 22, 1935, G8, ProQuest Historical Newspapers; "War Mothers Announce Features for Conven-

tion," *Washington Post*, September 15, 1935, ST6, ProQuest Historical Newspapers; "War Mothers Announce Features for Convention," *Washington Post*, September 15, 1935, ST6, ProQuest Historical Newspapers.

31. "Their Sons Died, but They Were Turned Down," *Baltimore Afro-American*, October 12, 1935, 5, ProQuest Historical Newspapers.

32. "Gold Star Mother Pays Respect to Deceased Heroes," *Baltimore Afro-American*, October 12, 1935, 4, ProQuest Historical Newspapers.

33. "American War Mothers," *Chicago Defender*, December 21, 1935, 7, ProQuest Historical Newspapers.

34. "American War Mothers," *Chicago Defender*, December 21, 1935, 7.

35. "Jim Crow Revealed in Group of War Mothers," *Baltimore Afro-American*, June 2, 1934, 20, ProQuest Historical Newspapers.

36. Scrapbook, box 1, Alice Moore French Papers, folder 10, handwritten with photographs and clippings, M458, Indiana Historical Society.

37. During the interwar era, the YWCA struggled with how to include African American women in the organization as some of its White members began to question segregation. See Robertson, *Christian Sisterhood*; Whalan, *Great War*.

38. Budreau, *Bodies of War*, 183–84. For more on republican motherhood, see Plant, *Mom*, 56–58; Kerber, *Women of the Republic*.

39. For more on motherhood as a form of service to the nation, see Plant, *Mom*, 56–62. For an in-depth analysis of the Gold Star pilgrimages in the context of motherhood and maternalism, see Plant, "Gold Star Mothers Pilgrimages."

40. Irwin, *Making the World Safe*, 86.

41. du Plessis, "Alice French," 101–6; Ladd-Taylor, *Mother-Work*, 3–4; Gordon, *Pitied but Not Entitled*, 55.

42. du Plessis, "Alice French," 101–6.

43. American War Mothers, "Rituals of the American War Mothers," adopted 1928, 32–34, Kentucky Historical Society Rare Books & Pamphlets, http://www.kyhistory.com.

44. "Meeting of National Executive Board of American War Mothers, Auditorium Hotel in Chicago, Illinois September 7th, 8th, & 9th, 1934," 13, MWMC.

45. Herbert Hoover, "Message to the American War Mother Magazine ," American Presidency Project, 1933, https://www.presidency.ucsb.edu.

46. "Years of Compassion 1914–1923," exhibits, n.d., Herbert Hoover Presidential Library and Museum, https://hoover.archives.gov; Sandra Trenholm, "Food Conservation during WWI: 'Food Will Win the War,'" Gilder Lehrman Institute of American History, October 16, 2012, https://www.gilderlehrman.org.

47. "Transcript of Proceedings: Second Biennial Convention of American War Mothers, 1921," 6–7.

48. "Transcript of Proceedings: Second Biennial Convention of American War Mothers, 1921," 7–9.

49. "Transcript of Proceedings: Second Biennial Convention of American War Mothers, 1921," 19–20.

50. "Invitation to the American War Mothers Twelfth Annual Mother's Day Services, 1936," box 14, General Correspondence, folder American War Mothers, John J. Pershing Papers, Manuscript Division, LOC; "Program of the American War Moth-

ers Thirteenth Annual Mother's Day Services, 1937," box 14, General Correspondence, folder American War Mothers, John J. Pershing Papers, Manuscript Division, LOC; *The American War Mothers Present Seventh Annual Mother's Day Ceremonies* (pamphlet), box 67, folder 1460-50-80-50, RG 79, National Capital Region, Subject Files, 1924–1951, NACP; "Meeting of National Executive Board of American War Mothers Auditorium Hotel in Chicago, Illinois September 7th, 8th, & 9th, 1934," 18–29, American War Mothers National Headquarters Collection, MWMC; "History of American War Mothers from October 1933 to September 1935, assembled by National Historian Mrs. J. E. Wilcox of Bancroft, Kansas," MWMC. Examples of some memorials erected by individual AWM chapters include the Inter-City American War Mothers Memorial outside Kansas City, Missouri; a memorial to those from Marshall County, Indiana, killed in the war, located in the Buck Cemetery; a memorial erected by the San Antonio Chapter of the AWM outside the Tobin Center for the Performing Arts in San Antonio; and a memorial in Philadelphia erected by the Philadelphia Chapter of the AWM intended to be titled "The American War Mother and Her Sons." James J. Heiman, *Voices in Bronze and Stone: Kansas City's World War I Monuments and Memorials* (Kansas City, MO: Kansas City Star Books, 2013), 61; "War Mothers Ass'n Breaks Ground for Soldier Memorial," unlabeled news clipping, n.d., box 1, Alice Moore French Papers, folder 8, AWM Indiana Chapter Scrapbook 1921-26, M458, Indiana Historical Society; "War Mothers Make Gift to Marshall County," May 31, 1923, box 1, Alice Moore French Papers, folder 8, AWM Indiana Chapter Scrapbook 1921-26, M458, Indiana Historical Society; "Proposed Monument to Be Erected by the Philadelphia Chapter in Honor of Those Who Served and Died in the World War," box 14, General Correspondence, John J. Pershing Papers, Manuscript Division, LOC; "Great War Monument, Philadelphia, Pennsylvania—World War I Memorials and Monuments on Waymarking.com," Waymarking.com, November 22, 2006, http://www.waymarking.com; "American War Mothers World War 1 Memorial Monument," United States World War One Centennial Commission, February 27, 2018, https://www.worldwar1centennial.org.

51. American War Mothers, "Rituals of the American War Mothers," adopted 1928, 32–34, Kentucky Historical Society Rare Books & Pamphlets, http://www.kyhistory.com.

52. "Capitol Bridge as It Will Appear When Built in Warrior's Memory," news clipping with no author or newspaper name listed, box 21, scrapbook 9, Kentucky State Chapter 1947-1948, American War Mothers Collection, MSS 127, Kentucky Historical Society; invitation to the dedication of the Memorial Bridge, box 11, series 22, 1938 dedication of the War Mothers Memorial Bridge Frankfort, American War Mothers Collection, MSS 127, Kentucky Historical Society; Mrs. Mary Moran to Governor Simeon Willis, February 14, 1945, box 17, scrapbook 1, American War Mothers Collection, MSS 127, Kentucky Historical Society.

53. "Fourth Annual Convention National American War Mothers, October 1-4, 1923, Kansas City, Missouri, Hotel Muhleback," 26, no folder, no box, MWMC.

54. "History of American War Mothers," 22–24, box 1, Alice Moore French Papers, folder 7, History of American War Mothers, M458, Indiana Historical Society.

55. "Fourth Annual Convention National American War Mothers October 1-4, 1923 Kansas City, Missouri, Hotel Muhleback," 25–26.

56. "Kansas City Chapter American War Mothers Yearbook 1928," 3, box 2004.100, no folder, American War Mothers Collection, National WWI Museum and Memorial Archives.

57. "Indiana," in scrapbook "American War Mothers History, September 1935 to September 1937, Corabelle G. Francis, Historian, Kansas Section," MWMC.

58. "Proceedings of the 5th Bi-ennial Convention (7th National Convention) of the American War Mothers," 168–75, MWMC.

59. "Proceedings of the 5th Bi-ennial Convention," 129–33.

60. "Proceedings of the 5th Bi-ennial Convention," 130.

61. "Proceedings of the 5th Bi-ennial Convention," 135–40.

62. "War Mothers in Favor of Bonus," *Waco City Times Herald*, October 3, 1923, box 2004.100, no folder, American War Mothers Collection, National WWI Museum and Memorial Archives.

63. Many pages of the AWM's scrapbook that recorded the organization's activities from 1935 to 1937 include news clippings of articles published in local newspapers about local chapters' carnation sales. For example, "Carnations Made by Vets," n.d., no author or newspaper, in scrapbook "American War Mothers History, September 1935 to September 1937, Corabelle G. Francis, Historian, Kansas Section," MWMC.

64. "Constitution and By-Laws, American War Mothers, Amended September 23, 1929," 14, in "American War Mothers First Annual Report Philadelphia, Pennsylvania Acceptance of Act of Incorporation 1925," MWMC; "The Poppy," Royal British Legion, n.d., https://www.britishlegion.org.uk; Veterans of Foreign Wars, "Buddy Poppy," n.d., http://www.vfw.org.

65. Executive vice chair to heads of services and offices of American Red Cross National Headquarters, May 5, 1943, box 935, folder 610, American War Mothers, RG 200, NACP; Vice chair in charge of domestic operations to all service heads, May 9, 1934, box 44, folder 041, American War Mothers, RG 200, NACP. Documentation shows that the AWM sold carnations at the Red Cross Headquarters in 1934, 1943, and probably throughout the 1930s, as it was an annual event.

66. Coolidge to Mrs. H. H. McCluer, March 4, 1924, box 14, General Correspondence, folder American War Mothers, John J. Pershing Papers, Manuscript Division, LOC; Pershing to Mrs. H. H. McCluer, April 14, 1924, box 14, General Correspondence, folder American War Mothers, John J. Pershing Papers, Manuscript Division, LOC.

67. "Carnations Made by Vets," n.d., no author or newspaper, in scrapbook "American War Mothers History, September 1935 to September 1937, Corabelle G. Francis, Historian, Kansas Section," MWMC.

68. "War Mothers Plan Sale of Carnations," n.d., no author or newspaper, in scrapbook "American War Mothers History, September 1935 to September 1937, Corabelle G. Francis, Historian, Kansas Section," MWMC.

69. "Meetings of the Executive Board of the American War Mothers, Claypool Hotel, Indianapolis, September 22–23, 1933," 4–8, no box, no folder, MWMC.

70. "Meetings of the Executive Board of the American War Mothers, Claypool Hotel, Indianapolis, September 22–23, 1933," 5–6.

71. "Mrs. Eva Price Chosen State's 'War Mother,'" *Washington Post*, May 14, 1944, M2.

72. "Eligible to Join 'War Mothers,'" *New York Times*, September 29, 1942, 20.

73. "Chapters Organized 1918–1943," box 17, scrapbook 1, American War Mothers Collection, MSS 127, Kentucky Historical Society.

74. Mrs. Mattie Madden to the State Board of American War Mothers, letter including "Report of Dorie Miller Chapter of American War Mothers, Lexington, Kentucky," April 19, 1944, box 8, folder 25, American War Mothers Collection, MSS 127, Kentucky Historical Society.

75. Mrs. Mattie Madden to the State Board of American War Mothers, October 10, 1944, box 8, folder 25, American War Mothers Collection, MSS127, Kentucky Historical Society.

76. "Veterans' Aid Described: War Mothers at Meeting Here Discuss Hospital Services," *New York Times*, September 13, 1947, 13.

77. Memorial Home section, "American War Mothers First Annual Report Philadelphia, Pennsylvania Acceptance of Act of Incorporation 1925," MWMC; "Fitzsimons General Hospital," *Colorado Encyclopedia*, last modified February 8, 2020, https://coloradoencyclopedia.org.

78. *Carry On* 5, no. 3 (August 1926): 17, box 1922–1932, folder 1926, Women's Overseas Service League, *Carry On* Periodical Collection, Gift of Carolyn Habgood, MWMC; "Fitzsimons General Hospital," *Colorado Encyclopedia*.

79. "Fitzsimons General Hospital," *Colorado Encyclopedia*.

80. Memorial Home section, "American War Mothers First Annual Report Philadelphia, Pennsylvania Acceptance of Act of Incorporation 1925," MWMC.

81. *Carry On* 5, no. 3 (August 1926): 17, box 1922–1932, folder 1926, *Carry On* Periodical Collection, Gift of Carolyn Habgood, MWMC.

82. For example, the Lincoln Capital (Nebraska) Chapter owned ten shares. Mrs. C. E. Burton to General Pershing, February 2, 1932, box 14, General Correspondence, folder American War Mothers, John J. Pershing Papers, Manuscripts Division, LOC; Memorial Home section, "American War Mothers First Annual Report Philadelphia, Pennsylvania Acceptance of Act of Incorporation 1925," MWMC.

83. Memorial Home section, "American War Mothers First Annual Report Philadelphia, Pennsylvania Acceptance of Act of Incorporation 1925," MWMC.

84. Home Operating Committee section, "American War Mothers First Annual Report Philadelphia, Pennsylvania Acceptance of Act of Incorporation 1925," MWMC.

85. Memorial Home section, "American War Mothers First Annual Report Philadelphia, Pennsylvania Acceptance of Act of Incorporation 1925," MWMC.

86. Memorial Home section, "American War Mothers First Annual Report Philadelphia, Pennsylvania Acceptance of Act of Incorporation 1925," MWMC. The Aurora, Colorado, historic nomination form for the home noted that it included a front walk inlaid with "memory stepping stones" that listed the names of chapters or individuals who donated to the home, but I have not confirmed this with other sources or during a 2015 visit to the home as seen from the street (I could not enter the property or grounds as it is now a private home). "Historic Nomination Form, City of Aurora, Colorado, Historic Preservation Commission, I.D. # HP87–102, Project Name: War Mothers Home," 4, April 2, 1987, application submitted by William C. Thomas, https://www.auroragov.org.

87. *Carry On* 5, no. 3 (August 1926): 17, box 1922–1932, folder 1926, *Carry On* Periodical Collection, Gift of Carolyn Habgood, MWMC.

88. *Carry On* 6, no. 2 (May 1927): 19, box 1922–1932, folder 1927, *Carry On* Periodical Collection, Gift of Carolyn Habgood, MWMC.

89. "Proceedings of the 5th Bi-ennial Convention," 209.

90. "Proceedings of the 5th Bi-ennial Convention," 209.

91. "Remarks of Brigadier General Omar H. Quade," framed, no folder, no box, MWMC.

92. "Remarks of Brigadier General Omar H. Quade," framed, no folder, no box, MWMC; Program "Dedication of Memory Trees," NACP.

93. "Remarks of Brigadier General Omar H. Quade," framed, no folder, no box, MWMC.

94. "Remarks of Brigadier General Omar H. Quade," framed, no folder, no box, MWMC.

95. "Proceedings of the 5th Bi-ennial Convention," 41.

96. "Meetings of the Executive Board of the American War Mothers Claypool Hotel, Indianapolis, September 22–23, 1933," 4–8.

97. "Penny Fund Plan for War Mothers," *Indianapolis News*, September 26, 1933, in scrapbook "History of American War Mothers from October 1933 to September 1935," MWMC.

98. "Proceedings Tenth National Convention American War Mothers, September 30–October 3, 1935, Wardman Park Hotel, Washington, D.C." 81, no folder, no box, MWMC.

99. While campaigning for the presidency, FDR coined the term the "Forgotten Man" in a radio address on April 7, 1932. In this address, known as "The Forgotten Man Speech," FDR referenced World War One and called on citizens to mobilize again as they had during the war, but this time against the Great Depression. Franklin D. Roosevelt, radio address from Albany, New York, "The 'Forgotten Man' Speech," April 7, 1932, American Presidency Project, https://www.presidency.ucsb.edu. For more about the "Forgotten Man" and the cultural power of this term during the Great Depression, see Finkelstein, "Carry On," 284–333; Martin Rubin, "The Crowd, the Collective, and the Chorus: Busby Berkeley and the New Deal," in *Movies and Mass Culture*, ed. John Belton (New Brunswick, NJ: Rutgers University Press, 1996), 59–92; Jeffrey Spivak, *Buzz: The Life and Art of Busby Berkeley* (Lexington: University Press of Kentucky, 2011), 76; Jonathan Kahana, "The Forgotten Man; or, How Hollywood Invented Welfare," *Camera Obscura* 62, no. 21(2) (2006): 81–82.

100. "Constitution and By-Laws, American War Mothers, Amended September 23, 1929," 3, 12.

101. In 1925, the AWM passed a resolution petitioning Congress to support an iteration of the pilgrimage bill that would have sent mothers and fathers of Americans buried overseas to those cemeteries. At the 1929 convention in Louisville, the AWM passed another resolution supporting the pilgrimage, but this time fathers were excluded, while mothers and wives of those buried at sea or missing in action, as well as women who had already visited the cemetery at their own expense, were included. "Proceedings of the

5th Bi-ennial Convention," 136, 195, 358; Resolution 10, "American War Mothers First Annual Report Philadelphia, Pennsylvania, Acceptance of Act of Incorporation, 1925."

102. "Proceedings of the 5th Bi-ennial Convention," 188–92.

103. "Proceedings of the 5th Bi-ennial Convention," 185.

104. "Proceedings of the 5th Bi-ennial Convention," 194.

105. "Transcript of Proceedings: Second Biennial Convention of American War Mothers, 1921," 30–32.

106. Eleanor Cresswell Wagner to Mrs. C. D. Brawner, May 21, 1940, box 935, folder 610, RG 200, NACP.

107. "Eligible to Join 'War Mothers,'" *New York Times*, September 29, 1942, 20.

108. "Veterans' Aid Described," *New York Times*, September 13, 1947, 19.

109. Since the Fitzsimons Hospital Building, opened in 1941, is on the National Register of Historic Places, the architectural elements of this particular building from the hospital's past have been preserved despite its new usage. In particular, the suite of rooms where President Eisenhower recovered from his 1955 heart attack are preserved and open to the public. Special thanks to Laura Steadman and Melissa Mezger for alerting me to this information. "Eisenhower Suite: The President's 1955 Heart Attack," University of Colorado Anschutz Medical Campus, n.d., https://medschool.cuanschutz.edu; "Fitzsimons General Hospital," *Colorado Encyclopedia*.

110. "Aurora Historic Preservation Landmarks," City of Aurora Historic Preservation Commission, 30, January 2016, https://www.auroragov.org; "Historic Nomination Form, City of Aurora, Colorado, Historic Preservation Commission I.D. # HP87–102, Project Name: War Mothers Home," April 2, 1987, application submitted by William C. Thomas, https://www.auroragov.org; "A Guide to Aurora Historic Preservation Landmarks," Aurora Historic Preservation, 31, https://e.issuu.com; Aurora TV, "Aurora History Tour—War Mother's Home," https://www.auroratv.org.

111. I viewed the exterior of the Memorial Home from the street in November 2015 and observed that it was extremely run-down and did not appear to be marked as a historic site. Email correspondence in November and December 2019 with T. Scott Williams, director of the Aurora History Museum, and Drake Brownfield, Aurora historic preservation specialist, confirmed that the home remained in a dilapidated state.

Chapter 5

1. "Hearing Before a Subcommittee of the Committee on Military Affairs, United States Senate, Seventieth Congress, Second Session, on H.R. 5494 S. 2681 S. 5332, Bills to Enable the Mothers and Unmarried Widows of the Deceased Soldiers, Sailors, and Marines of the American Forces Interred in the Cemeteries of Europe to make a Pilgrimage to These Cemeteries," part 2, February 12, 1929, 27, ProQuest Congressional Publications, https://congressional.proquest.com.

2. Budreau, *Bodies of War*, 21. During the Spanish-American War, the US repatriated the remains of its casualties, although there were far fewer casualties than in World War One. Dean W. Holt, *American Military Cemeteries: A Comprehensive Guide to the Hallowed Grounds of the United States, Including Cemeteries Overseas* (Jefferson, NC: McFarland, 1992), 3.

3. The number of American dead from World War One varies by source: the American Battle Monuments Commission and the US Department of Veterans Affairs list the total number as 116,516, while George Brown Tindall and David Emory Shi list it as 126,000. "World War I Burials and Memorializations," American Battle Monuments Commission (ABMC), n.d., https://www.abmc.gov; "America's War," US Department of Veterans Affairs, n.d., https://www.va.gov; George Brown Tindall and David Emory Shi, *America: A Narrative History 8th Edition*, 8th ed. (New York: W. W. Norton, 2010), 765; Budreau, *Bodies of War*, 21; Sledge, *Soldier Dead*, 135.

4. Sledge, *Soldier Dead*, 136; "World War I Burials and Memorializations," ABMC, n.d., https://www.abmc.gov. According to the ABMC, 30,973 Americans who died during World War One are buried at its cemeteries, and 4,446 who were missing in action, lost, or buried at sea are memorialized on Tablets of the Missing at the cemeteries, although exact figures for World War One unknowns remain hard to verify.

5. Drew Gilpin Faust, *This Republic of Suffering: Death and the American Civil War* (New York: Vintage Books, 2008), xiv, 61–63.

6. Faust, 86–87, 96–101; Budreau, *Bodies of War*, 87. See also Shannon Bontrager, *Death at the Edges of Empire: Fallen Soldiers, Cultural Memory, and the Making of an American Nation, 1863–1921* (Lincoln: University of Nebraska Press, 2020).

7. Quoted in Budreau, *Bodies of War*, 70. Original quotation from a letter from Roosevelt, "Roosevelt Objects to Removal of Son," *New York Times*, November 18, 1918, 11.

8. Budreau, *Bodies of War*, 13.

9. Mrs. Elizabeth Conley to the Quartermaster Corps, February 20, 1921, box 1008, Burial Case Files 1915–1939, folder 293, Conley, Francis X., Records of the Office of the Quartermaster General, Record Group 92 (RG 92), NACP. These burial files were located at the National Archives, College Park, when I conducted my research in the summer of 2012 but have since been relocated to the National Archives' National Personnel Records Center in St. Louis. Information regarding Mrs. Conley also came from box 5, American Gold Star Mothers, Inc., Records, folder "American Gold Star Mothers Applications for Membership Wa-We 1930–40," Manuscript Division, LOC.

10. Mrs. Elizabeth Conley to the Quartermaster Corps, n.d., box 1008, folder 293, RG 92, NACP.

11. Mrs. Katherine M. Gallagher to Captain A. D. Hughes, June 21, 1931, box 1784, Burial Case Files 1915–1939, folder Gallagher, Edward, RG 92, NACP.

12. "Burial and Memorialization Statistics," ABMC, n.d., https://www.abmc.gov.

13. Sledge, *Soldier Dead*, 136; Budreau, *Bodies of War*, 15; "Burial and Memorialization Statistics," ABMC, n.d., https://www.abmc.gov. While the exact number of unidentified and missing American service members from World War One remains unknown, at its sites, the ABMC memorializes 4,456 Americans from that war who were missing in action, lost, or buried at sea.

14. Grossman, *Civic Architecture of Paul Cret*, 143; Robin, *Enclaves of America*, 3–4, 30–31. For more on the diplomatic purposes of the pilgrimages, see Graham, *Gold Star Mother Pilgrimage*, 72–73; Budreau, *Bodies of War*, 100–106; Richard Hulver, "Remains in Peace: The Diplomacy of American Military Bodies in France, 1919–1972" (PhD diss., West Virginia University, 2015).

15. "Montfaucon American Monument," ABMC, n.d., http://www.abmc.gov.

16. Robin, *Enclaves of America*, 30, 60. Robin provides a detailed examination of the political and diplomatic meaning of the ABMC cemeteries and memorials.

17. Budreau, *Bodies of War*, 22.

18. *Commemorative Sites Booklet*, ABMC, n.d., 3, https://www.abmc.gov.

19. "The Commission: Intro," ABMC, n.d., https://www.abmc.gov. For a narrative history of the ABMC, see Thomas H. Conner, *War and Remembrance: The Story of the American Battle Monuments Commission* (Lexington: University Press of Kentucky, 2018).

20. *Commemorative Sites Booklet*, 3, 6–14.

21. "The Commission: Intro"; Conner, *War and Remembrance*, 1–2. As of December 2021, the ABMC administers twenty-six permanent overseas military cemeteries and thirty-one federal memorials, monuments, and markers and continues to carry out its mission of memorializing America's overseas war dead. In addition to cemeteries and memorials related to World War One and World War Two, the ABMC also acquired or created memorials and cemeteries related to a select few other conflicts, such as the Korean War, the Vietnam War, US forces in Mexico and Panama, and the Spanish American War. "Cemeteries and Memorials," ABMC, n.d., https://abmc.gov. For more about the history, design, and meaning of the ABMC World War Two cemeteries, see Kate Clarke Lemay, *Triumph of the Dead: American World War II Cemeteries, Monuments, and Diplomacy in France* (Tuscaloosa: University of Alabama Press, 2018). For more about the ABMC's Spanish American War site in Cuba, the Santiago Surrender Tree, see Bontrager, *Death at the Edges of Empire*.

22. Budreau, *Bodies of War*, 38–45; Conner, *War and Remembrance*, 20–23.

23. For a detailed examination of the American negotiations regarding the war dead and the negotiations with foreign countries regarding repatriation and the creation of American cemeteries, see Budreau, *Bodies of War*, 38–50, 66–69, 116–20. See also Conner, *War and Remembrance*, 20–23.

24. Faust, *This Republic of Suffering*, 248–49. For another discussion of the development of Civil War cemeteries, see, for example, Blair, *Cities of the Dead*. Prior to the Civil War, Congress had established the Mexico City National Cemetery for the remains of Americans killed during the Mexican War, many of whom were buried in a common grave. The ABMC became the steward of this cemetery in 1946. In 1982, the ABMC also acquired the Corozal American Cemetery in Panama, which contains the graves of American veterans and those who contributed to the construction of the Panama Canal. *Mexico City American Cemetery and Memorial* (pamphlet), ABMC, n.d., https://www.abmc.gov; "Mexico City National Cemetery," ABMC, https://www.abmc.gov; *Corozal American Cemetery and Memorial* (pamphlet), ABMC, n.d., https://www.abmc.gov; "Corozal American Cemetery," ABMC, https://www.abmc.gov.

25. Faust, *This Republic of Suffering*, 249. The careful organization of graves and architectural elements at the ABMC cemeteries originated from the earlier Civil War cemeteries and must also be understood as a result of the "search for order" in the US after the Civil War. In discussing the rise of civic art and architecture after the Civil War, Michele Bogart argued that sculptors and artists were influenced by this interest in the organization of society, which inspired ideas about civic art that impacted memorials and cemeteries both in the US and abroad, including the ABMC projects. See Bogart,

Public Sculpture and the Civic Ideal, 6; Robert H. Wiebe, *The Search for Order, 1877–1920* (New York: Hill and Wang, 1967).

26. Faust, *This Republic of Suffering*, 271.

27. Budreau, *Bodies of War*, 39–50.

28. For a full analysis of the architecture of the ABMC cemeteries and the Gold Star rest houses, see Allison S. Finkelstein, "A Female Sanctuary on the Former Western Front: The Gold Star Pilgrimage Rest Houses in France, 1930–33," *Buildings and Landscapes: The Journal of the Vernacular Architecture Forum* 23, no. 1 (Spring 2016): 56–57; Grossman, *Civic Architecture of Paul Cret*, 127.

29. The landscapes of the ABMC cemeteries also resemble parks, which ties them to the pastoral burial grounds popular in the nineteenth-century US as well as to the new memorial parks that emerged in the decades after 1917. Kenneth T. Jackson and Camilo José Vergara, *Silent Cities: The Evolution of the American Cemetery* (New York: Princeton Architectural Press, 1989), 5, 28–29. The ABMC cemeteries included office buildings and visitors' buildings, which were built in either the French eclectic style or the French Romanesque Revival style. The French eclectic style was popular in America from about 1915 to 1945. McAlester and McAlester, *Field Guide to American Houses*, 387.

30. "Hearing Before a Subcommittee of the Committee on Military Affairs, United States Senate, Seventieth Congress, Second Session, on H.R. 5494 S. 2681 S. 5332, Bills to Enable the Mothers and Unmarried Widows of the Deceased Soldiers, Sailors, and Marines of the American Forces Interred in the Cemeteries of Europe to Make a Pilgrimage to These Cemeteries," part 2, February 12, 1929, 6–7, ProQuest Congressional Publications, https://congressional.proquest.com; Graham, *Gold Star Mother Pilgrimages*, 76–77; "Proceedings of the 5th Bi-ennial Convention (7th National Convention) of the American War Mothers," 188–95, American War Mothers National Headquarters Collection, MWMC.

31. "Hearing Before a Subcommittee of the Committee on Military Affairs," 6–7.

32. The Gold Star pilgrimages have recently been the subject of several historical studies. However, only Budreau's work includes an in-depth historical analysis of the Gold Star pilgrimages in terms of memory and commemoration. Rebecca Jo Plant's work analyzes the pilgrimages in terms of maternalism and motherhood and situates the program within women's history. The works by John Graham, Holly S. Fenelon, and Lotte Larsen Meyer are focused more on summary than on analysis, and Constance Potter's article presents a history of the pilgrimages aimed at helping researchers use the associated records at the National Archives. Studies of the Gold Star pilgrimages include Budreau, *Bodies of War*; Budreau, "Politics of Remembrance"; Graham, *Gold Star Mother Pilgrimages*; Potter, "World War I Gold Star Mothers Pilgrimages, Part I"; Potter, "World War I Gold Star Mothers Pilgrimages, Part II"; Plant, *Mom*; Plant, "Gold Star Mothers Pilgrimages"; Plant and Clarke, "'Crowning Insult'"; and Meyer, "Mourning in a Distant Land."

33. Budreau, *Bodies of War*, 95.

34. Budreau, "Politics of Remembrance," 386.

35. Budreau, "Politics of Remembrance," 380.

36. For a detailed description and analysis of the lobbying efforts that led to the passage of the pilgrimage legislation, see Budreau, *Bodies of War*, 192–208.

37. Mrs. Ethel Stratton Nock to General Pershing, September 27, 1927, box 14, Gen-

eral Correspondence, 1904–48, folder American War Mothers, John J. Pershing Papers, Manuscript Division, LOC.

38. Budreau, "Politics of Remembrance," 373; Budreau, *Bodies of War*, 202–5; "American Cemeteries in Europe," Pub. L. No. 952, 45 Stat. 1508 (1929). For a detailed explanation of the entire pilgrimage program and legislation, see Graham, *Gold Star Mother Pilgrimages*, 7, 50–74; and Plant, *Mom*, 55–68.

39. The segregation of the Gold Star pilgrimages, the backlash against it, and the experiences of the African American pilgrims have already been well covered in depth by several authors and therefore will not be explored in greater detail in this chapter. For detailed studies of the segregation of the pilgrimage program and related public criticisms of the pilgrimages, see Budreau, *Bodies of War*, 210–17; Plant, *Mom*, 68–77; Plant and Clarke, "'Crowning Insult,'" 406–32; Graham, *Gold Star Mother Pilgrimages*, 116–38; Budreau, "Gold Star Mothers," 67–69; Plant, "Gold Star Mothers Pilgrimages," 132–35. Likewise, there is a finite amount of material in the pilgrimage files in the National Archives about the segregation of the pilgrimages, much of which has already been well mined by scholars. I examined and used this primary source material, which can be found in the National Archives II, College Park, MD, in box 345, miscellaneous file 1922–1935, Gold Star Pilgrimage, Amendments, Proposed, US Lined 1933, RG 92, NACP; box 379, miscellaneous file 1922–1935, 516 Pilgrimages Gold Star, Misc. Feb. 1930, Colored Cross References 1930–33, RG 92, NACP; box 380, miscellaneous file 1922–1935, 516 Pilgrimages Gold Star, Colored Meals 1930, Escadrille Lafayette 1930, 27th Div., RG 92, NACP.

40. Frank G. Allen to Herbert Hoover, February 21, 1930, box 379, folder 516 Pilgrimage Gold Star (Colored Vol. 1), RG 92, NACP.

41. Secretary of War to Frank G. Allen, circa March 19, 1930, box 379, folder 516 Pilgrimage Gold Star (Colored Vol. 1), RG 92, NACP.

42. Budreau, *Bodies of War*, 212–13; Budreau, "Gold Star Mothers," 69; Plant and Clarke, "'Crowning Insult,'" 422.

43. Budreau, *Bodies of War*, 213–15; Graham, *Gold Star Mother Pilgrimages*, 121, 126–27.

44. Budreau, *Bodies of War*, 211–12, 215–17; Plant, *Mom*, 68–71; Graham, *Gold Star Mother Pilgrimages*, 117–21.

45. It is difficult to know the exact number of African American pilgrims invited on the trips and how many accepted, declined, and actually traveled. Budreau estimated that about 1,593 African American women were eligible and that while 233 accepted the invitation, fewer than 200 actually went on the trips. Budreau also estimated that about 23 women refused the invitation at the behest of the NAACP. Plant and Clarke estimated that 279 Black women went on the trips and about 25 cancelled their reservations. The numbers provided by these authors support the estimates provided in this book. Budreau, *Bodies of War*, 215; Budreau, "Gold Star Mothers," 69; Graham, *Gold Star Mother Pilgrimages*, 123–37; Plant and Clarke, "'Crowning Insult,'" 407.

46. For an in-depth analysis of the pilgrimages in the context of motherhood and maternalism, see "Mothers of the Nation: Patriotic Maternalism and Its Critics," chap. 2 in Plant, *Mom*.

47. Graham, *Gold Star Mother Pilgrimages*, 71; Plant, *Mom*, 64–66.

48. Plant, *Mom*, 60, 68–77; Plant, "Gold Star Mothers."

49. Plant, *Mom*, 60, 68–77.

50. For more on women's roles in commemorating the Civil War, see, for example, Silber, *Romance of Reunion*; Cox, *Dixie's Daughters*; Mills and Simpson, *Monuments to the Lost Cause*; Janney, *Burying the Dead*.

51. Janney, *Burying the Dead*, 1–3; Blair, *Cities of the Dead*, 5–6.

52. Plant, *Mom*, 56–68; Budreau, *Bodies of War*, 88–94.

53. Graham, *Gold Star Mother Pilgrimages*, 59–60.

54. Graham, *Gold Star Mother Pilgrimages*, 59–60; Plant, *Mom*, 63–64; Meyer, "Mourning in a Distant Land," 40.

55. Blight, *Race and Reunion*, 154; Budreau, *Bodies of War*, 87.

56. Budreau, *Bodies of War*, 176–84, 188–89, 190–91. David W. Lloyd, *Battlefield Tourism: Pilgrimage and the Commemoration of the Great War in Britain, Australia and Canada, 1919–1939* (Oxford: Berg, 1998), 1–2.

57. Trout, *On the Battlefield of Memory*, xv–xviii.

58. Trout, *On the Battlefield of Memory*, xv–xxiv; American Battle Monuments Commission, *American Armies and Battlefields in Europe* (Washington, DC: Center of Military History, United States Army, 1995).

59. Lloyd, *Battlefield Tourism*, 5–7. Likewise, Ron Robin asserts that visits to World War One cemeteries were pilgrimages not so different from those to the holy shrines after the Crusades (*Enclaves of America*, 55); George Mosse discusses what he calls the "Myth of the War Experience," which depicted the war as a sacred event, as well as the "cult of the fallen soldier" (*Fallen Soldiers*, 7); and Annette Becker explains how parts of the front in France had been deemed sacred land (*War and Faith*, 124). For more about the intersection of religion and the commemoration of World War One in Europe, see Winter, *Sites of Memory*; Meyer, "Mourning in a Distant Land," 48; Harvey Levenstein, *Seductive Journeys: American Tourists in France from Jefferson to the Jazz Age* (Chicago: University of Chicago Press, 1998), 225–28.

60. Lloyd, *Battlefield Tourism*, 217.

61. Lloyd, 220–21.

62. The pilgrimage records at the National Archives include numerous documents and items that demonstrate the seriousness with which the Quartermaster Corps approached the planning of the pilgrimage. These records can be found in the National Archives II, College Park, MD (NACP), in RG 92, Office of the Quartermaster General, under various iterations of titles such as "Pilgrimage, Gold Star," "Gold Star Pilgrimage," and "American Pilgrimage Gold Star Mothers and Widows." The items described in this paragraph were found in box 391, entry 1897, folder 561, PILGRIMAGE GOLD STAR MOTHERS, 448–551, vol. 5 gm (REPORT), RG 92, NACP.

63. The army assigned an identifying letter to each party, for example Party "O." The size of the parties varied; the very first pilgrimage group, Party "A," included 234 women in its 1930 trip, while Party "E" in 1932 included just 79 women. Graham, *Gold Star Mother Pilgrimages*, 148, 159.

64. Graham, 202.

65. Graham, 19.

66. Itinerary of "Somme Cemetery Party B Group 5, and Group 2," box 391, folder 561, RG 92, NACP. Visits to Brookwood Cemetery in England also included stops at tourist sites.

67. Itinerary of "Somme Cemetery Party B Group 5, and Group 2," 222.

68. Report about the pilgrimages, March 7, 1931, box 360, folder 319.1, Pilgrimage Gold Star (Europe 1930, 1931, 1932, 1933PILG), RG 92, NACP.

69. "Scrapbook of Col. Richard T. Ellis," box 1, Gold Star Pilgrimages, 1930, Transportation Request, 1930, Gold Star Pilgrimage, Letters sent Relating to Provision of Subsistence Stores during Mexican War, Flood Sufferers in Miss. Valley, 1914–15 (box 1), RG 92, NACP.

70. John Ford, *Pilgrimage* (Hollywood: Fox Film Corporation, 1933), DVD. The film was loosely based on a short story with the same title (I. A. R. Wylie, "Pilgrimage," *American Magazine* 114, no. 5 [November 1932]: 44–47, 90–96). I found some evidence of Gold Star pilgrims' thoughts on the Fox film; they did not want to see the trips commercialized. Mrs. Katherine M. Gallagher to Fox Film, Inc., January 23, 1933, Pilgrimage (Fox, 19—) MPAA/PCA, Academy of Motion Picture Arts & Sciences, Margaret Herrick Library. For more detail, see Finkelstein, "Female Sanctuary," 68.

71. Budreau argues that the pilgrimages and American remembrance of World War One in general were politically motivated. *Bodies of War*, 241.

72. Plant provides a detailed assessment of women's political activism during the interwar period in the context of the pilgrimages. *Mom*, 55–57.

73. "A Man's Best Friend," *National Tribune*, May 14, 1931, in album titled "Press Clippings Mothers and Widows Pilgrimage to the Cemeteries of Europe," box 348, RG 92, NACP.

74. "Speeches made at tea-reception at Restaurant Laurent on May 26th, 1932, Party 'A'—Gold Star Mothers and Widows: Ambassador Walter E. Edge," box 369, folder 319.1, Pilgrimage Gold Star Party A. 1932, RG 92, NACP.

75. Budreau, *Bodies of War*, 37–50. For more on the World War One cemeteries established by the British, see David Crane, *Empires of the Dead: How One Man's Vision Led to the Creation of WWI's War Graves* (London: William Collins, 2013).

76. For more on how the bodies of American casualties were used for diplomatic purposes, see Hulver, "Remains in Peace."

77. "Hearing Before a Subcommittee of the Committee on Military Affairs," 27.

78. "Speech of General Pagezy at Reception, August 18, 1932," box 2012.94, Julia C. Underwood Pilgrimage Collection, National WWI Museum and Memorial Archives.

79. La Bienvenue Française to Pilgrims, Summer 1932, box 2012.94, Julia C. Underwood Pilgrimage Collection, National WWI Museum and Memorial Archives.

80. "Speeches made at tea-reception at Restaurant Laurent on May 26th, 1932, Party 'A'—Gold Star Mothers and Widows: Monsieur de Billy," box 369, folder 319.1, RG 92, NACP.

81. La Bienvenue Française to Pilgrims, Summer 1932, National WWI Museum and Memorial Archives.

82. Budreau, *Bodies of War*, 218; Medals and Program for Memorial Service on board the *SS Leviathan*, August 12, 1932, box 2012.94, Julia C. Underwood Pilgrimage Collection, National WWI Museum and Memorial Archives.

83. Medals and Program for Memorial Service on board the *SS Leviathan*, August 12, 1932, National WWI Museum and Memorial Archives.

84. Major Louis C. Wilson, Q.M.C., "The War Mother Goes 'Over There,'" *Quartermaster Review*, May–June 1930, 22, in album titled "Press Clippings Mothers and Widows Pilgrimage to the Cemeteries of Europe," box 348, RG 92, NACP. These medals and the way they made these civilian women part of the US military apparatus bear testament to the accuracy of Michael S. Sherry's argument about the militarization of the US after the 1930s. Though far different in their purpose, they are also unsettlingly similar to the military-style medals given to German women by the Nazis, such as the Cross of Honor of the German Mother given to women who bore a certain number of healthy children to serve the Reich, starting in 1938. Sherry, *In the Shadow of War*, ix–xii; "Cross of Honor of the German Mother, 3rd Class Order, Bronze Cross," US Holocaust Memorial Museum, https://collections.ushmm.org. For information on the World War One Victory Medal see, for example, "World War I Victory Medal," NHHC, November 10, 2016, https://www.history.navy.mil; Alexander J. Laslo, *The Interallied Victory Medals of World War I* (Albuquerque: Dorado, 1992), 86–123.

85. "Speeches made at tea-reception at Restaurant Laurent on May 26th, 1932, Party 'A'—Gold Star Mothers and Widows: General J. J. Pershing," box 369, folder 319.1, RG 92, NACP.

86. "A Guest of the Government," file 516—Pilgrimage, Gold Star, box 352, RG 92, NACP.

87. Mrs. Maud L. Reives to G. G. Bartlett, July 15, 1930, folder 330.13 Pilgrimage Gold Star 1930, box 376, RG 92, NACP.

88. Mrs. Callie M. Laird to the War Department, July 21, 1930, box 376, folder 330.1, Pilgrimage Gold Star 1930, RG 92, NACP.

89. Hilda A. Meystre, "Our Hearts O'erflow," in album titled "Press Clippings Mothers and Widows Pilgrimage to the Cemeteries of Europe," box 348, RG 92, NACP.

90. "Col. Ellis Report of 1930 Pilgrimage in Europe, Submitted March 7, 1931," 16, box 348, folder Reports Annual New York and Europe 1931, RG 92, NACP; Budreau, *Bodies of War*, 206. Ellis is a central figure in Budreau's book.

91. "Col. Ellis Report of 1930 Pilgrimage in Europe," 1–2. Colonel Ellis stated that the average age of the pilgrims was between sixty-one and sixty-five. See also Budreau, *Bodies of War*, 206. The Quartermaster Corps gathered detailed reports about each pilgrim's health prior to the trip and kept detailed records of their health during the journey. See box 59, folder 1932, RG 92, NACP. This folder contains medical reports from the pilgrims' doctors about their health conditions before the trip and official pilgrimage lists that state their condition of health.

92. The large number of newspaper clippings found in the Gold Star pilgrimage records in RG 92 suggests that the Gold Star pilgrimages received extensive coverage in newspapers across the country. Numerous boxes within this record group contain news-

paper clippings about the events. Rebecca Jo Plant's use of newspaper articles in *Mom: The Transformation of Motherhood in Modern America*, as well as my own newspaper research, also attests to the high level of media coverage focused on the pilgrimages.

93. See "Scrapbook of Col. Richard T. Ellis," box 1, RG 92, NACP.

94. Michael Sherry describes the early 1930s as a time when "the First World War's sour legacy of revolution, nationalism, and debt" were "fresh to Americans." *Shadow of War*, 15.

95. For more information on the architectural origins of the rest houses, see Finkelstein, "Female Sanctuary," 52–77. For information on ladies' rest rooms, see Britanik, "Where Are the Ladies' Rest Rooms?"; Carroll Van West, "Assessing Significance and Integrity in the National Register Process: Questions of Race, Class, and Gender," in *Preservation of What, for Whom? A Critical Look at Historical Significance*, ed. Michael A. Tomlan (Ithaca, NY: National Council for Preservation Education, 1998), 109–16. For more information on military base hostess houses, see Brandimarte, "Women on the Home Front," 202. For more information on early twentieth-century country clubs, see James M. Mayo, *The American Country Club: Its Origins and Development* (New Brunswick, NJ: Rutgers University Press, 1998), 134.

96. In considering how women fit into the male military landscape of commemoration, I took heed of Sally McMurry's call for scholars of vernacular architecture to integrate women's history more thoroughly into their work. Angel Kwolek-Folland's suggestions for using gender as a category of analysis in vernacular architecture studies and Joan W. Scott's concept of gender as a category of historical analysis were also influential. Sally McMurry, "Women in the American Vernacular Landscape," *Material Culture* 20, no. 1 (Spring 1988): 33–49; Angel Kwolek-Folland, "Gender as a Category of Analysis in Vernacular Architecture Studies," in *Gender, Class, and Shelter: Perspectives in Vernacular Architecture*, vol. 5, ed. Elizabeth Collins Cromley and Carter L. Hudgins (Knoxville: University of Tennessee Press, 1995), 3–10; Joan W. Scott, "Gender: A Useful Category of Historical Analysis," *American Historical Review* 91, no. 5 (December 1986): 1053–75.

97. Photographs and documentary evidence of the rest houses enable an architectural examination of the structures, even though no Gold Star rest houses or blueprints of them survive. For an in-depth architectural analysis of the rest houses, see Finkelstein, "Female Sanctuary."

98. McAlester and McAlester, *Field Guide*, 453; Finkelstein, "Female Sanctuary."

99. "Col. Ellis Report of 1930 Pilgrimage in Europe. Submitted March 7, 1931," 16, box 348, folder Reports Annual New York and Europe 1931, RG 92, NACP.

100. McAlester and McAlester, *Field Guide*, 454; Finkelstein, "Female Sanctuary."

101. I have not yet found documents that show the location of the rest houses in each cemetery. Records in the National Archives, College Park, at the ABMC's Headquarters in both Garches, France, and Arlington, Virginia, and at four ABMC cemeteries (Suresnes, Meuse-Argonne, St. Mihiel, and Brookwood) turned up nothing. In discussions with ABMC employees in 2012 and 2013, the general consensus was that the location of the rest houses is still a mystery. Additionally, while visiting the Meuse-

Argonne and St. Mihiel Cemeteries in 2012 I was unable to find any physical evidence or footprints of the rest houses visible to the naked eye.

102. "Col. Ellis Report of 1930 Pilgrimage in Europe, Submitted March 7, 1931," 16, box 348, folder Reports Annual New York and Europe 1931, RG 92, NACP. It is important to note that the rest houses did not contain any bedrooms, apartments, or spaces for the pilgrims to sleep; they were not for overnight accommodations. The pilgrims typically stayed at hotels in nearby towns, and the rest houses were used solely for rest, relaxation, and toilet needs during the cemetery visits.

103. "Col. Ellis Report of 1930 Pilgrimage in Europe," 17.

104. Mrs. Hattie B. Bisbee and Mrs. Sarah Parker to Ellis, n.d., box 376, folder 330.1, RG 92, NACP.

105. *Carry On* 10, no. 1 (February 1931): 13–14, box 1922–1932, folder 1931, Women's Overseas Service League *Carry On* Periodical Collection, Gift of Carolyn Habgood, MWMC.

106. Rebecca Jo Plant provides a few examples of women, such as a Gold Star mother, who opposed the trip based on its cost and criticized the government for its care of World War One veterans. *Mom*, 71–72; "Gold Star Mothers Pilgrimages," 135–38.

Conclusion

1. "Service Women Praised: Truman in Message to League Hails Aid in Wars," *New York Times*, July 2, 1946, 20.

2. Cartoon drawn by George Price, box WOSL-National History Projects, Service Projects, Rosters, 2, folder WOSL History Project, Women's Overseas Service League Collection, National WWI Museum and Memorial Archives; Glenn Collins, "George Price 93, Cartoonist of Oddities, Dies," *New York Times*, January 14, 1995, A30, http://www.nytimes.com. This cartoon likely appeared in the *New Yorker*, where most of Price's cartoons were published.

3. A brief review of Rogers's personal correspondence revealed numerous letters from women of both the World War One and World War Two generations who wrote to her regarding their status in the military, or lack thereof. She maintained her connections to these women and to the WOSL over the years and continued to be an advocate for them. Box 2, folder 23, Edith Nourse Rogers Papers, 1854–1961, MC 196, Schlesinger Library, Radcliffe Institute, Harvard University, Cambridge, MA.

4. Treadwell, *United States Army*, 18–19.

5. "Hearings Before the Committee on Military Affairs, House of Representatives, Seventy-Seventh Congress, 2nd Session, on H.R. 6293," Jan. 21–22, 1942, 6, ProQuest Legislative Insight, https://congressional.proquest.com.

6. "Hearings Before the Committee on Military Affairs, House of Representatives, Seventy-Seventh Congress, 2nd Session, on H.R. 6293," Jan. 21–22, 1942, 10.

7. "Congressional Record, House, March 17, 1942: Women's Army Auxiliary Corps," 2582, ProQuest Legislative Insight, https://congressional.proquest.com.

8. "Congressional Record, House, March 17, 1942: Women's Army Auxiliary Corps," 2584.

9. Mankin later served in the US House of Representatives. "Hearings Before the Committee on Military Affairs, House of Representatives, Seventy-Seventh Congress, 2nd Session, on H.R. 6293," May 1 and 4, 1942, 40–46; "Mankin, Helen Douglas," History, Art & Archives, US House of Representatives, https://history.house.gov.

10. "Hearings Before the Committee on Military Affairs, House of Representatives, Seventy-Seventh Congress, 2nd Session, on H.R. 6293," May 1 and 4, 1942, 40–46; Bettie J. Morden, *The Women's Army Corps, 1945–1978* (Washington, DC: Center of Military History, United States Army, 1990), 3–4. Morden notes that Rogers had added an amendment to the WAAC Act that would have given women military status.

11. "Hearings Before the Committee on Military Affairs, House of Representatives, Seventy-Seventh Congress, 2nd Session, on H.R. 6293," May 1 and 4, 1942, 40–46.

12. Morden, *Women's Army Corps*, 3–5; Wasniewski, *Women in Congress*, 72–74; Evelyn M. Monahan and Rosemary Neidel-Greenlee, *A Few Good Women: America's Military Women from World War I to the Wars in Iraq and Afghanistan* (New York: Alfred A. Knopf, 2010), 16–19; "Congressional Record, House, March 17, 1942: Women's Army Auxiliary Corps," 2580–608, ProQuest Legislative Insight, https://congressional.proquest.com; Treadwell, *United States Army*, 24–28.

13. "Congressional Record, House, March 17, 1942: Women's Army Auxiliary Corps," 2592–93, ProQuest Legislative Insight, https://congressional.proquest.com; "Hoffman, Clare Eugene," History, Art & Archives, US House of Representatives, https://history.house.gov.

14. "Asks Pay Equality for WAAC," *New York Times*, July 15, 1942, 22.

15. Morden, *Women's Army Corps*, 5.

16. Regina T. Akers, "The WAVES' 75th Birthday," NHHC, May 10, 2019, https://www.history.navy.mil; "Establishment of Women's Reserve," NHHC, November 30, 2017, https://www.history.navy.mil.

17. Godson, *Serving Proudly*, 112; Robin J. Thomson, "SPARS: The Coast Guard & the Women's Reserve in World War II," US Coast Guard Historian's Office, https://www.history.uscg.mil.

18. Godson, *Serving Proudly*, 112.

19. Morden, *Women's Army Corps*, 12.

20. Morden, *Women's Army Corps*, 12; Wasniewski, *Women in Congress*, 74; "Women's Army Corps," Pub. L. No. 110, 57 Stat. 371 (1943).

21. Treadwell, *United States Army*, x, 14, 17.

22. Quoted in Treadwell, *United States Army*, 14, 17.

23. "WAAC's Can Relax in Newly Dedicated Recreation Room at Bolling Field," *Washington Post*, April 22, 1943, B6.

24. "Foreseen in 1918," *Chicago Daily Tribune*, September 27, 1943, 12.

25. "Would Serve Overseas: Former Red Cross Aide in France Becomes WAC Here," *New York Times*, April 11, 1944, 9.

26. Eric W. Boyle, OHA 371, World War Reconstruction Aides Association Collection, Finding Aid, NMHM, 2012, 1; Paul A. Ussery, "COL Emma Vogel: First Chief of the Women's Medical Specialist Corps," *AMEDD Historian*, no. 2 (Spring 2013): 1–2.

27. Rebecca Robbins Raines, *Getting the Message Through: A Branch History of the*

U.S. Army Signal Corps (Washington, DC: Center of Military History, United States Army, 1999), 170, 204; Zeiger, *In Uncle Sam's Service*, 172–73.

28. The Hello Girls' fight for veteran status has already been analyzed in great detail in chapter 12 of Elizabeth Cobbs's book *The Hello Girls: America's First Women Soldiers* (273–303). As a result, it is not explored in depth in this book. See also Hello Girls Congressional Gold Medal Act of 2019, S. 206, 116th Congress, https://www.congress.gov /bill; Frahm, "Advance to the 'Fighting Lines.'"

29. "Who Is a 'Veteran'?—Basic Eligibility for Veterans' Benefits," Congressional Research Service, May 25, 2016, 4–5, https://crsreports.congress.gov.

30. Department of Defense, Office of the Secretary of the Air Force, "Determinations of Active Military Service and Discharge; Civilian or Contractual Personnel," *Federal Register* 46, no. 138 (July 20, 1981): 37306, https://cdn.loc.gov.

31. Thanks to Justin Buller for his help analyzing the *Federal Register* and the meaning of "active military service."

32. Wasniewski, *Women in Congress*, 73–74; Glenn C. Altschuler and Stuart M. Blumin, *The GI Bill: A New Deal for Veterans* (New York: Oxford University Press, 2009), 62–63; Michael J. Bennett, *When Dreams Came True: The GI Bill and the Making of Modern America* (Washington, DC: Brassey's, 1996), 29, 91, 115–17.

33. Altschuler and Blumin as well as Bennett include Rogers in their histories of the GI Bill's creation (though they misrepresent her involvement with the WOSL), but other studies either do not include her or overlook her and her World War One service, even though she is seen in the photos of FDR signing the bill. Such studies include Jennifer D. Keene, *Doughboys, the Great War, and the Remaking of America* (Baltimore: Johns Hopkins University Press, 2001); Ortiz, *Beyond the Bonus March*; Edward Humes, *Over Here: How the G.I. Bill Transformed the American Dream* (Orlando, FL: Harcourt, 2006); Milton Greenberg, *The GI Bill: The Law That Changed America* (New York: Lickle, 1997); Suzanne Mettler, *Soldiers to Citizens: The G.I. Bill and the Making of the Greatest Generation* (New York: Oxford University Press, 2005); Kathleen J. Frydl, *The GI Bill* (New York: Cambridge University Press, 2009).

34. Katherine Gray Kraft, "Rogers, Edith Nourse, 1881–1960, Papers, 1854–1961: A Finding Aid," Harvard University Library, 1974, https://hollisarchives.lib.harvard.edu; "Rogers, Edith Nourse," History, Art & Archives, US House of Representatives, https:// history.house.gov.

35. Captain Joseph Piggott to Edith Nourse Rogers, June 6, 1947, box 2, folder 23, Edith Nourse Rogers Papers, 1854–1961, MC 196, Schlesinger Library, Radcliffe Institute, Harvard University.

36. For an analysis of race and gender discrimination in relation to the GI Bill, see Altschuler and Blumin, *GI Bill*, 118–47; Lizabeth Cohen, *A Consumer's Republic: The Politics of Mass Consumption in Postwar America* (New York: Alfred A. Knopf, 2003); Ira Katznelson, *When Affirmative Action Was White: An Untold History of Racial Inequality in Twentieth-Century America* (New York: W. W. Norton, 2005).

37. "Servicemen's Readjustment Act of 1944," Pub. L. No. 346, 58 Stat. 284 (1944).

38. Keene, *Doughboys*, 205. Keene argued that the GI Bill was "the final legacy of World War I to the nation."

39. Shanken, "Planning Memory," 144–45.

40. During Honor Flight San Diego's trip to Washington, DC, on October 19, 2013, with my supervision, my undergraduate student Elliot Fitall interviewed fourteen of the World War Two veterans on the trip. He found that many veterans did not pay attention to the lack of a national World War Two memorial until they were older, as they were too busy using their GI Bill benefits to build their lives after the war. Elliot's analysis of these interviews came from his final paper. Elliot Fitall, "The World War II Memorial" (History 208 final paper, University of Maryland, 2013). Many thanks to him for his fine research and analysis.

41. For more on the impact of later versions of the GI Bill on subsequent generations of veterans, see Mark Boulton, *Failing Our Veterans: The G.I. Bill and the Vietnam Generation* (New York: New York University Press, 2014).

42. Ron Grandon, "Mural to Be Dedicated Honors Service Women," *Kansas City Times*, July 9, 1956, 1F, 3F, in unlabeled binder of Liberty Memorial Association News Clippings, National WWI Museum and Memorial Archives; "Their Service Is Cited," possibly from the *Kansas City Times*, found in unlabeled binder of Liberty Memorial Association News Clippings, National WWI Museum and Memorial Archives.

43. "Elements of the Museum and Memorial," National WWI Museum and Memorial, https://www.theworldwar.org; "Private Events," National WWI Museum and Memorial, https://www.theworldwar.org; Derek Donovan, *Lest the Ages Forget: Kansas City's Liberty Memorial* (Kansas City, MO: Kansas City Star Books, 2001), 108–9.

44. Ron Grandon, "Mural to Be Dedicated Honors Service Women," *Kansas City Times*, July 9, 1956, 1F, 3F.

45. Ron Grandon, "Mural to Be Dedicated Honors Service Women," *Kansas City Times*, July 9, 1956, 1F, 3F; "Their Service Is Cited," possibly from the *Kansas City Times*; Heiman, *Voices in Bronze and Stone*, 9; Donovan, *Lest the Ages Forget*, 102–8.

46. "Their Service Is Cited," possibly from the *Kansas City Times*.

47. "Mission," Women In Military Service For America Memorial Foundation, https://www.womensmemorial.org.

48. "The Register," Summer 1998, 6, box Women's Memorial Foundation Newsletters, "The Register," WIMSA History Collection, MWMC.

49. Wilma L. Vaught, *The Day the Nation Said "Thanks!": A History and Dedication Scrapbook of the Women In Military Service For America Memorial* (Washington, DC: Military Women's Press, 1999), 98–99.

50. Richard Goldstein, "Frieda Hardin, 103; Inspired Military Women," *New York Times*, August 15, 2000, B6.

Bibliography

ARCHIVAL COLLECTIONS

Academy of Motion Picture Arts & Sciences, Margaret Herrick Library, Beverly Hills, CA
Motion Picture Association of America/Production Code Administration Records
(MPAA/PCA Records)

American Red Cross Archives, National Headquarters, Washington, DC

Archives of American Art, Smithsonian Institution, Washington, DC
Anna Coleman Ladd Papers, ca. 1881–1950

Imperial War Museum, London, UK
Women's Work Collection, Museum Administrative Records

Indiana Historical Society, Indianapolis, IN
Alice Moore French Papers

Kentucky Historical Society, Frankfort, KY
American War Mothers Collection
Rare Books and Pamphlets

Library of Congress, Manuscript Division, Washington, DC
American Gold Star Mothers, Inc., Records
John J. Pershing Papers
Mabel Thorp Boardman Papers
Mary Church Terrell Papers

Michigan State University Libraries Digital Repository, East Lansing, MI
Women's Overseas Service League Oral Histories

National Archives II, College Park, MD
RG 79: Records of the National Park Service, National Capital Region
RG 92: Records of the Office of the Quartermaster General
RG 117: Records of the American Battle Monuments Commission
RG 200: National Archives Gift Collection, Records of the American National Red Cross

National Archives Building, Washington, DC
RG 66: Records of the Commission of Fine Arts

National Museum of American History, Armed Forces History Division, Smithsonian Institution, Washington, DC
Colonial Dames Collection Documents
Yeoman (F) Files

National Museum of Health and Medicine, Otis Historical Archives, Silver Spring, MD
OHA 97: Angier and Hitchcock Collection
OHA 353: Vogel Collection
OHA 371: World War Reconstruction Aides Association Collection

National WWI Museum and Memorial Archives, Kansas City, MO
American War Mothers Collection
Daniel MacMorris Papers, 1948–1962
Julia C. Underwood Pilgrimage Collection
Liberty Memorial Association Minute Book Collection
Liberty Memorial Association Records
Women's Overseas Service League Collection

Naval History and Heritage Command, Archives Branch, Washington, DC
Papers of Eunice C. Dessez (Collection 226)
Papers of Helen G. O'Neill (Collection 236)

Schlesinger Library, Radcliffe Institute, Harvard University, Cambridge, MA
Edith Nourse Rogers Papers, 1854–1961

Smithsonian Institution Archives, Washington, DC
George Washington Memorial Association Records, 1890–1922

University of Texas at San Antonio Libraries Special Collections, San Antonio, TX
Women's Overseas Service League Records

Women's Memorial Foundation Archives, Arlington, VA
American War Mothers National Headquarters Collection
WIMSA History Collection
Women's Overseas Service League (WOSL) *Carry On* Periodical Collection, Gift of Carolyn Habgood

PERIODICALS AND NEWSPAPERS
American City
American Legion Weekly
American Magazine
Baltimore Afro-American
Carry On
Carry On: A Magazine of the Reconstruction of Disabled Soldiers and Sailors
Chicago Daily Tribune

Chicago Defender
Indianan
Indianapolis News
Kansas City Times
Los Angeles Times
Miami Herald
National Tribune
New York Times
Quartermaster Review
Red Cross Courier
Seattle Post-Intelligencer
Seattle Times
VFW Magazine
Washington Post

PUBLISHED PRIMARY SOURCES

Addams, Jane. *The Long Road of Woman's Memory*. New York: Macmillan, 1916.
———. *Peace and Bread in Time of War* and *Patriotism and Pacifists in War Time*. New York: Garland, 1972.
Addams, Jane, Emily G. Balch, and Alice Hamilton. *Women at the Hague: The International Congress of Women and Its Results*. New York: Garland, 1972.
Building Age Publishing Corporation. *Beautiful Bungalows of the Twenties*. Mineola, NY: Dover, 2003.
Caldwell, A. B., ed. *History of the American Negro: Virginia Edition*. Vol. 5. Atlanta: A. B. Caldwell, 1921. https://archive.org.
Creel, George. *How We Advertised America*. New York: Harper & Brothers, 1920.
Dessez, Eunice C. *The First Enlisted Women: 1917–1918*. Philadelphia: Dorrance, 1955.
Duffield, Marcus. *King Legion*. New York: Jonathan Cape & Harrison Smith, 1931.
Evans, Anne M. "Rest Rooms for Women in Marketing Centers." In *Yearbook of the United States Department of Agriculture*, 217–24. Washington, DC: Government Printing Office, 1918.
Fitzgerald, Alice L. F. *The Edith Cavell Nurse from Massachusetts*. Boston: W. A. Butterfield, 1917.
Hancock, Joy Bright. *Lady in the Navy: A Personal Reminiscence*. Annapolis, MD: Naval Institute Press, 1972.
Hill, Frank Ernest. *The American Legion Auxiliary, A History: 1924–1934*. Indianapolis: American Legion Auxiliary, 1935.
Hoppin, Laura Brackett, ed. *History of the World War Reconstruction Aides*. Millbrook, NY: William Tyldsley, 1933.
Hunton, Addie W., and Kathryn M. Johnson. *Two Colored Women with the American Expeditionary Forces*. Brooklyn, NY: Brooklyn Eagle Press, n.d., ca. 1920. www.archive.org.
James, Bessie R. *For God, for Country, for Home: The National League for Women's Service*. New York: G. P. Putnam's Sons, 1920.

Lancaster, Clay. *The American Bungalow, 1880–1930*. New York: Abbeville Press, 1985.

National Committee on Voluntary Aid of the Women's Section of the Navy League. *Manual of Voluntary Aid*. 2nd ed. Washington, DC: National Committee on Voluntary Aid, 1916.

Radford Architectural Company. *Radford's Home Builder: Bungalows, Artistic Homes, Cottages, Cement Houses, Flats, Garages, Stores, &C. &C.* Chicago: Radford Architectural Company, 1908.

Roosevelt, Mrs. Theodore, Jr. *The Day before Yesterday: The Reminiscences of Mrs. Theodore Roosevelt, Jr.* Garden City, NY: Doubleday, 1959.

Saylor, Henry H. *Bungalows: Their Design, Construction and Furnishing, with Suggestions Also for Camps, Summer Homes and Cottages of Similar Character.* New York: Robert M. McBride, 1920.

Scott, Emmett J. *Scott's Official History of the American Negro in the World War.* Chicago: Homewood Press, 1919. https://archive.org.

Sillia, Helene M. *Women's Overseas Service League: History.* Women's Overseas Service League, 1978.

Thompson, Mrs. Jos. H. *History: National American Legion Auxiliary.* Vol. 1. Pittsburgh, PA: Jackson-Remlinger Printing, 1926.

Thucydides. *The Peloponnesian War.* Translated by Benjamin Jowett. Oxford: Clarendon Press, 1881. https://archive.org.

War Department. *Pilgrimage for the Mothers and Widows of Soldiers, Sailors, and Marines of the American Expeditionary Forces Now Interred in the Cemeteries of Europe.* Washington, DC: Government Printing Office, 1930.

War Work Council, National Board of the Young Women's Christian Association. *Report of the Hostess House Committee.* New York: Young Women's Christian Association, 1920.

Whitney, Gertrude Vanderbilt. "The Useless Memorial." *Arts and Decoration* 12, no. 6 (April 25, 1920): 421.

Wylie, I. A. R. "Pilgrimage." *American Magazine* 114, no. 5 (November 1932): 44–47, 90–96.

Secondary Sources

Adler, Jessica L. *Burdens of War: Creating the United States Veterans Health System.* Baltimore: Johns Hopkins University Press, 2017.

Akers, Regina T. *The Navy's First Enlisted Women: Patriotic Pioneers.* Washington, DC: Naval History and Heritage Command, 2019.

Alexander, Adele Logan. Introduction to *Two Colored Women with the American Expeditionary Forces*, by Addie W. Hunton and Kathryn M. Johnson, xv–xxix. New York: G. K. Hall, 1997.

Allen, Michael J. "Sacrilege of a Strange, Contemporary Kind": The Unknown Soldier and the Imagined Community after the Vietnam War." *History & Memory* 23, no. 2 (Fall/Winter 2011): 90–131.

Alonso, Harriet Hyman. *Peace as a Women's Issue: A History of the U.S. Movement for World Peace and Women's Rights.* Syracuse, NY: Syracuse University Press, 1993.

——. *The Women's Peace Union and the Outlawry of War, 1921–1942*. Syracuse, NY: Syracuse University Press, 1997.

Altschuler, Glenn C., and Stuart M. Blumin. *The GI Bill: A New Deal for Veterans*. New York: Oxford University Press, 2009.

American Battle Monuments Commission. *American Armies and Battlefields in Europe*. Washington, DC: Center of Military History, United States Army, 1995.

American Graves Registration Service. *History of the American Graves Registration Service, Q.M.C. in Europe*. Washington, DC: Adjutant General Center, 1976.

Anderson, Benedict. *Imagined Communities: Reflections on the Origin and Spread of Nationalism*. New York: Verso, 1991.

Antolini, Katharine Lane. "Memorializing Motherhood: Anna Jarvis and the Struggle for the Control of Mother's Day." PhD diss., West Virginia University, 2009.

Badger, Anthony J. *The New Deal: The Depression Years, 1933–40*. Chicago: Ivan R. Dee, 1989.

Baker, Roscoe. *The American Legion and American Foreign Policy*. New York: Bookman Associates, 1954.

Barthes, Roland. *The Fashion System*. Translated by Matthew Ward and Richard Howard. London: Jonathan Cape, 1985.

Beale, Helen E. "Women and First World War Memorials in Arles and la Provence mistralienne." *Modern and Contemporary France* 7, no. 2 (1999): 209–24.

Becker, Annette. *War and Faith: The Religious Imagination in France, 1914–1930*. Translated by Helen McPhail. New York: Berg, 1998.

Belton, John, ed. *Movies and Mass Culture*. New Brunswick, NJ: Rutgers University Press, 1996.

Bennett, Michael J. *When Dreams Came True: The GI Bill and the Making of Modern America*. Washington, DC: Brassey's, 1996.

Bennett, Tony. *The Birth of the Museum: History, Theory, Politics*. London: Routledge, 1995.

Bergman, Andrew. *We're in the Money: Depression America and Its Films*. New York: New York University Press, 1971.

Bevan, Robert. *The Destruction of Memory: Architecture at War*. London: Reaktion Books, 2006.

Biernoff, Suzannah. "The Face of War." In *Ugliness: The Non-beautiful in Art and Theory*, edited by Andrei Pop and Mechtild Widrich, 34–48. New York: I. B. Tauris, 2014.

——. "Flesh Poems: Henry Tonks and the Art of Surgery." *Visual Culture in Britain* 11, no. 1 (March 2010): 25–47.

——. "The Rhetoric of Disfigurement in First World War Britain." *Social History of Medicine* 24, no. 3 (December 2011): 666–85. https://doi.org/10.1093/shm/hkq095.

Biernoff, Suzannah, and Jane Tynan. "Making and Remaking the Civilian Soldier: The First World War Photographs of Horace Nicholls." In *Men at War*, special issue, *Journal of War and Culture Studies* 5, no. 3 (September 2012): 277–95.

Bird, William L., Jr. *Souvenir Nation: Relics, Keepsakes, and Curios from the Smithsonian's National Museum of American History*. New York: Princeton Architectural Press, 2013.

Black, Timuel D., Jr. *Bridges of Memory: Chicago's Second Generation of Black Migration.* Evanston, IL: Northwestern University Press, 2007.

Blackwell, Joyce. *No Peace Without Freedom: Race and the Women's International League for Peace and Freedom, 1915–1975.* Carbondale: Southern Illinois University Press, 2004.

Blair, Carole, V. William Balthrop, and Neil Michel. "The Arguments of the Tombs of the Unknown: Rationality and National Legitimation." *Argumentation* 25, no. 4 (2011): 449–68.

Blair, Karen J. *The Clubwoman as Feminist: True Womanhood Redefined, 1868–1914.* New York: Holmes & Meier, 1980.

———. *Joining In: Exploring the History of Voluntary Organizations.* Malabar, FL: Krieger, 2006.

———. *The Torchbearers: Women and Their Amateur Arts Associations in America, 1890–1930.* Bloomington: Indiana University Press, 1994.

Blair, William A. *Cities of the Dead: Contesting the Memory of the Civil War in the South, 1865–1914.* Chapel Hill: University of North Carolina Press, 2004.

Blakesley, Rosalind P. *The Arts and Crafts Movement.* London: Phaidon Press, 2006.

Blankenship, Janie, ed. *VFW Magazine: Women at War, from the Revolutionary War to the Present,* special publication, July 2011.

Blight, David. *Race and Reunion: The Civil War in American Memory.* Cambridge, MA: Belknap Press of Harvard University Press, 2001.

Bodnar, John. *The "Good War" in American Memory.* Baltimore: Johns Hopkins University Press, 2010.

———. *Remaking America: Public Memory, Commemoration, and Patriotism in the Twentieth Century.* Princeton, NJ: Princeton University Press, 1992.

Bogart, Michele H. *Public Sculpture and the Civic Ideal in New York City, 1890–1930.* Chicago: University of Chicago Press, 1989.

Bontrager, Shannon. *Death at the Edges of Empire: Fallen Soldiers, Cultural Memory, and the Making of an American Nation, 1863–1921.* Lincoln: University of Nebraska Press, 2020.

Borg, Alan. *War Memorials: From Antiquity to the Present.* London: Leo Cooper, 1991.

Boulton, Mark. *Failing Our Veterans: The G.I. Bill and the Vietnam Generation.* New York: New York University Press, 2014.

Bourke, Joanna. *Dismembering the Male: Men's Bodies, Britain and the Great War.* Chicago: University of Chicago Press, 1996.

Boyer, Paul S., Clifford E. Clark Jr., Sandra McNair Hawley, Joseph E. Kett, Neal Salisbury, Harvard Sitkoff, and Nancy Woloch. *The Enduring Vision: A History of the American People.* Vol. 2, *From 1865.* Boston: Houghton Mifflin, 2006.

Brandimarte, Cynthia A. "To Make the World Homelike": Gender, Space, and America's Tea Room Movement." *Winterthur Portfolio* 30, no. 1 (Spring 1995): 1–19.

———. "Women on the Home Front: Hostess Houses during World War I." *Winterthur Portfolio* 42, no. 4 (Winter 2008): 201–22.

Breen, William J. "Black Women and the Great War: Mobilization and Reform in the South." *Journal of Southern History* 44, no. 3 (August 1978): 421–40.

Breeze, Carla. *American Art Deco: Architecture and Regionalism*. New York: W. W. Norton, 2003.

Brewer, Susan A. *Why America Fights: Patriotism and War Propaganda from the Philippines to Iraq*. New York: Oxford University Press, 2009.

Brinkley, Alan. *The End of Reform: New Deal Liberalism in Recession and War*. New York: Vintage Books, 1996.

———. *Voices of Protest: Huey Long, Father Coughlin, and the Great Depression*. New York: Vintage Books, 1983.

Bristow, Nancy K. *Making Men Moral: Social Engineering during the Great War*. New York: New York University Press, 1996.

Britanik, Kristin L. "Where Are the Ladies' Rest Rooms?: The Evolution of Women-Only Resting Rooms amid Social Changes of the Early Twentieth-Century." Master's thesis, University of Maryland, College Park, 2012.

Brown, Carrie. *Rosie's Mom: Forgotten Women Workers of the First World War*. Boston: Northeastern University Press, 2002.

Brown, Nikki. *Private Politics and Public Voices: Black Women's Activism from World War I to the New Deal*. Bloomington: Indiana University Press, 2006.

Buckley, Thomas H. *The United States and the Washington Conference, 1921–1922*. Knoxville: University of Tennessee Press, 1970.

Budreau, Lisa M. *Bodies of War: World War I and the Politics of Commemoration in America, 1919–1933*. New York: New York University Press, 2010.

———. "Gold Star Mothers." In *We Return Fighting: World War I and the Shaping of Modern Black Identity*, edited by Kinshasha Holman Conwill, 67–69. Washington, DC: Smithsonian Books, 2019.

———. "The Politics of Remembrance: The Gold Star Mothers' Pilgrimage and America's Fading Memory of the Great War." *Journal of Military History* 72, no. 2 (April 2008): 371–411.

———. "War Service by African American Women at Home and Abroad." In *We Return Fighting: World War I and the Shaping of Modern Black Identity*, edited by Kinshasha Holman Conwill, 60–62. Washington, DC: Smithsonian Books, 2019.

Bunch, Lonnie G., III. "The Definitive Story of How the National Museum of African American History and Culture Came to Be." *Smithsonian*, September 2016. https://www.smithsonianmag.com.

———. *A Fool's Errand: Creating the National Museum of African American History and Culture in the Age of Bush, Obama, and Trump*. Washington, DC: Smithsonian Books, 2019.

———. "On the Horizon—toward Civil Rights." Epilogue to *We Return Fighting: World War I and the Shaping of Modern Black Identity*, edited by Kinshasha Holman Conwill, 137–40. Washington, DC: Smithsonian Books, 2019.

Burstein, Andrew. *America's Jubilee, July 4, 1826: A Generation Remembers the Revolution after Fifty Years of Independence*. New York: Alfred A. Knopf, 2001.

Bussey, Gertrude, and Margaret Tims. *Pioneers for Peace: Women's International League for Peace and Freedom, 1915–1965*. London: WILPF British Section, 1980.

Capozzola, Christopher. *Uncle Sam Wants You: World War I and the Making of the Modern American Citizen*. New York: Oxford University Press, 2008.

Chambers, John Whiteclay, II, ed. *The Eagle and the Dove: The American Peace Movement and United States Foreign Policy, 1900–1922*. New York: Garland, 1976.

Chandler, Susan. "Addie Hunton and the Construction of an African American Female Peace Perspective." *Affilia* 20, no. 3 (Fall 2005): 270–83.

Christman, Anastasia J. "The Best Laid Plans: Women's Clubs and City Planning in Los Angeles, 1890–1930." PhD diss., University of California, Los Angeles, 2000.

Christman, Robert. "A Guide to the Virginia War History Commission, 1915–1931." Richmond: Library of Virginia, 2004. https://ead.lib.virginia.edu.

———. "The Records of the Virginia War History Commission." *Virginia Cavalcade* 50, no. 3 (Summer 2001): 100–101.

City of Aurora Historic Preservation Commission. "Aurora Historic Landmarks." 2012. https://www.auroragov.org.

Clark, Mary Sine. "'If They Consent to Leave Them Over There'": The European Pilgrimages of World War I Mothers and Widows from Virginia." *Virginia Cavalcade* 50, no. 3 (Summer 2001): 135–41.

Clark, Robert Judson, ed. *The Arts and Crafts Movement in America, 1876–1916*. Princeton, NJ: Princeton University Press, 1972.

Clifford, John Garry. *The Citizen Soldiers: The Plattsburg Training Camp Movement, 1913–1920*. Lexington: University Press of Kentucky, 1972.

Clifford, J. Garry, and Samuel R. Spencer Jr. *The First Peacetime Draft*. Lawrence: University Press of Kansas, 1986.

Cobb, Ruth. *A Place We Called Home: A History of Illinois Soldiers' Orphans' Homes, 1864–1931, Illinois Soldiers' and Sailors' Children's School, 1931–1979*. Normal: Illinois State University, 2007.

Cobbs, Elizabeth. *The Hello Girls: America's First Women Soldiers*. Cambridge, MA: Harvard University Press, 2017.

Cohen, Lizabeth. *A Consumer's Republic: The Politics of Mass Consumption in Postwar America*. New York: Alfred A. Knopf, 2003.

Cole, Wayne S. *Senator Gerald P. Nye and American Foreign Relations*. Minneapolis: University of Minnesota Press, 1962.

Condell, Diana, and Jean Liddiard. *Working for Victory: Images of Women in the First World War, 1914–18*. London: Routledge & Kegan Paul, 1987.

Connelly, Mark. *The Great War, Memory and Ritual: Commemoration in the City and East London, 1916–1939*. Rochester, NY: Royal Historical Society, 2001.

Conner, Thomas H. *War and Remembrance: The Story of the American Battle Monuments Commission*. Lexington: University Press of Kentucky, 2018.

Cooper, Annabel, Robin Law, Jane Malthus, and Pamela Wood. "Rooms of Their Own: Public Toilets and Gendered Citizens in a New Zealand City, 1860–1940." *Gender, Place & Culture: A Journal of Feminist Geography* 7, no. 4 (July 14, 2010): 417–33.

Cooper, Brittany. "Mary Church Terrell and Ida B. Wells." In *We Return Fighting: World War I and the Shaping of Modern Black Identity*, edited by Kinshasha Holman Conwill, 102–5. Washington, DC: Smithsonian Books, 2019.

Cott, Nancy F. *The Grounding of Modern Feminism*. New Haven, CT: Yale University Press, 1987.

Cox, Karen L. *Dixie's Daughters: The United Daughters of the Confederacy and the Preservation of Confederate Culture*. Gainesville: University Press of Florida, 2003.

Craik, Jennifer. *Uniforms Exposed: From Conformity to Transgression*. Oxford, UK: Berg, 2005.

Crane, David. *Empires of the Dead: How One Man's Vision Led to the Creation of WWI's War Graves*. London: William Collins, 2013.

Crellin, Sarah. "Hollow Men: Francis Derwent Wood's Masks and Memorials, 1915–1925." *Sculpture Journal* 6 (2001): 75–88.

Crowdus, Gary, ed. *The Political Companion to American Film*. Chicago: Lakeview Press, 1994.

Crownshaw, Richard, Jane Kilby, and Antony Rowland, eds. *The Future of Memory*. New York: Berghahn Books, 2010.

Cumming, Elizabeth, and Wendy Kaplan. *The Arts and Crafts Movement*. London: Thames and Hudson, 1991.

Dalessandro, Robert J., and Michael G. Knapp. *Organization and Insignia of the American Expeditionary Force, 1917–1923*. Atglen, PA: Schiffer Military History, 2008.

Daniels, Caroline. "'The Feminine Touch Has Not Been Wanting': Women Librarians at Camp Zachary Taylor, 1917–1919." *Libraries & the Cultural Record* 43, no. 3 (2008): 286–307.

Daniels, Roger. *The Bonus March: An Episode of the Great Depression*. Westport, CT: Greenwood, 1971.

Davis, Allen F. *American Heroine: The Life and Legend of Jane Addams*. New York: Oxford University Press, 1973.

de Certeau, Michel. *The Practice of Everyday Life*. Translated by Steven Rendall. Berkeley: University of California Press, 1984.

Delegard, Kirsten Marie. *Battling Miss Bolsheviki: The Origins of Female Conservatism in the United States*. Philadelphia: University of Pennsylvania Press, 2012.

Denning, Michael. *The Cultural Front: The Laboring of American Culture in the Twentieth Century*. New York: Verso, 1998.

Dickinson, Greg, Carole Blair, and Brian L. Ott, eds. *Places of Public Memory: The Rhetoric of Museums and Memorials*. Tuscaloosa: University of Alabama Press, 2010.

Dickon, Chris. *The Foreign Burial of American War Dead: A History*. Jefferson, NC: McFarland, 2011.

Dickson, Paul, and Thomas B. Allen. *The Bonus Army: An American Epic*. New York: Walker, 2004.

Dickstein, Morris. *Dancing in the Dark: A Cultural History of the Great Depression*. New York: W. W. Norton, 2009.

Doenecke, Justus D., and Mark A. Stoler. *Debating Franklin D. Roosevelt's Foreign Politics, 1933–1945*. Lanham, MD: Rowman & Littlefield, 2005.

Doherty, Thomas. *Pre-code Hollywood: Sex, Immorality, and Insurrection in American Cinema, 1930–1934*. New York: Columbia University Press, 1999.

Donovan, Derek. *Lest the Ages Forget: Kansas City's Liberty Memorial*. Kansas City, MO: Kansas City Star Books, 2001.

Doss, Erika. *Memorial Mania: Public Feeling in America*. Chicago: University of Chicago Press, 2010.

Douglas, Allen. *War, Memory, and the Politics of Humor: The Canard Echaîné and World War I*. Berkeley: University of California Press, 2002.

Dowling, Elizabeth Meredith. *New Classicism: The Rebirth of Traditional Architecture*. New York: Rizzoli International Publications, 2004.

Dubin, Steven C. *Displays of Power: Memory and Amnesia in the American Museum*. New York: New York University Press, 1999.

DuBois, Ellen Carol. *Harriot Stanton Blatch and the Winning of Woman Suffrage*. New Haven, CT: Yale University Press, 1997.

Dumbrowski, Nicole Ann, ed. *Women and War in the Twentieth Century: Enlisted with or without Consent*. New York: Garland, 1999.

Dumenil, Lynn. *The Second Line of Defense: American Women and World War I*. Chapel Hill: University of North Carolina Press, 2017.

du Plessis, Elizabeth Cafer. "Alice French, Indiana War Mothers: From World War I 'Kitchen Soldiers' to Postwar Immigrant Reformers." In *Feminist Frontiers: Women Who Shaped the Midwest*, edited by Yvonne J. Johnson, 99–118. Kirksville, MO: Truman State University Press, 2010.

———. "Meatless Days and Sleepless Nights: Food, Agriculture, and Environment in World War I America." PhD diss., Indiana University, 2009.

Dusch, Charles D., Jr. "Great War Aviation and Commemoration: Louis Bennett, Jr., Commander of the West Virginia Flying Corps." PhD diss., West Virginia University, 2009.

Early, Frances H. *A World Without War: How U.S. Feminists and Pacifists Resisted World War I*. Syracuse, NY: Syracuse University Press, 1997.

Ebbert, Jean, and Marie-Beth Hall. *The First, the Few, the Forgotten: Navy and Marine Corps Women in World War I*. Annapolis, MD: Naval Institute Press, 2002.

Edwards, John Carver. *Patriots in Pinstripe: Men of the National Security League*. Washington, DC: University Press of America, 1982.

Eichenberg, Julia, and John Paul Newman, eds. *The Great War and Veterans' Internationalism*. Basingstoke, UK: Palgrave Macmillan, 2013.

Eisenhower, John S. D., and Joanne Thompson Eisenhower. *Yanks: The Epic Story of the American Army in World War I*. New York: Touchstone, 2001.

Elshtain, Jean Bethke. *Jane Addams and the Dream of American Democracy*. New York: Basic Books, 2002.

Elshtain, Jean Bethke, and Sheila Tobias, eds. *Women, Militarism, and War: Essays in History, Politics, and Social Theory*. Savage, MD: Rowman & Littlefield, 1990.

Enloe, Cynthia. *Does Khaki Become You? The Militarization of Women's Lives*. Boston: South End Press, 1983.

Ewing, Elizabeth. *Women in Uniform through the Centuries*. London: B. T. Batsford, 1975.

Farwell, Bryan. *Over There: The United States in the Great War, 1917–1918*. New York: W. W. Norton, 1999.

Faust, Drew Gilpin. *This Republic of Suffering: Death and the American Civil War*. New York: Vintage Books, 2008.

Fenelon, Holly S. *That Knock on the Door: The History of Gold Star Mothers in America*. Bloomington, IN: iUniverse, 2012.

Finkelstein, Allison S. "American Women in the War." In *World War I Remembered*, edited by Robert J. Dalessandro and Robert K. Sutton, 97–107. N.p., Eastern National, 2017.

——. "Carry On: American Women and the Veteranist-Commemoration of the First World War, 1917–1945." PhD diss., University of Maryland, College Park, 2015.

——. "A Female Sanctuary on the Former Western Front: The Gold Star Pilgrimage Rest Houses of 1930–33." *Buildings and Landscapes: The Journal of the Vernacular Architecture Forum* 23, no. 1 (Spring 2016): 52–77.

Finnegan, John Patrick. *Against the Specter of a Dragon: The Campaign for American Military Preparedness, 1914–1917*. Westport, CT: Greenwood Press, 1974.

Fischer, Marilyn, Carol Nackenoff, and Wendy Chmielewski, eds. *Jane Addams and the Practice of Democracy*. Urbana: University of Illinois Press, 2009.

Fitall, Elliot. "The World War II Memorial." History 208 final paper, University of Maryland, College Park, 2013.

Flanagan, Maureen A. "Gender and Urban Political Reform: The City Club and the Woman's City Club of Chicago in the Progressive Era." *American Historical Review* 95, no. 4 (October 1990): 1032–50.

——. *Seeing with Their Hearts: Chicago Women and the Vision of the Good City, 1871–1933*. Princeton, NJ: Princeton University Press, 2002.

Ford, Liam T. A. *Soldier Field: A Stadium and Its City*. Chicago: University of Chicago Press, 2009.

Foster, Carrie A. *The Women and the Warriors: The U.S. Section of the Women's International League for Peace and Freedom, 1915–1946*. Syracuse, NY: Syracuse University Press, 1995.

Foster, Catherine. *Women for All Seasons: The Story of the Women's International League for Peace and Freedom*. Athens: University of Georgia Press, 1989.

Foster, Gaines M. *Ghosts of the Confederacy: Defeat, the Lost Cause, and the Emergence of the New South*. New York: Oxford University Press, 1985.

Frahm, Jill. "Advance to the 'Fighting Lines': The Changing Role of Women Telephone Operators in France During the First World War." *Federal History* 8 (2016): 95–108.

——. "The Hello Girls: Women Telephone Operators with the American Expeditionary Forces during World War I." *Journal of the Gilded Age and Progressive Era* 3, no. 3 (July 2004): 272–93.

Frank, Lisa Tendrich, ed. *An Encyclopedia of American Women at War: From the Home Front to the Battlefields*. Santa Barbara, CA: ABC-CLIO, 2013.

Frankel, Noralee, and Nancy S. Dye, eds. *Gender, Class, Race, and Reform in the Progressive Era*. Lexington: University Press of Kentucky, 1991.

Fraser, Steve, and Gary Gerstle, eds. *The Rise and Fall of the New Deal Order, 1930–1980*. Princeton, NJ: Princeton University Press, 1989.

Friedl, Vicki L. *Women in the United States Military, 1901–1995: A Research Guide and Annotated Bibliography*. Westport, CT: Greenwood Press, 1996.

Frydl, Kathleen J. *The GI Bill*. New York: Cambridge University Press, 2009.

Furstenberg, Francois. *In the Name of the Father: Washington's Legacy, Slavery, and the Making of a Nation*. New York, Penguin Press, 2006.

Fussell, Paul. *The Great War and Modern Memory*. New York: Oxford University Press, 1975.

Gaffney, Angela. *Aftermath: Remembering the Great War in Wales*. Cardiff: University of Wales Press, 1998.

Gallagher, Gary W. *Causes Won, Lost, & Forgotten: How Hollywood and Popular Art Shape What We Know about the Civil War*. Chapel Hill: University of North Carolina Press, 2008.

Gavin, Lettie. *American Women in World War One: They Also Served*. Niwot: University Press of Colorado, 2006.

Gibson, Thomas J. "The Nye Committee and American Isolationism." Master's thesis, Claremont Graduate School, 1958.

Gilbert, James. *Whose Fair? Experience, Memory, and the History of the Great St. Louis Exposition*. Chicago: University of Chicago Press, 2009.

Gilbert, Martin. *The First World War: A Complete History*. New York: Owl Books, Henry Holt, 1994.

Gillis, John R., ed. *Commemorations: The Politics of National Identity*. Princeton, NJ: Princeton University Press, 1994.

Giovacchini, Saverio. *Hollywood Modernism: Film and Politics in the Age of the New Deal*. Philadelphia: Temple University Press, 2001.

Glassberg, David. *American Historical Pageantry: The Uses of Tradition in the Early Twentieth Century*. Chapel Hill: University of North Carolina Press, 1990.

———. *Sense of History: The Place of the Past in American Life*. Amherst: University of Massachusetts Press, 2001.

Glassford, Sara, and Amy Shaw, eds. *A Sisterhood of Suffering and Service: Women and Girls of Canada and Newfoundland during the First World War*. Vancouver: University of British Columbia Press, 2012.

Glazer, Nathan, and Cynthia R. Field, eds. *The National Mall: Rethinking Washington's Monumental Core*. Baltimore: Johns Hopkins University Press, 2008.

Gobel, David, and Daves Rossell, eds. *Commemoration in America: Essays on Monuments, Memorialization, and Memory*. Charlottesville: University of Virginia Press, 2013.

Godson, Susan H. *Serving Proudly: A History of Women in the U.S. Navy*. Annapolis, MD: Naval Institute Press, 2001.

Goebel, Stefan. *The Great War and Medieval Memory: War, Remembrance and Medievalism in Britain and Germany, 1914–1940*. Cambridge: Cambridge University Press, 2007.

Goldberg, David J. *Discontented America: The United States in the 1920s*. Baltimore: Johns Hopkins University Press, 1999.

Goode, James M. *Washington Sculpture: A Cultural History of Outdoor Sculpture in the Nation's Capital*. Baltimore: Johns Hopkins University Press, 2008.

Gordon, Linda. "Black and White Visions of Welfare: Women's Welfare Activism, 1890–1945." *Journal of American History* 78, no. 2 (September 1991): 559–90.

———. *Pitied but Not Entitled: Single Mothers and the History of Welfare, 1890–1935*. New York: Free Press, 1994.

———. "Social Insurance and Public Assistance: The Influence of Gender in Welfare Thought in the United States, 1890–1935." *American Historical Review* 97, no. 1 (February 1992): 19–54.

Graham, John. *The Gold Star Mother Pilgrimages of the 1930s: Overseas Grave Visitations by Mothers and Widows of Fallen U.S. World War I Soldiers*. Jefferson, NC: McFarland, 2005.

Grayzel, Susan. *Women's Identities at War: Gender, Motherhood, and Politics in Britain and France During the First World War*. Chapel Hill: University of North Carolina Press, 1999.

Green, Nancy L. *The Other Americans in Paris: Businessmen, Countesses, Wayward Youth, 1880–1941*. Chicago: University of Chicago Press, 2014.

Greenberg, Milton. *The GI Bill: The Law That Changed America*. New York: Lickle, 1997.

Gregory, Adrian. *The Silence of Memory: Armistice Day, 1919–1946*. Oxford, UK: Berg, 1994.

Grossman, Elizabeth G. "Architecture for a Public Client: The Monuments and Chapels of the American Battle Monuments Commission." *Journal of the Society of Architectural Historians* 43, no. 2 (May 1984): 119–43.

———. *The Civic Architecture of Paul Cret*. New York: Cambridge University Press, 1996.

Gullace, Nicoletta F. "White Feathers and Wounded Men: Female Patriotism and the Memory of the Great War." *Journal of British Studies* 36, no. 2 (April 1997): 178–206.

Gutman, Sharon A. "Influence of the U.S. Military and Occupational Therapy Reconstruction Aides in World War I on the Development of Occupational Therapy." *American Journal of Occupational Therapy* 49, no. 3 (March 1995): 256–62.

Hacker, Barton C. "Control, Utility, Status, Symbolism: Suffragists, Boy Scouts, Blackshirts, and Other Politicians in Uniform." In *Proceedings of the 2006 ICOMAM Symposium, Uniforms: Yesterday, Today, and Tomorrow*, 72–81. Brussels: Musée Royal de l'Armée et d'Histoire Militaire, for ICOMAM, 2006.

Hacker, Barton C., and Margaret Vining. *A Companion to Women's Military History*. Boston: Brill, 2012.

———, eds. *Cutting a New Pattern: Uniformed Women in the Great War*. Washington, DC: Smithsonian Institution Scholarly Press, 2020.

Hagopian, Patrick. *The Vietnam War in American Memory: Veterans, Memorials, and the Politics of Healing*. Amherst: University of Massachusetts Press, 2009.

Halbwachs, Maurice. *On Collective Memory*. Translated by Lewis A. Coser. Chicago: University of Chicago Press, 1992.

Haley, Bruce. *Living Forms: Romantics and the Monumental Figure*. Albany: State University of New York Press, 2003.

Hämmerle, Christa, Oswald Überegger, and Birgitta Bader Zaar, eds. *Gender and the First World War*. London: Palgrave Macmillan, 2014.

Hanson, Neil. *Unknown Soldiers: The Story of the Missing of the First World War*. New York: Alfred A. Knopf, 2006.

Hartwick, Ann M. Ritchie. *The Army Medical Specialist Corps: The 45th Anniversary*. Washington, DC: Center of Military History, 1993. https://history.army.mil.

Hass, Kristin Ann. *Carried to the Wall: American Memory and the Vietnam Veterans Memorial*. Berkeley: University of California Press, 1998.

——. *Sacrificing Soldiers on the National Mall*. Berkeley: University of California Press, 2013.

Hawley, Ellis W. *The Great War and the Search for Modern Order: A History of the American People and Their Institutions, 1917–1933*. New York: St. Martin's Press, 1979.

Heiman, James J. *Voices in Bronze and Stone: Kansas City's World War I Monuments and Memorials*. Kansas City, MO: Kansas City Star Books, 2013.

Henry, Marilène Patten. *Monumental Accusations: The monuments aux morts as Expressions of Popular Resentment*. New York: Peter Lang, 1996.

Higonnet, Margaret R., ed. *Letters and Photographs from the Battle Country: The World War I Memoir of Margaret Hall*. Charlottesville: University of Virginia Press, 2014.

——, ed. *Lines of Fire: Women Writers of World War I*. New York: Plume, 1999.

——, ed. *Nurses at the Front: Writing the Wounds of the Great War*. Boston: Northeastern University Press, 2001.

Higonnet, Margaret Randolph, Jane Jenson, Sonya Michel, and Margaret Collins Weitz, eds. *Behind the Lines: Gender and the Two World Wars*. New Haven, CT: Yale University Press, 1987.

Hine, Darlene Clark. *Black Women in White: Racial Conflict and Cooperation in the Nursing Profession, 1890–1950*. Bloomington: Indiana University Press, 1989.

Hoagland, Alison K. "Introducing the Bathroom: Space and Change in Working-Class Houses." *Buildings & Landscapes: Journal of the Vernacular Architecture Forum* 18, no. 2 (Fall 2011): 15–42.

Holm, Jeanne. *Women in the Military: An Unfinished Revolution*. Novato, CA: Presidio Press, 1982.

Holt, Dean W. *American Military Cemeteries: A Comprehensive Guide to the Hallowed Grounds of the United States, Including Overseas*. Jefferson, NC: McFarland, 1992.

Hulver, Richard. "Remains in Peace: The Diplomacy of American Military Bodies in France, 1919–1972." PhD diss., West Virginia University, 2015.

Humes, Edward. *Over Here: How the G.I. Bill Transformed the American Dream*. Orlando, FL: Harcourt, 2006.

Hurt, R. Douglas. *The Dust Bowl: An Agricultural and Social History*. Chicago: Nelson-Hall, 1981.

Irwin, Julia F. *Making the World Safe: The American Red Cross and a Nation's Humanitarian Awakening*. New York: Oxford University Press, 2013.

Isenberg, Michael T. *War on Film: The American Cinema and World War I, 1914–1941*. East Brunswick, NJ: Associated University Presses, 1981.

Jackson, Kenneth T., and Camilo José Vergara. *Silent Cities: The Evolution of the American Cemetery*. New York: Princeton Architectural Press, 1989.

Jakeman, Robert J. "Memorializing World War I in Alabama." In *The Great War in the Heart of Dixie: Alabama During World War I*, edited by Martin T. Oliff, 201–20. Tuscaloosa: University of Alabama Press, 2008.

James, Pearl, ed. *The New Death: American Modernism and World War I*. Charlottesville: University of Virginia Press, 2013.

———. *Picture This: World War I Posters and Visual Culture*. Lincoln: University of Nebraska Press, 2009.

Janney, Caroline E. *Burying the Dead but Not the Past: Ladies' Memorial Associations & the Lost Cause*. Chapel Hill: University of North Carolina Press, 2008.

Jeansonne, Glen. *Women of the Far Right: The Mothers' Movement and World War II*. Chicago: University of Chicago Press, 1996.

Jeffreys-Jones, Rhodri. *Changing Differences: Women and the Shaping of American Foreign Policy, 1917–1994*. New Brunswick, NJ: Rutgers University Press, 1995.

Jensen, Kimberly. *Mobilizing Minerva: American Women in the First World War*. Urbana: University of Illinois Press, 2008.

Johnson, Kathleen Burger. "Delano, Jane Arminda (1862–1919)." In *An Encyclopedia of American Women at War: From the Home Front to the Battlefields*, edited by Lisa Tendrich Frank, 186–88. Santa Barbara, CA: ABC-CLIO, 2013.

Jonas, Manfred. *Isolationism in America, 1935–1941*. Ithaca, NY: Cornell University Press, 1966.

Jones, Marian Moser. *The American Red Cross from Clara Barton to the New Deal*. Baltimore: Johns Hopkins University Press, 2013.

Jones, Marian Moser, and Matilda Saines. "The Eighteen of 1918–1919: Black Nurses and the Great Flu Pandemic in the United States." *American Journal of Public Health* 109, no. 6 (June 2019): 877–84.

Joseph, Nathan. *Uniforms and Nonuniforms: Communication through Clothing*. Westport, CT: Greenwood Press, 1986.

Kahana, Jonathan. "The Forgotten Man; or, How Hollywood Invented Welfare." *Camera Obscura* 62, no. 21(2) (2006): 74–107.

Kammen, Michael. *Mystic Chords of Memory: The Transformation of Tradition in American Culture*. New York: Alfred A. Knopf, 1991.

———. *A Season of Youth: The American Revolution and the Historical Imagination*. New York: Oxford University Press, 1978.

Katznelson, Ira. *When Affirmative Action Was White: An Untold History of Racial Inequality in Twentieth-Century America*. New York: W. W. Norton, 2005.

Kavanagh, Gaynor. *Museums and the First World War: A Social History*. London: Leicester University Press, 1994.

Keene, Jennifer D. *Doughboys, the Great War, and the Remaking of America*. Baltimore: Johns Hopkins University Press, 2001.

Kelly, Andrew. *Cinema and the Great War*. London: Routledge, 1997.

Kelly, Patrick J. *Creating a National Home: Building the Veteran's Welfare State, 1860–1900*. Cambridge, MA: Harvard University Press, 1997.

Kelman, Ari. *A Misplaced Massacre: Struggling over the Memory of Sand Creek*. Cambridge, MA: Harvard University Press, 2013.

Kendrick, Kathleen M. *Official Guide to the Smithsonian National Museum of African American History & Culture*. Washington, DC: Smithsonian Books, 2017.

Kennedy, David M. *Freedom from Fear: The American People in Depression and War, 1929–1945*. New York: Oxford University Press, 1999.

———. *Over Here: The First World War and American Society*. New York: Oxford University Press, 1980.

Kennedy, Kathleen. *Disloyal Mothers and Scurrilous Citizens: Women and Subversion during World War I*. Bloomington: Indiana University Press, 1999.

Kerber, Linda K. *No Constitutional Right to Be Ladies: Women and the Obligations of Citizenship*. New York: Hill and Wang, 1998.

———. *Women of the Republic: Intellect and Ideology in Revolutionary America*. Chapel Hill: University of North Carolina Press, 1980.

Kidd, William, and Brian Murdoch, eds. *Memory and Memorials: The Commemorative Century*. Bodmin, UK: Ashgate, 2004.

Kieran, David. *Forever Vietnam: How a Divisive War Changed American Public Memory*. Amherst: University of Massachusetts Press, 2014.

Kinder, John M. "Iconography of Injury: Encountering the Wounded Soldier's Body in American Poster Art and Photography of World War I." In *Picture This: World War I Posters and Visual Culture*, edited by Pearl James, 340–68. Lincoln: University of Nebraska Press, 2009.

Kington, Donald M. *Forgotten Summers: The Story of the Citizens' Military Training Camps, 1921–1940*. San Francisco: Two Decades Publishing, 1995.

Kleinberg, S. J. *Widows and Orphans First: The Family Economy and Social Welfare Policy, 1880–1939*. Urbana: University of Illinois Press, 2006.

Koistinen, Paul A. C. *Planning War, Pursuing Peace: The Political Economy of American Warfare, 1920–1939*. Lawrence: University Press of Kansas, 1998.

Koven, Seth. "Remembering and Dismemberment: Crippled Children, Wounded Soldiers, and the Great War in Great Britain." *American Historical Review* 99, no. 4 (October 1994): 1167–202.

Koven, Seth, and Sonya Michel, eds. *Mothers of a New World: Maternalist Politics and the Origins of Welfare States*. New York: Routledge, 1993.

———. "Womanly Duties: Maternalist Politics and the Origins of Welfare States in France, Germany, Great Britain, and the United States, 1880–1920." *American Historical Review* 95, no. 3 (October 1990): 1076–108.

Krasner, James. "Doubtful Arms and Phantom Limbs: Literary Portrayals of Embodied Grief." *PMLA* 119 (March 2004): 218–32.

Kuhlman, Erika A. *Of Little Comfort: War Widows, Fallen Soldiers, and the Remaking of the Nation after the Great War*. New York: New York University Press, 2012.

———. *Petticoats and White Feathers: Gender Conformity, Race, the Progressive Peace Movement, and the Debate over War, 1895–1919*. Westport, CT: Greenwood Press, 1997.

Kwolek-Folland, Angel. "Gender as a Category of Analysis in Vernacular Architecture

Studies." In *Gender, Class, and Shelter: Perspectives in Vernacular Architecture*, vol. 5, edited by Elizabeth Collins Cromley and Carter L. Hudgins, 3–10. Knoxville: University of Tennessee Press, 1995.

Ladd-Taylor, Molly. *Mother-Work: Women, Child Welfare, and the State, 1890–1930*. Urbana: University of Illinois Press, 1994.

Lamberti, Elena, and Vita Fortunati, eds. *Memories and Representations of War: The Case of World War I and World War II*. New York: Rodopi, 2009.

Landsberg, Alison. *Prosthetic Memory: The Transformation of American Remembrance in the Age of Mass Culture*. New York: Columbia University Press, 2004.

Larsson, Marina. "A Disenfranchised Grief: Post-war Death and Memorialisation in Australia after the First World War." *Australian Historical Studies* 40, no. 1 (March 2009): 79–95.

———. *Shattered Anzacs: Living with the Scars of War*. Sydney, Australia: University of New South Wales Press, 2009.

Laslo, Alexander J. *The Interallied Victory Medals of World War I*. Albuquerque: Dorado, 1992.

Lemay, Kate Clarke. *Triumph of the Dead: American World War II Cemeteries, Monuments, and Diplomacy in France*. Tuscaloosa: University of Alabama Press, 2018.

Lembcke, Jerry. *The Spitting Image: Myth, Memory, and the Legacy of Vietnam*. New York: New York University Press, 2000.

Lemons, J. Stanley. *The Woman Citizen: Social Feminism in the 1920s*. Charlottesville: University Press of Virginia, 1990.

Lengel, Edward G. *To Conquer Hell: The Meuse-Argonne, 1918 The Epic Battle That Ended the First World War*. New York: Henry Holt, 2008.

Levenstein, Harvey. *Seductive Journeys: American Tourists in France from Jefferson to the Jazz Age*. Chicago: University of Chicago Press, 1998.

———. *We'll Always Have Paris: American Tourists in France since 1930*. Chicago: University of Chicago Press, 2004.

Levitch, Mark. *Panthéon de la Guerre: Reconfiguring a Panorama of the Great War*. Columbia: University of Missouri Press, 2006.

Lewis, Pierce. "The Monument and the Bungalow." *Geographical Review* 88, no. 4 (October 1998): 507–27.

Licursi, Kimberly J. Lamay. *Remembering World War I in America*. Lincoln: University of Nebraska Press, 2018.

Linenthal, Edward T., and Tom Engelhardt, eds. *History Wars: The Enola Gay and Other Battles for the American Past*. New York: Henry Holt, 1996.

Linker, Beth. "Strength and Science: Gender, Physiotherapy, and Medicine in Early-Twentieth-Century America." *Journal of Women's History* 17, no. 3 (Fall 2005): 106–32.

———. *War's Waste: Rehabilitation in World War I America*. Chicago: University of Chicago Press, 2011.

Lisio, Donald J. *The President and Protest: Hoover, MacArthur, and the Bonus Riot*. New York: Fordham University Press, 1994.

Lloyd, David W. *Battlefield Tourism: Pilgrimage and the Commemoration of the Great War in Britain, Australia and Canada, 1919–1939*. Oxford, UK: Berg, 1998.

Looney, J. Jefferson. "'I Really Never Thought War Was So Cruel': The Veterans' Questionnaires of the Virginia War History Commission." *Virginia Cavalcade* 50, no. 3 (Summer 2001): 125–33.

Lorentzen, Lois Ann, and Jennifer Turpin, eds. *The Women and War Reader.* New York: New York University Press, 1998.

Lowe, Jaclyn Faglie. "The Reconstruction Aides." *American Journal of Occupational Therapy* 46, no. 1 (January 1992): 38–43.

Luebke, Thomas E., ed. *Civic Art: A Centennial History of the U.S. Commission of Fine Arts.* Washington, DC: US Commission of Fine Arts, 2013.

Lupkin, Paula. *Manhood Factories: YMCA Architecture and the Making of Modern Urban Culture.* Minneapolis: University of Minnesota Press, 2010.

Lupton, Ellen, and J. Abbott Miller. *The Bathroom, the Kitchen, and the Aesthetics of Waste: A Process of Elimination.* New York: Princeton Architectural Press, 1992.

Margalit, Avishai. *The Ethics of Memory.* Cambridge, MA: Harvard University Press, 2002.

Mason, Ann Michele. "Nannie H. Burroughs' Rhetorical Leadership during the Interwar Period." PhD diss., University of Maryland, College Park, 2008.

Mason, Herbert Molloy, Jr. *VFW: Our First Century.* Lenexa, KS: Addax, 1999.

May, Lary. *The Big Tomorrow: Hollywood and the Politics of the American Way.* Chicago: University of Chicago Press, 2000.

Mayo, James M. *The American Country Club: Its Origins and Development.* New Brunswick, NJ: Rutgers University Press, 1998.

McAlester, Virginia, and Lee McAlester. *A Field Guide to American Houses.* New York: Alfred A. Knopf, 1996.

McDaid, Jennifer Davis. "'Our Share in the War Is No Small One': Virginia Women and World War I." *Virginia Cavalcade* 50, no. 3 (Summer 2001): 100–123.

McDowell, Peggy, and Richard E. Meyer. *The Revival Styles in American Memorial Art.* Bowling Green, OH: Bowling Green State University Popular Press, 1994.

McElya, Micki. *The Politics of Mourning: Death and Honor in Arlington National Cemetery.* Cambridge, MA: Harvard University Press, 2016.

McMurry, Sally. "Women in the American Vernacular Landscape." *Material Culture* 20, no. 1 (Spring 1998): 33–49.

McNeil, Karen Ann. "Building the California Women's Movement: Architecture, Space, and Gender in the Life and Work of Julia Morgan." PhD diss., University of California, Berkeley, 2006.

———. "'Women Who Build': Julia Morgan & Women's Institutions." *California History* 89, no. 3 (2012): 41–74.

Mettler, Susan. *Soldiers to Citizens: The G.I. Bill and the Making of the Greatest Generation.* New York: Oxford University Press, 2005.

Meyer, Leisa D. *Creating G.I. Jane: Sexuality and Power in the Women's Army Corps During World War II.* New York: Columbia University Press, 1996.

Meyer, Lotte Larsen. "Mourning in a Distant Land: Gold Star Pilgrimages to American Military Cemeteries in Europe, 1930–33." *Markers* 20 (2003): 31–75.

Michel, Sonya. *Children's Interests/Mother's Rights: The Shaping of America's Child Care Policy.* New Haven, CT: Yale University Press, 1999.

Miller, Richard E. "The Golden Fourteen, Plus: Black Navy Women in World War One." *Minerva* 13, no. 3 (December 31, 1995).

Mills, Cynthia, and Pamela H. Simpson, eds. *Monuments to the Lost Cause: Women, Art, and the Landscapes of Southern Memory.* Knoxville: University of Tennessee Press, 2003.

Mock, James R., and Cedric Larson. *Words That Won the War: The Story of the Committee on Public Information, 1917–1919.* Princeton, NJ: Princeton University Press, 1939.

Monahan, Evelyn M., and Rosemary Neidel-Greenlee. *A Few Good Women: America's Military Women from World War I to the Wars in Iraq and Afghanistan.* New York: Alfred A. Knopf, 2010.

Morden, Bettie J. *The Women's Army Corps, 1945–1978.* Washington, DC: Center of Military History, United States Army, 1990.

Morgan, Francesca. *Women and Patriotism in Jim Crow America.* Chapel Hill: University of North Carolina Press, 2005.

Mosse, George L. *Fallen Soldiers: Reshaping the Memory of the World Wars.* New York: Oxford University Press, 1990.

Muncy, Robyn. *Creating a Female Dominion in American Reform, 1890–1935.* New York: Oxford University Press, 1991.

Murphy, Mary-Elizabeth B. *Jim Crow Capital: Women and Black Freedom Struggles in Washington, D.C., 1920–1945.* Chapel Hill: University of North Carolina Press, 2018.

Neal, Arthur G. *National Trauma & Collective Memory: Major Events in the American Century.* Armonk, NY: M. E. Sharpe, 1998.

Nehls, Christopher Courtney. "'A Grand and Glorious Feeling': The American Legion and American Nationalism between the World Wars." PhD diss., University of Virginia, 2007.

Nielsen, Kim E. *Un-American Womanhood: Antiradicalism, Antifeminism, and the First Red Scare.* Columbus: Ohio State University Press, 2001.

Nora, Pierre. "Between Memory and History: *Les Lieux de Mémoire*." *Representations* 26 (Spring 1999): 7–24.

——, ed. *Realms of Memory: The Construction of the French Past.* Vol. 2, *Traditions.* Translated by Arthur Goldhammer. New York: Columbia University Press, 1997.

——, ed. *Realms of Memory: The Construction of the French Past.* Vol. 3, *Symbols.* Translated by Arthur Goldhammer. New York: Columbia University Press, 1998.

——, ed. *Rethinking France: Les Lieux de Mémoire.* Vol. 2, *Space.* Translated by David P. Jordan. Chicago: University of Chicago Press, 2009.

——, ed. *Rethinking France: Les Lieux de Mémoire.* Vol. 3, *Legacies.* Translated by David P. Jordan. Chicago: University of Chicago Press, 2009.

Norkunas, Martha. *Monuments and Memory: History and Representation in Lowell, Massachusetts.* Washington, DC: Smithsonian Institution Press, 2002.

O'Bryan, Katherine Merzbacher. "Gender, Politics, and Power: The Development of the

Ladies Rest Room and Lounge in Rural America, 1900–1945." PhD diss., Middle Tennessee State University, 2013.

O'Leary, Cecelia Elizabeth. *To Die For: The Paradox of American Patriotism.* Princeton, NJ: Princeton University Press, 1999.

Olick, Jeffrey K., Vered Vinitzky-Seroussi, and Daniel Levy, eds. *The Collective Memory Reader.* New York: Oxford University Press, 2011.

Ortiz, Stephen R. *Beyond the Bonus March and GI Bill: How Veteran Politics Shaped the New Deal Era.* New York: New York University Press, 2010.

———, ed. *Veterans' Policies, Veterans' Politics: New Perspectives on Veterans in the Modern United States.* Gainesville: University Press of Florida, 2012.

Ouditt, Sharon. *Fighting Forces, Writing Women: Identity and Ideology in the First World War.* New York: Routledge, 1994.

Patch, Nathaniel. "The Story of the Female Yeoman during the First World War." *Prologue* 38, no. 3 (Fall 2006): 54–59.

Patterson, David S. *The Search for Negotiated Peace: Women's Activism and Citizen Diplomacy in World War I.* New York: Routledge, 2008.

Pencak, William. *For God & Country: The American Legion, 1919–1941.* Boston: Northeastern University Press, 1989.

Perrett, Geoffrey. *America in the Twenties: A History.* New York: Simon and Schuster, 1982.

Perry, Elisabeth Israels. *Belle Moskowitz: Feminine Politics and the Exercise of Power in the Age of Alfred E. Smith.* New York: Oxford University Press, 1987.

Pessen, Edward. "The Great Songwriters of Tin Pan Alley's Golden Age: A Social, Occupational, and Aesthetics Inquiry." *American Music* 3, no. 2 (Summer 1985): 180–97.

Petrone, Karen. *The Great War in Russian Memory.* Bloomington: Indiana University Press, 2011.

Pettigrew, Judith, Katie Robinson, and Stephanie Moloney. "The Bluebirds: World War I Soldiers' Experiences of Occupational Therapy." *American Journal of Occupational Therapy* 71, no. 1 (January/February 2017): 1–9.

Piehler, G. Kurt. "Remembering the War to End All Wars." In *Unknown Soldiers: The American Expeditionary Forces in Memory and Remembrance,* edited by Mark Snell, 28–59. Kent, OH: Kent State University Press, 2008.

———. *Remembering War the American Way.* Washington, DC: Smithsonian Institution Press, 1995.

Placzek, Adolf F. *Macmillan Encyclopedia of Architects.* London: Free Press, 1982.

Plant, Rebecca Jo. "Anti-maternalism: A New Perspective on the Transformation of Gender Ideology in the Twentieth-Century United States." *Social Politics* 22, no. 3 (Fall 2015): 283–88.

———. "The Gold Star Mothers Pilgrimages: Patriotic Maternalists and Their Critics in Interwar America." In *Maternalism Reconsidered: Motherhood, Welfare, and Social Policy in the Twentieth Century,* edited by Marian van der Klein, Rebecca Jo Plant, Nicole Sanders, and Lori R. Weintrob, 121–47. New York: Berghahn Books, 2012.

———. *Mom: The Transformation of Motherhood in Modern America.* Chicago: University of Chicago Press, 2010.

Plant, Rebecca Jo, and Frances M. Clarke. "'The Crowning Insult': Federal Segregation and the Gold Star Mother and Widow Pilgrimages of the Early 1930s." *Journal of American History* 102, no. 2 (September 2015): 406–32.

Plastas, Melinda. *A Band of Noble Women: Racial Politics in the Women's Peace Movement*. Syracuse, NY: Syracuse University Press, 2011.

Poole, Robert M. *On Hallowed Ground: The Story of Arlington National Cemetery*. New York: Walker, 2010.

Pop, Andrei, and Mechtild Widrich, eds. *Ugliness: The Non-beautiful in Art and Theory*. New York: I. B. Taurus, 2014.

Potter, Constance. "World War I Gold Star Mothers Pilgrimages, Part I." *Prologue* 31, no. 2 (Summer 1999): 140–45.

———. "World War I Gold Star Mothers Pilgrimages, Part II." *Prologue* 31, no. 3 (Fall 1999): 210–15.

Powaski, Ronald E. *Toward an Entangling Alliance: American Isolationism, Internationalism, and Europe, 1901–1950*. Westport, CT: Greenwood Press, 1991.

Powell, Michelle Rene. "Tiffany Memorial Windows: How They Unified a Region and a Nation through Women's Associations from the North and the South at the Turn of the Twentieth Century." Master's thesis, Corcoran College of Art and Design, 2012.

Price, George. *The World of George Price: A 55-Year Retrospective*. New York: Beaufort Books, 1988.

Purcell, Sarah. *Sealed with Blood: War, Sacrifice, and Memory in Revolutionary America*. Philadelphia: University of Pennsylvania Press, 2002.

Pursell, Carroll W., Jr. *The Military-Industrial Complex*. New York: Harper & Row, 1972.

Quigley, Joan. *Just Another Southern Town: Mary Church Terrell and the Struggle for Racial Justice in the Nation's Capital*. New York: Oxford University Press, 2016.

Quintana, Maria. "Addie Waites Hunton (1866–1943)." *Black Past*, January 7, 2010. https://www.blackpast.org.

Raines, Rebecca Robbins. *Getting the Message Through: A Branch History of the U.S. Army Signal Corps*. Washington, DC: Center of Military History, United States Army, 1999.

Reardon, Carol. *Pickett's Charge in History and Memory*. Chapel Hill: University of North Carolina Press, 1997.

Reynolds, David. *The Long Shadow: The Legacies of the Great War in the Twentieth Century*. New York: W. W. Norton, 2014.

Rhodes, Benjamin D. *United States Foreign Policy in the Interwar Period, 1918–1941: The Golden Age of American Diplomatic and Military Complacency*. Westport, CT: Praeger, 2001.

Richter, Amy G. *Home on the Rails: Women, the Railroad, and the Rise of Public Domesticity*. Chapel Hill: University of North Carolina Press, 2005.

Rieselbach, Leroy N. *The Roots of Isolationism: Congressional Voting and Presidential Leadership in Foreign Policy*. Indianapolis: Bobbs-Merrill, 1966.

Robb, George. *British Culture and the First World War*. Basingstoke, UK: Palgrave, 2002.

Robertson, Nancy Marie. *Christian Sisterhood, Race Relations, and the YWCA, 1906–46*. Urbana: University of Illinois Press, 2007.

Robin, Ron. *Enclaves of America: The Rhetoric of American Political Architecture Abroad, 1900–1965*. Princeton, NJ: Princeton University Press, 1992.

Robinson, Patricia Dawn. "From Pedestal to Platform: The American Women's Club Movement, 1800–1920." PhD diss., University of California, Davis, 1993.

Rogers, Daniel T. *Atlantic Crossings: Social Politics in a Progressive Age*. Cambridge, MA: Belknap Press of Harvard University Press, 1998.

Rollins, Peter C., and John E. O'Connor, eds. *Hollywood's World War I: Motion Picture Images*. Bowling Green, OH: Bowling Green State University Popular Press, 1997.

Rosenberg, R. B. *Living Monuments: Confederate Soldiers' Homes in the New South*. Chapel Hill: University of North Carolina Press, 1993.

Rossini, Daniela, ed. *From Theodore Roosevelt to FDR: Internationalism and Isolationism in American Foreign Policy*. Staffordshire, UK: Ryburn, 1995.

Rubin, Martin. "The Crowd, the Collective, and the Chorus: Busby Berkeley and the New Deal." In *Movies and Mass Culture*, edited by John Belton, 59–92. New Brunswick, NJ: Rutgers University Press, 1996.

Rubin, Richard. *The Last of the Doughboys: The Forgotten Generation and Their Forgotten World War*. New York: Houghton Mifflin Harcourt, 2013.

Rumer, Thomas A. *The American Legion: An Official History, 1919–1989*. New York: M. Evan, 1990.

Sacchi, Livio. "Jefferson & Co.: The Influence of the Italian Architectural Culture in Washington D.C. and Virginia." In *The Italian Legacy in Washington, D.C.: Architecture, Design, Art, and Culture*, edited by Luca Molinari and Andrea Canepari, 25–36. Milan, Italy: Skira Editore, 2007.

Salter, Krewasky A. "From Civil War to World War: African American Soldiers and the Roots of the Civil Rights Movement." In *We Return Fighting: World War I and the Shaping of Modern Black Identity*, edited by Kinshasha Holman Conwill, 51–95. Washington, DC: Smithsonian Books, 2019.

Sammons, Jeffrey T., and John H. Morrow Jr. *Harlem's Rattlers and the Great War: The Undaunted 369th Regiment & the African American Quest for Equality*. Lawrence: University Press of Kansas, 2014.

Saunders, Nicholas J., ed. *Matters of Conflict: Material Culture, Memory and the First World War*. Abingdon, UK: Routledge, 2004.

———. *Trench Art: Materialities and Memories of War*. Oxford, UK: Berg, 2003.

Savage, Kirk. *Monument Wars: Washington, D.C., the National Mall, and the Transformation of the Memorial Landscape*. Berkeley: University of California Press, 2009.

———. *Standing Soldier, Kneeling Slave: Race, War and National Identity in Nineteenth-Century America*. Princeton, NJ: Princeton University Press, 1997.

Schaffer, Ronald. *America in the Great War: The Rise of the War Welfare State*. New York: Oxford University Press, 1991.

Schneider, Dorothy, and Carl J. Schneider. *Into the Breach: American Women Overseas in World War I*. New York: Viking Adult, 1991.

Scott, Anne Fior. *Natural Allies: Women's Associations in American History*. Urbana: University of Illinois Press, 1991.

Scott, Joan W. "Gender: A Useful Category of Historical Analysis." *American Historical Review* 91, no. 5 (December 1986): 1053–75.

Sewall, Jessica. "Sidewalks and Store Windows as Political Landscapes." In *Constructing Image, Identity, and Place: Perspectives in Vernacular Architecture*, edited by Alison K. Hoagland and Kenneth A. Breisch, 85–98. Knoxville: University of Tennessee Press, 2003.

Shackel, Paul A., ed. *Myth, Memory, and the Making of the American Landscape*. Gainesville: University Press of Florida, 2001.

Shanken, Andrew M. *194X: Architecture, Planning, and Consumer Culture on the American Homefront*. Minneapolis: University of Minnesota Press, 2009.

———. "Planning Memory: Living Memorials in the United States during World War II." *Art Bulletin* 84, no. 1 (March 2002): 130–47.

Sheftall, Mark David. *Altered Memories of the Great War: Divergent Narratives of Britain, Australia, New Zealand and Canada*. London: I. B. Tauris, 2010.

Sherman, Daniel J. *The Construction of Memory in Interwar France*. Chicago: University of Chicago Press, 1999.

Sherry, Michael G. *In the Shadow of War: The United States since the 1930s*. New Haven, CT: Yale University Press, 1995.

Shipton, Elisabeth. *Female Tommies: The Frontline Women of the First World War*. Stroud, UK: History Press, 2014.

Shlaes, Amity. *The Forgotten Man: A New History of the Great Depression*. New York: Harper Collins, 2007.

Silber, Nina. *The Romance of Reunion: Northerners and the South, 1865–1900*. Chapel Hill: University of North Carolina Press, 1993.

Sillia, Helene M. *Lest We Forget: A History of the Women's Overseas Service League*. Privately published, 1978.

Sklar, Kathryn Kish. "Hull House: A Community of Women Reformers." *Signs* 10, no. 4 (Summer 1985): 658–77.

Sklaroff, Lauren Rebecca. *Black Culture and the New Deal: The Quest for Civil Rights in the Roosevelt Era*. Chapel Hill: University of North Carolina Press, 2009.

Skocpol, Theda. *Protecting Soldiers and Mothers: The Political Origins of Social Policy in the United States*. Cambridge, MA: Harvard University Press, 1992.

Sledge, Michael. *Soldier Dead: How We Recover, Identify, Bury, & Honor Our Military Fallen*. New York: Columbia University Press, 2005.

Sloane, David Charles. *The Last Great Necessity: Cemeteries in American History*. Baltimore: Johns Hopkins University Press, 1991.

Slotkin, Richard. *Lost Battalions: The Great War and the Crisis of American Nationality*. New York: Henry Holt, 2005.

Smith, Jill Halcomb. *Dressed for Duty: America's Women in Uniform, 1898–1973*. San Jose, CA: T. James Bender, 2001.

Smith, Steven D. *The African American Soldier at Fort Huachuca, Arizona, 1892–1946*. Fort Huachuca, AZ, and Seattle: US Army Fort Huachuca, AZ, and Center of Expertise for Preservation of Historic Structures & Buildings, US Army Corps of Engineers, Seattle District, 2001.

Smith, Timothy. *A Chickamauga Memorial: The Establishment of America's First Civil War National Military Park*. Knoxville: University of Tennessee Press, 2009.

——. *The Golden Age of Battlefield Preservation: The Decade of the 1890s and the Establishment of America's First Five Military Parks*. Knoxville: University of Tennessee Press, 2008.

Smyth, J. E., ed. *Hollywood and the American Historical Film*. Basingstoke, UK: Palgrave Macmillan, 2012.

Snell, Mark A., ed., *Unknown Soldiers: The American Expeditionary Forces in Memory and Remembrance*. Kent, OH: Kent State University Press, 2008.

Sokołowska-Paryż, Marzena. *Reimagining the War Memorial, Reinterpreting the Great War: The Formats of British Commemorative Fiction*. Newcastle upon Tyne, UK: Cambridge Scholars Publishing, 2012.

Spivak, Jeffrey. *Buzz: The Life and Art of Busby Berkeley*. Lexington: University Press of Kentucky, 2011.

Sprague, Charles A. "Oregon's New Capitol." *Oregon Historical Quarterly* 37, no. 2 (June 1936): 130–36.

Spring, Peter, trans. and ed. *Guide to the Vatican: Museums and City*. Vatican City: Edizioni Musei Vaticani, 2007.

Spritzer, Lorraine Nelson. *The Belle of Ashby Street: Helen Douglas Mankin and Georgia Politics*. Athens: University of Georgia Press, 1982.

Sturken, Marita. *Tangled Memories: The Vietnam War, the AIDS Epidemic, and the Politics of Remembering*. Berkeley: University of California Press, 1997.

——. *Tourists of History: Memory, Kitsch, and Consumerism from Oklahoma City to Ground Zero*. Durham, NC: Duke University Press, 2007.

Susman, Warren I. *Culture as History: The Transformation of American Society in the Twentieth Century*. Washington, DC: Smithsonian Institution Press, 2003.

Swift, Earl. *Where They Lay: Searching for America's Lost Soldiers*. Boston: Houghton Mifflin, 2003.

Thelen, David. "Memory and American History." *Journal of American History* 75, no. 4 (March 1998): 1117–29.

Thom, Deborah. *Nice Girls and Rude Girls: Women Workers in World War I*. London: I. B. Tauris, 1998.

Tindall, George Brown, and David Emory Shi. *America: A Narrative History*. 8th ed. New York: W. W. Norton, 2010.

Tindall, George B., David E. Shi, and Thomas Lee Pearcy. *The Essential America*. New York: W. W. Norton, 2001.

Todman, Dan. *The Great War: Myth and Memory*. London: Hambledon and London, 2005.

Tompkins, Sally Kress. *A Quest for Grandeur: Charles Moore and the Federal Triangle*. Washington, DC: Smithsonian Institution Press, 1993.

Treadwell, Mattie E. *United States Army in World War II, Special Studies: The Women's Army Corps*. Washington, DC: Center of Military History, 1995.

Trouillot, Michel-Rolph. *Silencing the Past: Power and the Production of History*. Boston: Beacon Press, 1995.

Trout, Steven. *Memorial Fictions: Willa Cather and the First World War*. Lincoln: University of Nebraska Press, 2002.

———. *On the Battlefield of Memory: The First World War and American Remembrance, 1919–1941*. Tuscaloosa: University of Alabama Press, 2010.

Truett, Randall Bond, ed. *Washington, D.C.: A Guide to the Nation's Capital*. New York: Hastings House, 1968.

Ussery, Paul A. "COL Emma Vogel: First Chief of the Women's Medical Specialist Corps." *AMEDD Historian*, no. 2 (Spring 2013): 1–2.

Vance, Jonathon F. *Death So Noble: Memory, Meaning, and the First World War*. Vancouver: University of British Columbia Press, 1997.

van Emden, Richard. *The Quick and the Dead: Fallen Soldiers and Their Families in the Great War*. London: Bloomsbury, 2011.

Van West, Carroll. "Assessing Significance and Integrity in the National Register Process: Questions of Race, Class, and Gender." In *Preservation of What, for Whom? A Critical Look at Historical Significance*, edited by Michael A. Tomlan, 109–16. Ithaca, NY: National Council for Preservation Education, 1997.

Vaught, Wilma L. *The Day the Nation Said "Thanks!": A History and Dedication Scrapbook of the Women in Military Service for America Memorial*. Washington, DC: Military Women's Press, 1999.

Vining, Margaret, and Barton C. Hacker. "Displaying the Great War in America: The War Exhibition of the United States National Museum (Smithsonian Institution), 1918 and Beyond." In *The Universal Heritage of Arms and Military History: Challenges and Choices in a Changing World*, 27–32. Vienna: Heeresgeschichtliches Museum, 2008.

———. "From Camp Follower to Lady in Uniform: Women, Social Class and Military Institutions before 1920." *Contemporary European History* 10 (2001): 353–73.

———. "Uniforms Make the Woman." In *Materializing the Military*, vol. 5 of *Artefacts: Studies in the History of Science and Technology*, edited by Bernard Finn and Barton C. Hacker, 65–76. London: Science Museum Press, 2005.

———. "Volunteers Inspired by Conscription—Uniformed Women in World War I." In *The Total War, The Total Defense, 1789–2000*, edited by Per Iko, Lars Ericson, and Gunnar Aselius, 346–52. Stockholm: Swedish Commission on Military History, 2001.

Vogel, Emma E. "Physical Therapists before World War II (1917–1949)." In *Army Medical Specialist Corps*, edited by Robert S. Anderson, 41–67. Washington, DC: Office of the Surgeon General, Department of the Army, 1968.

Vogel, Emma E., and Helen B. Gearin. "Events Leading to the Formation of the Women's Medical Specialist Corps." In *Army Medical Specialist Corps*, edited by Robert S. Anderson, 1–22. Washington, DC: Office of the Surgeon General, Department of the Army, 1968.

Vogel, Emma E., Katharine E. Manchester, Helen B. Gearin, and Wilma L. West. "Training in World War II." In *Army Medical Specialist Corps*, edited by Robert S. Anderson, 137–82. Washington, DC: Office of the Surgeon General, Department of the Army, 1968.

Wagner-Pacifici, Robin, and Barry Schwartz. "The Vietnam Veterans Memorial: Commemorating a Difficult Past." *American Journal of Sociology* 97, no. 2 (September 1991): 376–420.

Ward, Stephen R., ed. *The War Generation: Veterans of the First World War.* Port Washington, NY: National University Publications, 1975.

Ware, Susan. *Beyond Suffrage: Women in the New Deal.* Cambridge, MA: Harvard University Press, 1981.

———. *Holding Their Own: American Women in the 1930s.* Boston: Twayne, 1982.

———. *Partner and I: Molly Dewson, Feminism, and New Deal Politics.* New Haven, CT: Yale University Press, 1987.

Warren, Harris Gaylord. *Herbert Hoover and the Great Depression.* New York: Oxford University Press, 1959.

Wasniewski, Matthew A., ed. *Women in Congress, 1917–2006.* Washington, DC: Government Printing Office, 2006.

Waters, W. W. *B.E.F.: The Whole Story of the Bonus Army.* With William C. White. New York: Arno Press and the New York Times, 1969.

West, Patricia. *Domesticating History: The Political Origins of America's House Museums.* Washington, DC: Smithsonian Books, 1999.

Weyeneth, Robert R. "The Architecture of Racial Segregation: The Challenges of Preserving the Problematical Past." *Public Historian* 27, no. 4 (Fall 2005): 11–44.

Whalan, Mark. *The Great War and the Culture of the New Negro.* Gainesville: University Press of Florida, 2008.

White, Marguerite. *American War Mothers: Fifty Year History, 1917–1967.* Indianapolis: American War Mothers, 1981.

Wiebe, Robert H. *The Search for Order, 1877–1920.* New York: Hill and Wang, 1967.

Wilkinson, Mary. "Patriotism and Duty: The Women's Work Collection at the Imperial War Museum." *Imperial War Museum Review* 6 (1991): 31–38.

Williams, David. *Media, Memory, and the First World War.* Montreal: McGill-Queen's University Press, 2009.

Williams, Noel T. St. John. *Judy O'Grady and the Colonel's Lady: The Army Wife and Camp Follower since 1660.* London: Brassey's, 1988.

Wilson, Charles Reagan. *Baptized in Blood: The Religion of the Lost Cause, 1865–1920.* Athens: University of Georgia Press, 1980.

Wilson, Mabel O. *Begin with the Past: Building the National Museum of African American History and Culture.* Washington, DC: Smithsonian Books, 2016.

Wiltsher, Anne. *Most Dangerous Women: Feminist Peace Campaigners of the Great War.* Boston: Pandora, 1985.

Wiltz, John E. *From Isolation to War, 1931–1941.* New York: Thomas Y. Crowell, 1968.

Wingate, Jennifer. "Doughboys, Art Worlds, and Identities: Sculpted Memories of World War I in the United States." PhD diss., Stony Brook University, 2002.

———. "Motherhood, Memorials, and Anti-militarism: Bashka Paeff's 'Sacrifices of War.'" *Woman's Art Journal* 29, no. 2 (Fall–Winter 2008): 31–40.

———. "Over the Top: The Doughboy in World War I Memorials and Visual Culture." *American Art* 19, no. 2 (Summer 2005): 26–47.

———. "Real Art, War Art and the Politics of Peace Memorials in the United States after World War I." *Public Art Dialogue* 2, no. 2 (September 2012): 162–89.

———. *Sculpting Doughboys: Memory, Gender, and Taste in America's World War I Memorials.* Farnham, UK: Ashgate, 2013.

Winter, Jay. *Remembering War: The Great War between Memory and History in the Twentieth Century.* New Haven, CT: Yale University Press, 2006.

———. *Sites of Memory, Sites of Mourning: The Great War in European Cultural History.* Cambridge: Cambridge University Press, 1995.

Winter, Jay, Geoffrey Parker, and Mary R. Habeck, eds. *The Great War and the Twentieth Century.* New Haven, CT: Yale University Press, 2000.

Winter, Jay, and Antoine Prost. *The Great War in History: Debates, Controversies, 1914 to the Present.* New York: Cambridge University Press, 2005.

Yalom, Marilyn. *The American Resting Place: Four Hundred Years of History through Our Cemeteries and Burial Grounds.* New York: Houghton Mifflin, 2008.

Young, Alfred F. *The Shoemaker and the Tea Party: Memory and the American Revolution.* Boston: Beacon Press, 2000.

Young, James E. *The Texture of Memory: Holocaust Memorials and Meaning.* New Haven, CT: Yale University Press, 1993.

Young, Nancy Beck. *Lou Henry Hoover: Activist First Lady.* Lawrence: University Press of Kansas, 2004.

Young, Vivian Lea. "'Petticoats Are Part of This Uniform': American Women Volunteers of the First World War and Their Uniforms." Master's thesis, George Washington University, 1987.

Zeiger, Robert H. *America's Great War: World War I and the American Experience.* Lanham, MD: Rowman & Littlefield, 2000.

Zeiger, Susan. *In Uncle Sam's Service: Women Workers with the American Expeditionary Force, 1917–1919.* Ithaca, NY: Cornell University Press, 1999.

Index